RACE FOR THE SOUTH POLE

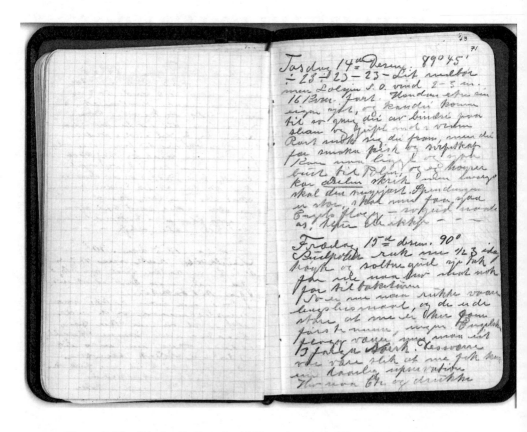

Figure 1 Olav Bjaaland's diary for 15 December 1911. 'We reached the South Pole at 2.30 today, tired and hungry', the entry begins, 'thank God we have enough food for the return journey. So now we have attained the goal of our desires.'

— Margit Bjåland

RACE FOR THE SOUTH POLE

THE EXPEDITION DIARIES OF SCOTT AND AMUNDSEN

Roland Huntford

continuum

Published by the Continuum International Publishing Group

The Tower Building	80 Maiden Lane
11 York Road	Suite 704
London	New York
SE1 7NX	NY 10038

www.continuumbooks.com

Editorial matter and translation of the diaries of Roald Amundsen and Olav Bjaaland copyright © Roland Huntford, 2010.

First published 2010

British Library Cataloguing-in-Publication Data
A catalogue record for this book is available from the British Library.

ISBN 978-1441-16982-2

Designed and typeset by Pindar NZ, Auckland, New Zealand
Printed and bound in Great Britain by the MPG Books Group

CONTENTS

To my wife, Anita

FIGURES

ACKNOWLEDGEMENTS

First of all, I want to thank Margit Bjåland of Morgedal in Telemark for kindly making available the Antarctic diaries of her kinsman, Olav Olavson Bjaaland. This book would have been immeasurably poorer without her permission to publish and translate.

As ever, I must thank Dr Gordon Johnson, the President, and the fellows of Wolfson, my Cambridge college, for providing a congenial scholarly atmosphere and access to the resources of the university.

I am grateful to the Cambridge University Library for unfailing help and courtesy. The same holds for the University Computing Service Help Desk, which is really worthy of its name.

Once more I must thank the National Library of Norway in Oslo for much patient help, especially with illustrations. I am particularly grateful to the Manuscripts Collection for generously giving copies of Amundsen's Antarctic diaries. I also wish to thank the Fram Museum in Oslo for assistance with Norwegian pictures and sources.

Thanks are due to Ben Hayes, my editor at Continuum. David Michael, my copy-editor, has done much to shape the book, for which I also thank him.

I must thank Dr. Charles Swithinbank for sharing his knowledge of Antarctica and help with illustrations. Thanks also go to Nick Lambourne, of Christie's.

I thank Susie Nixon for continuing to keep me on an even keel.

And of course, yet again, I must thank my wife, Anita, to whom this book is dedicated and to whom I owe everything. As usual, she has borne literary strain with unbelievable patience. Our sons, Nicholas and Anthony, have also continued their support.

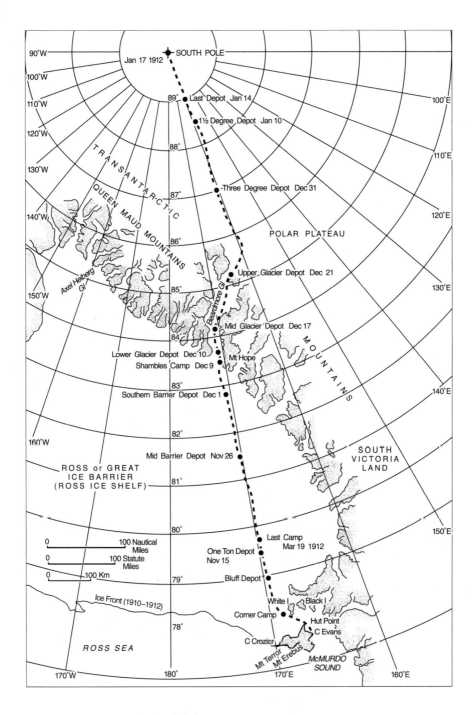

Map 1 Scott's route to the South Pole

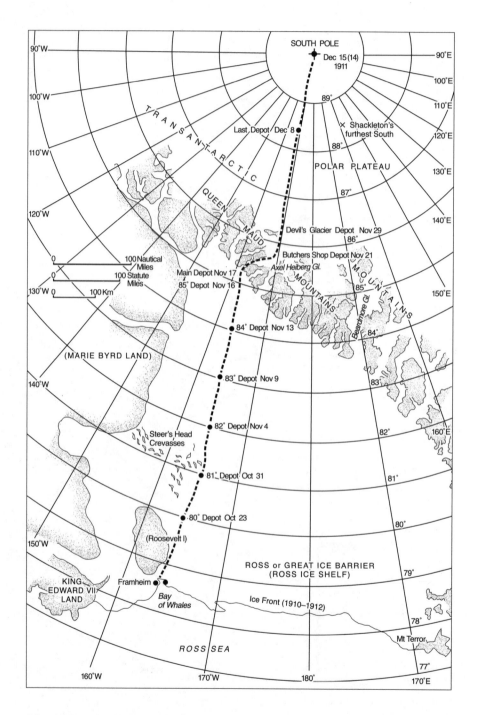

Map 2 Amundsen's route to the South Pole

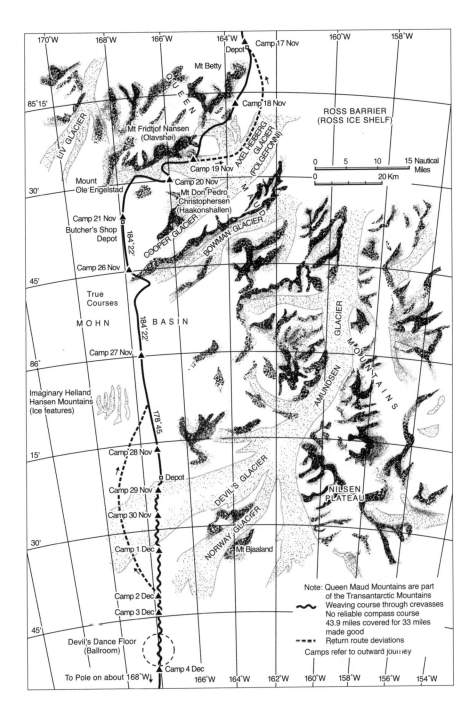

Map 3 Amundsen's crossing of the Transantarctic Mountains

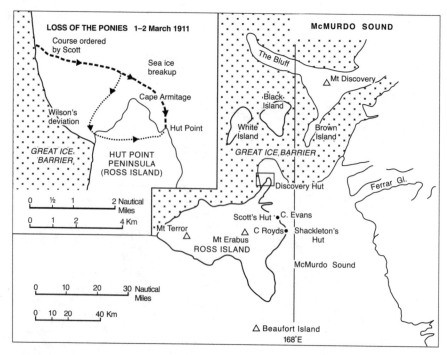

Map 4 McMurdo Sound

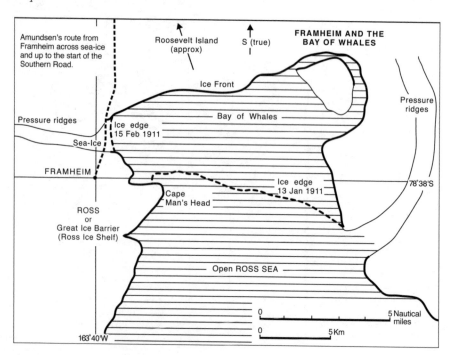

Map 5 Framheim and the Bay of Whales

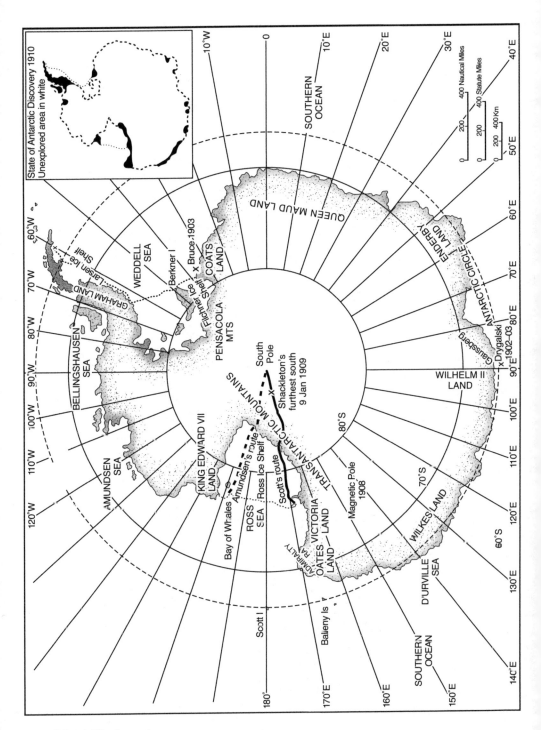

Map 6 The Antarctic

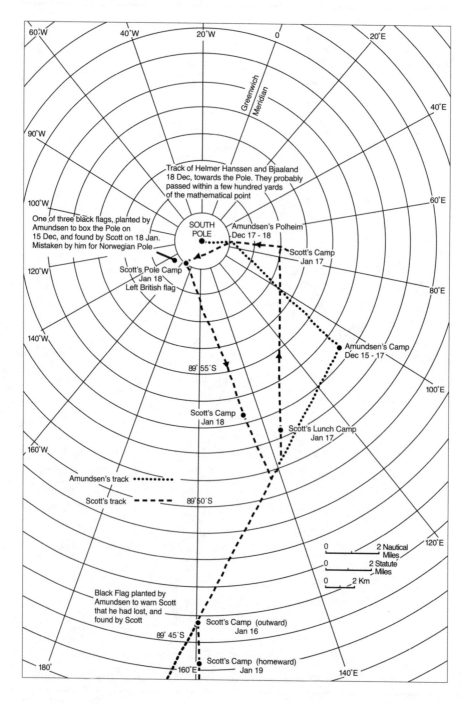

60°W 40°W 20°W 0 20°E

Greenwich Meridian

40°E

90°W

Track of Helmer Hanssen and Bjaaland
18 Dec, towards the Pole. They probably
passed within a few hundred yards
of the mathematical point

60°E

100°W

One of three black flags, planted by
Amundsen to box the Pole on
15 Dec, and found by Scott on 18 Jan.
Mistaken by him for Norwegian Pole

SOUTH
POLE

Amundsen's Polheim
Dec 17 - 18

Scott's Camp
Jan 17

Scott's Pole Camp
Jan 18
Left British flag

120°W

80°E

140°W

Amundsen's Camp
Dec 15 - 17

89° 55′S

100°E

Scott's Camp
Jan 18

Scott's Lunch Camp
Jan 17

160°W

Amundsen's track ••••••••

Scott's track – – – – 89° 50′S

0   2 Nautical
         Miles

0   2 Statute
         Miles

0   2 Km

120°E

Black Flag planted by
Amundsen to warn Scott
that he had lost, and
found by Scott

Scott's Camp (outward)
Jan 16

89° 45′S

180°

160°E

Scott's Camp (homeward)
Jan 19

140°E

Map 7 The tracks of Amundsen and Scott at the South Pole. After Hinks (1944).

NOTE ON THE TEXT

In the interests of historical authenticity, original forms have been preserved where possible. In Scott's diaries, his own spelling and punctuation have been kept. Amundsen's spelling was erratic, but trying to convey this in translation would have confused the reader. Bjaaland only used the degree sign for latitudes, omitting it in temperatures.

Christiania, sometimes spelled Kristiania, is the present-day Oslo, capital of Norway. The name was changed in 1925.

Bjaaland is also spelled Bjåland. The pronunciation is the same, roughly 'aw'. The Norwegian letter ø is pronounced like 'pearl'.

In the Antarctic, what the diaries variously call the Great Ice Barrier, the Ice Barrier, or simply the Barrier is today known as the Ross Ice Shelf. King Edward VII Land is now the Edward VII Peninsula.

'R.' in Scott's diary stands for a return camp on his way back from the Pole. Cuts in the original printed edition of the diary are identified by ***bold italic*** type.

Units are a bugbear. For distance, both Amundsen and Scott, being seamen, use the nautical or geographical mile. It is equivalent to one-sixtieth of a degree, or one minute of latitude. It is fixed at 1.85 kilometres or, in imperial measure, 6.080 feet, equivalent to 1⅐ statute miles. The statute mile is 1.6 km. It is sometimes uncertain which mile Scott is using. Amundsen sticks to the nautical mile.

For obvious reasons, Scott consistently uses imperial measures. The pound (lb) for weight, equals 454 grams, and the ton of 2,240 pounds, is equivalent to 1.017 metric tonnes of 1,000 kilograms. For length, there is the foot, corresponding to 30.48 cm, the yard of 3 feet (0.91 m) and, for depths at sea, the fathom or 6 ft (1.82 m). In the case of volume, the imperial gallon equals 4.55 litres or 1.2 US gallons of 3.79 litres.

The Norwegians were still imperfectly metricated. For mass, volume, and everyday length they used metric units. The nautical mile for distance was one exception; altitude another. They still measured this in feet. This was an ancient but variable Scandinavian unit, standardized in 1875 to the so-called metric foot of 30 centimetres, divided, like the imperial system, into 12 inches. One reason for continuing with the unit was the fact that their own maps still gave altitude in feet; another, that pocket altimeters were mainly of English origin, and therefore preserved imperial measurement.

For temperature, Scott used Fahrenheit, Amundsen, centigrade (Celsius) throughout. The conversion is simple but tedious. The freezing point of water, 0°C. is 32°F; the boiling point 100°C. and 212°F. respectively, so that 1°F. is equal to 0.56°C. Some useful equivalents are:

F	+35°	10°	0°	−10°	−20°	−30°	−40°	−50°	−60°	−70°
C	+1.7°	+12.1°	−17.8°	−23.3°	−28.9°	−34.4°	−40°	−45.6°	−51.1°	−56.7°

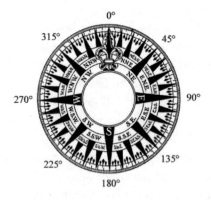

Figure 2   Traditional mariner's compass dial, with the main equivalents in degrees. This is to make sense of compass bearings in the diaries.

Direction can be even more confusing. Both expeditions used the traditional mariner's compass, with its 32 points. A 'point' is 11¼°, and ¼ point is the smallest practical unit, about 2.81°. To complicate matters, Amundsen uses plain degrees to express magnetic variation.

Translations are the author's own.

DRAMATIS PERSONAE

NORWEGIAN LAND PARTY

Roald Engebreth Gravning Amundsen (1872–1928). Ship's captain and expedition leader. He was on the *Belgica* Antarctic expedition 1897–9 and commanded the North-West Passage expedition, 1903–6.

Olav Olavson Bjaaland (1873–1961). Ski-racer, ski-maker, farmer, carpenter. He was the winner of the Nordic combination (cross-country and ski jumping) at Holmenkollen in 1894 and 1902 and the runner-up in the 50 km cross-country ski race at Holmenkollen in 1908.

Julius Helmer Hanssen (1870–1956). Ship's mate, skier, dog driver. He gained his polar experience Arctic sealing in 1896 8. He was on the North West Passage expedition, under Amundsen, 1903–6.

Sverre Hassel (1876–1928). Ship's mate, skier, dog driver. Norwegian marine, and later in the customs service. He was on the second *Fram* expedition to the Canadian Arctic under Otto Sverdrup, 1898–1902.

Fr Hjalmar Johansen (1867–1913). International gymnast, skier, dog-driver, army officer. He was on the first *Fram* expedition, 1893–96, and served under various explorers on Spitsbergen, 1907–09.

Adolf Henrik Lindstrøm (1866–1939). Ship's cook. From boyhood, he went sealing and whaling in the Arctic. He joined the second *Fram* expedition, 1898–1902, and was on the North-West Passage expedition under Amundsen, 1903–6.

Kristian Prestrud (1881–1927). Lieutenant, Norwegian Navy. Navigational specialist.

Jørgen Stubberud (1883–1978). Carpenter, builder and cabinet maker.

Oscar Wisting (1871–1936). Hunter, skier, went to sea at the age of 14. Petty Officer, Norwegian Navy. Polar experience: Arctic whaling, 1903–6.

BRITISH LAND PARTY

W. W. Archer (18??–1944). Chief Steward, late RN.

Edward L. Atkinson (1881–1929). Surgeon, RN.

Henry Robertson Bowers (1883–1912). Lieutenant, Royal Indian Marine.

Apsley Cherry-Garrard (1886–1959). Winchester and Christ Church, Oxford, where he read modern history. Subscribing volunteer, mustered as assistant zoologist.

Thomas Clissold (1886–1963). Cook, late RN.

Thomas Crean (1877–1938). Petty officer, RN. He was on the *Discovery* expedition, 1901–4.

Bernard Day (1884–1952). Motor mechanic. Drove and maintained Scott's motor sledges. He looked after the motor car on Shackleton's *Nimrod* expedition, 1907–9 – the first attempt at motorized transport in the Antarctic.

Frank Debenham (1883–1965). Australian geologist.

Edgar Evans (1876–1912). Petty officer, RN. He was on the *Discovery* expedition, 1901–4.

Edward Ratcliffe Garth Russell Evans (1881–1957). Lieutenant, RN (later Admiral Lord Mountevans), second in command of the expedition.

Robert Forde (1875–1959). Petty officer, RN.

Demetri Gerof (Dmitriy Semenovich Girov) (1888–1932[?]). Born in Sakhalin, Russian Far East. Dog driver, recruited by Meares (q.v.).

Tryggve Gran (1889–1980). The Norwegian with Scott. Ski instructor and youngest member of Scott's landing party. After the expedition he became a pioneering airman and, in 1914, made the first flight over the North Sea.

Frederick J. Hooper (1891–1955). Steward, Late RN.

Patrick Keohane (1879–1950). Petty Officer, RN.

William Lashly (1867–1940). Chief Stoker, RN. Driver and mechanic for Scott's motor sledges. He had been on the *Discovery* expedition, 1901–4.

Cecil Henry Meares (1877–1937). Dog driver. Cold climate experience: Siberia and Russian Far East. In 1910, went to Siberia and Manchuria to buy dogs and ponies for the expedition.

Edward W. Nelson (1883–1923). Biologist.

Lawrence Edward Grace Oates (1880–1912). Eton and Captain, 6th Inniskilling Dragoons. Cavalryman and subscribing volunteer, appointed to care for Scott's ponies.

Anton Omelchenko (Anton Lukich Omel'chenko) (1883–1932). Born in the Ukraine. Russian jockey. Recruited by Meares (q.v.) in Harbin (Manchuria) to help manage the ponies in transport. In the Antarctic, Anton served as a groom or stable boy.

Herbert George Ponting (1870–1935). Photo journalist.

Robert Falcon Scott (1868–1912). Captain, RN and expedition leader. Commanded the *Discovery* expedition to the Antarctic, 1901–4.

George Clarke Simpson (1878–1965). DSc (Manchester), India Meteorological Department, meteorologist on Scott's expedition.

Thomas Griffith Taylor (1880–1963). University of Sydney and Emmanuel College, Cambridge. Australian geologist.

Thomas Soulsby Williamson (1877–1940). Petty Officer , RN. He was on the *Discovery* expedition, 1901–4.

Dr Edward Adrian Wilson (1872–1912). Gonville and Caius College, Cambridge and St George's Hospital, London, Chief of the Scientific Staff. He had been on the *Discovery* expedition, 1901–4.

Charles Seymour Wright (later Sir Charles Wright) (1887–1975). University of Toronto and Gonville and Caius College, Cambridge. Canadian physicist.

ABBREVIATIONS

asl – above sea level
Bj. – Bjaaland
BL – The British Library, London
Christie's – Christie's auction house, London
Has., Hass., Hs. or H. – Hassel
HH – Helmer Hanssen
Joh. – Johansen
Jørg, Jg., or Jørgen – Stubberud (his Christian name is 'George' in English)
l. – litres
m – nautical miles or metres, according to context
m/s – metres per second
NBO – National Library of Norway in Oslo
Pem. or P. – Pemmican
Pr. – Prestrud
RGS – Royal Geographical Society
RN – Royal Navy
SPRI – Scott Polar Research Institute, Cambridge.
W. – Wisting

INTRODUCTION

The race to the South Pole has had an enduring fascination. Its blend of triumph and calamity is unique. It began in 1910, with the departure of two ships. One was *Terra Nova*, carrying British explorers under Robert Falcon Scott. *Fram* was the other vessel, sailing with the rival Norwegian expedition led by Roald Engebreth Gravning Amundsen on board.

Controversy has muffled the voices of both men from the start. The heart of the matter is their overland journey from the base ashore to the Pole and back, of which their personal records are the substance of this book. Through their diaries they have spoken for themselves.

Scott made the running, as his diary was the first to appear in print; generally with small misleading cuts which, following modern practice, are now restored. Amundsen's journal has never yet been published in its entirety outside the original Norwegian, and appears here for the first time in English. The diaries of both men are laid out in parallel for direct comparison. They are arranged here, day by day, so that the protagonists, who never met in person, finally confront each other across the printed page.

To balance Scott's flow of words, but not only on that account, Amundsen's diary appears together with that of his companion, Olav Olavson Bjaaland. This is the first unabridged publication and the first translation into English. It introduces a great double act in polar exploration. Amundsen was the determined pioneer; Bjaaland a ski champion, with no previous interest in the Polar Regions, but from a certain point of view the star of the show.

While the British were seeking adventure, the Norwegians saw the affair as a kind of sporting contest. That meant skiing, which, in its modern guise was their invention and their national sport. The Antarctic being full of snow, it seemed an extension of the home terrain. Understandably therefore, Amundsen considered the fight for the South Pole to be a ski race writ large. This made Bjaaland a natural choice. Born in 1873, he was a talented ski racer with an enviable record at Holmenkollen, the classic Norwegian international event and, to this day, a kind of Nordic Olympia. In 1894 and 1902, he won the Nordic combination of jumping and cross-country and, in 1908, was runner-up in the 50 km cross-country event, the Nordic marathon. All this was before the invention of the Winter Olympics, and today his achievement would be the equivalent of winning multiple Olympic medals. Besides this, Bjaaland came from Morgedal in the province of Telemark. Both were names to conjure with. Widely considered a cradle of modern skiing, Telemark provided most Norwegian ski champions of the age. (It was also the birthplace of Henrik Ibsen, with whom Bjaaland shares a streak of poetic vision and an ironic sense of humour, rare among polar explorers, which sets off Amundsen's straight-faced style.) Out of Morgedal, a secluded mountain village, came a disproportionate number of skiing champions and pioneers. Bjaaland's presence fortified his companions with the knowledge that Scott had nobody in the same league.

Bjaaland was also a character in his own right. Unimpressed by rank, he had a disarming way of puncturing pomposity, and a gift for defusing conflict with a wry little joke. He had his own take on a Norwegian proverb that 'Nordic men must rove and roam.' He only left the country twice: to demonstrate skiing in Chamonix, and to run in the race for the South Pole. It was enough for him. By profession a yeoman farmer, he was tied to his native soil, with his skiing a part-time accomplishment. He was a kind of Sancho Panza, bringing everyone down to earth. Above all, Bjaaland did not write his diary looking over his shoulder at the world. It was a record for himself alone. He had trenchancy and wit to set against the outpouring of a readier pen. His comments can be taken at face value.

Apart from personalities, national prestige was at stake. In the age of empires the British, with the biggest one on earth, wanted to add the South Pole to their imperial dominion. For their part the Norwegians, newly independent, having only separated from Sweden in 1905, saw in the polar outlands the chance for a small country to build an empire of its own.

None of this by itself explains the abiding interest in Amundsen and Scott. It is rather more personal. It was a duel between two very different men. Scott, born in 1868 and Amundsen, in 1872, belonged to the same generation, but they had little more in common. Scott was burdened with heroic ideals; Amundsen simply wanted to attain the Pole. Scott followed the Romantic tradition of heroism as suffering; Amundsen came from a culture which saw no virtue in unnecessary risk to life and limb. Amundsen, like most Scandinavians, had an affinity with Nature, and a proper humility before her powers, so that he was suited to his task. Scott came from a society divorced from Nature and which thought it knew best, disqualifying him from the land he had chosen to invade. To this, he added a mental rigidity of his own. He did have social poise, however. Amundsen proved once again that the qualities of leadership do not necessarily make for a comfortable presence.

In character and appearance Scott could never have been anything but a contemporary Englishman. He was an Edwardian – although King Edward VII had died just before he sailed, succeeded by George V – with the characteristic blend of heroic longings and a neurotic fear of decadence in a time of change and looming threat of war. Amundsen, for his part, with his long, hawk nose, was not exactly a model Nordic figure. Beyond nationality, he seemed out of time and out of place; a throwback to a distant age. He might almost have stepped out of some ancient epic. He was the Homeric hero, a survivor, 'the man of many wiles', in the wonderful opening words of the Odyssey, who 'saw the cities of many men and knew their minds'.

When Amundsen and Scott sailed for the south, they were already polar explorers of repute. In 1902–4, Scott commanded an Antarctic expedition – usually

Figure 3 Portrait of Olav Bjaaland. Taken 1910, before Fram sailed.

– Author's collection

called *Discovery*, after the expedition ship on which he broke the record for the Furthest South. Amundsen had been to Antarctica before Scott. That was with a cosmopolitan party which, in 1897–9, under a Belgian leader, Adrien de Gerlache, on a ship called – naturally – *Belgica*, spent the first known winter in the Antarctic. More famously, at the other end of the world, during 1903–6 Amundsen, now in command of his own expedition, with a tiny fishing smack called *Gjøa*, became the first man to navigate the legendary North West Passage through the Canadian Arctic on one and the same keel.

Both men were ships' captains, but Scott was a naval officer whereas Amundsen came from the mercantile marine. Amundsen was running his expedition as a private enterprise, a bit of a Viking marauder perhaps, with a prejudice against being caught with his pants down. He was a professional polar explorer, among the first of his kind in the modern sense. From late adolescence, he had systematically prepared himself. With various comical or menacing interludes,[1] he practised mountain skiing, also a Norwegian invention, under a teacher from the generation of pioneers. In other words, Amundsen made his beginner's mistakes at home, where they mattered least, before taking to the snows in dead earnest. His seagoing career, to obtain his master's certificate, was also a means to an end. He saw polar exploration as a blend of the sailor's and the skier's art. This was quite in character since, constrained by the geography of the country, the Norwegian often lived among the fjords between mountains and the sea.

Scott was the opposite in every way. Although his expedition was also a private venture, he ran it like a warship, with rigid naval discipline, and as many naval men as he could get hold of, perpetuating the unfortunate naval hold on British polar exploration. He was the last in a Royal Navy tradition of using polar exploration as a path to advancement when there was no facilitating war at sea. An amateur in snow travel, he did not prepare in advance, but relied on improvisation in the field. He owed his rank to two quick promotions rooted in the snows. He was the protégé of Sir Clements Markham, the manipulative President of the Royal Geographical Society, who pointed him in the right direction, and secured him his command of *Discovery*.[2]

Scott was heir to the long British history of polar exploration, stretching back to Elizabethan times. Amundsen had no such tradition behind him. Norwegian polar exploration began in his own lifetime with the first crossing of Greenland by his great compatriot Fridtjof Nansen in 1888, a mere two decades before. By the same token, Amundsen was spared the disturbing power of the past that is a theme of Greek tragedy and, closer to his own times, the dramas of his compatriot, Henrik Ibsen.

Since the South Pole lies on a continent encircled by the waters of another hemisphere, the approach belongs to tales of the sea. The contrast between the men heading south in 1910 was mirrored in their ships. *Terra Nova* was an ordinary weather-beaten Newfoundland sealer bought straight off the sealing grounds, as she was. *Fram* – 'forwards' – was going through a comprehensive refit. A masterpiece of the shipbuilder's art, she was a piece of living history. She had been specially built to a unique design for Nansen to try to reach the North Pole by freezing her into the Arctic pack ice and letting her drift with a presumed current across the top of the world. It was a revolutionary experiment. Sailing in 1893, *Fram* fell short of her theoretical destination by some 250 miles, Nansen meanwhile having left the ship with one companion on an audacious attempt to attain his goal using dogs and skis. He only reached a latitude of 86°14' but it was a record for the furthest north, and his retreat across the shifting pack became a saga of survival. Nansen and *Fram* returned to civilization within a week of each other in August 1896. He, having been given up for dead, became a hero of his times and *Fram* one of the most famous ships afloat.

From the outset there was hidden drama in the rivalry of Amundsen and Scott. They were facing each other by a trick of fate. When *Terra Nova* finally headed south from Cardiff on 15 June 1910, Scott did not know that he had the Norwegians on his tail. Hardly anyone else knew either when *Fram* left Norway, at Flekkerø, on the south coast of the country, and stood out to sea through the Skagerrak nearly seven weeks later on 9 August. Her voyage had actually begun at midnight on 6 June, when she raised anchor in the fjord beside Amundsen's home near Christiania, and sailed out on a month's oceanic trials in the North Atlantic, to correct any faults before starting off in earnest. *Terra Nova* put to sea after a sketchy refit without a preliminary cruise.

The first hint to Scott of a rival in the field came when he landed in Australia at Melbourne on 12 October. Awaiting him was a cable from Amundsen to say that he too was heading for Antarctica. The prelude had been played out at Madeira. *Ao pólo-sul*[3] – 'To the South Pole' – was the front-page headline that greeted *Fram* in *Diario de Noticias*, the main local newspaper, reporting that *Fram* had dropped anchor out in Funchal roads, on 6 September. It was a natural assumption, since the visit of *Terra Nova* late in June. It was the last thing that Amundsen wanted to read.

Originally, Amundsen planned to be the first man at the North Pole. Meanwhile in September 1909, the American explorers F. A. Cook and R. E. Peary returned to civilization, each claiming to have forestalled him. Disbelief in both lingers to this day. Whatever the truth, this was, as Amundsen himself baldly put it, 'the death blow to my enterprise.'[4] John Scott Keltie, Secretary of the Royal Geographical Society in London, who wrote on exploration for *The Times*, declared that Cook and Peary would 'largely discount Amundsen's expedition from the newspaper point of view.'[5] Even then, besides the money involved, the press was creating its own reality. In the Arctic, there was nothing left to conquer. The Pole-seeker suffered the pangs of disappointed ambition. A very human craving for conspicuous achievement survived. Amundsen sought another field of conquest. In an historic about turn, he pretended still to be going north, while in reality switching to the other, as yet untrodden, Pole.

Amundsen kept up the pretence even with his men. With careful planning to mask his true intention, he only shared the secret with the ship's officers and a few strategic confidantes in Norway. His secrecy had many strands. In part it derived from a constitutional fear of tempting fate; more prosaically by concerns that his private patrons would withdraw their support. Besides, Amundsen was in debt, and at all costs had to keep his creditors at bay. Then too as Nansen with some justification said afterwards: 'It was evidently me [Amundsen] was most

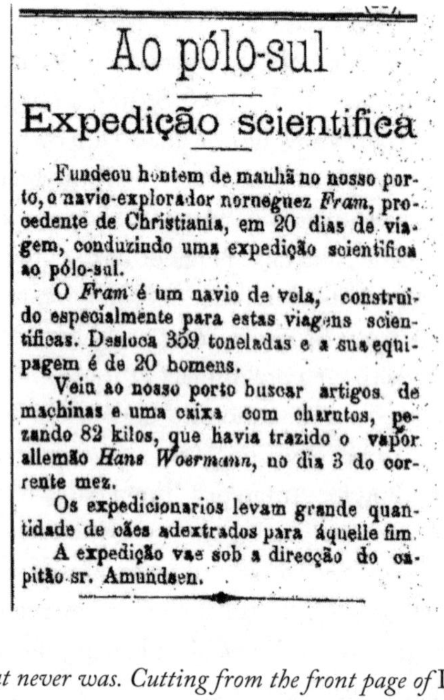

Ao pólo-sul

Expedição scientifica

Fundeou hontem de manhã no nosso porto, o navio-explorador norneguez *Fram*, procedente de Christiania, em 20 dias de viagem, conduzindo uma expedição scientifica ao pólo-sul.

O *Fram* é um navio de vela, construido especialmente para estas viagens scientificas. Desloca 359 toneladas e a sua equipagem é de 20 homens.

Veiu ao nosso porto buscar artigos de machinas e uma caixa com charutos, pezando 82 kilos, que havia trazido o vapor allemão *Hans Woermann*, no dia 3 do corrente mez.

Os expedicionarios levam grande quantidade de cães adextrados para áquelle fim.

A expedição vae sob a direcção do capitão sr. Amundsen.

Figure 4 The scoop that never was. Cutting from the front page of Diario de Noticias, *the chief Madeira newspaper, for 7 September 1910 declaring that Amundsen was going to the South Pole,* Ao pólo-sul. *He only revealed his switch from north to south two days later, when Fram was about to sail. Luckily for Amundsen the inspired guess remained on the island. This is probably the first time that the piece has been reproduced since its original publication.*

– Nesos database, Funchal, Madeira

afraid of . . .'[6] Now a professor of oceanography, and still a power in the land, in the half-world of his imagination, Nansen clung to an old desire, laced with self-delusion – what Ibsen calls the 'life-lie' – for the South Pole himself. Still Nansen had supported Amundsen, as the younger man, in his original Arctic plans, and ceded his claim to *Fram*. She was state property, so the Norwegian government could stop Amundsen because they had lent him the ship to go north.

One of the many ironies of the story is that to begin with, it was Amundsen who did not know that he was faced with a contender. He had decided to go South by 9 September 1909, a Thursday.[7] Scott only announced his expedition on the following Monday. For one thing, this shows that the threat of Scott played no part in Amundsen's change of mind. In any case, Scott's appearance on the stage still left Amundsen with the strategic advantage. He knew his rival's every move, whereas Scott was kept in the dark until late in the game.

Scott had in fact been harbouring designs on the South Pole since 1904, when he returned from the *Discovery* expedition. Because he had returned to naval duties his preparations, too, were discreetly veiled. In another ironical twist, the same affair of Cook and Peary that had driven Amundsen to act as he did also precipitated Scott's announcement – to forestall, among others, an *American* descent on the South Pole. The greater goad, however, was the near success of Sir Ernest Shackleton. He returned from the Antarctic in the spring of 1909, a national hero, having sensationally set a new record for the furthest south, to come within 100 miles or so of the Pole itself. Sir Ernest had been with Scott on the *Discovery* expedition. There they had quarrelled, and ever since cordially loathed each other. Scott wanted to avenge his eclipse by the man whom he both envied and despised. So between Shackleton, Peary, Cook and, be it said, a masterful wife of a year's standing, Scott found himself setting off in haste earlier than he might otherwise have wished.

There was reason in all this urgency. Time was running out. After centuries of exploration, almost the whole earth was known. The Polar Regions were the last great blanks upon the map. The first crossing of Greenland, the North West Passage, and now the South Pole belonged to the handful of factitious goals that marked the end of an age. The South Pole was the last great symbol of terrestrial discovery before the leap into space, and the first men on the moon. Shackleton had left what Amundsen called a 'little patch'[8] behind. That patch, however, was the last remaining chance of original achievement. The whole race turned on those few unaccomplished miles. Not only Amundsen and Scott were in the running. Peary was rumoured to be turning south; so too Dr Jean Charcot, a French explorer who had already been to Antarctica. A German and a Japanese expedition were actually preparing to set off. Both Amundsen and Scott had every incentive to strike as quickly as they could.

For centuries, the British had been attempting the emblematic polar goals, only to be forestalled in every one. They suffered mainly from the Scandinavian ascendancy of the late nineteenth century. It began with the North-East Passage, the fabled short cut to the Orient along the coast of Siberia. An aim of the Elizabethan navigators, it was finally accomplished by Baron Erik Adolf Nordenskiöld, the illustrious Finnish-born Swede, pioneer of modern polar exploration, in his ship *Vega* in 1878–9. Amundsen, of course, achieved the North-West passage and Nansen the first crossing of Greenland. The North Pole ceased to be a British affair in 1876, when a Royal Navy expedition failed, although it did set a new record for the Furthest North of 83°20'. The setbacks were all due fundamentally to the twin drawbacks of estrangement from Nature and worship of mediocrity. The South Pole was the last chance for the British to redeem a litany of failure. By the same token, Amundsen merely had to finish the hat trick, as it were.

There had been scattered reports of Scott's preparations, but his unexpected announcement made secrecy even more imperative for Amundsen. If the Norwegian authorities had an inkling of the truth, they would have had another reason to stop Amundsen in his tracks. This was a fear of antagonizing the British upon whom, as a Great Power, the security of a newly independent Norway might depend, and who looked on the Antarctic as their own preserve. Had that Funchal *Ao pólo-sul* headline leaked out, it could have disrupted Amundsen's careful plans. Luckily for him, although Madeira was a cablehead, the unintended scoop stayed on the island, no doubt to some journalist's everlasting regret.

Until Madeira, no one could tell where Amundsen was really heading – not even the men on board. His published aim was to repeat the first drift of the *Fram*, but reach the Pole itself by carrying out Nansen's original intention. This had been to enter the Arctic via the Bering Strait. Nansen, however, sailing from northern Norway, was stopped by the ice well short of his goal, and was obliged to begin his drift off the Siberian coast. Amundsen proposed reaching the Strait via the Pacific instead. As the Panama Canal was not yet open, this meant rounding Cape Horn. So until Madeira, the course, whether north or south, was the same. It was only afterwards that the truth would emerge when *Fram* changed direction and, instead of Cape Horn for the Arctic, she would head the other way, eastwards by the Cape of Good Hope across the Indian Ocean, making for the Antarctic.

Madeira was consequently the turning point. As he had planned all along, it was there, just before leaving, that Amundsen now told his men where he was really bound. That was on 9 September. Stunned, intrigued or downright amused by the sheer impertinence of it all, the whole crew agreed to carry on. Amundsen allowed no time for second thoughts. He immediately weighed anchor, and *Fram*, swinging in the roadstead, stood out to sea.

Among seafarers, Madeira has always had an historic role. One of the Portuguese Atlantic islands, it is the sentinel of the Trade Winds, and it was a last port of call for bunkering and filling up with water and fresh food when heading south. Amundsen's brother Leon was there to see him off. Leon was his confidential agent. He had come to Madeira to help with the arrangements, and now returned to Norway to break the news, on 1 October as it happened. Leon had with him a letter of agonized explanation to Nansen from his brother. It was also Leon who had sent the cable that caught Scott at Melbourne.

Fram was then still far behind in the South Atlantic, approaching the island of South Trinidad, off the coast of Brazil. She had been carried there in a wide westerly swing by the south-east trade winds, making unavoidable leeway. Like *Terra Nova*, *Fram* was a wooden sailing ship with auxiliary power but, unlike her, it did not touch at the island. The race for the South Pole was, after all, an amphibious operation and the approach by sea was the first, critical lap.

A bleak uninhabited outcrop of fractile, volcanic rock breaking the waters of the South Atlantic, South Trinidad looked like an engraving by Gustav Doré of Mount Purgatory from Dante's *Inferno*. *Terra Nova* dropped anchor off the island on 26 July, staying for two days. This was a diversion to collect zoological and botanical specimens ashore. It was an episode of what was billed as a scientific expedition, with a staff of practising scientists distinct from the explorers. Dr Edward Wilson organized the excursion. Wilson was one of the expedition doctors, and its scientific director. He had been on the *Discovery* expedition with Scott, and was now his spiritual prop. The landing on South Trinidad somehow reflected the whole undertaking. 'We want the Scientific work to make the bagging of the Pole merely an item in the results',[9] Wilson wrote, with unthinking hubris, to his father. The landing party resembled a shipload of Peter Pans on a jaunt. From Wilson down, they cheerfully ignored the risks of a rocky shore in an unprotected anchorage. Disaster duly struck when, coming off in boats to return to the ship, some of the party were nearly drowned or dashed to pieces on the rocks by an unexpected rise in the surge and backwash of the South Atlantic swell. Wilson was an onlooker, and someone recorded him as saying 'it was . . . curious . . . that a number of men, knowing that there was nothing they could do, could quietly watch a man fighting for his life, and he did not think that any but the British temperament could do so.'[10] Their luck held – on this occasion – and it all passed off with a wholesale ducking, a few grazes, and only a little damage to valuable equipment.

Following nearly three months later, *Fram* hurried along to gain on *Terra Nova*, keeping well clear of the island. That neatly symbolized the difference between the expeditions. Scott was leading a cumbrous undertaking with unclear aims Amundsen, a raid focused on a single goal. 'At all costs we had to be first at the finish', as Amundsen himself put it. 'Everything had to be concentrated on that.'[11] Science, he declared 'would have to look after itself.' But, he gently added, 'We could not reach the Pole by the route I had decided on, without . . . enriching different branches of science.'[12]

Amundsen had a point. 'Science', in the sense used by Scott and his like, was a moralistic fig leaf; even a pseudo religion. In its true sense of probing the unknown, geographical exploration is in itself a branch of science. What Amundsen did grasp was that the South Pole had a symbolism beyond pure geography. It meant closing one chapter in the advance of knowledge and, in a broader context, opening another, of which space travel was only one aspect. It was a demon that had to be exorcized.

There is something else. For all his faults, Amundsen was no hypocrite. He had no need of moralistic window dressing. He came from a culture that admired conspicuous achievement. He wanted the Pole; that was good enough for him. The deed was its own justification. Amundsen did not need to play at being Darwin on a South Atlantic island.

Fram passed within sight of South Trinidad to rate the chronometers. That is to say, they were checked against a geographical feature whose longitude was *known*, and hence the relation to Greenwich Mean Time. Without radio, this was a way of finding the time away from the civilized world. It is difficult now to conceive of the isolation possible on earth before time and space were annihilated by instant communication. To the men on *Fram*, as the humpbacked silhouette of Madeira sank wanly into the sea astern, it was their last contact with the outside for a long time to come. They had passed beyond human ken. Marine radio did exist, but not everywhere, and certainly not on *Fram*. She might have been adrift out in the cosmos. She was more alone than any space capsule today, constantly in touch with its control centre back on Earth. This suited Amundsen. To avoid the slightest possibility of recall, not to mention the clutches of his creditors, he was going to sail without stopping. He would round the Cape of Good Hope far out to sea, giving ships and civilization a wide berth before making his landfall in the south. Now you can fly to Antarctica in a matter of days; Amundsen was going to sail for months on end over an unforgiving sea.

Terra Nova was following a more leisurely course. After Madeira and South

Trinidad, she put in at Simonstown, near Cape Town on the Cape of Good Hope, and then a British naval base. Scott meanwhile had stayed behind in England to follow on by mailboat with his wife, Kathleen. She had decided to accompany her husband and see him off at the world's end, leaving their ten-month-old son, Peter, to be looked after by a nurse. Originally, they were supposed to sail on together to New Zealand but, at the Cape, Scott unexpectedly left Kathleen to travel on without him, while he, exerting rank, and status of leading the expedition, took command of *Terra Nova* for the crossing of the Indian Ocean to Melbourne. Such erratic changes are unsettling, and make another contrast with Amundsen. As captain of *Fram*, he had appointed a naval officer called Thorvald Nilsen and, even though Amundsen was himself a qualified Master, and leader of the expedition, he never challenged Nilsen's authority on board.

From Melbourne, *Terra Nova* sailed on to New Zealand. There, at Lyttelton,

Figure 5 Fram *in high seas, two men at the helm, to stop her flying up into the wind. In the Roaring Forties on the way to the Antarctic, October-November 1910.*

– National Library of Norway

she was restowed, finally to gather the various threads of an intricate enterprise. Scott wanted to be the first man at the South Pole but, following the precept that 'gentlemen don't practice', he had done nothing since *Discovery* to learn more about snow travel. Succumbing to the national vice, dishonesty of purpose, he also disclaimed anything so unseemly as a race. Either way, snow travel was the crux, and here the cargo that *Terra Nova* took on board at Lyttelton told its own tale.

Three crates on deck each held a motor sledge, shipped from England. They were the outcome of Scott's experiments with motors in the snow. These went back to his return from the *Discovery* expedition. In the spirit of the age, Scott thought that technology would be a short-cut to success, obviating the need systematically to acquire a mastery of the polar environment that, on *Discovery*, he had conspicuously lacked. Mechanized snow travel, however, did not yet exist. A new technology could not be devised in haste, and it eventually dawned on Scott that his motor sledges would be no panacea. He needed other forms of transport in reserve.

One result was that *Terra Nova* loaded 19 Manchurian ponies, shipped all the way from Central Asia. As an enemy can become an obsession, Scott was copying Shackleton in this. Ignoring the compact evidence of history, Shackleton had decided that sledge dogs were useless in polar travel, and turned to horses for his own heroic attempt on the South Pole. This resulted from the failure of dogs on the *Discovery* expedition. In such cases, one Norwegian polar explorer crassly remarked, 'we can safely assume that it is the masters who need training.'[13] Nonetheless Scott followed Shackleton and blamed the dogs for failings of his own.

When *Terra Nova* finally left New Zealand for the Antarctic on 29 November 1910, she was overcrowded – all of 747 tons with 65 men on board – grossly overloaded, and top heavy with assorted cargo including bales of fodder on her decks. In ice-clad Antarctica there was no grazing, and all feed for the ponies had to be brought along. Dogs of course, being carnivores, could live off the seals crowding the coast. Raked from stem to stern by violent seas a day or two out from New Zealand, *Terra Nova* nearly foundered in a storm. Because of a slovenly refit, her pumps failed, and water slopped around the bilges to threaten her with capsizing. Somehow she scraped through. Deep-laden, she lumbered on southwards in uncertain weather and heavy seas.

Fram, meanwhile, was some 3,800 miles astern, having already gained 2,000 miles since the start, and still bearing down. She was a floating kennel. One hundred Eskimo dogs were draped about the ship, with fecund bitches holding more on the way. The 19 men on board pandered to their every whim, for the animals were the key to *their* enterprise. Amundsen at least had no doubts over technique. He had staked all on sledge dogs to get him quickly to the Pole, and back home safely again. His dogs came from northern Greenland, because they were thought to be the best. He had ordered them through the Danish authorities, who obligingly shipped them straight to Norway, where they were transferred to *Fram* for the long voyage south.

Dogs were only part of the tale. Skis were the remainder. Amundsen was going to run sledge dogs with men on skis. Dog driving was not native to Norway, so he had no inherent advantage over Scott. The difference was that Amundsen belonged to a school that did not believe that civilization had all the answers, but was prepared to learn from primitive tribes who had anything to teach. As a draught animal, the dog belonged to native Arctic peoples, notably Eskimos in America and Greenland, and various tribes strung out along Siberia down to Kamchatka and the Ainus of Sakhalin. It was from them that Nansen and his successors learned the technique. Dog driving was ancient; so too the ski. The combination was occasionally found among Siberian tribes, but its modern use in polar exploration was specifically Norwegian.

Fram herself had been the cradle of that technique. On her first voyage, under Nansen in the north, the men on board would practise dog sledging on the pack ice round the ship, learning as they went. Norway being the birthplace of modern skiing, they were naturally on skis. Nansen himself was the grand example. He had already revolutionized polar exploration on the first crossing of Greenland by doing so on skis. He also thereby demythologized the polar environment besides, unintentionally, popularizing the ski abroad. Unfortunately for him, he man-hauled on that occasion, but swore never to do so again.

One day, on *Fram*, someone wrote in his diary that 'We can say that skiers and dog sledge kept up with each other.'[14] This was the momentous discovery that the natural speeds of a cross-country skier and a loaded dog sledge were the same. For the record, the date was 18 February 1894 and the diarist, Sigurd Scott Hansen, a naval lieutenant on board. (Incidentally he also noted that his skis were coming apart. He was using an early, experimental form of laminated construction, while solid wood was still the rule.)

This was the origin of the whole system of polar travel that Amundsen was going to apply. *Fram* herself was also home to its advance. Between 1898 and 1902 she sailed on another expedition, now to the Canadian Arctic, commanded by Otto Sverdrup, who had captained her on her first voyage under Nansen. Sverdrup travelled perhaps 2,000 miles running skiers and dog sledges together, perfecting the technique. 'Polar exploration', so Sverdrup summed up, 'has two natural requirements: *Skis* and *dogs*.'[15] On *Fram* now there was a direct link with all this. Sverre Hassel, whom Amundsen had earmarked as a dog driver for the coming polar journey, had been on the selfsame ship under Sverdrup. Likewise Hjalmar Johansen was on board, and he had been on the first voyage of the *Fram*. In fact he had been Nansen's companion on the dash to the furthest north, the pioneering effort using skis and dogs. Besides, Amundsen had also used the technique on his traverse of the North West Passage. Helmer Hanssen, a gifted dog driver from that expedition, was also now on *Fram*, so the circle was complete.

The advantage of using skis and dogs was, firstly, that by skiing instead of riding on the sledges, the men saved that much useful load. Secondly, only a skier could comfortably keep up with the dogs and maintain a proper speed. The ski, properly used, also gave mobility and saved energy, favouring survival. Then Shackleton had proved that the Pole almost certainly lay high up across mountains on the ice cap. On that account, it would be best to know how to negotiate downhill runs on the way home. Amundsen had trained himself in mountain skiing for an occasion such as this. He and his men were mostly practised skiers with decades of experience and Olav Bjaaland at their head.

Bjaaland was an outstanding example of how Amundsen chose his men. In Amundsen's own words, he wanted 'experienced people' who were 'adapted to working outside in cold weather to the highest degree.'[16] Another example was Adolf Henrik Lindstrøm, the cook and major domo, he too a veteran of the North-West Passage. Lindstrøm came from Hammerfest in the extreme north of Norway. He was a specialist polar cook, well versed in preparing seal meat and other dishes so that, as we would say, vitamin C was preserved, and scurvy prevented. He was also a self-taught cabinet maker, mechanic, and in general the man of many talents that Amundsen particularly wanted.

Amundsen saw the human factor as nine parts of the game. He was, however, no luddite. He had a technical bent, but understood the limitations of technology. He eschewed motorized snow transport, because it was still too unreliable, and in the polar environment, at the limits of survival, he could not accept another risk, so he stuck to the proven method of dogs and skis.

Where Amundsen could reasonably exploit new technology he did so. For example, he replaced *Fram*'s steam engines with a new type of marine diesel engine[17] – a Swedish invention – making her one of the first ocean-going vessels ever with diesel propulsion. This gave quick starting and instant power without wasting fuel to keep up a head of steam. *Fram*'s chief engineer, Knut Sundbeck (a brave man, being the only Swede in a shipload of Norwegians, and whose hobby was building a perpetual motion machine) saved her many an awkward moment thereby.

According to received wisdom, *Fram* was not a good sea boat, having been designed for survival in the ice. Broad in the beam, with a rounded hull like an eggshell and no keel, to let her rise when squeezed by the pack ice, instead of being crushed, she wallowed and rolled mercilessly in the long waves of the Southern Ocean. She added the whimsical trick of flying up into the wind, so that she often needed two men at the helm. Her designer, Colin Archer, a Norwegian of Scottish descent, was a pioneering naval architect who knew all about seaworthiness. He worked with an advanced mathematical model, and all the way from Norway to the Antarctic *Fram* never shipped a sea. She was a dry ship so the dogs at least were happy. The contrast with *Terra Nova* was great. Even in a storm, when waves towered far up the mainmast, threatening to swamp her, *Fram* gave a little kick with her stern at the last moment, and the sea swept harmlessly beneath.

Running before the westerly gales of the roaring forties, *Fram*, like a tubby Viking ship sailing on a raid, swooped and yawed onwards to Antarctica. To avoid boredom Amundsen had originally left making equipment like tents and paraffin tanks for the stable drift in the ice; now the same work had to be done with the pitching and tossing of a seaway underfoot. It was finished by the end of the oceanic part of the voyage and arrival at the pack ice guarding the Ross Sea.

In the space of three-and-a-half days, by a combination of Colin Archer's talent, the accumulated expertise of the specialized ice pilots on board, and the skill of the ship's captain, Thorvald Nilsen, not to mention Sundbeck and his diesel, *Fram* cantered through the ice and emerged into the open waters beyond. She had found exactly the right point in the pack ice at the right time of year. On 14 January 1911, *Fram* reached her destination at the Bay of Whales, where Amundsen proposed to put his base. It was near the Eastern end of what is now called the Ross Ice Shelf, but was then known as the Great Ice Barrier.

The name 'Ross' commemorates Admiral Sir James Clark Ross, a British naval officer, arguably one of the greatest polar explorers, and the moving spirit of this story. In 1841 Ross discovered the open sea and the ice shelf that bear his name, in addition to several hundred miles of the adjacent coast. Amundsen recognized the greatness of his predecessor. With only sails and the power of the wind, Ross 'plunged into the heart of a pack which all previous polar explorers regarded as certain death,' Amundsen admiringly wrote. 'It is difficult for us to understand . . . We who only need a signal to start the propeller, and wriggle out of the first difficulty we meet.'[18]

It was the book that Ross wrote about his expedition that persuaded Amundsen to put his base on the ice shelf itself. The ice shelf is, in effect, a huge glacier abutting the Antarctic continent, continually flowing onwards to calve icebergs now and then. Conventional wisdom predicted that this process would send Amundsen's base out to sea. Amundsen however understood the uses of history. He had read his Ross, and identified the Bay of Whales with an inlet that Ross discovered in the Barrier around 165° W. longitude in 1841. One of his officers called it The Barrier Bight.[19] Later sightings, including one by Ross himself in 1842, then Scott on *Discovery* in 1902, and Shackleton in 1908, all confirmed an opening at the position of Ross's Barrier Bight. It periodically changed shape being now what Shackleton had called the Bay of Whales, but it was essentially the same permanent formation.

From the masthead, Ross had also observed an undulating rise in the Barrier to the South. Amundsen interpreted this as the shape of ice flowing over a solid obstacle. He reasoned that the Barrier must be grounded at that point, which explained the existence of the Bay of Whales and made it relatively safe. He was right for the wrong reasons. The Bay of Whales was afloat, but in the lee of Roosevelt Island, a shoal which was subsequently discovered. The ice does indeed flow over it, to be slowed in its advance but also divided into two streams that rejoin each other downstream in a violent clash like standing waves in a cataract. That is what explains the feature called the Bay of Whales, permanent in its underlying formation, but breaking off now and then as the ice moves inexorably on towards the open sea.

Long before, while still planning his campaign, Amundsen had decided that the advantages of the location outweighed the risks of the ice shelf calving precisely at that point. It lay directly on the field of action, with no danger of being cut off. It was closer to the Pole than Scott's base at the other end of the Barrier by a whole degree of latitude. Fate had pointed Amundsen in that direction. He knew that Scott was heading for McMurdo Sound, at the western end of the Barrier, so that was out of bounds. In any case, along the whole ice front, 400 miles long, almost at the eastern end, the Bay of Whales was about the only place where it was low enough for landing. Elsewhere it was, as Bjaaland put it, 'this Great Wall of China [that] glitters . . . It is a strange feeling that grips one [at] the sight.'[20]

Having started 5,000 miles behind, Amundsen was now 60 miles ahead. Through a strategic decision, he had secured a tactical advantage. He might already have won the battle before it began. Whatever the circumstances, he understood the relation between strategy and tactics – and of how many generals can that be said?

Terra Nova, meanwhile, spent three weeks beset in the pack ice, wasting coal to keep up steam for her antiquated engines. Unlike *Fram*, she had no

Figure 6 Framheim, Amundsen's base at the Bay of Whales.

– Author's collection

ice pilot. That was symptomatic. Amundsen wanted the best men of their kind, and tried to match their personalities. It is difficult to detect any pattern in Scott's method of selection, beyond ignoring the lessons of the past, and minimal experience of snow and ice, with a preference for naval men. They were a company 'shoved together at random',[21] as Dr Wilson himself cheerfully admitted. Eventually, *Terra Nova* emerged from the pack, found the Ross Sea and, on the 4th January 1911, finally reached her destination in McMurdo Sound. She was unable to break through the bay ice to reach terra firma at the edge of the Ice Barrier, so Scott settled in haste for a promontory further out on Ross Island. It was named for the occasion Cape Evans, after Edward Ratcliffe Garth Russell Evans ('Teddy' to his intimates), a naval lieutenant (later Admiral Lord Mountevans) second in command of the expedition. Unloading began immediately, over a strip of bay ice anchored to the land.

Rising up nearby, a landmark with a wisp of smoke, was Mount Erebus, the only active volcano in Antarctica, and gloomily named by Ross after one of his ships – *Terror* was the other[22] – which in turn had been baptized after the ancient Greek figure of primeval darkness. Scott had been there before, on the *Discovery* expedition, so to him it was all familiar. Nonetheless through persistent ignorance of sea ice, one of the motor sledges broke through on unloading,

and irretrievably sank to the bottom of McMurdo Sound. That too was symptomatic. Moreover Cape Evans itself boded ill as Erebus. The base hut being built
there was connected with the edge of the Ice Barrier by a temperamental sheet
of bay ice that could unexpectedly go out and therefore, because of obstructive
ice falls from Erebus, risked being cut off from the field of action.

Meanwhile, at the other end of the Ice Barrier, the road to the South began
on the doorstep of the Norwegian base hut that was being assembled from pre-
fabricated sections. It was a modest structure, just big enough to house the nine
men who made up Amundsen's shore party. Scott's hut was more elaborate, with
twenty seven inhabitants. Moreover, the space was divided by an improvised
wall into two sections, one for officers and gentlemen, and another for ratings.
In Amundsen's quarters, there were no such distinctions. It made good sense
to preserve the customs of each society. The real distinction was this. Most of
Scott's men had hardly seen snow before, while all of Amundsen's companions
were inured to a cold climate, and several knew the Arctic as well.

Amundsen and his men had quickly settled down. The hut was about two nautical miles from the water's edge, so *Fram*'s cargo had to be taken there by sledge.
Amundsen used this to teach dog driving to the tyros. That included Bjaaland,
and a naval gunner called Oscar Wisting, who was to play a leading role in the
story. Running back and forth, they each covered perhaps 500 miles in all, which
enabled men and dogs to learn each other's foibles. Amundsen had anticipated
this shuttle between ship and hut, so had prepared pennants on low sticks in
advance to mark the course. Faced with the same circumstances, but without the
same forethought, Scott had had to improvise markers with empty paraffin tins.
It was a contrast that some of his men were soon able personally to observe.

In the small hours of 4 February 1911, *Terra Nova* appeared at the Bay of
Whales and lay to at the edge of the ice just ahead of *Fram*. It was the sole
encounter between the two expeditions, and thus historic in its way.

The Norwegians had long expected the British, but to say that the British
were thunderstruck would be an understatement. They were not expecting
the Norwegians there at all. Scott had tried to conceal Amundsen's cable at
Melbourne, even from his own men, but the news of course leaked out. Scott
then did the next best thing, and discouraged all speculation about Amundsen's
intentions. In Amundsen's mental world, his cable to Scott at Melbourne – 'Beg
leave to inform you *Fram* proceeding Antarctic' – was a polite way of issuing
a challenge. Scott was too English to understand a foreigner or allow for lin-
guistic difference, so he could not grasp the implications of what he read. In any
case Amundsen had unequivocally stated his intention. He was going to 'take
part in the fight for the South Pole',[23] as he put it in a press release. His brother

Leon, after returning from Madeira, gave this to journalists in Christiania on 1 October 1910. It was front-page stuff in the Norwegian capital but, through a combination of execrable staff work by Scott's supporters, and the dubious judgement of Fleet Street foreign news editors, it was slow in filtering through to the English-speaking world.

Even so, Amundsen remained impenetrably discreet. He 'could not yet say with certainty' where he would land, as he announced. There was a reason for keeping this secret within a secret. In his published plans, Scott had revealed that he would have two bases: besides McMurdo Sound at the Western end of the Ice Barrier, also King Edward VII Land to the East.[24] King Edward VII Land was too close for comfort to the Bay of Whales. Amundsen had to avoid provoking his rival into forestalling him. He did find the Bay of Whales untenanted, but it was a close run thing. A bare three weeks separated the arrival of *Fram* and *Terra Nova*.

Scott had let slip his opinion that Amundsen was bound for the Weddell Sea, on the other side of Antarctica. Hence the sense of shock when *Terra Nova* stumbled on the Norwegians at the Bay of Whales. Amundsen himself may have encouraged that misconception. In his statement to the Press, he said that on returning from the Antarctic, after putting the landing party ashore, *Fram* would first put in at Punta Arenas, in the Straits of Magellan. That certainly pointed to the Weddell Sea. However, it was also a natural stop on the way from the Bay of Whales to Buenos Aires, *Fram*'s destination for the southern winter.

That is a story of its own. Before leaving Norway, Amundsen was not only in debt but – what seemed to be his fate – quite simply broke. His compatriots were uninterested. He could not even afford the cost of a relief voyage to fetch him back from Antarctica. At the eleventh hour, Providence duly intervened. A wealthy expatriate Norwegian in the Argentine known as Don Pedro Christophersen wanted to do something for the old country, and one way was to offer Amundsen the help he might require. *Fram* would head for Buenos Aires to receive Don Pedro's generosity.

Meanwhile, at the Bay of Whales, *Terra Nova* at last discovered Amundsen's presence in the Ross Sea, and his real intentions. The shock of the truth following concealment from on high was almost a paradigm of British public life. 'It appears that . . . Capt. Amundsen . . . is going to have a run for the Pole so it will prove a very exciting affair', one astonished *Terra Nova* seaman wrote in his diary, summing up the general feeling on board. 'He has dogs for sledge work and all his men are good on ski.'[25]

Terra Nova had arrived, because swirling ice had stopped her landing a party on King Edward VII Land, and the Bay of Whales offered an alternative approach. The visitors were shown all over *Fram*, being suitably awestruck by treading the deck of 'the famous ship'. They could also observe the quiet efficiency around them compared with the amateurish muddle at McMurdo Sound. Amundsen, who nursed no feelings of prescriptive right, personally told the Englishmen to land where they liked and make themselves at home. The Englishmen, however, taking a high moral stance over Amundsen's 'intrusion', gallantly spurned his well-intentioned offer. So on the same afternoon of arrival, *Terra Nova* sailed off.

The following day Amundsen's hut was formally named Framheim – 'The home of *Fram*' – a word play on Jotunheimen, 'The Home of the Giants', the highest mountain range in Norway. Soon after, on 10 February, Amundsen, with three companions, three sledges and 18 dogs, set off on their first tour to put out a depot for the next season's polar journey.

Antarctica is one of the few places on earth where Man comes close to controlling his own fate. It is an ice cap resting on continental land and, away from the marine life along its shores, it is a freezing desert. Snow rarely falls; it is simply blown from one place to another. The lifeless hinterland is clinically free of hostile bacteria and hostile men, although which is worse must remain a moot point. A man is thrown on his own resources. He must carry all supplies with him, and create the conditions to support life. It can only be compared with travel out in space, for which it also holds some lessons. Survival is a simple matter of logistics. Depots of food and fuel of the right size, properly spaced, are the means; hence the importance of preliminary journeys to put them out.

Amundsen understood this. He and his companions were back in five days, having moved half a ton of supplies to 80° S. They had pushed their advanced base forward some 80 nautical miles. There was also something more. Scott was following a route surveyed by Shackleton to within 100 miles of the goal. Amundsen was faced by the unknown, bedevilled by the whims and vagaries of moving ice. He could only be certain of where he had already trodden. He eschewed Scott's advertised route. Instead he was going to make a beeline for the Pole, following a meridian of longitude – a Great Circle course in navigating parlance – for the shortest possible distance. He would have to pioneer a completely new route. That meant exploring and racing at the same time. In the depot journey he had managed to reconcile that conflict.

The psychological consequences were arguably greater. This was part of a plan that Amundsen had devised at the beginning in his home by the fjord in Christiania. It was Amundsen's style of leadership to share his plans in all their detail with his men, so that everyone understood what was happening, and grasped their own function in relation to the whole. In fact he had posted an

Figure 7 The fateful encounter. Scott's Terra Nova *(l.) and Amundsen's* Fram *meet at the Bay of Whales, 4th February 1911.*

– National Library of Norway

exposition of his polar campaign in *Fram's* charthouse, so that his companions had the whole voyage to familiarize themselves with the details before landing, and understand what was expected of them. That first depot journey proved that now the plans were also working in the field, and seen to be working.

There was also a psychological victory over Amundsen's Antarctic predecessors, Shackleton and Scott. After a few miles the dreadful Barrier turned out to be just a snowfield, like any other. Snow, after all, to Amundsen, like anyone who understands it, is simply Nature in another form. It is a versatile, complex and friendly substance. It is building material, insulation, water supply, a refrigerator for preserving food and, to a skier, an efficient means of travel, making all the frozen world a highway. Scott, by contrast, saw snow as an enemy to be conquered, with himself as the invader, making another distinction between the two expeditions.

Amundsen and his highly adapted companions soon felt at home. 'The skiing on the Barrier', Amundsen wrote disbelievingly in his diary, 'is splendid'.[26] It was merely an extension of familiar surroundings. Almost as an afterthought, Amundsen had proved, on the first serious journey, that the Norwegian system of running dogs together with men on skis did work in Antarctica as well. The going was much easier than on the shifting pack ice of the Arctic. There was a scintilla of relief that Fate had sent them South.

When all is said and done, however, the dogs were an auxiliary; it was the ski that lay at the heart of the system. In Amundsen's own words:

> Every day we had reason to praise our skis. We often asked each other where we would have been without these excellent devices. The answer was mostly: probably at the bottom of some crevasse or hole. Already on reading the various reports of the Barrier's appearance and nature, it was clear to all of us, who were bred and born with skis on our feet, that these must be considered indispensable. This opinion was fortified day by day, and it is not saying too much that they played . . . the most important . . . rôle . . . on our . . . expedition. Many a time we moved over parts so crevassed and broken that it would have been impossible to negotiate on foot. I need not elaborate on the advantage of skis in deep, loose snow.[27]

Returning to Framheim, Amundsen found that *Fram* herself had already left for the Southern winter. He felt an ambivalent aftertaste of *Terra Nova*, with the distant threat of Scott's motor sledges, but the bizarre presence of two ponies on board. Of the dogs on the last day's run, Amundsen wrote: '51½ nautical miles, [hauling] 50 kg per dog . . . they will hold their own with the ponies on the Barrier all right.'[28]

If only he had known.

The Norwegians and their dogs had done a return trip of 160 nautical miles or so in five days. By a suitable coincidence, they arrived home on 15 February, and the next day Scott reached the limit of his first, and only depot journey, having taken 24 days for the outward journey of a bare 120 nautical miles, or about one-fifth Amundsen's speed. Scott too had wanted to reach 80° S, but now stopped at 79°28½'. The ponies had been his undoing. They were clearly unadapted to the circumstances. They suffered in the Antarctic cold. They could not move against a blizzard, and wilted in the kind of temperatures – a modest –20°C. that they were now facing. They needed irksome and time-consuming care. At each camp, they had to be rubbed down and covered with blankets for the night, while snow walls were built to shield them from the wind. To save his own feelings Scott, squeamish to a degree, had shrunk from driving them further, although with every mile his own fate might be hanging in the balance.

For want of snowshoes, the ponies sank in snowdrifts up to their bellies, while dogs tripped happily on top. This was understandable. A pony exerts a pressure of 15 lbs per square inch on its hooves, but for a dog's paw the figure is 3½ – and a man on ski only ½. On the trail, the dog trotted unconcernedly in fair weather and in foul. In camp, he kept warm on his own and generally looked after himself.

Scott illogically resented Nature for having adapted dogs to the conditions and not his favoured ponies. He gave as one reason that when the beasts were hungry they 'eat their own excrement. With the ponies it does not seem so horrid, as there must be a good deal of grain, &c., which is not fully digested. It is the worst side of dog driving.'[29] He was able to make comparisons because, against his will, he had also brought dogs along. Nansen, and others, had persuaded him to do so as an extra precaution on top of motor sledges and ponies. Scott had ordered about 35 from Siberia, of whom 30 had survived to land at McMurdo Sound. He was now using them together with the ponies.

The depot journey therefore turned into a cumbrous procession. Captain Lawrence Edward Grace Oates, a British Army cavalry officer, appointed to look after the ponies, was quietly appalled at the folly of running two kinds of transport. It meant staggered starts to allow for different speeds. The dogs, being quickest, would set off last. Timing was ragged. Most days were marred by confusion and misunderstanding. This had much to do with Scott's style of leadership. Unlike Amundsen, he kept his intentions to himself. He depended on the old naval system of blind obedience to orders and, as a Captain, R. N., treated any questioning or initiative as tantamount to mutiny.

Captain Oates, of the Sixth Inniskilling Dragoons, was one of two paying volunteers. The other was Apsley Cherry Garrard, a young, impressionable Oxford graduate who, it was felt, needed toughening. They each subscribed £1000, about £75,000 today. In the nicest possible way, they had bought their way into the expedition for some adventure and a change of scene; something that Amundsen would never have countenanced.

Scott's dog driver was an eclectic traveller called Cecil Meares. A habitué of Central Asia, somehow connected with the War Office, probably through Intelligence, Meares was well acquainted with distant snows. He had crossed Siberia in winter from south to north, driving dogs and sledges. For unclear reasons someone at the Admiralty had pressed him on Scott. At any rate, Meares had much in common with Oates – who had served in India – and shared his contempt for Scott's bungled travelling.

Also taken aback was the incongruous figure of a Norwegian called Tryggve Gran. Scott had brought him as a ski expert. The origins of that were also rooted in the Discovery expedition. Scott had then tried skis, failed and, echoing his experience with the dogs, blamed the skis, dismissing them for polar travel. Then in March 1910, Scott had visited Norway to test his motor sledges. He met Nansen who, in a spirit of charity, arranged a demonstration of skiing by practised, native skiers, which Scott, oddly enough, had never seen before. Scott swung to the other extreme. From the depths of disbelief, he now invested the ski with quasi-magical powers and, at Nansen's suggestion, appointed Gran to imprint the virtues of skiing on recalcitrant acolytes. When he reached the ice, Scott's attitude to skis vacillated again. On the depot journey, Gran found himself ignominiously ordered to wade through the snow *on foot* and lead a pony, while his skis were dragged behind on a sledge. He had a Sisyphean task in trying to make competent skiers out of reluctant beginners in a few weeks. In a telling comparison, Amundsen's shore party had nearly two centuries of skiing between them; Scott, with three times the number, could barely muster five years.

Nonetheless both were Nansen's heirs, because he had introduced the ski to polar exploration. He gave it even more. For the first crossing of Greenland, he had invented a new kind of sledge. Hitherto, polar explorers had used a heavy model with narrow wooden runners, descended from the polar Eskimos. Nansen introduced a light, flexible pattern with broad, ski-like runners. He based it on an ancient type used by Norwegian farmers, but also found among Siberian tribes, the Samoyeds in particular. It ran more easily, and generally floated on soft snow. It proved so superior that, dubbed the Nansen sledge, it was universally adopted. Both Amundsen and Scott used it as a matter of course. So in skis and sledges, each followed the same basic travelling technique inherited from Nansen. That they applied it in different ways, and Scott reluctantly, is another matter altogether. Amundsen experimented and modified in the search for technical perfection. Scott simply bought skis and sledges off the shelf in Christiania. This is what he was now using on his depot journey.

Having built the depot – called One Ton, after the weight of its contents – Scott, goaded by some obscure presentiment, was seized with impatience to return to base. Despite his lingering suspicion of dogs, he ordered Meares to rush him back instantly as quickly as he could, leaving his subordinates straggling behind to cope with the ponies alone. On 22 February, Scott reached the old *Discovery* hut at the edge of the Barrier. The distance that had taken over three weeks with ponies, he had covered in five days with dogs. That left him unimpressed. Against all the evidence, he still obdurately preferred his ponies, as if he could not bear to admit that he might be wrong. Nor did he yet grasp that he was confronted with a race.

'I shall do everything possible to meet [Scott] down there and tell him my decision', Amundsen had written to Nansen en route to Madeira, 'and then he can act accordingly.'[30] *Terra Nova* offered an acceptable proxy in Lt (later Captain) Victor Campbell, a Royal Navy officer, who was temporarily in

Figure 8   Unusual picture of Amundsen (centre) at Framheim, the Norwegian base at the Bay of Whales during the southern winter of 1911.

– National Library of Norway

command, before leading the now abortive expedition to King Edward VII Land.

Campbell had Norwegian connections. He owned salmon fishing rights in western Norway, spoke the language, and was a passable skier. For some reason, he was not in the main landing party. Regretfully he sailed away from the Bay of Whales to find another field of action, eventually going ashore for the winter at Cape Adare, on the tip of South Victoria Land and there passes out of the story. Along the way, on 8 February, *Terra Nova* put in at McMurdo Sound, to land Campbell's two ponies, for which he now felt he had no further use. At the old *Discovery* hut Campbell also left a letter with the news of Amundsen.

That was what was awaiting Scott when he arrived from his depot journey on 22 February. Amundsen was lucky not to have delivered his message in person. Scott's reaction was to 'proceed as though this had not happened. To go forward and do our best for the honour of the country without fear or panic.'[31] That at least was how he put it in his diary. To his companions he presented a different aspect. 'For many hours Scott cd. think of nothing else not talk of anything else. Evidently a great shock for him', Cherry-Garrard noted. 'I think Scott had a bad night.'[32] Mental collapse is not pleasant to behold, even in a rival, and the effect on Amundsen might have been unsettling.

Scott's agitation was at least partly explained by his naval career. He was the everlasting subaltern, who had been promoted above his level. Amundsen suffered from a different kind of pressure. His was a classic case of a big man from a small country, with all the claustrophobia and mental suffocation that that implied. Henrik Ibsen, no slavish admirer of his fellow-Norwegians, expressed it in these lines:

> They all agree on one thing alone,
> That every great man must be toppled and stoned[33]

Scott was also disturbed by the collapse of self-delusion. Until then, he had succumbed to the old habit of British politicians and officialdom in pretending that a threat did not exist. The authorities at home had reassured him. Sir Clements Markham, now retired from the RGS, but still devoted to Scott, and obstinate as ever, took a different view. Alone, he used his Norwegian contacts to ferret out information. As a result he persuaded the RGS to cable Scott on 4 November 1910 – erroneously – that Amundsen was heading for McMurdo Sound. Scott also concealed that cable from his companions at the time. When he arrived at McMurdo Sound to find no Amundsen, he decided that the Norwegian threat had disappeared. Now Scott had been outmanoeuvred. Amundsen was on his doorstep, and there *was* to be a race after all.

It did not help that Campbell reported that the Norwegians were 'a tough looking lot'[34] or that Scott thought it 'very unsporting since our plans of landing a party there were known.' That expressed the general view. Captain Oates begged to differ. One of two Etonians on the expedition (Campbell being the other), he was less prone to other-worldly considerations. 'They say that Amundsen has been underhand' Oates had characteristically written to his mother on first hearing the news, 'but I personally don't see it is underhand to keep your mouth shut.'[35]

At least Oates had a sense of proportion. More blows followed Campbell's letter further to distress Scott. When his depot party returned, one of the ponies died, probably from exposure. Others then perished in a breakup of the ice near the *Discovery* hut. This resulted from Scott's orders to march offshore, showing persistent ignorance of sea ice, and a disregard for working cracks that foretold imminent disaster. The outcome of the depot journey was that seven out of eight ponies had been lost. The travel had been abysmal, the goal unattained.

Campbell's letter almost seemed like Fate knocking at the door. 'Scott thinks

[Amundsen] will get to the Pole – said so in as many words', Cherry-Garrard observed. Scott now grasped that he had underestimated his opponent. Because of the ponies, he would have to start later than Amundsen, besides which Amundsen's base was closer to the Pole. And revealingly, as Scott put it, 'I never thought [Amundsen] could get so many dogs on to the Barrier.' In other words, Scott now understood that the Norwegians would also travel faster than himself. He seemed almost doomed before the race had begun. When the expedition was reunited in the hut at Cape Evans towards the end of April, Scott had given up for the season, passively awaiting events. Fatalism was in the air.

Meanwhile, at the other end of the Barrier, Amundsen, with fewer men but more dogs, was working far later in the season to consolidate his position before winter came down. On 22 February, when Scott was learning of his threat through Campbell's letter, Amundsen set out on his second depot journey. It lasted exactly a month, during which he put out two more depots, one at 81° S. and another at 82° S. He wanted a good start for the polar journey; his real concern was to secure his line of retreat. He had driven his men, his dogs and himself hard because he did understand that, in the end, every mile would count. He achieved his aim, but eight dogs paid with their lives. In a cold snap that injured their paws and drained their strength, he had mercilessly lashed them on. It left him and his companions with lingering remorse.

There was one more trip before the sun set for the Antarctic winter on 21 April, not to reappear for another four months. This was to add a ton of seal meat and other supplies to the depot at 80° S.; also to mark the route there with pennants like a mountain ski touring track at home.

Devoid of radio, each expedition was isolated from the other, so that Amundsen could not know that his forward base at 82° S. was now 150 naut- ical miles ahead of Scott; nor that he had put out three times Scott's single ton of supplies. What Amundsen did know was that he was better prepared for the cold, because he had fur clothing, but Scott did not. Amundsen had learned from the Eskimos on the North West Passage. His teachers were the Netsilik tribe, highly adapted to a polar environment. They had had little contact with Europeans, and therefore had best preserved their native lore. Amundsen cop- ied the pattern of their garments, inner and outer, loose-fitting, with plenty of air pockets and air circulation. This was to prevent sweating, the enemy of insulation, and keeping warm and dry. He had them made up in reindeer fur, like the Netsiliks, besides sealskin, and Burberry cloth for kinder weather. So far the reindeer fur had kept him warm; too warm even below −40°C. when skiing fast.

It was now, in the long Antarctic winter, that Amundsen's style of leadership came into its own. Among polar explorers, he was a pioneer in psychological screening. He tried to eliminate misfits and adventurers. He understood the psychology of small groups. He had chosen his men for their skills and personality, but they were individualists and not team players in the usual sense, subsumed into the collective. Amundsen aimed to harness individual talent to a common end without stifling enterprise. By contrast, Scott understood only 'the patter of many feet on deck', and exercised an authoritarian system of blind obedience that crushed initiative and drained mental energy.

Two American academics, Boynton and Fischer, call Amundsen's method the 'virtuoso team'; the antithesis of Scott's hierarchical discipline and today's corporate mentality. They cite Amundsen as one example; others range from Jerome Robbins, who created *West Side Story*, to Colonel Groves, who led the Manhattan Project, which produced the atom bomb.[36]

Amundsen resolved his problem by treating his men as individuals. 'I . . . let everybody have the feeling of being independent within his own sphere', as he himself put it. 'In that way [everyone] is treated as a rational being, not as a machine.'[37]

Nature gave a helping hand. The hut had been drifted up. Instead of clearing the snow, someone proposed burrowing into it and digging out workshops and stores (and a sauna) to relieve congestion in the hut. It was, as Amundsen said, working with Nature instead of against her – his philosophy (and that of the Scandinavian school of polar exploration) in a nutshell. A whole warren of snow caves sprang up, so that the party was separated during working hours, gathering only at mealtimes and in the evening. Much friction was avoided thereby. The dogs slept in their own bell tents, cased about with snow for insulation. They were the lucky ones. They had halcyon days with nothing to do but eat, sleep, drink and chase bitches to their heart's content. Until the spring, it was their masters who would have to do all the work.

Now Amundsen proved that he had the moral and material reserves to overcome his setbacks. For all their success, the depot journeys had exposed a plethora of failings. Among the more troubling were the tents. Amundsen had originally decided on a two-man model, reasoning that it would be warmer. In practice, it turned out to be crowded at mealtimes, and generally oppressive. Hassel suggested sewing them together to make four or five-man tents. He and Wisting, seamen both, having the necessary skill, did the work in a few days.

The sledges had also failed. Misled by his predecessors, Amundsen had ordered models to cope with rough terrain. They were too stiff and heavy for the gentle snowfield the Barrier turned out to be. They ran badly. They had to be made lighter and more flexible. This involved planing down the runners, by hand naturally. Bjaaland did the work. Besides being a ski champion, Bjaaland was a skilled carpenter, ski maker, and violin maker into the bargain. He also made four new extra-light sledges for speed on the ice cap. Critically, he overhauled the specially made skis, of solid hickory, 2½ m long, like jumping skis today. They were broad, with flaring tips to give a large bearing surface for safe passage over crevasses, across sastrugi and other little devilments of snow and ice.

Another drawback was the weight of the sledging cases for holding supplies. They were made to Amundsen's novel design, with a circular press-lid of aluminium, like a tea caddy, for ease of opening without undoing the lashings on the sledge. Made of solid ash for strength and resistance to cold, they were far too heavy. They had to be lightened. The other carpenter, Jørgen Stubberud, did the work. He had already made the hut in Norway, and now dismantled all the packing cases, planing down each single board by hand, before reassembling them.

The most serious failure was the ski boots. Received wisdom had it that soft footwear was the only pattern for deep cold. *Finnesko* were commonly used, notably by Scott. They only suited simple toestraps on the skis however. Amundsen wanted a stiff-soled boot to use with the Huitfeldt binding and the Høyer-Ellefsen tensioned heelstrap.[38] This was the first modern binding with fixed metal toe irons. It gave absolute lateral control, essential for good technique and saving energy. It would also ease any downhill runs from the polar plateau. Ordinary stiff-soled boots, however, impeded circulation, risking frostbite at low temperature.

Amundsen set out to remove that drawback, and design a stiff-soled boot adapted to deep cold. It had never been done before. He began by ordering extra large ski boots with space for multiple inner soles and socks. There was no time to experiment at home. They quickly proved defective in the field. They were too small, the soles too thick, and leather uppers too stiff. So a classic process of development ensued. Various members of the party turned themselves into cobblers. They successively enlarged the boots and thinned the soles so that they still bore the lateral strain of the bindings and the longitudinal pressure of the heelstrap without restricting movement of the heel and risking frostbite. Leather in the uppers was cut away and replaced with thin canvas, which was softer and more flexible. In the end, leather remained only in the sole and toecaps. What emerged was the first stiff-soled, cold-weather footwear, and an ancestor of the modern cross-country racing boot. Part of the system was seven layers of insulating material, especially fur, worn within the boot.

Besides sledges, skis and boots, there was much else to be done. Every last item of equipment had to be overhauled or improved. Working a six-hour day, six days a week, the expedition took all winter to prepare for the polar journey. Kristian Prestrud, the only ship's officer to go ashore, gave a refresher course in navigation, attendance at which was compulsory, Amundsen included. Prestrud also gave an optional refresher course in English for those who wished to study the comprehensive library of polar literature that Amundsen had somehow acquired.

Back at McMurdo Sound, meanwhile, things were rather different. A leisurely air of insouciance prevailed. Preparations for the sledging season began after the southern midwinter, and then only by the ratings, working part time.

In one of their few points of resemblance, both Amundsen and Scott overtly ignored each other's presence for most of the winter. As spring approached, with the return of the sun after the winter on 24 August 1911 their attitudes diverged. Scott continued with his declared pretence that Amundsen did not exist. Anyway, he knew that if he did not succeed, he might still be forgiven a 'glorious failure'.

Amundsen had no such comfort. For him, it was victory or nothing. Underestimating an opponent was not one of Amundsen's failings, and he was ever conscious of the looming figure of Scott. Scott had announced that he would reach the Pole on 22 December. That was barely four months off . Somehow Amundsen had to forestall him. Not only Amundsen, but his companions were now growing restive beneath their habitual calm. They imagined Scott's motor sledges, impervious to the weather, already on their way.

Thus plagued, and against all experience, Amundsen decided on an early start. At first he suggested the return of the sun after the Antarctic winter. He was voted down. He knew his men. He could not simply give orders and rely on unthinking obedience. He discussed his plans openly at every stage – even the possibility of waiting until 1 November – because he could lead only with consent. He now proposed some time early in September. The sun was not yet wholly above the horizon and, as if on a distant planet, its rays held no warmth. His companions reluctantly agreed, including one vote by secret ballot. Eight men were to make the attempt, leaving only Lindstrøm behind, to look after the hut on his own. One day, about a fortnight after the sun returned, when the temperature rose from −50°C. to the relatively humane level of −37°C. (mercury freezes at −38.9°C.), Amundsen finally set off. About the same time, Scott was making his first moves toward the Pole. Now the diaries take up the tale. Like many historical documents, they are superficially unimpressive. Those from the polar journey itself are written in pencil, and naturally reflect the diarists.

Scott chose Winsor and Newton's artists sketchbooks; his arrangement is unsystematic. Amundsen and Bjaaland used ordinary notebooks, keeping their entries in strict chronological order.

RACE FOR THE SOUTH POLE

FRIDAY, SEPTEMBER 1ST, 1911
Scott

Friday, Sept. 1st. A very windy night, dropping to gusts in morning, preceding beautifully calm, bright day. If September holds as good as August we shall not have cause of complaint. Meares and Demetri started for Hut Point just before noon. The dogs were in fine form. Demetri's team came over the hummocky tide crack at full gallop, depositing the driver on the snow. Luckily some of us were standing on the floe. I made a dash at the bow of the sledge as it dashed past and happily landed on top; Atkinson grasped at the same object, but fell, and was dragged merrily over the ice. The weight reduced the pace, and others soon came up and stopped the team. Demetri was very crestfallen. He is extremely active and it's the first time he's been unseated.

There is no real reason for Meares' departure yet awhile, but he chose to go and probably hopes to train the animals better when he has them by themselves. As things are, this seems like throwing out the advance guard for the summer campaign.

I have been working very hard at sledging figures with Bowers' able assistance. The scheme develops itself in the light of these figures, and I feel that our organization will not be found wanting, yet there is an immense amount of detail, and every arrangement has to be more than usually elastic to admit of extreme possibilities of the full success or complete failure of the motors.

I think our plan will carry us through without the motors (though in that case nothing else must fail), and will take full advantage of such help as the motors may give. Our spring travelling is to be limited order. E. Evans, Gran, and Ford [sic] will go out to find and remark 'Corner Camp.' Meares will then carry out as much fodder as possible with the dogs. Simpson, Bowers, and I are going to stretch our legs across to the Western Mountains. There is no choice but to keep the rest at home to exercise the ponies. It's not going to be a light task to keep all these frisky little beasts in order, as their food is increased. To-day the change in masters has taken place: by the new arrangement

Wilson takes Nobby
Cherry-Garrard takes Michael
Wright takes Chinaman
Atkinson takes Jehu.

The new comers seem very pleased with their animals, though they are by no means the pick of the bunch.

Scott is writing for an audience, yet being unintentionally revealing. The departure of Meares was, in effect, the start of the polar journey. In Scott's disciplinary system, Meares' freedom of action was unique, and beyond the curious phraseology lie undertones of discord. They were at loggerheads, Meares being openly contemptuous of Scott's leadership. Scott seemed almost afraid of Meares, perhaps because Meares stood his ground, or had contacts in high places, or both.[39]

'Demetri' is Dmitryi Girov. His falling off the sledge reveals a vital difference from the Norwegians. Neither Demetri nor Meares were on ski. They either rode on the sledges or trotted by the side. Amundsen was alone in using a combination of dogs and ski. It gave him a critical advantage.

Simpson's presence was an oddity. In private, Scott called him 'old maidish', and had once rejected him from the Discovery *expedition. Bowers was a Clydeside Scot. He belonged to the Royal Indian Marine, the Indian Navy, when it was still part of the British Empire. Its officers came from the United Kingdom. Bowers was Scott's devoted servant.*

SUNDAY, SEPTEMBER 3RD, 1911
Scott

Sunday, Sept. 3rd The weather still remains fine, the temperature down in the minus thirties. All going well and everyone in splendid spirits. Last night Bowers lectured on Polar clothing. He had worked the subject up from our Polar library with critical and humorous ability, and since his recent journey he must be considered as entitled to an authoritative opinion of his own. The points in our clothing problems are too technical and too frequently discussed to need special notice at present, but as a result of a new study of Arctic precedents it is satisfactory to find it becomes more and more evident that our equipment is the best that has been devised for the purpose, always excepting the possible alternative of skins for spring journeys, an alternative we have no power to adopt. In spite of this we are making minor improvements all the time.

Bowers' research was about seven years after Amundsen's own formative experience of the North West Passage. It seems designed to bolster Scott's belief that his clothing was the 'best that has been devised for the purpose', as he put it. Nonetheless his anoraks, for example, lacking fur, and with separate hoods, were simply repeating old mistakes. Likewise the dismissal of 'skins for spring journeys' reveals an old prejudice, as recorded by Amundsen: 'The English have loudly and openly told the world that . . . fur clothes are rubbish. We will see.'[40] This was rooted in the association of fur with primitive tribes, which, to British explorers of the age, disqualified it for civilized men. The disdain applied only to clothes. Fur sleeping bags were acceptable. They were the warmest then in use.

Bowers' 'recent journey' meant one at midwinter by Bowers himself, Wilson and Cherry-Garrard. They went to Cape Crozier on Ross Island to fetch an incubating egg of the Emperor Penguin. It was Wilson's idea, connected with Darwin's theory of evolution. That gave the enterprise a scientific sheen. Ill-clothed, ill-fed, and bizarrely man-hauling on foot, because they could not use skis properly, they stumbled back after five weeks, for a total distance of a bare 70 nautical miles, within an ace of freezing to death, as if they had courted suffering for its own sake. All this too makes a contrast with Amundsen, the kernel of whose creed was to keep something in reserve and never willingly approach the limits of endurance.

FRIDAY, SEPTEMBER 8ᵀᴴ, 1911
Amundsen

Friday 8 Sept.
Today we got off at last – but not without setbacks. When the dog teams were harnessed to all the sledges, HH's and W.'s dogs bolted, as a result of which they had to chase them for a long distance before catching up with them. It was only at 12.30 p.m. that we could set off from the starting place. The skiing has been brilliant today. I have rarely had such good skiing. I myself am in the lead, while

the others follow, each with their dog team. Halted at 3.30 p.m. after having covered 10.4 nautical miles from Framheim. Unfortunately 3 of Kamilla's children have followed us and they will have to be put down as quickly as possible. The weather was lovely all the way here. Calm, partly clear –38°. We have strayed a little too far W'wards so tomorrow we must keep more E'ly in order to rejoin our old tracks.

Bjaaland

8 September
Well at last the day arrived when the great sledge journey to the south had its beginning. The weather was fine –37 with NE'ly breeze. The dogs were crazy as coots, and Hanssen's and Wisting's teams bolted over the ice towards the south and a whole hour [was wasted]. It was difficult to get going and W. capsized his sledge. Distance 10.4 nautical miles. Dogs restless. I slept badly.

SATURDAY, SEPTEMBER 9TH, 1911

Amundsen

Saturday – 9 Sept.
Off at 7.30 a.m. after a horrible night. As it happens 'Kaisa', a bitch belonging to Pr. is on heat, and that set all emotions on edge. None of us slept a minute. Have shot her today, as it was impossible to manoeuvre with her. Kamilla's three little ones were also shot. We will now have some peace at night, I imagine. We have done relatively well, considering that it is the second day – 13.5 nautical miles. We have followed all the flags previously laid out. They have not undergone any change in the course of the winter. The skiing has been the same brilliant kind as yesterday. We have climbed considerably. Have crossed a number of crevasses.

Bjaaland

9th
Fine weather and skiing. Covered 13.4 nautical miles. The dogs were crazy and confused. Seven little pups were killed. Kaisa was shot for loose living.

SUNDAY, SEPTEMBER 10TH, 1911

Amundsen

Sunday 10 Sept.

Changeable weather. At 6 a.m. Pr. and Bj. went back to the place where 'Kaisa' was shot, to fetch a pup that had stayed there. It was ca. 3 nautical miles away. They returned at 8.30 and we were then just about ready to go. The dogs were rabid in their rush this morning at the start. *No one* could control their team. They rushed off like a babbling flock of wild geese. The one team ran into the other, and a lot of time was lost in disentangling. During the disentangling, Hass.'s team ran off, and only after a long chase were we able to get hold of them again. It was only at 10 a.m. that we finally departed. But then everything went brilliantly. Those with the strongest teams bound some dogs on their sledges. Now all was well, and they stormed ahead. Halted at 3 p.m. when we had done 16.3 nautical miles. We followed the flags until the p.m. We then followed a more E'ly course to avoid the misery that we stumbled into on the last depot journey to 80°.

Bjaaland

10th –39 deg. Fine weather. Went out today with Pr. at 5.30 to fetch Kaisa's little one, that was lying 3½ nautical miles away next to its mother's carcass. The dogs were quite mad today and went on the rampage. Hassel's dogs rushed away from him after almost a whole nautical mile, when they reached me they streaked past, and probably would have gone home if I had not got hold of them. The day's run was 16.3 nautical miles. Southerly breeze –40. Nippy.

Scott

Sunday, Sept. 11th. [sic.] – A whole week since the last entry in my diary. I feel very negligent of duty, but my whole time has been occupied in making detailed plans for the Southern journey. These are finished at last, I am glad to say; every figure has been checked by Bowers, who has been an enormous help to me. If the motors are successful, we shall have no difficulty in getting to the Glacier, and if they fail, we shall still get there with any ordinary degree of good fortune. To work three units of four men from that point onwards requires no small provision, but with the proper provision it should take a good deal to stop the attainment of our object. I have tried to take every reasonable possibility of misfortune into consideration, and to so organise the parties as to be prepared to meet them. I fear to be too sanguine, yet taking everything into consideration I feel that our chances ought to be good. The animals are in splendid form. Day by day the ponies get fitter as their exercise increases, and the stronger, harder food toughens their muscles. They are very different animals from those which we took south last year, and with another month of training I feel there is not one of them but will make light of the loads we shall ask them to draw. But we cannot spare any of the ten, and so there must always be anxiety of the disablement of one or more before their work is done.

E. R. Evans, Forde, and Gran left early on Saturday for Corner Camp. I hope they will have no difficulty in finding it. Meares and Demetri came back from Hut Point the same afternoon – the dogs are wonderfully fit and strong, but Meares reports no seals up in the region, and as he went to make seal pemmican, there was little object in his staying. I leave him to come and go as he pleases, merely setting out the work he has to do in the simplest form. I want him to take fourteen bags of forage (130 lbs each) to Corner Camp before the end of October and to be ready to start for his supporting work soon after the pony party – a light task for his healthy teams. Of hopeful signs for the future none are more remarkable than the health and spirit of our people. It would be impossible to imagine a more vigorous community, and there does not seem to be a single weak spot in the twelve good men and true who are chosen for the Southern advance. All are now experienced sledge travellers, knit together with a bond of friendship that has never been equalled under such circumstances. Thanks to these people, and more especially to Bowers and Petty Officer Evans, there is not a single detail of our equipment which is not arranged with the utmost care and in accordance with the tests of experience.

It is good to have arrived at a point where one can run over facts and figures again and again without detecting a flaw or foreseeing a difficulty.

I do not count on the motors – that is a strong point in our case – but should they work well our earlier task of reaching the Glacier will be made quite easy. Apart from such help I am anxious that these machines should enjoy some measure of success and justify the time, money and thought which have been given to their construction. I am still very confident of the possibility of motor traction, whilst realizing that reliance cannot be placed on it in its present untried evolutionary state – it is satisfactory to add that my own view is the most cautious one held in our party. Day is quite convinced he will go a long way and is prepared to accept much heavier weights than I have given him. Lashly's opinion is perhaps more doubtful, but on the whole hopeful. Clissold is to make the fourth man of the motor party. I have already mentioned his mechanical capabilities. He has had a great deal of experience with motors, and Day is delighted to have his assistance.

We had two lectures last week – the first from Debenham dealing with General Geology and having special reference to the structures of our region. It cleared up a good many points in my mind concerning the gneissic base rocks, the Beacon sandstone, and the dolerite intrusions. I think we shall be in a position to make fairly good field observations when we reach the southern land.

The scientific people have taken keen interest in making their lectures interesting, and the custom has grown of illustrating them with lantern slides made from our own photographs, from books, or from drawings of the lecturer. The custom adds to the interest of the subject, but robs the reporter of notes. The second weekly lecture was given by Ponting. His store of pictures seems unending and has been an immense source of entertainment to us during the winter. His lectures appeal to all and are fully attended. This time we had pictures of the Great Wall and other stupendous monuments of North China. Ponting always manages to work in detail concerning the manners and customs of the peoples in the countries of his travels; on Friday he told us of Chinese farms and industries, of hawking and other sports, most curious of all, of the pretty amusement of flying pigeons with Aeolian whistling pipes attached to their tail feathers.

Ponting would have been a great asset to our party if only on account of his lectures, but his value as pictorial recorder of events becomes daily more apparent. No expedition has ever been illustrated so extensively, and the only difficulty will be to select from the countless subjects that have been recorded by his camera-and yet not a single subject is treated with haste; the first picture is rarely counted good enough, and in some cases five or six plates are exposed before our very critical artist is satisfied.

This way of going to work would perhaps be more striking if it were not common to all our workers here; a very demon of unrest seems to stir them to effort, and there is now not a single man who is not striving his utmost to get good results in his own particular department. *Nelson took very long to make a start but for the last month or two he has made great strides and now I have every hope that the biological results will rank with those obtained by other workers.*

It is a really satisfactory state of affairs all round. If the Southern journey comes off, nothing, not even priority at the Pole, can prevent the Expedition ranking as one of the most important that ever entered the Polar regions.

On Friday Cherry-Garrard produced the second volume of the *S. P. T.* – on the whole an improvement on the first. Poor Cherry perspired over the editorial, and it bears the signs of labour-the letterpress otherwise is in the lighter strain:

Taylor again the most important contributor, but now at rather too great a length; Nelson has supplied a very humorous trifle; the illustrations are quite delightful, the highwater mark of Wilson's ability. The humour is local, of course, but I've come to the conclusion that there can be no other form of popular journal.

The weather has not been good of late, but not sufficiently bad to interfere with exercise, &c.

E. R. Evans is Lt Evans, whose trip to Corner Camp – 88 nautical miles there and back, man-hauling again, on foot, without skis – was the next stage in the involved beginnings of the British polar journey. His namesake, Petty Officer Edgar Evans, together with Bowers, were Scott's most devoted and unquestioning followers.

It was rather late to start planning the polar journey. Scott almost seems to glory in his last-minute rush as proof of activity and an act of faith in improvisation. It was two years after launching his expedition. It was also two years since Amundsen had sat preparing his detailed plans for the Pole at home by the fjord in Christiania before sailing off.

What Scott calls 'the Glacier' is the Beardmore Glacier. This was the road to the heights, discovered and named by Shackleton after one of his patrons. Scott rarely mentions that glacier in any other way. By omitting the name of Beardmore, it is as if Scott is willing to accept Shackleton's pioneering, but grudges him the credit. Amundsen, by contrast is quite happy to give the glacier its full name, as it appeared on the map.

Scott is glossing over the state of the ponies. He had asked Meares, the dog driver, to buy the ponies, on the grounds that he happened to be in the region. Oddly enough Captain Oates, the cavalryman, and no mean judge of horseflesh, was not there, but on the ship. He first saw the animals in New Zealand, pronouncing them crocks.

Debenham's and Ponting's lectures were part of an unbroken after-dinner series, all winter long, attendance at which Scott made more-or-less compulsory, and most of which had nothing to do with polar travel. According to Tryggve Gran, the participants themselves dubbed it 'Little Oxford and Cambridge'.[41] *Scott now appears as an academic manqué; and rather more at ease, presiding over the simulacrum of an Oxford or Cambridge High Table, far removed from the impending push for the Pole.*

All winter, meanwhile, Framheim had been one big workshop, preparing for the Pole. Prestrud was working on specialized navigation at high latitudes to ease calculation on the trail. 'If we are to win', Amundsen once famously said, 'not a trouser button must be missing.'

'S.P.T.' is the South Polar Times, the expedition mag., that absolutely indispensable accessory of self-respecting polar explorers; but not, be it said, at the Bay of Whales.

The complaint about Nelson, a marine biologist, is psychologically interesting. Scott, like any senior academic wanted lots of data from his scientists, because of the kudos he hoped personally to win thereby. He did not understand contemplation and the world behind the human brow where thoughts arise. He had a mania for conspicuous activity, and treated its absence as insubordination.

MONDAY, SEPTEMBER 11TH, 1911

Amundsen

Monday 11 Sept.

−55.5° in the morning. Calm and clear. Luckily it was calm all day, so it has not felt cold in any way. We encountered some crevasses in the a.m. HH's sledge fell in badly together with me, but we hauled it right up again. Breath has formed so thickly round the sledges that sometimes we could not see the sledges. HH mostly runs ahead. For the moment, no forerunner is needed. Passed several flags yesterday. Continually bad skiing.

Bjaaland

11 September −55.5. Fine and clear. Was up and ready to go at 10 to 8. The skiing was sluggish the whole time. Hanssen's sledge ran into a crevasse and 4 men had to go to the rescue. It was bloody cold in the sleeping bag. Everything damp with the rime that forms everywhere. God knows where it will end. Have done 5.5 nautical miles.

Helmer Hanssen ('HH') was the navigator. A sailor on skis, he had before him a small ship's compass, liquid damped and mounted on gimbals in a protective box at the back of the sledge. This was the standard compass, by which the other ones were calibrated. To avoid deflecting the standard compass, Amundsen had made Helmer Hanssen's sledge non-magnetic. There was no ferrous material in its construction or its load. Steering at least was as simple as being at the helm of a ship at sea, with constant indication of course, whatever the weather or visibility, and no effect on speed.

At the time, the magnetic compass was the only practical instrument for showing direction. Unfortunately it had an inherent error. It pointed towards the magnetic pole – south in the Antarctic – so that south by compass differed from true south by an angle called the magnetic variation. Knowledge of its value was essential in following a true course. Changing with time and place, it was found by a particular observation of the sun known as the azimuth [see Glossary p. 315]. On the featureless, unexplored Barrier, bounded only by the horizon, Amundsen was like a deep sea mariner in uncharted waters, navigating by sun and compass alone.

TUESDAY, SEPTEMBER 12ᵀᴴ, 1911

Amundsen

Tuesday 12 Sept.
Poor visibility. Horrible breeze from S. −52° Dogs obviously weakened by the cold. People stiff in their frozen clothes – more or less content after a night of frost – prospects of milder weather doubtful – all this persuaded me to settle for reaching the depot at 80° this time – deposit our things and then return as quickly as possible to await the arrival of spring. To risk men and animals out of sheer obstinacy and continue, just because we have started on our way – that would never occur to me. If we are to win this game, the pieces must be moved carefully – one false move, and everything can be lost. After an hour's travel today, the liquid in our damped compasses turned out to have become so viscous that the compasses were utterly useless. To start with, we tried to steer with the fragment of sun that we had. Found it advisable to make camp at 10 a.m. The sun was then almost invisible, and air thick with impenetrable mist blocked all sight ahead. Instead of pitching the tents, we made two igloos, and were nice and warm inside despite the inhospitable weather outside. Will carry on as soon as we can see.

Bjaaland

Tuesday 12 September. It was a cold night and the same sort of day. Some wind and fog so we had to stop and build an igloo, where we are now sitting and eating and drinking. The Chief's mood is at freezing point and he made the decision to turn for home, and just as well, otherwise we would have frozen to death. This igloo is nice and warm unlike the tent which was full of rime frost. Sleeping bags and clothes are wet through; in fact stiff as iron, but when one has finally got into them, one just has to stay there. God help me it was just shit and best forgotten.

Here Amundsen reveals his view of exploration as a game of chess 'If your opponent moves a piece, you must be able to answer with a counter-move,' he had once remarked. 'Everything must be planned ahead, so that one is not surprised by anything unforeseen'.[42] It is not a bad philosophy for a Nordic ski race either.

Both Amundsen and Bjaaland, meanwhile, record the peculiarities of fur in a polar environment. Fur is adapted to dry cold. Moisture is anathema. Eskimos have always understood this, and therefore, at low temperatures, refused to hurry as a matter of self preservation. Excess speed means sweat, which condenses on the fur, destroying its insulating properties, with the consequences that Bjaaland succinctly describes. It was a lesson that Amundsen had learned from the Netsiliks but, not being Eskimo himself, had been unable to apply under extreme conditions when it mattered most.

WEDNESDAY, SEPTEMBER 13TH, 1911
Amundsen

Wednesday 13 Sept.
We had a splendid night in our igloo. It could not have been better. The ice was rather noisy – banging and cracking that woke us now and then. Around 7.30 we were ready to depart. It was then –52°. Clear and calm. Odd how little one notices these low temperatures. Even a light flurry in one's face, which can happen now and then, does not feel particularly cold. But when all is said and done, the greatest danger of these low T. is the damage to one's clothes. If we only had a chance to dry out, things would be completely different. We stopped at 3 p.m., and had then done 16 nautical miles. This evening we have –56.2°, calm and clear. It is cold in the tents, but luckily we have enough paraffin. I wanted to serve some Geneva, but oddly enough it had frozen solid and the bottle was shattered. But helpless we were not. We also had some Lysholm in our stores. It was also frozen solid, but luckily the bottle was undamaged. It seems that it might possibly be thawed out. When we have got into our sleeping bags, we take a swig to cope with the –60° that will surely come during the night.

Bjaaland

13th. Today the weather was calm and clear here, so the journey continues, we could see two summits, at the same time we caught sight of two flags on the right which were put up on the last tour in the autumn. The cold is foul –52.5 m. –51 evening –56.2 extra chocolate and a tot we are now 5.1 nautical miles from the depot.

The paraffin was fuel for the Primus. A Swedish invention, the Primus was the first efficient portable stove. It worked by vaporizing paraffin under pressure in a burner ('burns without a wick' was its original slogan) to produce an intense, roaring flame. Working the Primus was a little more involved than a modern bottle gas stove. It had to be started by filling a dish with alcohol, which, igniting at very low temperatures, was lit to heat the burner and begin vaporizing the paraffin That in turn meant carrying two kinds of fuel. Also it was vital to maintain the pressure by means of a built-in hand pump and an exhaust valve. It was worth the trouble. Light and compact, the Primus was vastly more effective than anything before. It could bring a litre of water to the boil in 4 or 5 minutes. Its fuel consumption was low, greatly increasing the range of unsupported travel. A product of the 1890s, it was the technical breakthrough that made long polar journeys possible. Nansen on the Fram *was the first polar explorer to use the Primus. It was now the standard expedition stove. Both Amundsen and Scott used it, as they shared skis, ski bindings and Nansen sledges. The Scandinavians not only founded the modern school of polar exploration, but more or less invented its equipment.*

Lysholm is a superior Norwegian aquavit. It would have been brought, inter alia, *to toast memorable occasions along the way.*

THURSDAY, SEPTEMBER 14TH, 1911

Amundsen

Thursday 14 Sept.
−56° Calm and clear. After a few hours on the march, we caught sight of our depot along our course. Now that wasn't bad without a compass. All honour to HH, who has steered the whole time. Reached the depot 10.15 p.m. Everything was in good order there. Deposited all our things, drank a cup of hot milk, and then turned back. It is grim to get going in such weather – but it has to be done. Skiing very sluggish.

Bjaaland

14th. Came to the depot ¼ past 10, we discharged our loads, and swung home-wards. It is a bloody cold job driving here in 55–56 degrees of frost, and partly tired and sick dogs. We found the depot a little drifted over. I took two photos of the caravan. We did 14.6 m., but did not reach the igloos as intended. This evening it is −54 deg. here, and God help me miserably cold.

Scott

Thursday, Sept. 14th. Another interregnum. I have been exceedingly busy finishing up the Southern plans, getting instruction in photographing, and preparing for our jaunt to the west. I held forth on the 'Southern Plans' yesterday; everyone was enthusiastic, and the feeling is general that our arrangements are calculated to make the best of our resources. Although people have given a good deal of thought to various branches of the subject, there was not a suggestion offered for improvement. The scheme seems to have earned full confidence: it remains to play the game out.

The last lectures of the season have been given. On Monday Nelson gave us an interesting little resume [sic] of biological questions, tracing the evolutionary development of forms from the simplest single-cell animals.

Tonight Wright tackled 'The Constitution of Matter', with the latest ideas from the Cavendish Laboratory: it was a tough subject, yet one carries away ideas of the trend of the work of the great physicists, of the ends they achieve and the means they employ. Wright is inclined to explain matter as velocity; Simpson claims to be with J. J. Thomson in stressing the fact that gravity is not explained.

These lectures have been a real amusement and one would be sorry enough that they should end, were it not for so good a reason. I am determined to make some better show of our photographic work on the Southern trip than has yet been accomplished – with Ponting as a teacher it should be easy. He is prepared to take any pains to ensure good results, not only with his own work but with that of others-showing indeed what a very good chap he is.

To-day I have been trying a colour screen – it is an extraordinary addition to one's powers.

To-morrow Bowers, Simpson, Petty Officer Evans, and I are off to the West. I want to have another look at the Ferrar Glacier, to measure the stakes put out by Wright last year, to bring my sledging impressions up to date (one loses details of technique very easily), and finally to see what we can do with our cameras. I haven't decided how long we shall stay away or precisely where we shall go; such vague arrangements have an attractive side.

We have had a fine week, but the temperature remains low in the twenties, and to-day has dropped to −35°. I shouldn't wonder if we get a cold snap.

Scott is here expounding his complex plan for the Pole, as prepared with Bowers. It involved four kinds of transport; motors, ponies, dogs and man-hauling, with different parties weaving back and forth. Margin of error there was none. Some of his listeners

– officers and scientists – had a sense of unease laced with foreboding. They kept their counsel, for they had long since learnt that Scott did not take kindly to criticism. His manner was that of an autocratic senior officer briefing subordinates. He took silence as consent.

This was the first time that Scott had revealed his plans, although on 8 May, he did lecture in general on the polar journey. He could trust Bowers not to leak their deliberations.

FRIDAY, SEPTEMBER 15TH, 1911
Amundsen

Friday 15 Sept.
Off at 7 a.m. To start with, an unpleasant breeze from the N. It soon dropped, and then we had the most glorious weather – calm and clear. I have ski-jored with W. all day. It was brilliant. The skiing was sluggish during the first half, but later of the very best kind. Have followed our tracks until we stopped during the afternoon at one of the flags we had planted. Steering by compass from here. Have been forced to abandon several of our dogs along the way – those who have fallen ill or those who simply gave up. Oddly enough 'Sarikken' collapsed during the march. This surprised us, because she had not shown any symptoms of disease. Poor creature, she has given birth to good children, pulled well, and now she is lying dead on the Barrier. The past few days have seen quite extraordinary snow formations. They consist of extremely fine drift snow collected in small cylinder-shaped bales. These bales are so fine and light that it is difficult to take them in one's hand. However, if one seizes them, all that remains of a rather large cylindrical formation is some viscous, snow-like substance between the fingers, which almost completely vanishes. They roll away like small wheels across the ice. In appearance they completely resemble the dandelion seeds which flutter around in the form of eiderdown during the autumn. Both Jørg. and HH had their right heels frostbitten last night in the tent – this could not happen when moving.

Bjaaland

15 September
The second day of the homeward run is at an end, and it was bitter as vinegar –47.5 with NW wind right in my mug; delightful. The dogs are suffering

horribly in the cold and are miserable, in agony with frostbitten paws. Adam and Lazarus froze to death when they lay down, Karenius likewise, also Sofie, although the latter was shot. We travelled 31 nautical miles from 7 to 3 p.m. This evening the temperature was –35°, and it has clouded over. Intend reaching home tomorrow.

SATURDAY, SEPTEMBER 16TH, 1911

Amundsen

16 Sept – Saturday

Here again – Left the last camp at 7 a.m. HH went first, and then W., with whom I ski-jored. The skiing was brilliant until we came down on to the last part here at the edge of the Barrier. Here the skiing was like sand. By 4 p.m. the first two sledges were home – W. and HH. Bj. came at 6 p.m., and Hass. & Jørg. at 6.30 p.m. It does not seem that Joh. and Pr. will arrive this evening. The time is now 9 p.m. and they are still out. Joh. was last seen ca. 15 nautical miles away. Pr. was then behind on ski. They have tent and sleeping bags so they cannot be in trouble – The dogs were worn out on arriving here – All well here – Ca. 40 nautical miles today. T. 8 o'clock –51° – When we set off this morning T. was –40.2°.

Bjaaland

16 September

Ready to go 7 o'clock, weather was good –44.5. As we wanted to get home, it was a wild chase and we well and truly outdistanced each other. Helmer and Wisting and the Chief went off at full speed, so we saw them as just a white dot far away, they reached home at 4 p.m. Luckily Hassel overtook me after 7 nautical miles, equipped with a long pole which the dogs were dead scared of. Johansen and Prestrud will have a bad night without food and without warmth so that it is uncertain what will happen to them. One way or another, Prestrud had fallen behind on ski, and Johansen having sped away from him, he decided to wait at the flagpost 15 m away, and many dogs must be lying there, worn out by the frost, perhaps for ever. 11 o'clock to night. The missing men have not come, they will surely be here by midday tomorrow.

SUNDAY, SEPTEMBER 17TH, 1911

Amundsen

17 Sept. – Sunday
Pr. and Joh. came in at 12.30 this morning. At the breakfast table this morning I asked the reasons for their long delay. To my surprise, Joh. thought it appropriate to utter some scarcely flattering opinions of me in my capacity of leader of the proceedings here. It was not only our return journey yesterday that he found indefensible to the highest degree etc. etc. but also much else that I had taken the liberty of doing as leader in the course of things. However I received no answer to my request for justification for these statements. The gross and unforgivable part of these statements is that they were made in everybody's hearing. The bull must be taken by the horns; I had to make an example immediately. At the dinner table, I announced that after his statements, I decided that it was best to dismiss him from the journey to the Pole. Instead I have ordered him in writing to take part in a reconnaissance exp. to King Edward the 7th Land under Pr.'s command. This document was handed over at the same time. He immediately replied that he refused to take part in anything of the kind. I await his written justification.

The reason that I drove on yesterday without waiting for the others, which I normally did, was that both HH and Jørg. had frostbitten left heels, and it was therefore vital for us to reach shelter as quickly as possible so that they could receive the necessary treatment. It now turns out that Pr. also has one heel badly frostbitten. But he had not uttered a single word about it. Had he brought it to my attention, I would immediately have given him my place on W.'s sledge, which I knew would be one of the first to reach home. At the dinner table I asked each individual what he thought of my course of action. They unanimously agreed that I had acted correctly. This was a sad end to our splendid unity. But I decided that as a result of his behaviour, the only alternative was to dismiss him. There must be no elements of criticism on our southern journey. Especially coming from an old polar explorer like him, they would be doubly dangerous. – We are dealing with the heels as best we can. Bathe them in boiling hot water. They seem quite good now. I have provisionally fixed our departure for 15 October. Don't believe in any improvement in the t. conditions before then.

Judging by comments made today it seems that many have criticized our early departure. Well, it is easy to do so afterwards. – Looking back, when I headed South as early as the beginning of September, the reason was that I assumed that we might possibly find more reasonable temperatures further in the Barrier than here. Temperature graphs from *all* previous expeditions show consistently milder temperatures than we have found. Likewise, with one exception, they all showed a sharp rise in September. I have asked myself several times in the course of the winter: have we stumbled on a local cold pole? Without trying, we could not decide with any certainty. Now we have tried, but found no improvement in the conditions. On that account, we must now simply wait to see what happens. To sit still without doing anything would never occur to me, criticize me who will. With the exception of the three frostbitten heels, and some dogs, our little journey has not caused us any loss. It was a good trial run. Besides, we got everything up to 80°. Still and clear but cold. –51°

Bjaaland

Sunday

17ᵗʰ. Second day after homecoming. Prestrud and Johansen turned up at midnight nonetheless. They had straggled and gone astray because they had lost the track. Prestrud was miserably frozen, and his feet full of blisters. Johansen had been careless enough to race away from him. There was a real settling of accounts today, it was bad for those who had been left behind and Johansen then uttered words that would have been best left unsaid. The consequence was that the Chief adopted a plan whereby Prestrud, accompanied by Johansen, would travel eastwards and try to find King Edward VII's Land. The Chief justified this by saying that Johansen could intrigue with the others during the journey and everything would grind to a halt. Johansen protested, he received written orders, so will just have to obey. Prestrud was more sensible, and said that he was willing. Hanssen and Stubberud and Hassel and Prestrud are in trouble with their legs, and it will be a good three weeks before they are well. In the middle of October we others will go south again and preferably reach the Pole, which will really be a hard nut to crack, as it will need an incredibly careful advance if dogs and men are to hold out. The cold was the real reason that the dogs weakened as quickly as they did. The tour was instructive and we were able to test our equipment, some of which will be altered a little.

Bjaaland, as usual, had got it right. Men, Amundsen liked to say, are the unknown factor on an expedition, and this abortive start was a test in good time to avoid disaster on the trail. Johansen had always been a disturbing element. His outburst was the culmination of smouldering discontent. Since his saga with Nansen in the north, he had been unable to settle down. An outcast from society and, by his own account, bur-dened by some shadow hanging over him, he found relief only in the snows, away from civilization. On that account Nansen, who felt some responsibility, more or less forced Johansen on Amundsen. It was against Amundsen's better judgement but he, being in a false position over his secret switch from North to South, was unable to resist.

Johansen had privately been comparing Amundsen unfavourably with Nansen all along. He quarrelled with some of his companions. The cause of his wrath was Amundsen's behaviour on the last day's race for home.

Amundsen's diary hints at self-justification. His remark about a 'local cold pole' at least was close to the truth. The compensation was relatively little wind, often dead calm, allowing him to enjoy in comfort the shimmering curtains of the southern aurora weaving across the winter sky. With Scott it was the other way about. He had far more blizzards and storms, but somewhat higher temperatures. This had something to do with the proximity of mountains at McMurdo Sound, compared with the endless plain behind the Bay of Whales. Being the first to winter on the Barrier, Amundsen had no local data to guide him. He mistakenly assumed similar conditions everywhere. Scott's and Shackleton's previous observations at McMurdo Sound had misled him into starting as early as he did.

In any case, on that last fateful day, Amundsen had acted out of character. Instead of waiting for the stragglers to keep everyone together, he had simply thrown himself on the leading sledge, and sauve qui peut. *No doubt he was blinded by self-disgust at the check to his plans. Whatever the explanation, to quote Stubberud, it was 'quite simply a mistake.'*[43]

If so, it was a fortunate one. Amundsen's 'panic', as Johansen called it,[44] *had exposed the party's human failings in time. Prestrud now grasped that the Pole was physically beyond him. He was relieved to be going on a lesser journey. Taking Johansen towards the Pole would have been a mortal risk. For the good of the enterprise, he had to be discarded. This apparent setback was arguably Amundsen's greatest stroke of luck. The price, as he said was the 'end to our splendid unity'. In fact, he had kept his men reason-ably content all winter, and now the cross-currents were swirling.*

Compared with the mental turmoil, rectifying the material defects was child's play. Physically, the only consequence was frostbitten feet. This was due to faults in the still imperfect ski boots. For the fourth time they were unpicked, enlarged and modified. Other deficiencies in equipment were corrected. Ever the perfectionist, Amundsen was making alterations until the last minute.

Nonetheless it was not a happy interlude. The quarrel with Johansen had left a dis-mal atmosphere. It was not helped by the threat of Scott, or rather his motor-sledges, that continued to haunt the hut at the Bay of Whales.

MONDAY, SEPTEMBER 18ᵀᴴ, 1911

Amundsen

18 Sept. – Monday

Calm and clear. –49 this morning. –45 this evening. Have again assumed the met. obs. W. and Bj. went into the Barrier at 10 a.m., each with his dog team – to fetch those dogs that had stayed behind. They did the tour – 30 nautical miles – in six hours and collected about 10 dogs. Most of them would probably have returned of their own accord in the course of time. Most of them were fit and frisky. A couple of them had sore legs. The loss of dogs on the tour was thus three bitches and two dogs. The only one of these that was worth anything was 'Kaisa'. We are now in full spate again drying our equipment. The ceiling is full of hanging sleeping bags and doggy harnesses. As far as I can see, the frostbitten heels are making good progress. Have now changed from wet to dry poultices. HH's heel is the worst affected.

TUESDAY, SEPTEMBER 19ᵀᴴ, 1911

Amundsen

19 Sept. – Tuesday

Glorious weather today. Ca. –45°. Clear and calm. It began to blow from the E. this evening and clouded over somewhat. We are occupied with drying. The heels are being nursed. They look better.

WEDNESDAY, SEPTEMBER 20ᵀᴴ, 1911

Amundsen

20 Sept. – Wednesday.

Overcast with a breeze from NE quarter. Ca. –32°. In the forenoon brought home supplies from the store. The dogs pulled 100 kg each. They manage this over a short distance. Carry on with the heels. Change boracic acid poultices morning and evening. The patients spend most of the time on their backs.

Well now I have taken the last, and I hope the final decision on our forthcoming work. We will be divided into two parties. HH, W., Hass., Bj. and I go South. Pr. and Jørg. go E. to determine the position of King E. VII's Land. Furthermore they will map the bay and investigate a major disturbance that we have observed in the Barrier in a SW'ly direction – 16 nautical miles away. – Joh.

has unfortunately refused to obey the orders I have given him, and will therefore have to pass the time here at home as best he can. His justification for this will be found in the iron document box – received yesterday. It is self-evident that after what has happened, he must be excluded from the third voyage of the *Fram*. – Departure is set for the 15 October. But the intention is also to wait longer if wind and weather so decide. – Onwards we must go – but prudence is the watchword.

Prestrud could hardly travel on his own, so Amundsen had asked Stubberud, as a personal favour, if he would also go to King Edward VII Land. Nobody had yet been ashore there, and it was reinsurance against failure of the southern journey, but still it was not the Pole. With a twinge of disappointment, Stubberud agreed. In the end, as Bjaaland had surmised, Johansen did obey orders, and followed Prestrud as well.

Earlier in the spring, when persistent thought of Scott disturbed Amundsen's calm exterior with vacillation, he had proposed a side trip to King Edward VII Land to test equipment. The compact majority stopped it, on the grounds that it was a waste of energy. It is odd how the two expedition mirrored each other. Scott's 'jaunt' to the western mountains was also an irrelevant side trip, but with his rigid discipline, and intimidating manner, there were no dissenting voices to save him from himself.

Amongst other things, Amundsen's false start had proved that eight was too unwieldy for a single party. Those chosen for the Pole formed a cohesive group. Also the smaller number meant an appreciably greater margin of safety: Five men would now share food and fuel calculated for eight. The supplies were packed in modules, so rearrangement was easy.

THURSDAY, SEPTEMBER 21ST, 1911

Amundsen

21 Sept. – Thursday
Stiff breeze from E. – Partly overcast. Ca. –25°. Busy with drying and equipment. Heels dressed morning and evening.

FRIDAY, SEPTEMBER 22ND, 1911
Amundsen

22 Sept. – Friday.
Ca. –40° Calm and clear. Lovely weather. Busy with various small chores.
Unfortunately it turns out that navigation watch No.8 – which Joh. had in his
keeping – has been made absolutely useless by careless treatment. This watch has
proved to be our most reliable one the whole time, so we have suffered a heavy
loss. I thought that it would be in the best hands by trusting it to a man with his
experience. But I was sadly mistaken. I gave him a belt to hold it, and keep it next
to his skin. In that way one can manage to keep watches at a reasonably constant
temperature. But that experienced man thought he knew better, discarding the
belt, and then putting the watch in his coat pocket, as a consequence of which
it was exposed to extremes of heat and –57°. – We cannot even get it going and
have had to throw it away. Those watches which have been treated with care – it
now turns out – have kept going as usual, despite the low t. we met.

SATURDAY, SEPTEMBER 23RD, 1911
Amundsen

23 Sept. – Saturday.
Glorious weather. Calm and partly clear. Ca. –37°. The dogs are content now.
Lie in the sunshine and doze. There is rarely any fighting among them. A great
number of them still have sore legs after the trip. It will take time alright before
the legs of the four-legged ones are healed. The heels are improving. Pierced
some of the old skin today in order to let air and boracic acid on to the new skin.

SUNDAY, SEPTEMBER 24TH, 1911
Amundsen

24 Sept. – Sunday
Fog all day. Ca. –35° Calm. Light SW'ly breeze this evening. We have seen the
first signs of spring today. Bj. came back after a trip to the sea ice, and reported
that two big seals were lying there. Later in the afternoon he, Hass. and I went
down to get hold of them, but just imagine, they had disappeared. Meanwhile
Bj. managed to find one far out at 'Man's Head' and shot it. It was a giant. So
now we have got fresh meat again, and I hope that we will have plenty of it

henceforth. There has been movement in the [sea] ice, which has enabled the seals to climb up. These last few days the ice has undergone violent screwing along the edge of the barrier where we had our first transport [from the ship]. It must have happened during the small hours of the 21st, when we had a gale from E. – probably NE later. The ice had been forced high up the Barrier face – to a height of 30 to 40 ft. It was quite impressive to see. One could see many seracs. It is among these that the seals find holes through which they can emerge. – We go out tomorrow to fetch the meat. – We have had a big concert this evening – HH's birthday. 'Michaelorva' and 'Borghild Bryn' are our favourites. Ah, how good it was to hear them. They have surely never had a more grateful audience. The patients are improving. Pr. resumed looking after his dogs today. The others start tomorrow. Yesterday I began taking the evening observ. without a lamp for the first time.

'Man's Head' is Cape Man's Head, a feature in the Barrier ice that marked the western entry to the Bay of Whales. By 'concert', Amundsen meant playing the gramophone, driven by clockwork and periodically wound up. It was hollow and tinny because the sound was mechanically transmitted by the needle on the pickup from the swiftly turning records and faintly amplified by the iconic acoustic horn, but it was music nonetheless.

MONDAY, SEPTEMBER 25TH, 1911

Amundsen

25 Sept. – Monday.
Fog. NE'ly breeze. Ca. –30°. Without doubt spring has arrived. And the first signs of spring had to pay with their lives. Two huge seals – Wedell – have been brought in, and we have all eaten absolutely fresh meat. All of us greatly appreciate it – man and beast. They were incredibly fat. Blubber 4 inches thick. These monsters presumably weighed 300 kg. each. We will get three ample feeds out of these two. But then we have 100 animals that must be fed. Bj. and W., who went out to fetch these animals, report that outside Man's Head the ice ran in huge wave formations as far as the eye could see. The pressure from outside has been enormous, but has not yet managed to break up this part. There are gigantic seracs along the whole Barrier here inside the bay. Outside Man's Head the ice had nearly forced its way up to the height of the Barrier – ca. 80 ft. – that is an impressive height – The heels are making good progress, but it was only today

that HH got back any feeling. I doubt whether I dare take him out on a serious trip before 1 November. It is a long time to wait, but it is better thus and have everything in order. From today, the patients have resumed looking after their respective dogs. – It is strange that we have heard so little of the violent screwing of the ice in our vicinity. Pr. believes that he heard something in the small hours of the 21st, but he could not be certain. In this, I maintain that I can see proof that we are resting on solid ground. If this part of the Barrier had been a swimming mass of ice, I really believe that we would have felt the blow. It will be interesting to see further developments.

TUESDAY, SEPTEMBER 26TH, 1911
Amundsen

26 Sept. – Tuesday.
Spring has really arrived in earnest. –18° this evening. We have had a little snow today for a change. The wind is also blowing from an unusual quarter – from N. in fact. Now blowing 6.6 m. Extensive water sky to the NW. We have allowed daylight into the kitchen today. It looks really snug and cosy. The main room will be opened to daylight tomorrow. Have done some work outside today. It feels quite like summer outside. Continue dressing the heels.

By 'blowing 6.6 m.', Amundsen meant 6.6 metres a second; measured by an anemometer. To admit daylight involved digging out the snowdrift blocking the windows, and removing the shutters.

WEDNESDAY, SEPTEMBER 27TH, 1911
Amundsen

27 Sept. – Wednesday
Gale from E. with thick drift all day. –18°. We have let daylight into the main room today. Had dinner in daylight – Quite homely. Yesterday we had the pleasure of welcoming back one of our straggling dogs. It was 'Kamilla'. She was left behind ca. 60 nautical miles away. She was just as round and pleasant as usual. She is good at having children – otherwise of no use. Attend to the heels morning and evening.

THURSDAY, SEPTEMBER 28TH, 1911

Amundsen

28 Sept. – Thursday.

The wind has veered between E and SE today at a strength of 5–10 m. It is fresher this evening (10 m.) from ESE and –9°. A little snow also fell this evening. There is no longer any doubt that it is spring. Have done some outdoor work. Built snow walls on the side both of the common room and kitchen to prevent drift building up. In weather like this – partly clear – we can be without lamps right up until 4 p.m. – Have dug out the meteorological cage this morning and moved it a few metres towards the E. It is now in the lee of the hut's long wall, and will probably no longer be drifted over. The weather-cock was moved at the same time. – Bj. and I took a walk to 'Man's Head' in the afternoon to see if any seals had appeared. It was interesting to see how the pressure has distorted the ice. Some huge wave formations in the ice were strangest of all. It looks as if the pressure ceased just as the ice in these formations was about to break up and form seracs. The biggest waves were ca. 30 f. high. The ice had piled up to a height of 40 ft. against the Barrier. We crossed a channel recently frozen over. Otherwise the ice further out gives the impression of being quite undisturbed. Big dark water sky to the NW. Just as we were about to turn home with mission unaccomplished where hunting seal was concerned, we caught sight of a year-old Weddell seal just under 'Man's Head'. Bj., who had a carbine, was just about to despatch it, when he noticed that the barrel was full of hard packed snow. We had nothing with which to remove it, and the gun was unuseable. But naturally we could not let the seal get away. Bj. attacked the seal with a good knife, and in the space of a quarter of an hour, he managed to kill it. This was not a good, hunter's way of killing game, but here it didn't matter here after all. We had to have some venison – by a decent method if possible – if not, we must have it anyway. We cut it open – took fillets and sirloin with us. We will carry the carcass home at the first opportunity. We had ca. 20 dogs with us but, oddly enough none of them stayed behind to regale themselves. They all followed us home.

FRIDAY, SEPTEMBER 29TH, 1911

Amundsen

29 Sept. – Friday

Storm (19 m.) from NE. T.–19°. The drift was so thick that we could not see the immediate surroundings. HH's dog tent was blown flat. All the dogs had to be dug out. They were safe and sound. He has now appropriated the 'maternity home'. In future an igloo will serve as a 'larder'. The wind eased somewhat (14 m.) after dinner. At 3 o'clock it was dead calm. Soon after, it blew from the E, but moderately. The second and even greater sign of spring appeared this afternoon in the form of a flock of 'Antarctic petrels'. It was sheer pleasure for us all to see them again. Not least for the dogs – the silly idiots. They ran about like madmen – probably in order to get a catch. The hunt dissolved into a wild battle among themselves. So spring has arrived in dead earnest!

Seal, birds and –57° in the same month! That is indeed a record.

Bjaaland

29 September

For some days, it has now been nice and mild. On the 24th, H.H.'s birthday, I did a ski tour down to the sea ice and suddenly bumped into a seal, a monstrous thing, big and fat, it was just by the run up to the depot. A ½ m from another one that followed. There has been vile screwing and huge floes have forced themselves up and pressed right up on to the Barrier. I shot a seal out at Man's Head that day. It was the first this year. The Chief and I were out yesterday on ski to look for seal, we went round the serac near M. Head and past the two tiny capes. Saw many fine caves and screwing and crevasses and nastiness which I must really photograph. On the return journey, we suddenly came upon a little seal next to [Man's] Head, I wanted to finish it off, but because there was snow in the barrel, and the cartridge would not go in, I then drew my knife and gave it a stab, so that the blood spurted out, and then we had to flee to the serac, and there he found a way up to the other side, where we lived, we were caught by a snow storm, but we found our way home. The storm has raged all night and today, the worst we have had, 19 to 20 m wind from N. About 3 o'clock the wind suddenly dropped and it cleared up. A new sign of spring came around 5 o'clock, three *ice petrels*, which fluttered round the camp and then they sped off to sea again. It is building up to bad weather again, here it is mild and pleasant, –9 pure summer.

SATURDAY, SEPTEMBER 30TH, 1911

Amundsen

30 Sept. – Saturday
Calm and overcast Ca. –12°. It feels just like summer. Bj. and I went out in the
forenoon to fetch the seal we shot the day before yesterday. Five huge beasts had
climbed up along the barrier, and they were all dispatched. They were all Weddell.
One was a female with a fully developed embryo. To his great surprise, Bj. saw
the embryo crawl out when he cut a hole in the womb. It was 118 cm long and
82 cm round the waist. L. has already skinned it for the collection. It was quite
interesting to see this poor little wretch crawl about. When it saw us moving,
it fixed its big eyes on us and set a course directly for us. In the afternoon we
went down with five sledges each with eight dogs in front. But my word it was
hard enough for the dogs with a seal on the sledge. They are so unbelievably
fat – ca. 4 inches blubber that they must presumably weigh 3–400 kg. When
we got them up here, fillets and sirloin were carved out for domestic use – also
meat for a whole feed for the animals was carved out and put in the meat tent.
We have now got 10 whole feeds from these five. All the dogs gather around
when they were being carved, and ate what they wanted. Only finished all this
work at 7 p.m. The wood and coal tent fell down during the p.m. Have put it
up again as best we could.

Bjaaland

30 September
Well it was a lovely day –23 deg. and the Chief and I went hunting for seal. We
did the trip to Man's Head, there on the other side we found five huge beasts,
Weddell seal, which were soon picked off. While I was standing next to the dead
one, I shot another seal, and when I got to grips with the former, God help me
I found a live young seal in her carcass 1.18 m long, still it wasn't fully formed,
but there was a lot of life in it, and we had to use three bullets on it. Lindstrøm
skinned it. Believe me, I needed a Lysholm at dinner after that.

SUNDAY, OCTOBER 1ST, 1911

Amundsen

1 Oct. – Sunday
Gale from the N. quarter, with thick drift. Ca. –12°. Apart from those looking after the dogs, we stay indoors in such weather.

Scott

Sunday, Oct.1st. –Returned on Thursday from a remarkably pleasant and instructive little spring journey, after an absence of thirteen days from September 15. We covered 152 geographical miles by sledgemeter (175 statute miles) in 10 marching days. It took us 2½ days to reach Butter Point (28½ miles geog.), carrying a part of the Western Party stores which brought our load to 180 lbs. a man.

After depositing this extra load we proceeded, reaching Cathedral Rocks on the 19th. Here we found the stakes placed by Wright across the glacier, and spent the remainder of the day and the whole of the 20th in plotting their position accurately. We saw that there had been movement and roughly measured it as about 30 feet. After plotting the figures it turns out that the movement varies from 24 to 32 feet at different stakes – this is 7½ months. This is an extremely important observation, the first made on the movement of the coastal glaciers; it is more than I expected to find, but small enough to show that the idea of comparative stagnation was correct. Bowers and I exposed a number of plates and films in the glacier which have turned out very well, auguring well for the management of the camera on the Southern Journey.

On the 21st we came down the glacier and camped at the northern end of the foot. From thence we jogged up the coast on the following days, dipping into New Harbour and climbing the moraine, taking angles and collecting rock specimens. At Cape Bernacchi we found a quantity of pure quartz in situ, and in it veins of copper ore. I got a specimen with two or three large lumps of copper included. This is the first find of minerals suggestive of the possibility of working. The next day we sighted a long, low ice wall, and took it at first for a long glacier tongue stretching seaward from the land. As we approached we saw a dark mark on it. Suddenly it dawned on us that the tongue was detached from the land, and we turned towards it half recognizing familiar features. As we got close we saw similarity to our old Erebus Glacier Tongue, and finally caught sight of a flag on it, and suddenly realised that it might be the piece broken off our old Erebus Glacier Tongue. Sure enough it was; we camped near the outer end, and climbing on to it soon found the depôt of fodder left by Campbell and the line of stakes planted to guide our ponies in the autumn.

The piece which is about 2 miles long, has turned through half a circle, so that the old western end is now towards the east. Considering the many cracks in the ice mass it is most astonishing that it should have remained intact throughout its sea voyage.

At one time it was suggested that the hut should be placed on this Tongue. What an adventurous voyage the occupants would have had! The Tongue which was 5 miles south of C. Evans is now 40 miles W. N. W. of it. From the Glacier Tongue we still pushed north. *David writes that Granite Harbour was incorrectly charted by the Discovery but its old position is retained in the later maps.*

We reached Dunlop Island on the 24th just before the fog descended on us, and got a view along the stretch of coast to the north which turns at this point.

We saw enough to show that Granite Harbour cannot be South of the position we assigned to it – One can imagine a rather tired and bewildered sledge party getting confused as to land marks – but it was a pity David did not correct his impression before printing his narrative.

Dunlop Island has undoubtedly been under the sea. We found regular terrace beaches with rounded water – worn stones all over it; its height is 65 feet. After visiting the island it was easy for us to trace the same terrace formation on the coast; in one place we found water – worn stones over 100 feet above sea-level. Nearly all these stones are erratic and, unlike ordinary beach pebbles, the under sides which lie buried have remained angular.

Unlike the region of the Ferrar Glacier and New Harbour, the coast to the north of C. Bernacchi runs on in a succession of rounded bays fringed with low ice walls. At the headlands and in irregular spots the gneissic base rock and portions of moraines lie exposed, offering a succession of interesting spots for a visit in search of geological specimens. Behind this fringe there is a long undulating plateau of snow rounding down to the coast; behind this again are a succession of mountain ranges with deep-cut valleys between. As far as we went, these valleys seem to radiate from the region of the summit reached at the head of the Ferrar Glacier.

As one approaches the coast, the 'tablecloth' of snow in the foreground cuts off more and more of the inland peaks, and even at a distance it is impossible to get a good view of the inland valleys. To explore these over the ice cap is one of the objects of the Western Party.

On the afternoon of the 24th we turned back, and covering nearly eleven miles, camped inside the Glacier Tongue. After noon on the 25th we made a direct course for C. Evans, and in the evening camped well out in the Sound.

Bowers got angles from our lunch camp and I took a photographic panorama; which is a good deal over exposed.

We only got 2½ miles on the 26th when a heavy blizzard descended on us and we were obliged to camp. It continued to blow hard throughout the 27th, and the 28th proved the most unpleasant day of the trip. We started facing a very keen, frostbiting wind. Although this slowly increased in force, we pushed doggedly on, halting now and again to bring our frozen features round. It was 2 o'clock before we could find a decent site for a lunch camp under a pressure ridge. The fatigue of the prolonged march told on Simpson, whose whole face was frostbitten at one time – it is still much blistered. It came on to drift as we sat in our tent, and again we were weather-bound. At 3 the drift ceased, and we marched on, wind as bad as ever; then I saw an ominous yellow fuzzy appearance on the southern ridges of Erebus, and knew that another snowstorm approached. Foolishly hoping it would pass us by I kept on until Inaccessible Island was suddenly blotted out. Then we rushed for a camp site, but the blizzard was on us. In the driving snow we found it impossible to set up the inner tent, and were obliged to unbend it. It was a long job getting the outer tent set, but thanks to Evans and Bowers it was done at last. We had to risk frostbitten fingers and hang on to the tent with all our energy: got it secured inch by inch, and not such a bad speed all things considered. We had some cocoa and waited. At 9 p.m. the snow drift again took off, and we were now so snowed up, we decided to push on in spite of the wind.

We arrived in at 1.15 a.m., pretty well done. The wind never let up for an instant; the temperature remained about −16°, and the 21 statute miles which we marched in the day must be remembered amongst the most strenuous in my memory.

Except for the last few days, we enjoyed a degree of comfort which I had not imagined possible on a spring journey. The temperature was not particularly high, at the mouth of the Ferrar it was −40°, and it varied between −15° and −40° throughout. Of course this is much higher than it would be on the Barrier, but it does not in itself promise much comfort. The amelioration of such conditions we owe to experience. We used one-third more than the summer allowance of fuel. This, with our double tent, allowed a cosy hour after breakfast and supper in which we could dry our socks, &c., and put them on in comfort. We shifted our footgear immediately after the camp was pitched, and by this means kept our feet glowingly warm throughout the night. Nearly all the time we carried our sleeping-bags open on the sledges. Although the sun does not appear to have much effect, I believe this device is of great benefit even in the coldest weather – certainly by this means our bags were kept much freer of moisture than they would have been had they been rolled up in the daytime. The inner tent gets a good deal of ice on it, and I don't see any easy way to prevent this.

The journey enables me to advise the Geological Party on their best route to Granite Harbour: this is along the shore, where for the main part the protection of a chain of grounded bergs has preserved the ice from all pressure. Outside these, and occasionally reaching to the headlands, there is a good deal of pressed up ice of this season, together with the latest of the old broken pack. Travelling through this is difficult, as we found on our return journey. Beyond this belt we passed through irregular patches where the ice, freezing at later intervals in the season, has been much screwed. The whole shows the general tendency of the ice to pack along the coast.

The objects of our little journey were satisfactorily accomplished, but the greatest source of pleasure to me is to realise that I have such men as Bowers and P.O. Evans for the Southern journey. I do not think that harder men or better sledge travellers ever took the trail. Bowers is a little wonder. I realised all that he must have done for the C. Crozier Party in their far severer experience.

In spite of the late hour of our return everyone was soon afoot, and I learned the news at once. E. R. Evans, Gran, and Ford had returned from the Corner Camp journey the day after we left. They were away six nights, four spent on the Barrier under very severe conditions – the minimum for one night registered −73°.

I am glad to find that Corner Camp showed up well; in fact, in more than one place remains of last year's pony walls were seen. This removes all anxiety as to the chance of finding the One Ton Camp.

On this journey Ford got his hand badly frostbitten. I am annoyed at this, as it argues want of care; moreover there is a good chance that the tip of one of the fingers will be lost, and if this happens or if the hand is slow in recovery, Forde cannot take part in the Western Party. I have no one to replace him.

E. R. Evans looks remarkably well, as also Gran. *Evans says that Gran has behaved very well indeed, took his share in all the work and was eager to do all aright – This is a great relief after my experience of last year and confirms the idea that the first troubles were due to youth. With the winter he has found his feet and developed into a thoroughly good boy ready to face hardship with the best.*

The ponies look very well and all are reported to be very buckish.

Here Scott uncovers the true reason for his side trip, a distraction that puzzled even his followers. Never mind geology; it is the spectre of his ghostly rival Shackleton that beckons. 'David' is Edgeworth David, Shackleton's geologist on his expedition of 1907–9, when he came close to the Pole. Scott was rather sensitive about the mapping under his leadership on the Discovery *expedition; Griffith Taylor, his own Australian*

Figure 9 Adolf Henrik Lindstrøm, Amundsen's cook and major-domo, in the galley at Framheim.

– National Library of Norway

geologist, having said that it was a 'disgrace'. Scott had gone in the wrong direction to settle a minor point in his obsessive feud with Shackleton.

Given the Norwegian threat, the 152 geographical (i.e. nautical) miles in this diversion to the west would have been better spent moving supplies southwards to concentrate on the road to the Pole. Lt Evans had had the temerity to say so, only to be snubbed by Scott on the grounds that he, Scott, refused to diverge from his stated course of acting as if Amundsen did not exist. Bravado, obstinacy and muddled thinking all played a part.

Scott also demonstrates his mania for interference, while perversely shifting responsibility to a willing horse like Bowers. At one level Scott just seemed to be playing the amateur geologist. Then again perhaps, like Amundsen, he was seeking reinsurance against failure at the Pole, but doing it through science. From a certain point of view, the whole side-trip was simply another exercise in self-punishment, since it was man-hauling a heavy sledge, on foot, without skis. Its one material outcome was to weaken men for the main Polar journey.

The reference to Gran was Scott's way of making amends. Amundsen's arrival on the scene precipitated Gran into a state of acute embarrassment because of their shared nationality. Scott did not help by venting his irritation with Amundsen on Gran as 'his' Norwegian. Lt Evans, an understanding officer and a good messmate, took Gran *under his wing, and smoothed over the difficulties. For his part, Gran behaved with great tact and dignity, winning much sympathy thereby. On that account or other-wise, Evans later married a Norwegian girl.*

Scott's sledgemeter was a device for registering the distance travelled. It was sim-ply a bicycle wheel with a revolution counter attached to the back of the sledges. Both British and Norwegians used it. The difference was this. Amundsen's revolution coun-ters were larger, and hence more legible – a consideration under stress. Then drift snow, the desert sand of a cold climate, penetrated the mechanism of the revolution counters to compromise their accuracy. This was unfortunate, since a precise measure of distance was vital to navigation. The problem was recognized at the Bay of Whales alone. After slaving all winter, Lindstrøm made the sledgemeters drift-proof. These are details, but it was a cumulative succession of detail that would decide the outcome of the race.

MONDAY, OCTOBER 2ND, 1911

Amundsen

2 Oct. – Monday
Gale from the E. quarter. Ca. –13°. Working indoors. The heels are steadily improving, but it will take time to get the new skin strong enough to stand heavy work – Doubt whether it will be possible to leave before the end of the month.

TUESDAY, OCTOBER 3RD, 1911

Amundsen

3 Oct. – Tuesday.
Gale from the E. quarter Ca. –12° Eased somewhat this evening. Also had some snow today. Average t. for Sept. = –37°. Have started my written work today. In case I do not return in time for *Fram's* departure from this place, I am prepar-ing telegram and report with everything that has happened here. The necessary orders must also be drafted.

Scott

Wednesday, Oct. 3rd. – We have had a very bad weather spell. Friday, the day after we returned, was gloriously fine – it might have been a December day, and an inexperienced visitor might have wondered why on earth we had not started to the South. Saturday supplied a reason; the wind blew cold and cheerless; on

Sunday it grew worse, with very thick snow, which continued to fall and drift throughout the whole of Monday. The hut is more drifted up than it has ever been, huge piles of snow behind every heap of boxes, &c., all our paths a foot higher; yet in spite of this the rocks are rather freer of snow. This is due to melting, which is now quite considerable. Wilson tells me the first signs of thaw were seen on the 17th.

Yesterday the weather gradually improved, and to-day has been fine and warm again. One fine day in eight is the record immediately previous to this morning.

Evans, Debenham, and Gran set off to the Turk's Head on Friday morning, Evans to take angles and Debenham to geologise; they have been in their tent pretty well all the time since, but have managed to get through some work. Gran returned last night for more provisions and set off again this morning, Taylor going with him for the day. Debenham has just returned for food. He is immensely pleased at having discovered a huge slicken-sided fault in the lavas of the Turk's Head. This appears to be an unusual occurrence in volcanic rocks, and argues that they are of considerable age. He has taken a heap of photographs and is greatly pleased with all his geological observations. He is building up much evidence to show volcanic disturbance independent of Erebus and perhaps prior to its first upheaval.

Meares has been at Hut Point for more than a week; seals seem to be plentiful there now. Demetri was back with letters on Friday and left on Sunday. He is an excellent boy, full of intelligence.

Ponting has been doing some wonderfully fine cinematograph work. My incursion into photography has brought me in close touch with him and I realise what a very good fellow he is; no pains are too great for him to take to help and instruct others, whilst his enthusiasm for his own work is unlimited.

His results are wonderfully good, and if he is able to carry out the whole of his programme, we shall have a cinematograph and photographic record which will be absolutely new in expeditionary work.

A very serious bit of news to-day. Atkinson says that Jehu is still too weak to pull a load. The pony was bad on the ship and almost died after swimming ashore from the ship – he was one of the ponies returned by Campbell. He has been improving the whole of the winter and Oates has been surprised at the apparent recovery; he looks well and feeds well, though a very weedily built animal compared with the others. I had not expected him to last long, but it will be a bad blow if he fails at the start. I'm afraid there is much pony trouble in store for us.

Oates is having great trouble with Christopher, who didn't at all appreciate being harnessed on Sunday, and again to-day he broke away and galloped off over the floe. On such occasions Oates trudges manfully after him, rounds him up to within a few hundred yards of the stable and approaches cautiously; the animal looks at him for a minute or two and canters off over the floe again. When Christopher and indeed both of them have had enough of the game, the pony calmly stops at the stable door. If not too late he is then put into the sledge, but this can only be done by tying up one of his forelegs; when harnessed and after he has hopped along on three legs for a few paces, he is again allowed to use the fourth. He is going to be a trial, but he is a good strong pony and should do yeoman service.

Day is increasingly hopeful about the motors. He is an ingenious person and has been turning up new rollers out of a baulk of oak supplied by Meares, and with Simpson's small motor as a lathe. The motors *may* save the situation. I have been busy drawing up instructions and making arrangements for the ship, shore station, and sledge parties in the coming season. There is still much work to be done and much, far too much, writing before me.

Time simply flies and the sun steadily climbs the heavens. Breakfast, lunch, and supper are now all enjoyed by sunlight, whilst the night is no longer dark.

WEDNESDAY, OCTOBER 4TH, 1911

Amundsen

4 Oct. – Wednesday
At last the weather has eased. Light breeze from the E. quarter. Ca. –19°. – HH has converted the 'larder' to his own dog tent. Now he has all his dogs there permanently. Hass. has begun reinforcing the wood and coal tent. Jørg. has dug out the dogs' entrance as a W.C. It has been closed for the winter. Again they run in and out disposing of the night-soil. Shot the 'Knave', one of Joh. doggies today. It has been sick all winter – big open sores. It was beginning now to recover, but on that account became so aggressive that I decided it was better to finish it off. Anyway it would never be of any use to us. All three patients have now grown new skin on their heels. Now it is just a question of getting the skin strong enough.

THURSDAY, OCTOBER 5TH, 1911

Amundsen

5 Oct. – Thursday.
Light SSW'ly breeze. Today the T. has dropped from –17° at 8 a.m. to –32° at 8 p.m. It will be interesting to see how far it drops. Various outside jobs done today.

FRIDAY, OCTOBER 6ᵀᴴ, 1911

Amundsen

6 Oct. – Friday. A glorious day. Calm, and glittering sun. –36°. Today one could clearly feel the warmth of the sun. Everyone has tidied up the food store today. All boxes were arranged in square piles. Our experience during the winter has shown that this shape best resists drift. We will see. A few doggies came up from the sea ice today with very bloodstained heads. Probably they got hold of something. Will go down and investigate tomorrow. Joh. believes that he felt vibration in the hut some time ago – he maintained that it was the pressure of the sea ice on the Barrier. Pr., who was sitting and writing at the time, maintained that with the best will in the world, he noticed nothing at all. HH., who was also present, could notice nothing either.

Bjaaland

6 October 1911

–30 Fine, clear weather. Move the store today. Surely have food for 100 years. The Idiot has disappeared this evening, unfortunately fallen in a crevasse. The Chief is in a miserable mood. But it isn't my fault. He can thank his wanderlust for that. Anyway, I think of the Pole just as much as he does. God knows if I will ever get there or what K. will do to me. The boys' heels are better. Departure set for the 15ᵗʰ. Dear God, wherever you are, how will it go?

Scott

Friday, Oct. 6th.

With the rise of temperature there has been a slight thaw in the hut; the drips come down the walls and one has found my diary, as its pages show. The drips are already decreasing, and if they represent the whole accumulation of winter moisture it is extraordinarily little, and speaks highly for the design of the hut. There cannot be very much more or the stains would be more significant.

Yesterday I had a good look at Jehu and became convinced that he is useless; he is much too weak to pull a load, and three weeks can make no difference. It is necessary to face the facts and I've decided to leave him behind – we must do with nine ponies. Chinaman is rather a doubtful quantity and James Pigg is not a tower of strength, but the other seven are in fine form and must bear the brunt of the work somehow.

If we suffer more loss we shall depend on the motor, and then! . . . well, one must face the bad as well as the good.

It is some comfort to know that six of the animals at least are in splendid condition-Victor, Snippets, Christopher, Nobby, Bones are as fit as ponies could well be and are naturally strong, well-shaped beasts, whilst little Michael, though not so shapely, is as strong as he will ever be.

To-day Wilson, Oates, Cherry-Garrard, and Crean have gone to Hut Point with their ponies, Oates getting off with Christopher after some difficulty. At 5 o'clock the Hut Point telephone bell suddenly rang (the line was laid by Meares some time ago, but hitherto there has been no communication). In a minute or two we heard a voice, and behold! communication was established. I had quite a talk with Meares and afterwards with Oates. Not a very wonderful fact, perhaps, but it seems wonderful in this primitive land to be talking to one's fellow beings 15 miles away. Oates told me that the ponies had arrived in fine order, Christopher a little done, but carrying the heaviest load.

If we can keep the telephone going it will be a great boon, especially to Meares later in the season.

The weather is extraordinarily unsettled; the last two days have been fairly fine, but every now and again we get a burst of wind with drift, and to-night it is overcast and very gloomy in appearance.

The photography craze is in full swing. Ponting's mastery is ever more impressive, and his pupils improve day by day; nearly all of us have produced good negatives. Debenham and Wright are the most promising, but Taylor, Bowers and I are also getting the hang of the tricky [exposures].

Meares' later Service career in communications suggests that the Admiralty or War Office had asked him to test field telephony in extreme conditions. The Great War, after all, was only three years off. Meares used a single aluminium wire, laid on the ice by paying out a reel mounted on a dog sledge. The wire was uninsulated, using an earth return. The 12 nautical miles between Cape Evans and Hut Point was not a bad result with primitive equipment.

SATURDAY, OCTOBER 7TH, 1911

Amundsen

7 Oct. – Saturday.
Same splendid weather. –32°. Bj. and I went out on ski this morning to look for seal. We followed the usual track down to 'Man's Head'. It seemed that the doggies had gone out to hunt on their own account. We could follow the tracks a long way. We continued along the Barrier further towards the NE. We found a seal along the way, and it had to pay the price. A lonely 'Antarctic petrel' stayed in the vicinity. We continued along the Barrier in a N'ly direction. Cape after cape, bay after bay. At one point the pressure had overturned a promontory. It was a grand confusion to see. Will take a photo of it. We came to a little bay formation where the Barrier formed a right angle – a wall running N., and one across, E-W. We went into the bay, a splendid little bay where the Barrier front sloped right down to the sea. We went up that way and over the Barrier again. The trip took us 3 hours – ca. 10 nautical miles. It was a really fine round and well worth doing. We made the same trip in the afternoon and brought in the seal – one had a splendid picture of the Barrier on this trip and we will get many good photos of it.

Bjaaland

7 October
Was out hunting seal. Went 5 m., and then found one. The Chief wanted to see the innermost part of the bay. The Barrier has calved 2½ m. from Man's Head. It has happened in this way, it seems to have sunk down in there and raised the bay further out so that ice which is lying 30 feet underwater is visible and the top is sticking some 20 feet up the edge of the Barrier. It was possible to climb the B. nonetheless. There are many beautiful grottoes and ice screwing. Saw an Antarctic Petrel, which we took as a sign of spring. We went to the bottom of the bay, which ended in a narrow wedge, and the edge is drifted up so we had a fine ascent thence and straight home.

Scott

Saturday, Oct. 7th. As though to contradict the suggestion of incompetence, friend 'Jehu' pulled with a will this morning – he covered 3½ miles without a stop, the surface being much worse than it was two days ago. He was not at all distressed when he stopped. If he goes on like this he comes into practical politics again, and I am arranging to give 10-feet sledges to him and Chinaman instead of 12-feet. Probably they will not do much, but if they go on as at present we shall get something out of them.

Long and cheerful conversations with Hut Point and of course an opportunity for the exchange of witticisms. We are told it was blowing and drifting at Hut Point last night, whereas here it was calm and snowing; the wind only reached us this afternoon.

SUNDAY, OCTOBER 8TH, 1911

Amundsen

8 Oct. – Sunday
Same fine weather. Everyone went out on a trip during the forenoon to look at the part of the Barrier Bj. and I went along yesterday. Pr. has obtained many excellent photos of it. Is that little bay we have found – Balloon Bight? It agrees well with the distance between the big bay and Balloon B. Against that, the direction of the little bay, which is E-W, does not seem to be consistent; but some sliding and compression can do a lot. A seal came up today, but its life was spared, due to a lack of killing instruments.

Bjaaland

8 October Sunday evening.
–36 Fine day. Everyone out, some on ski, some ski-joring, others riding. The trip was to see the huge calved piece which has stuck its head above the sea ice to the N. I skied towards the Barrier and climbed on to the huge calved piece after we had taken pictures of it from above and below. Saw an Antarctic petrel.

Scott

Sunday, Oct. 8th. A very beautiful day. Everyone out and about after Service, all ponies going well. Went to Pressure Ridge with Ponting and took a number of photographs.

So far good, but the afternoon has brought much worry. About five a telephone message from Nelson's igloo reported that Clissold had fallen from a berg and hurt his back. Bowers organised a sledge party in three minutes, and fortunately Atkinson was on the spot and able to join it. I posted out over the land and found Ponting much distressed and Clissold practically insensible. At this moment the Hut Point ponies were approaching and I ran over to intercept one in case of necessity. But the man party was on the spot first, and after putting the patient in a sleeping-bag, quickly brought him home to the hut. It appears that Clissold was acting as Ponting's 'model' and that the two had been climbing about the berg to get pictures. As far as I can make out Ponting did his best to keep Clissold in safety by lending him his crampons and ice axe, but the latter seems to have missed his footing after one of his 'poses'; he slid over a rounded surface of ice for some 12 feet, then dropped 6 feet on to a sharp angle in the wall of the berg.

He must have struck his back and his head; the latter is contused and he is certainly suffering from slight concussion. He complained of his back before he grew unconscious and groaned a good deal when moved in the hut. He came to about an hour after getting to the hut, and was evidently in a good deal of pain; neither Atkinson nor Wilson thinks there is anything very serious, but he has not yet been properly examined and has had a fearful shock at the least. I still feel very anxious. To-night Atkinson has injected morphia and will watch by his patient.

Troubles rarely come singly, and it occurred to me after Clissold had been brought in that Taylor, who had been bicycling to the Turk's Head, was overdue. We were relieved to hear that with glasses two figures could be seen approaching in South Bay, but at supper Wright appeared very hot and said that Taylor was exhausted in South Bay – he wanted brandy and hot drink. I thought it best to despatch another relief party, but before they were well round the point Taylor was seen coming over the land. He was fearfully done *but that is no great matter – The serious thing to face is that here is a man going in charge of a party who cannot look after himself – I have suspected the possibility of this sort of thing for some time – Taylor is extremely excitable & nervous, flies off on a mission without any reflection on his ability to accomplish it – today he* must have pressed on towards his objective long after his reason should have warned him that it was time to turn; *I really dont know what to do about it* with this *matter to settle* and a good deal of anxiety about Clissold, the day terminates very unpleasantly.

MONDAY, OCTOBER 9TH, 1911

Amundsen

9 Oct. – Monday.
Fresh breeze from ENE (9 m) with drift this morning. Cleared up in the course of the day. Almost completely clear this evening. −30°. Have finished the work

on the store. It will probably remain standing as it is for a long time. Bj. saw an 'Antarctic petrel' up here. Unfortunately Bj. has lost his best dog, 'The Idiot'. It has been missing for several days, and has probably fallen into a crevasse. – The photos that Pr. took yesterday were splendid.

TUESDAY, OCTOBER 10ᵀᴴ, 1911

Amundsen

10 Oct. – Tuesday.
Light gale this morning from the E. (13.5 m) Dropped completely in the course of the day. M.T. –30°. Preparing ourselves for departure – 16 Oct.

Scott

Tuesday, Oct. 10ᵗʰ. Still anxious about Clissold. He has passed two fairly good nights but is barely able to move. He is unnaturally irritable, but I am told this is a symptom of concussion. This morning he asked for food, which is a good sign, and he was anxious to know if his sledging gear was being got ready. In order not to disappoint him he was assured that all would be ready, but there is scarce a slender chance that he can fill his place in the programme. *I took Taylor to task very candidly today – He was very humble and quite ready to admit his error – Perhaps it is well that I should have had the opportunity to talk straight – I am pretty sure some of my remarks sank in.*

Meares came from Hut Point yesterday at the front end of a blizzard. Half an hour after his arrival it was as thick as a hedge. He reports another loss – Deek, one of the best pulling dogs, developed the same symptoms which have so unaccountably robbed us before, spent a night in pain, and died in the morning. Wilson thinks the cause is a worm which gets into the blood and thence to the brain. It is trying, but I am past despondency. Things must take their course.

Fords fingers improve, but not very rapidly; it is hard to have two sick men after all the care which has been taken.

The weather is very poor – I had hoped for better things this month. So far we have had more days with wind and drift than without. It interferes badly with the ponies' exercise.

WEDNESDAY, OCTOBER 11TH, 1911

Amundsen

11 Oct. – Wednesday.
Glorious weather. Clear and calm most of the day. Has clouded over this evening.
Light breeze from SW M.T –39°

THURSDAY, OCTOBER 12TH, 1911

Amundsen

12 Oct. – Thursday
Bitterly cold day. M.t. –36° Breeze from ENE with fog. –

FRIDAY, OCTOBER 13TH, 1911

Amundsen

13 Oct. – Friday.
M.t. –28° Overcast. Light breeze from the E. 'Kamilla' had babies during the
night. – all well.

Scott

Friday, Oct. 13th. – The past three days have seen a marked improvement in both
our invalids. Clissold's inside has been got into working order after a good deal
of difficulty; he improves rapidly in spirits as well as towards immunity from
pain. The fiction of his preparation to join the motor sledge party is still kept
up, but Atkinson says there is not the smallest chance of his being ready. I shall
have to be satisfied if he practically recovers by the time we leave with the ponies.

Fords hand took a turn for the better two days ago and he maintains this
progress. Atkinson thinks he will be ready to start in 10 days' time, but the hand
must be carefully nursed till the weather becomes really summery.

The weather has continued bad till to-day, which has been perfectly beautiful. A fine warm sun all day – so warm that one could sit about outside in the
afternoon, and photographic work was a real pleasure.

The ponies have been behaving well, with exceptions. Victor is now quite easy
to manage, thanks to Bowers' patience. Chinaman goes along very steadily and is

not going to be the crock we expected. He has a slow pace, which may be trouble-some, but when the weather is fine that won't matter if he can get along steadily.

The most troublesome animal is Christopher. He is only a source of amuse-ment as long as there is no accident, but I am always a little anxious that he will kick or bite someone. The curious thing is that he is quiet enough to handle for walking or riding exercise or in the stable, but as soon as a sledge comes into the programme he is seized with a very demon of viciousness, and bites and kicks with every intent to do injury. It seems to be getting harder rather than easier to get him into the traces; the last two turns, he has had to be thrown, as he is unmanageable even on three legs. Oates, Bowers, and Anton gather round the beast and lash up one foreleg, then with his head held on both sides Oates gathers back the traces; quick as lightning the little beast flashes round with heels flying aloft. This goes on till some degree of exhaustion gives the men a better chance. But, as I have mentioned, during the last two days the period has been so prolonged that Oates has had to hasten matters by tying a short line to the other foreleg and throwing the beast when he lashes out. Even when on his knees he continues to struggle, and one of those nimble hind legs may fly out at any time. Once in the sledge and started on three legs all is well and the fourth leg can be released. At least, all has been well until to-day, when quite a comedy was enacted. He was going along quietly with Oates when a dog frightened him: he flung up his head, twitched the rope out of Oates' hands and dashed away. It was not a question of blind fright, as immediately after gaining freedom he set about most systematically to get rid of his load. At first he gave sudden twists, and in this manner succeeded in dislodging two bales of hay; then he caught sight of other sledges and dashed for them. They could scarcely get out of his way in time; the fell intention was evident all through, to dash his load against some other pony and sledge and so free himself of it. He ran for Bowers two or three times with this design, then made for Keohane, never going off far and dashing inward with teeth bared and heels flying all over the place. By this time people were gathering round, and first one and then another succeeded in clambering on to the sledge as it flew by, till Oates, Bowers, Nelson, and Atkinson were all sitting on it. He tried to rid himself of this human burden as he had of the hay bales, and succeeded in dislodging Atkinson with violence, but the remainder dug their heels into the snow and finally the little brute was tired out. Even then he tried to savage anyone approaching his leading line, and it was some time before Oates could get hold of it. Such is the tale of Christopher. I am exceedingly glad there are not other ponies like him. These capers promise trouble, but I think a little soft snow on the Barrier may effectually cure them.

Evans and Gran return to-night. We received notice of their departure from

Hut Point through the telephone, which also informed us that Meares had departed for his first trip to Corner Camp. Evans says he carried eight bags of forage and that the dogs went away at a great pace.

In spite of the weather Evans has managed to complete his survey to Hut Point. He has evidently been very careful with it and has therefore done a very useful bit of work.

SATURDAY, OCTOBER 14TH, 1911

Amundsen

14 Oct. – Saturday.

Fine weather this morning. Overcast, but clear. Thickened afterwards with mist and foggy air. E'ly breeze. M.t. –26°. Cinematograph in action today. Took scenes of pitching and collapsing tent. Pr. developed a photo of it this evening, It was excellent. His last photo of the Barrier was also excellent. We are now ready to get going again on Monday.

SUNDAY, OCTOBER 15TH, 1911

Amundsen

15 Oct. – Sunday

Light E'ly breeze. A little misty M.t. –27° Now ready to depart.

Bjaaland

15th

Now we are ready again. I hope it won't be a fiasco like the last time. I think that the prospects are better now than on the previous occasion. The dog teams are strong and the equipment is very good. We ought to go far in 100 days. If I emerge unscathed from this journey, I must see that I get out of polar exploration. It's hardly worth the trouble. So farewell Framheim and people and an easy life and if I should be caught out there, well, my tenderest wishes to friends and acquaintances, my fellow-countrymen and the Fatherland.

Scott

Sunday, Oct. 15th – Both of our invalids progress favourably. Clissold has had two good nights without the aid of drugs and has recovered his good spirits; pains have departed except from his back.

The weather is very decidedly warmer and for the past three days has been fine. The thermometer stands but a degree or two below zero and the air feels delightfully mild. Everything of importance is now ready for our start and the ponies improve daily.

Clissold's work of cooking has fallen on Hooper and Lashly, and it is satisfactory to find that the various dishes and bread bakings maintain their excellence. It is splendid to have people who refuse to recognise difficulties.

By now, the sun was continually above the horizon. The midnight sun had returned, and it was light round the clock. It was surely time to go. Bjaaland's '100 days' was the time allotted by Amundsen to the polar journey.

MONDAY, OCTOBER 16TH, 1911

Amundsen

16 Oct. – Monday
Fog this morning. Light SW'ly breeze. M.t. –28°. Lifted around midday. Everyone ready to depart. As we were standing ready – 2 p.m., the weather came down again completely and we had to give up getting off. Bj. and HH went down to the sea ice later and shot two seals. One of them had fully developed embryos.

TUESDAY, OCTOBER 17TH, 1911

Amundsen

17 Oct. – Tuesday
Gale from SW. M.t. –31° It is clear to see that the cold has eased. We had our lowest temperatures from that quarter previously. It has been thick all day, and there is no question of getting off. The wind has dropped this evening and we hope for tomorrow.

Scott

Tuesday, Oct. 17th. Things not going very well; with ponies all pretty well. Animals are improving in form rapidly, even Jehu, though I have ceased to count on that animal. To-night the motors were to be taken on to the floe. The drifts make the road very uneven, and the first and best motor overrode its chain; the chain was replaced and the machine proceeded, but just short of the floe was thrust to a steep inclination by a ridge, and the chain again overrode the sprockets; this time by ill fortune Day slipped at the critical moment and without intention jammed the throttle full on. The engine brought up, but there was an ominous trickle of oil under the back axle, and investigation showed that the axle casing (aluminium) had split. The casing has been stripped and brought into the hut; we may be able to do something to it, but time presses. It all goes to show that we want more experience and workshops.

I am secretly convinced that we shall not get much help from the motors, yet nothing has ever happened to them that was unavoidable. A little more care and foresight would make them splendid allies. The trouble is that if they fail, no one will ever believe this.

Meares got back from Corner Camp at 8 a.m. Sunday morning – he got through on the telephone to report in the afternoon. He must have made the pace, which is promising for the dogs. Sixty geographical miles in two days and a night is good going – about as good as can be.

I have had to tell Clissold that he cannot go out with the Motor Party, to his great disappointment. He improves very steadily, however, and I trust will be fit before we leave with the ponies. Hooper replaces him with the motors. I am kept very busy writing and preparing details.

We have had two days of northerly wind, a very unusual occurrence; yesterday it was blowing S.E., force 8, temp. −16°, whilst here the wind was north, force 4, temp. −6°. This continued for some hours – a curious meteorological combination. We are pretty certain of a southerly blizzard to follow, I should think.

Scott's lack of 'care and foresight' was his own fault. He had ordered the designer not to bother with extra testing and low temperature trials in a freezing chamber. The designer was a fellow officer, Engineer Commander R. W. Skelton, later Chief Engineer of the Navy. He had been with Scott on the Discovery expedition, but for reasons of naval etiquette had been dropped from this one. Lt Evans had objected to having anyone of a superior rank under him as nominally second-in-command. Skelton reproached Scott with using him and then casting him aside. His design was among the first snow vehicles to use the caterpillar track, an American invention. In the hurry demanded by Scott, turning was unresolved. Only later was it achieved by letting one track move faster than the other. Scott's men turned their sledges by main force, heaving on a shaft attached to the front.

WEDNESDAY, OCTOBER 18ᵀᴴ, 1911
Amundsen

18 Oct. – Wednesday.
Were ready again this morning. The same comedy again – gale and fog. Again we had to give up. Patience, patience, that is what we need here. In spite of the fog managed to fetch the last two seals we shot. M.t. –16°.

Scott

Wednesday, Oct.18ᵗʰ – The southerly blizzard has burst on us. The air is thick with snow.

A close investigation of the motor axle case shows that repair is possible. It looks as though a good strong job could be made of it. Yesterday Taylor and Debenham went to Cape Royds with the object of staying a night or two.

THURSDAY, OCTOBER 19ᵀᴴ, 1911
Amundsen

19 October – Thursday
Storm during the night and gale today from the E. quarter (16.6 m/sec) M.T. –19° No possibility of starting off. It has calmed down completely this evening. Barom. jumping up and down, but there is a possibility of starting off tomorrow.

FRIDAY, OCTOBER 20ᵀᴴ, 1911
Amundsen

Friday 20 October
At long last we managed to get off. The weather was not quite settled. Breeze first from one quarter, then another. Fog and mist. 9.30 a.m. it cleared a little

to the E. with a light breeze thence. We saddled our steeds, 13 before each of the four sledges, and set out. Pr. stood with the cine camera at the foot of the run down to the sea ice and filmed us all. Twenty seal lay in a group shielding a couple of new-born pups. He shot us again on the climb on the other side of the bay. The fog came down again after we had covered a little ground. HH ran first and set a course with his compass. For some reason we ran too far East, and into an unknown maze of cracks and crevasses. I sat together with W. His sledge was last. Suddenly a large piece of the surface fell away next to the sledge and exposed a gruesome abyss – big enough to swallow us all. Luckily we were so far to the side that we were saved. We understood from the surroundings that we had strayed too far to the East, and therefore set a course directly East by the compass (S. by W. true). That soon brought us within sight of some flags, and a short time afterwards reached the place where we shot 'Kaisa' on our last trip – 20.2 nautical miles. We managed splendidly in our improved tent. Although we were five, there is plenty of space.

Bjaaland

20 October 1911
Second start.

Well at long last we were ready, and the weather calmed down after eight days' storm. Pr. and I set off first, he was to film the troop. A lot of seals lay around. In one place, 10 to 15 seals were lying, among them two with pups – unfortunately I couldn't photograph them. Distance 20.2 m. Temperature –17.5. The dogs were too strong, so they were unharnessed, and some had to be carted along. Hanssen is cook. Sledge journey's members Capt. R. Amundsen Wisting Hassel and me O. Bjaaland.

Watching his estranged companions cross the frozen bay to the edge of the Barrier was Hjalmar Johansen, a truly tragic figure, whose outward personality seemed somehow fractured from a sensitive inner being. It was he who had best expressed the philosophy of the men now scurrying over the snow and dissolving into the mist. He had challenged the might of Nature, and learned that 'mankind is a miserable insect', as he wrote in his diary on returning to civilization in 1896 after his great journey over the Arctic ice with Nansen. 'And yet it is wonderful to be a human being!'[45]

SATURDAY, OCTOBER 21ST, 1911

Amundsen

Saturday 21 October

Gale during the night from E., eased somewhat during the forenoon. Set off at 10 a.m. It was not long before the wind rose again from the same quarter, now with thick driving snow. However we made good progress. Passed flag after flag for each nautical mile, and after having covered 17 nautical miles, we found a snow cairn erected at the beginning of April. It has thus lasted for seven months and is still in good condition. From this cairn we changed course a point northwards – ENE – so as not to get mixed up in 'filth'. – The wind dropped as the day went on. We drove on to the south-east. Luckily we had no wind from this quarter – It was really bitter to drive on, in spite of the temperature only being –24.2° Many of our dogs: Neptune, Rotta, Uranus, Ulrik, Bjørn and Fudis are exhausted; some have sore feet, the reason is unclear.

Bjaaland

21st. A gale blew up during the night, so hard that the tent was in convulsions, and around 5 o'clock, it was so violent that we feared what the day would bring, around 6 o'clock it eased, at 10 o'clock we drove off although it was blowing 10 m/sec, this evening wind from East 6 m/sec. Distance 20.3 m. Halted at 3.30. 10–15 dogs are bad.

SUNDAY, OCTOBER 22ND, 1911

Amundsen

Sunday 22 October

Thick fog. Stiff breeze from SE. Snowing and snowdrift. It was not a good day for travelling. But since we had just found our old tracks yesterday evening, I felt that we were absolutely justified when we set a course thence of NE by E. We raced ahead at a gallop. The dogs were simply mad to get through. Everything went well for a couple of hours. And then suddenly we reached classical crevassed terrain. We could not see many metres around us. I was ski-joring with W. and we were the last. Suddenly we saw that Bj.'s sledge – he was running just ahead of us – had tilted. We stopped our sledge. In the meantime, Bj.'s sledge had completely disappeared into the crevasse. With great presence of mind he himself had flung himself off, and now sat a couple of feet from the edge, and held the sledge by the trace. It took some time – 5 minutes I think – before we fetched the alpine rope, which was in the leading sledge – HH's – made it ready, and attached it to the trace. It was high time. Every moment it became heavier and heavier for Bj. A minute more, and he would have had to let the sledge disappear into the depths. Where the sledge had fallen into the crevasse, it was about 1 m wide, and deep – well in fact, we couldn't see the bottom. When we had attached the alpine rope, Bj. W. and I succeeded in holding the sledge. HH. and Has. then fetched another sledge, which we placed across the crevasse, and to which we anchored the hanging sledge. Thereafter W. was lowered on the alpine rope, and down there he managed to fix straps to the various boxes, and from that position we managed to haul them right up to the top. It took us a good 1½ hours to get the sledge up again. W., who had been down in the crevasse, could report that a short distance from where the sledge had fallen in, there was a huge widening under the surface which could have swallowed all sledges with full complement, if they had strayed broadside on. On closer investigation, it turned out that the terrain around us consisted entirely of crevasse after crevasse and enormous chasms. To continue in such terrain in thick fog, we decided was best avoided. It was difficult to find space for the tent, but with the aid of the tent pole, we were finally able to arrange a reasonably secure site. The tiny place on which we now have the tent standing is surrounded by crevasses and chasms on all sides, and our tent is certainly on the worst of them. The time is now 1 p.m. We are cooking lobscouse, and waiting for the fog to lift. At 4 o'clock it lifted. Then we could see seracs surrounding us – quite small, but enough to signal the 'filthy terrain'. Bj. W. and I went ahead on the alpine rope to find a way out. By going eastwards, we were soon out of it. At 5 o'clock we started off again at full tilt. The doggies ran like lightning. Too hastily however we resumed a course of E. by N. and once more it brought us among the crevasses. Four of HH's dogs fell into a hideous crevasse, which would easily have swallowed them and their cargo also, if he had not managed to stop. We were forced to retrace our steps out again and then make a wide detour to avoid the little seracs. This place had been crumpled with such violence, that huge slabs were piled up against each other like rafting in the pack ice. When we had worked our way round the 'filth', we caught sight of one of our flags *to the E*. In spite of everything we had strayed too far to the west – right into the 'filth'. It is quite extraordinary. Although even on the previous day we had struggled to keep N. of our course, and although we crossed the tracks we had followed the previous time, and although we even steered a point more northerly – NE by E, despite all this we bloody well came too far over to the W. We have had several opportunities of checking the compass on this journey, and it has proved to be absolutely in order. What could the reason be? I know only one answer – local disturbance. It must be this – cannot be anything else. That the compass is reliable was shown this evening when we found the two little igloos we built on our previous trip. – The going has been consistently good. A little loose snow the first 10 nautical miles from the edge of the Barrier but mostly hard.

Bjaaland

22 October

Among the crevasses.

On departure today, it was snowing and foggy so one couldn't see anything. We went at a frightening speed, but our course was too far west and 1-2-3 we were in crevassed terrain, and my sledge broke through along a crevasse, and fell in, and I flung myself to one side, and I grabbed the traces, and held on and screamed for help, but it was touch and go for the sledge, sinking and sinking and threatening to drag the doggies with it. Five men were unable to haul it up, so we put a sledge across, and anchored it, and Wisting let himself down and sent up little by little so everything was saved. The hole looked foul and bottomless, room for 100 sledges. We made camp close by. Hope that it will soon clear up and we can get away. At 3–4 in the morning the fog cleared and the sun broke through. We found that we had come to the seracs where we were last season. We got out safely, but because of the mistaken idea of where we were, we moved to the west, we shouldn't have done that, for there was crevasse after crevasse, and bang! Four of H.'s dogs fell in. H-H came and we got all of them up. Now we are in the igloo and –29.

Scott

Sunday, Oct. 22nd. The motor axle case was completed by Thursday morning, and, as far as one can see, Day made a very excellent job of it. Since that the Motor Party has been steadily preparing for its departure. To-day everything is ready. The loads are ranged on the sea ice, the motors are having a trial run, and, all remaining well with the weather, the party will get away to-morrow.

Meares and Demetri came down on Thursday through the last of the blizzard. At one time they were running without sight of the leading dogs – they did not see Tent Island at all, but burst into sunshine and comparative calm a mile from the station. Another of the best of the dogs, Cigan, was smitten with the unaccountable sickness; he was given laxative medicine and appears to be a little better, but we are still anxious. If he really has the disease, whatever it may be, the rally is probably only temporary and the end will be swift.

The teams left on Friday afternoon, Cigan included; to-day Meares telephones that he is setting out for his second journey to Corner Camp without him. On the whole the weather continues wretchedly bad; the ponies could not be exercised either on Thursday or Friday; they were very fresh yesterday and to-day in consequence. When unexercised, their allowance of oats has to be cut down. This is annoying, as just at present they ought to be doing a moderate amount of work and getting into condition on full rations.

The temperature is up to zero about; this probably means about −20° on the Barrier. I wonder how the motors will face the drop if and when they encounter it. Day and Lashly are both hopeful of the machines, and they really ought to do something after all the trouble that has been taken.

The wretched state of the weather has prevented the transport of emergency stores to Hut Point. These stores are for the returning depôts and to provision the *Discovery* hut in case the *Terra Nova* does not arrive. The most important stores have been taken to the Glacier Tongue by the ponies to-day.

In spite of all the care I have taken to make the details of my plan clear by lucid explanation, I find that Bowers is the only man on whom I can thoroughly rely to carry out the work without mistake, *I intended Oates to superintend the forage arrangements but arrays of figures however simply expressed are too much for him and I have had to hand this part also to Bowers – But for* the practical consistent work of pony training Oates is especially capable, and his heart is very much in the business.

It promised to be very fine to-day, but the wind has already sprung up and clouds are gathering again. There was a very beautiful curved 'banner' cloud south of Erebus this morning, perhaps a warning of what is to come.

Another accident – At one o'clock 'Snatcher,' one of the three ponies laying the depôt, arrived with single trace and dangling sledge in a welter of sweat. Forty minutes after [P.O.] Evans, his driver, came in almost as hot; simultaneously Wilson arrived with Nobby and a tale of events not complete. He said that after the loads were removed Bowers had been holding the three ponies, who appeared to be quiet; suddenly one had tossed his head and all three had stampeded – Snatcher making for home, Nobby for the Western Mountains, Victor, with Bowers still hanging to him, in an indefinite direction. Running for two miles, he eventually rounded up Nobby west of Tent Island and brought him in. Half an hour after Wilson's return, Bowers came in with Victor distressed, bleeding at the nose, from which a considerable fragment hung semi-detached.

Bowers himself was covered with blood and supplied the missing link-the cause of the incident. It appears that the ponies were fairly quiet when Victor tossed his head and caught his nostril in the trace hook on the hame of Snatcher's harness. The hook tore skin and flesh and of course the animal got out of hand. Bowers hung to him, but couldn't possibly keep hold of the other two as well. Victor had bled a good deal, and the blood congealing on the detached skin not only gave the wound a dismal appearance but greatly increased its irritation. I don't know how Bowers managed to hang on to the frightened animal; I don't believe anyone else would have done so. On the way back the dangling weight on the poor creature's nose would get on the swing and make him increasingly restive; it was necessary to stop him repeatedly. Since his return the piece of skin has been snipped off and proves the wound not so serious as it looked. The animal is still trembling, but quite on his feed, which is a good sign. I don't know why our Sundays should always bring these excitements.

Two lessons arise. First, however quiet the animals appear, they must not be left by their drivers – no chance must be taken; secondly, the hooks on the hames of the harness must be altered in shape.

I suppose such incidents as this were to be expected, one cannot have ponies very fresh and vigorous and expect them to behave like lambs, but I shall be glad when we are off and can know more definitely what resources we can count on.

Another trying incident has occurred. We have avoided football this season especially to keep clear of accidents, but on Friday afternoon a match was got up for the cinematograph and Debenham developed a football knee (an old hurt, I have since learnt, or he should not have played). Wilson thinks it will be a week before he is fit to travel, so here we have the Western Party on our hands and wasting the precious hours for that period. The only single compensation is that it gives Forde's hand a better chance. If this waiting were to continue it looks as though we should become a regular party of 'crocks.' Clissold was out of the hut for the first time to-day; he is better but still suffers in his back.

MONDAY, OCTOBER 23RD, 1911

Amundsen

Monday 23 October

Overcast and thick when we started at 8 a.m. After a little while it cleared overhead but the whole horizon remained thick. Soon we have a stiff breeze from the S.W. quarter with heavy drift, so we could see absolutely nothing – 100 m. ahead was all. According to the distance we covered yesterday, we should have another

22.8 nautical miles to 80°. We had a good test of both sledgemeter and compass. Without having seen our hands in front of our faces, so to speak, we ran close up to the depot 1.30 p.m. It was brilliant proof: a single point on this huge space, guided by sledgemeter and compass in the thickest spindrift. Everything was in good order, as we had left it. Snowdrifts had naturally formed round our sledge cases. We have now fed the doggies liberally with seal meat, and the carcasses are placed out on the snow to be used at will.

Bjaaland

23rd –28. Stratus. A wind of 8–9 m/s with drift soon blew up. Visibility nil. Found the depot precisely and now we will enjoy ourselves for two days and then the tour goes on further into the unknown. The south-wester continues.

TUESDAY, OCTOBER 24TH, 1911

Amundsen

Tuesday 24 October

Pure mess during the night. N'ly wind and snow. Eased enough during the morning so that we could get out in reasonably respectable weather and hack up meat for the dogs. They are having a good time now. As much fresh meat as they can eat. And then they can sleep to their heart's content. Now we have four dogs fewer than when we set out. These four were let loose on the way, because they could not keep up, presumably overfed. Consequently we now have 48 dogs left, or four teams of 12 each. We are having a splendid time in our tent. We stumbled on the brilliant idea of sewing an outer tent out of our 10 bunk curtains. This improvised outer tent proved excellent, in that it reduces the heat from the sun to a great extent, and holds the warmth inside. It is hugely different from the first trip. Now we always lie in loose bedclothes, warm and comfortable. Another great advantage is that it is always dark inside the tent – and that is desirable when one has been in the glare of the snow all day – Wind dropped during the day. Have spent p.m. packing the sledges and rebuilding the depot. Thus we are quite ready. The dogs are enjoying life.

Bjaaland

24th. The wind continued all day then dropped. We have now fed our dogs and eaten and drunk and the day after tomorrow head southwards.

Scott

Tuesday, Oct. 24th. Two fine days for a wonder. Yesterday the motors seemed ready to start and we all went out on the floe to give them a 'send off.' But the inevitable little defects cropped up, and the machines only got as far as the Cape. A change made by Day in the exhaust arrangements had neglected the heating jackets of the carburetters; one float valve was bent and one clutch troublesome. Day and Lashly spent the afternoon making good these defects in a satisfactory manner.

This morning the engines were set going again, and shortly after 10 a.m. a fresh start was made. At first there were a good many stops, but on the whole the engines seemed to be improving all the time. They are not by any means working up to full power yet, and so the pace is very slow. The weights seem to me a good deal heavier than we bargained for. Day sets his motor going, climbs off the car, and walks alongside with an occasional finger on the throttle. Lashly hasn't yet quite got hold of the nice adjustments of his control levers, but I hope will have done so after a day's practice. The only alarming incident was the slipping of the chains when Day tried to start on some ice very thinly covered with snow. The starting effort on such heavily laden sledges is very heavy, but I thought the grip of the pattens and studs would have been good enough on any surface. Looking at the place afterwards I found that the studs had grooved the ice.

Now as I write at 12.30 the machines are about a mile out in the South Bay; both can be seen still under weigh, progressing steadily if slowly.

I find myself immensely eager that these tractors should succeed, even though they may not be of great help to our southern advance. A small measure of success will be enough to show their possibilities, their ability to revolutionise Polar transport. Seeing the machines at work to-day, and remembering that every defect so far shown is purely mechanical, it is impossible not to be convinced of their value. But the trifling mechanical defects and lack of experience show the risk of cutting out trials. A season of experiment with a small workshop at hand may be all that stands between success and failure.

At any rate before we start we shall certainly know if the worst has happened, or if some measure of success attends this unique effort.

The ponies are in fine form. Victor, practically recovered from his wound, has been rushing round with a sledge at a great rate. Even Jehu has been buckish, kicking up his heels and gambolling awkwardly. The invalids progress, Clissold a little alarmed about his back, but without cause.

Atkinson and Keohane have turned cooks, and do the job splendidly.

This morning Meares announced his return from Corner Camp, so that all stores are now out there. The run occupied the same time as the first, when the routine was: first day 17 miles out; second day 13 out, and 13 home; early third day run in. If only one could trust the dogs to keep going like this it would be splendid. On the whole things look hopeful.

1 p.m. motors reported off Razor Back Island, nearly 3 miles out – come, come!

Amundsen's reference to being 'dark inside the tent' touches on another paradox of high latitudes. Shade is as essential as in the tropics. Heat threatens as much as cold; glare even more so. The explanation lies in the low altitude of the sun even at midsummer. The sun's rays bounce off the snow at just the right angle to cause maximum burning from above and beneath, and maximum discomfort to the eyes. What is more, the midnight sun is mildly confusing. Light round the clock disrupts the sense of time. This in turn threatens sleep patterns, and regular sleep belongs to the armament of survival.

WEDNESDAY, OCTOBER 25TH, 1911
Amundsen

Wednesday 25 October
Spent the day at rest. Dogs bursting with health. Tomorrow we go on further south. This time we have brought to the depot 200 kg dog pemmican +30 l. paraffin (130°) + 2 tins of biscuits + 3 alpine ropes + 3 complete units of food for 100 days. We have taken from the depot: 1 case of paraffin (150°) + 5 seals + 15 kg filets + 1 case of dog pemmican + 8 packets of chocolate.

Bjaaland

25th –20.5 Gale from S.E. which dropped towards 4 o'clock. It has now cleared up and the prospects for tomorrow are good. Dogs are hale and hearty. Dinner today consisted of boneless chicken, *dessert* plum pudding. The load is heavy, ca. 400 kg I think it is wrong, and a pity for the dogs to overload them but . . .

Heated and mixed with water, pemmican makes a sustaining stew – called 'hoosh' by the English – appreciated by those exerting themselves in a cold climate, but few others. Amundsen's dog pemmican was made with fish; at a pinch, the men could eat it too. Biscuits were the other staple. Based on ship's biscuits, they provided calories and carbohydrates.

Pemmican and biscuits were the core of both Scott's and Amundsen's diets. Scott added tea, butter, cocoa and sugar. Amundsen took chocolate and powdered milk. He thought that tea and coffee were useless weight, because they held no nourishment. (His men, all coffee addicts, suffered for that.) He reasoned that the chocolate would provide sugar, and the dried milk extra fat and protein. Combined, they formed the hot sweet, nourishing drink everyone needs in a cold climate. Amundsen also preferred simplicity in diet as in everything else. With only four ingredients, manipulation and accounting were easier.

Amundsen was working with huge margins of safety, while Scott had none. Not even that, however, could avert the overhanging threat of scurvy, the historical killer of sailors and polar explorers. Scurvy is an acute vitamin C deficiency. That was not understood at the time – vitamins had not yet been discovered – but fresh food was known to prevent the disease. Vitamin C was absent from the basic travelling diets of both Amundsen and Scott. This was potentially fatal, because Man is one of the few living creatures that cannot synthesize the vitamin, but needs an external source. The difference was this. Amundsen had some vitamin C from the frozen seal meat in his depots. This was not enough by itself to prevent scurvy, but he saw safety in speed which, although he did not know it, meant diet as well. The 100 days he had allowed for his polar journey also happens to be the maximum time that the human organism can store vitamin C.

THURSDAY, OCTOBER 26TH, 1911

Amundsen

Thursday 26 October.
N'ly breeze. Clear. Wonderful for travelling. First we got everything in order. Gathered all seal meat in one place. It is the flesh of 4 big seals. Collected all the pieces of blubber which lay strewn around, and put the finishing touches to the depot. At 9 a.m. we got going. The dogs were completely wild. Covered the stage, 15 nautical miles by 1 p.m. Pure luxury. Lovely weather. On this stretch, the Barrier has been absolutely even. Wonderful skiing.

Bjaaland

26th –31. Fine weather, westerly wind. Drove off 9 o'clock. Dogs in good spirits and flew like maniacs. Going good, and terrain fine and flat. Distance 15.6 m. from 9 o'clock to 1.30.

Scott

Thursday, Oct. 26th. Couldn't see the motors yesterday till I walked well out on the South Bay, when I discovered them with glasses off the Glacier Tongue. There had been a strong wind in the forenoon, but it seemed to me they ought to have got further – annoyingly the telephone gave no news from Hut Point, evidently something was wrong. After dinner Simpson and Gran started for Hut Point.

This morning Simpson has just rung up. He says the motors are in difficulties with the surface. The trouble is just that which I noted as alarming on Monday – the chains slip on the very light snow covering of hard ice. The engines are working well, and all goes well when the machines get on to snow.

I have organised a party of eight men including myself, and we are just off to see what can be done to help.

The laconic pleasure of Amundsen and Bjaaland reveals the essence of their system of snow travel. The speed of dogs before a loaded sledge matches that of a cross country skier idling; Bjaaland especially so. This means that they were operating well within their limits, and never drawing on physical and mental reserves. In fact they were better off than appears at first sight. Much of the time they were ski-joring; pulled along, as if on a drag-lift, by the surplus energy of the dogs. In other words, they were conserving their strength for what lay ahead. Barring accidents their survival was assured.

The comparison with Scott is obvious. He and his followers were straining at their limits of endurance. This seems to follow from something in the English psyche which equates achievement with self-punishment. It is an interesting cultural difference. A Norwegian once said to the author that 'you must never forget that a Norwegian will only give 99% of himself, never 100%.' Bjaaland, for one, lived up to that spectacularly.

FRIDAY, OCTOBER 27TH, 1911

Amundsen

Friday 27 October
Continued in the same glorious weather. Dead calm – Clear. Flat – fine without a single sastruga. Wonderful going. We took only 4½ hours for our allotted 15 nautical miles per day. It goes like greased lightning. The doggies are in better condition with every passing day. They are getting rid of their superfluous fat. Already in the forenoon we glimpsed the huge seracs in the east, which we saw for the first time between 81° and 82° S. latitude. Now we have them NE by N. From the dept at 81° S. latitude they bear NE by ¾ N. Now the sun is very strong. Forced the temperature up many degrees in the course of the day. Here in the tent it is like in a little oven. It is also quite dark. Everybody in brilliant form. Built our first snow cairn today at 80° 23.5'. They will be built at a man's height every 7th or 8th nautical mile. A little note with the position of the cairn and the bearing of the next cairn to the north will be inserted in the uppermost block of snow.

Bjaaland

27th –34 –28. Sunshine and calm. Set off at 8.20 and made camp at 1 o'clock. Distance 14.5 m. Built a cairn 24 m. from 80° and left a note in it. We ought to have found a cairn and an empty sledge case, but didn't find them. Can see signs of disturbance in the ice far ahead to the right. Today it has been absolutely flat and the going was good.

Scott

Friday, Oct. 28th [sic should be 27th]. We were away by 10.30 yesterday. Walked to the Glacier Tongue with gloomy forebodings; but for one gust a beautifully bright inspiriting day. Seals were about and were frequently mistaken for the motors. As we approached the Glacier Tongue, however, and became more alive to such mistakes, we realised that the motors were not in sight. At first I thought they must have sought better surface on the other side of the Tongue, but this theory was soon demolished and we were puzzled to know what had happened. At length walking onward they were descried far away over the floe towards Hut Point; soon after we saw good firm tracks over a snow surface, a pleasant

Figure 10 Amundsen's party at rest on the way to the Pole, October–November 1911.
                                                    – National Library of Norway

change from the double tracks and slippery places we had seen on the bare ice. Our spirits went up at once, for it was not only evident that the machines were going, but that they were negotiating a very rough surface without difficulty. We marched on and overtook them about 2½ miles from Hut Point, passing Simpson and Gran returning to Cape Evans. From the motors we learnt that things were going pretty well. The engines were working well when once in tune, but the cylinders, especially the two after ones, tended to get too hot, whilst the fan or wind playing on the carburettor tended to make it too cold. The trouble was to get a balance between the two, and this is effected by starting up the engines, then stopping and covering them and allowing the heat to spread by conductivity-of course, a rather clumsy device. We camped ahead of the motors as they camped for lunch. Directly after, Lashly brought his machine along on low gear and without difficulty ran it on to Cape Armitage. Meanwhile Day was having trouble with some bad surface; we had offered help and been refused, and with Evans alone his difficulties grew, whilst the wind sprang up and the snow started to drift. We had walked into the hut and found Meares, but now we all came out again. I sent for Lashly and Hooper and went back to help Day along. We had exasperating delays and false starts for an hour and then suddenly the machine tuned up, and off she went faster than one could walk, reaching Cape Armitage without further hitch. It was blizzing by this time; a fine sight to see the motor forging away through the mist as the snow flew by. We all went back to the hut; Meares and Demetri have been busy, the hut is tidy and comfortable and a splendid brick fireplace had just been built with a bran new stove-pipe leading from it directly upward through the roof. This is really a most credit-able bit of work. Instead of the ramshackle temporary structures of last season we have now a solid permanent fireplace which should last for many a year. We spent a most comfortable night.

This morning we were away over the floe about 9 a.m. I was anxious to see how the motors started up and agreeably surprised to find that neither driver took more than 20 to 30 minutes to get his machine going, in spite of the dif-ficulties of working a blow lamp in a keen cold wind.

Lashly got away very soon, made a short run of about ½ a mile, and then after a short halt to cool, a long non-stop for quite 3 miles. The Barrier, five geographical miles from Cape Armitage, now looked very close, but Lashly had overdone matters a bit, run out of lubricant and got his engine too hot. The next run yielded a little over a mile, and he was forced to stop within a few hundred yards of the snow slope leading to the Barrier and wait for more lubricant, as well as for the heat balance in his engine to be restored.

This motor was going on second gear, and this gives a nice easy walking speed, 2½ to 3 miles an hour; it would be a splendid rate of progress if it was not necessary to halt for cooling. This is the old motor which was used in Norway; the other machine has modified gears.

Meanwhile Day had had the usual balancing trouble and had dropped to a speck, but towards the end of our second run it was evident he had overcome these and was coming along at a fine speed. One soon saw that the men beside the sledges were running. To make a long story short, he stopped to hand over lubricating oil, started at a gallop again, and dashed up the slope without a hitch on his top speed – the first man to run a motor on the Great Barrier! There was great cheering from all assembled, but the motor party was not wasting time on jubilation. On dashed the motor, and it and the running men beside it soon grew small in the distance. We went back to help Lashly, who had restarted his engine. If not so dashingly, on account of his slower speed, he also now took the slope without hitch and got a last handshake as he clattered forward. His engine was not working so well as the other, but I think mainly owing to the first overheating and a want of adjustment resulting therefrom.

Thus the motors left us, travelling on the best surface they have yet encountered – hard windswept snow without sastrugi a surface which Meares reports to extend to Corner Camp at least.

Providing there is no serious accident, the engine troubles will gradually be got over; of that I feel pretty confident. Every day will see improvement as it has done to date, every day the men will get greater confidence with larger experience of the machines and the conditions. But it is not easy to foretell the extent of the result of older and earlier troubles with the rollers. The new rollers turned up by Day are already splitting, and one of Lashly's chains is in a bad way; it may be possible to make temporary repairs good enough to cope with the improved surface, but it seems probable that Lashly's car will not get very far.

It is already evident that had the rollers been metal cased and the runners metal covered, they would now be as good as new. I cannot think why we had not the sense to have this done. As things are I am satisfied we have the right men to deal with the difficulties of the situation. The motor programme is not of vital importance to our plan and it is possible the machines will do little to help us, but already they have vindicated themselves. Even the seamen, who have remained very sceptical of them, have been profoundly impressed. Evans said, 'Lord, sir, I reckon if them things can go on like that you wouldn't want nothing else' – but like everything else of a novel nature, it is the actual sight of them at work that is impressive, and nothing short of a hundred miles over the Barrier will carry conviction to outsiders.

Parting with the motors, we made haste back to Hut Point and had tea there. My feet had got very sore with the unaccustomed soft foot-gear and crinkly surface, but we decided to get back to Cape Evans. We came along in splendid weather, and after stopping for a cup of tea at Razor Back, reached the hut at 9 p.m., averaging 3½ stat. miles an hour. During the day we walked 26½ stat. miles, not a bad day's work considering condition, but I'm afraid my feet are going to suffer for it.

Bjaaland simply recorded air temperatures at the beginning of each day's entry, without identifying them as such; or specifying the time. Where appropriate, he preceded the temperatures by latitude; again simple figures without identification. He generally omitted the degree sign in the temperatures. After all, he was only jotting down notes for his own use, and no one else.

SATURDAY, OCTOBER 28TH, 1911

Amundsen

Saturday 28th October
SE gale with thick drift during the night, continuing all day. Have been forced to stay put.

Bjaaland

28th Saturday −22 −19.8 −16.5. Unfortunately the good weather ended abruptly. Around 10 o'clock, a gale blew up and has lasted all day with drift so thick that you couldn't see far, and we just lie and rest in the sleeping bags and are bored. There's little to do, hope it will soon finish. The little devil has eaten my ski binding. Sastrugi 1 m. high, unheard of in these parts.

Scott

Saturday, Oct. 29th [sic – should be 28th.] My feet sore and one 'tendon Achillis' strained (synovitis); shall be right in a day or so, however. Last night tremendous row in the stables. Christopher and Chinaman discovered fighting. Gran nearly got kicked. These ponies are getting above themselves with their high feeding. Oates says that Snippets is still lame and has one leg a little 'heated'; not a pleasant item of news. Debenham is progressing, but not very fast; the Western Party will leave after us, of that there is no doubt now. It is trying that they should be wasting the season in this way. All things considered, I shall be glad to get away and put our fortune to the test.

SUNDAY, OCTOBER 29TH, 1911

Amundsen

Sunday 29 October
Brilliant weather. Light n'ly breeze. Cleared up −19°. Snow a little looser today. No sastrugi. Going excellent. Dogs healthy. All well.

Bjaaland

29 [October] Sunday −19.8 −18.5. Left at 8.30, fine weather, the going a little soft, terrain flat, perhaps climbing a little. Distance 15 m. Made camp 1.30 p.m. Built a cairn at 80°30' Course ENE.

MONDAY, OCTOBER 30ᵀᴴ, 1911

Amundsen

Monday 30 October

Gale during the night with thick drift. Eased during the morning. We turned out as usual at 6 o'clock and were ready to start around 8. Before we left, HH shot one of his dogs − Bone. It was too old and couldn't keep up. It was big and fat. It was cut open, the innards taken out and the carcass put in the snow cairn we had built − The weather was not of the best kind when we set off. Fairly thick and wind from the northerly quarter. The going has not been of the best kind today − minor sastrugi and loose snow. Luckily it cleared gradually and at 1 p.m. we caught sight of the depot. At that point our course was almost exactly in its direction. Reached it at 2 p.m. Everything in order. Judging by appearances, very little snow has fallen. The snowdrift around the dept is about 1½ ft. high. Our average speed is now 3 nautical miles an hour.

Bjaaland

30 October −13.5 −12.5. Yesterday evening there was a gale, which caused big sastrugi and perhaps some snowfall. The wind dropped around 7–8 o'clock, and the weather was clear, skiing was heavy with loose snow. Hanssen shot a dog today and put it on a cairn at 80°45'. The sun broke through around nine o'clock. We saw the depot at 81° from a ridge 4 miles off. Passed two big crevasses running in a NE direction.

Scott

Monday, Oct. 30ᵗʰ. We had another beautiful day yesterday, and one began to feel that the summer really had come; but to-day, after a fine morning, we have a return to blizzard conditions. It is blowing a howling gale as I write. Yesterday

Wilson, Crean, Evans, and I donned our sledging kit and camped by the bergs for the benefit of Ponting and his cinematograph; he got a series of films which should be about the most interesting of all his collection. I imagine nothing will take so well as these scenes of camp life.

On our return we found Meares had returned; he and the dogs well. He told us that [Lieut.] Evans had come into Hut Point on Saturday to fetch a personal bag left behind there. Evans reported that Lashly's motor had broken down near Safety Camp; they found the big end smashed up in one cylinder and traced it to a faulty casting; they luckily had spare parts, and Day and Lashly worked all night on repairs in a temperature of −25°. By the morning repairs were completed and they had a satisfactory trial run, dragging on loads with both motors. Then Evans found out his loss and returned on ski, whilst, as I gather, the motors proceeded; I don't quite know how, but I suppose they ran one on at a time.

On account of this accident and because some of our hardest worked people were badly hit by the two days' absence helping the machines, I have decided to start on Wednesday instead of to-morrow.

If the blizzard should blow out, Atkinson and Keohane will set off to-morrow for Hut Point, so that we may see how far Jehu is to be counted on.

TUESDAY, OCTOBER 31ST, 1911
Amundsen

Tuesday 31 October

A wonderful rest day at 81°. Calm and clear. Have put our sleeping bags out to dry. They had become a little damp. Bj. and I went out to look at our transverse marks. These marks were narrow planks from boxes about 2½ long and were placed out at the beginning of March 1911. There they stood now, at the end of October, about ½ ft. lower – presumably caused by drift snow. They were so clear and visible that we could not have passed them without seeing them. Have profited by the fine day to take a number of observations and check the compasses. We have taken a number of photos. The doggies are in splendid form. We went past two crevasses yesterday, a short time before arriving here. There now remain in the depot five cases of meat pem.= 200 kg (net) and four cases of fish pem = 160 kg (net). In all = 360 kg. The depot has been completely rebuilt, and is now considerably higher. The flag that was planted on it in March is just as good. It almost seems not to have been used. There cannot have been much strong wind. Everybody has filled their cases with dog pemmican. Go on further tomorrow.

Bjaaland

31 October −19.5 −18 −24. Fine weather, too fine for a rest day. On examining the markings to the east, covered 8 m., we found that they were quite visible, drifted up by about ½ foot snow. At dinner today had caramel pudding for dessert.

Scott

Tuesday, Oct. 31ˢᵗ. The blizzard has blown itself out this morning, and this afternoon it has cleared; the sun is shining and the wind dropping. Meares and Ponting are just off to Hut Point. Atkinson and Keohane will probably leave in an hour or so as arranged, and if the weather holds, we shall all get off to-morrow. So here end the entries in this diary with the first chapter of our History. The future is in the lap of the gods; I can think of nothing left undone to deserve success.

WEDNESDAY, NOVEMBER 1ˢᵀ, 1911

Amundsen

Wednesday 1 November
Set off in thick fog. We had an eventful march. When we ran over here the first time, we only found one crevasse in which two of HH's dogs fell. Different this time. In the fog, we strayed into a long depression, and here we found crevasse after crevasse. They were not particularly wide − ca. 3 feet, and luckily ran athwart our course. If such beasts become parallel, then they are dangerous. When we had covered 12.5 nautical miles HH, who always goes first, ran over a crevasse, and was unfortunate enough to catch his ski tip in a dog trace, with the result that he fell, and remained lying right across the crevasse. A fairly unpleasant situation. The dogs had reached the other side, and started a dreadful brawl at the edge of the abyss. In the meanwhile the sledge was half way into the crevasse, and threatened to sink at any moment. I was able to stop the dogfight. W. dragged HH out of his perilous position, and by our combined effort, we managed to get the sledge out, and away from the dangerous neighbourhood. The others had crossed a little way off, where the snow bridge was stronger. Hass. also fell right in the middle of a crevasse, and came within an ace of ending badly.

These crevasses are impressive when one lies at the edge and stares down in them. A bottomless chasm goes from light blue into the thickest darkness. The ugliest formations we have found here are huge holes that could swallow *Fram* and a lot more besides. These holes are covered by a thin wind crust, and the little hole that is visible doesn't seem so menacing. But if one gets on to such a delightful spot, one is irrevocably lost. We passed one of these holes in the 'pea souper' today. Luckily HH saw it in time. There is not much that escapes his sharp eye. We are all clear. What risk do we not run in our march over such unpleasant places. We go with our lives in our hands each day. But it is pleasant to hear – nobody wants to turn back. No – these boys want to press on, cost what it will.

Bjaaland

Wednesday 1 November –19 –19. Thick fog and crevasse after crevasse. After travelling 8 m we reached some low ice mounds and a depression running south. We passed a vile hole in the end Hanssen ran into a foul crevasse. Distance 15 m.

Scott

Southern Journey Vol. I

Southern Journey

Nov. 1 Last night we heard that Jehu had reached Hut Point in about 5½ hours. This morning we got away in detachments – Michael, Nobby, Chinaman were first to get away about 11 a.m. The little devil Christopher was harnessed with the usual difficulty and started in kicking mood, Oates holding on for all he was worth.

Bones ambled off gently with Crean, and I led Snippets in his wake. Ten minutes after Evans and Snatcher passed at the usual full speed.

The wind blew very strong at the Razor Back and the sky was threatening – the ponies hate the wind. A mile south of this island Bowers and Victor passed me, leaving me where I best wished to be – at the tail of the line.

About this place I saw that one of the animals ahead had stopped and was obstinately refusing to go forward again. I had a great fear it was Chinaman, the unknown quantity, but to my relief found it was my old friend, Nobby, in obstinate mood. As he is very strong and fit the matter was soon adjusted with a little persuasion from Anton behind. Poor little Anton found it difficult to keep the pace with short legs.

Snatcher soon led the party and covered the distance in four hours. Evans said he could see no difference at the end from the start – the little animal simply romped in. Bones and Christopher arrived almost equally fresh, in fact the latter had been bucking and kicking the whole way, for the present there is no end to his devilment, and the great consideration is how to safeguard Oates. Some quiet ponies should always be near him, a difficult matter to arrange with such varying rates of walking. A little later I came up to a batch, Bowers, Wilson, Cherry, and Wright, and was happy to see Chinaman going very strong. He is not fast, but very steady, and I think should go a long way.

Victor and Michael forged ahead again, and the remaining three of us came in after taking a little under five hours to cover the distance.

We were none too soon, as the weather had been steadily getting worse, and soon after our arrival it was blowing a gale.

Amundsen was now 200 nautical miles ahead. Scott had lost the race before he began. Scott had 12 men, who would successively turn back, leaving the polar party alone for the final lap. This compares with the simplicity of Amundsen's five men, who – other things being equal – would start and finish together as a single group. Scott had eight ponies, equivalent to 48 dogs' pulling power and 30 dogs. Amundsen had 52 dogs to begin with. By contrast, he set off with ten times more supplies per man than Scott.

Amundsen among the crevasses graphically depicts the danger of unknown terrain in the treacherous substance that is ice. You can only be sure of where you have planted your feet before, and you stray at your peril. Scott had the easier navigation. His route had been surveyed before; by Shackleton in 1908–9, and himself partially on the Discovery *expedition in 1902–3. The dangers were well charted. Moreover, Scott had landmarks on the mapped adjacent mountains by which to steer. Amundsen did not. No one had been his way before.*

Amundsen and Bjaaland rarely touch on the mechanics of starting off. It was too simple and all routine. They merely harnessed the dogs and set off together in line ahead, Helmer Hanssen, as the navigator, always leading. Amundsen did not have a sledge or dog team of his own. As the leader, he wanted to roam up and down the line, so as to have an overview, and give help when needed. Sometimes he was forerunner, to assist Helmer Hanssen in making his dogs follow the course. Helmer Hanssen probably relished his constant nagging of Amundsen to veer left or right and ski straight, because it was difficult on a plain with no landmarks by which to steer. Besides which, Amundsen had to stay ahead of the dogs, who had taken up the chase. With someone in front, boredom vanished, and they could indulge their sense of humour. Usually Amundsen brought up the rear, to pick up anything that fell off the sledges. Since this was a highly responsible task, he believed that it fell to him, as leader, to perform.

THURSDAY, NOVEMBER 2ND, 1911

Amundsen

Thursday 2 November

Light breeze from SSE – 34½° To begin with, it seemed quite cold, but one gets used to anything. A rather narrow crevasse was all the horror today. The skiing has been rather firmer and better today than yesterday. By the way, we always take the same time – ca. 2½ hours for 5 nautical miles. We now stop every 5th nautical mile to build a cairn. When building the second cairn (10 nautical miles), we eat 3–4 biscuits. That's our lunch. It was a little hazy this morning, but it soon blew away and became absolutely clear. We have now passed the big seracs to the E., and otherwise the terrain seems nice and easy.

Bjaaland

2 Nov. –33 5 –24 –22. Very fine weather with a cold wind from ESE. Had fine terrain today, it seemed as if we were driving into a wind, 9 to 10 m/sec. for am now really frozen. Now building a cairn every 5 m. Passed high ice peaks to the east. 81°23'.

Scott

Nov. 2 Thursday. Hut Point. The march teaches a good deal as to the paces of the ponies. It reminded me of a regatta or a somewhat disorganised fleet with ships of very unequal speed. The plan of further advance has now been evolved. We shall start in three parties-the very slow ponies, the medium paced, and the fliers. Snatcher starting last will probably overtake the leading unit. All this requires a good deal of arranging. We have decided to begin night marching, and shall get away after supper, I hope. The weather is hourly improving, but at this season that does not count for much. At present our ponies are very comfortably stabled. Michael, Chinaman and James Pigg are actually in the hut. Chinaman kept us alive last night by stamping on the floor. Meares and Demetri are here with the dog team, and Ponting with a great photographic outfit. I fear he won't get much chance to get results.

FRIDAY, NOVEMBER 3RD, 1911

Amundsen

Friday 3 November

Stiff breeze with thick drift. The going has been extraordinarily heavy, and the dogs have struggled hard to move the sledges forward. Well now we have a gale from the south (force 6) and we have −15°. What on earth does this mean? We are having a splendid time in the tent. The tent is even and flat as a pancake. I started wearing snow goggles at 80°. The others have not yet started.

Bjaaland

3 Nov. 81°45' −18.5 − 10. Clear weather with snowdrift from south for a long time and much loose snow and dogs struggling.

Scott

Nov. 3rd Friday. Camp 1. A keen wind with some drift at Hut Point, but we sailed away in detachments. Atkinson's party, Jehu, Chinaman and Jimmy Pigg led off at eight. Just before ten Wilson, Cherry-Garrard and I left. Our ponies marched steadily and well together over the sea ice. The wind dropped a good deal, but the temperature with it, so that the little remaining was very cutting. We found Atkinson at Safety Camp. He had lunched and was just ready to march out again; he reports Chinaman and Jehu tired. Ponting arrived soon after we had camped with Demetri and a small dog team. The cinematograph was up in time to catch the flying rearguard which came along in fine form, Snatcher leading and being stopped every now and again − a wonderful little beast. Christopher had given the usual trouble when harnessed, but was evidently subdued by the Barrier Surface. However, it was not thought advisable to halt him, and so the party fled through in the wake of the advance guard.

After lunch we packed up and marched on steadily as before. I don't like these midnight lunches, but for man the march that follows is pleasant when, as to-day, the wind falls and the sun steadily increases its heat. The two parties in front of us camped 5 miles beyond Safety Camp, and we reached their camp some half or three-quarters of an hour later. All the ponies are tethered in good order, but most of them are tired − Chinaman and Jehu very tired. Nearly all are inclined to be off feed, but this is very temporary, I think. We have built walls, but there is no wind and the sun gets warmer every minute.

Mirage. Very marked waving effect to east. Small objects greatly exaggerated and showing as dark vertical lines.

1 p.m. Feeding time. Woke the party, and Oates served out the rations – all ponies feeding well. It is a sweltering day, the air breathless, the glare intense – one loses sight of the fact that the temperature is low (+22°) – one's mind seeks comparison in hot sunlit streets and schorching [sic] pavements, yet six hours ago my thumb was frostbitten. All the inconveniences of frozen footwear and damp clothes and sleeping-bags have vanished entirely. A petrol tin is near the camp and a note stating that the motor passed at 9 p.m. 28th, going strong – they have 4 to 5 days' lead and should surely keep it.

'Bones has eaten Christopher's goggles.' This announcement by Crean, meaning that Bones had demolished the protecting fringe on Christopher's bridle. These fringes promise very well – Christopher without his is blinking in the hot sun.

SATURDAY, NOVEMBER 4TH, 1911

Amundsen

Saturday 4 November
The S'ly wind eased during the night. Towards morning, it backed N'ly and the weather closed in. Driven in a 'pea souper' all day. Brilliant going, could not be better. Great change from one day to the other. Yesterday the skiing was sticky as fish glue. We halted after having done 16 nautical miles. In so doing, we have covered the distance to 82°. We saw no sign of the depot, but that is only to be expected, since the weather absolutely thick, with no visibility.

Bjaaland

4 Nov. –24 –21 Wind from the East. Thick misty weather, but the going was brilliant, and I have ski-jored all day. Distance 16 m. Couldn't find any depot or flags because we couldn't see far. Our course was ENE by ½ N for 9.5 m and ENE by ½ m for 6.5 m. Flat, flat.

Scott

Nov. 4th Sat. Camp 2. Led march – started in what I think will now become the settled order. Atkinson went at 8, ours at 10, Bowers, Oates and Co. at 11.15. Just after starting picked up cheerful note – and saw cheerful notices saying all well with motors, both going excellently. Day wrote 'Hope to meet in 80° 30' (Lat.).' Poor chap, within 2 miles he must have had to sing a different tale. It appears they had a bad ground on the morning of the 29th. I suppose the surface was bad and everything seemed to be going wrong. They 'dumped' a good deal of petrol and lubricant. Worse was to follow. Some 4 miles out we met a tin pathetically inscribed, 'Big end Day's motor No.2 cylinder broken.' Half a mile beyond, as I expected, we found the motor, its tracking sledges and all. Notes from Evans and Day told the tale. The only spare had been used for Lashly's machine, and it would have taken a long time to strip Day's engine so that it could run on three cylinders. They had decided to abandon it and push on with the other alone. They had taken the six bags of forage and some odds and ends, besides their petrol and lubricant. So the dream of great help from the machines is at an end! The track of the remaining motor goes steadily forward, but now, of course, I shall expect to see it every hour of the march.

The ponies did pretty well – a cruel soft surface most of the time, but light loads, of course. Jehu is better than I expected to find him, Chinaman not so well. They are bad crocks both of them.

It was pretty cold during the night, −7° when we camped, with a crisp breeze blowing. The ponies don't like it, but now, as I write, the sun is shining through a white haze, the wind has dropped, and the picketing line is comfortable for the poor beasts.

This, 1 p.m., is the feeding hour-the animals are not yet on feed, but they are coming on.

The wind vane left here in the spring shows a predominance of wind from the S.W quarter. Maximum scratching, about S.W. by W.

SUNDAY, NOVEMBER 5TH, 1911

Amundsen

Sunday 5 November

At 4 a.m. the sun came out for a moment and we were not slow in getting out of our sleeping bags. There the depot loomed up about 2 nautical miles ESE. The small flags were just as they had been left, standing out beautifully against

*Figure 11   Amundsen at a depot on the way to the South Pole, probably on the Ross Ice Shelf.
A snapshot by Bjaaland.*

— Author's collection

the white background. This is a victory for us. We have shown that it is possible to put out depots on these endless expanses and mark them so that with careful navigation we can find them again. We took the depot's bearings and went back to bed again. After breakfast we packed up and set off. The weather had then closed in again, but we had our bearing and after 2½ nautical miles' march we stood by our southernmost depot. Everything was in perfect order. The surrounding snowdrift was ca. 1½ ft. high. The flag had broken off, but that was due to a weak bamboo pole. We have spent the day getting the sledges in the same state as they were on leaving Framheim – in other words full to the brim. We are now fully fitted out for 100 days and everything – both men animals and equipment is in the finest condition. The doggies are now in a far better state than when we started off. All the sore feet have healed, and a little of the superfluous obesity has gone. W. shot Uranus. It was worth nothing, and ate an unreasonable amount. It was fat as a pig. The depot here was exactly the right size. No dog pemmican was left. Only Uranus. We have just enough human pemmican to take us back to 80°. The day gradually became fine. Now this afternoon we have brilliant clear weather, almost calm, boiling sun and –10°. I am now sitting in the tent and writing and it is so warm that thoughts stray now and then to the tropics.

Bjaaland

5th. At 4 o'clock early this morning, the fog lifted, and Wisting went out and caught sight of the depot to the NE. We had arrived 1 m. to the right. On getting up at 8 o'clock, it was thick again, but we arrived after having covered 2.5 m., now it has cleared up and we take on our loads and put everything in order.

Scott

Nov. 5th. Sunday – Camp 3. 'Corner Camp.' We came over the last lap of the first journey in good order – ponies doing well in soft surface, but, of course, lightly loaded. To-night will show what we can do with the heavier weights. A very troubled note from Evans (with motor) written on morning of 2nd, saying maximum speed was about 7 miles per day. They have taken on nine bags of forage, but there are three black dots to the south which we can only imagine are the deserted motor with its loaded sledges. The men have gone on as a supporting party, as directed. It is a disappointment. I had hoped better of the machines once they got away on the Barrier Surface.

The appetites of the ponies are very fanciful. They do not like the oil cake, but for the moment seem to take to some fodder left here. However, they are off that again to-day. It is a sad pity they won't eat well now, because later on one can imagine how ravenous they will become. Chinaman and Jehu will not go far I fear .

Amundsen is congratulating himself on his success in marking the depots. His 'small flags' belonged to a transverse line of flags running 5 nautical miles on each side. The idea was to find a depot even if one was off course. It seems an obvious device on a featureless plain, but Amundsen was the first to think of it.

It is illuminating of character that having got their bearings, Amundsen and his companions finished their night's sleep before heading for the depot, instead of rushing there immediately.

This was the last depot at 82° S, put out the previous autumn. Henceforth, all was unknown.

MONDAY, NOVEMBER 6TH, 1911

Amundsen

Monday 6 November

Better weather cannot be found. Absolutely calm. Burning sunshine and lovely warmth ca. −14°. The doggies are lying stretched out and enjoying themselves. Have taken the opportunity to take all possible obs. The compass variation has increased somewhat since 81°. There it was 119° NE. Here we have 129° NE. We have checked the variation in every conceivable way, with the same result. We go further s'wards tomorrow; build snow cairns every third nautical mile, and lay a depot every degree – for the return journey. From the latest calculation, it appears that we cannot count on traction further than back to 86°. Thereafter we will have to haul ourselves. The small packing case slats with blue-black pennants which were set up here transversely remain just as high as when they were placed out. The pennants show no signs of wear and tear. This seems to suggest little snowfall and wind. The day has been spent in patching. Put a report in the cairn here. Have taken zero point observation and boiling point observation. Shot Jålå this evening. She was heavily pregnant and could not continue. She is lying on the depot.

Bjaaland

6th. −18. Wonderful weather, have spent the day drying fur clothes and organizing our equipment. I have soldered a tap on a paraffin tin, and seen to my skis. Now we will travel 20 m. a day to cover a degree in three days, and do everything to reach 86° as fast as we can because dog food is short.

Scott

Nov. 6th. Monday – Camp 4. We started in the usual order, arranging so that full loads should be carried if the black dots to the south prove to be the motor. On arrival at these we found our fears confirmed. A note from Evans stated a recurrence of the old trouble. The big end of No. 1 cylinder had cracked, the machine otherwise in good order. Evidently the engines are not fitted for working in this climate, a fact that should be certainly capable of correction. One thing is proved; the system of propulsion is altogether satisfactory. The motor party has proceeded as a manhauling party as arranged.

With their full loads the ponies did splendidly, even Jehu and Chinaman with loads over 450 lbs. stepped out well and have finished as fit as when they started. Atkinson and Wright both think that these animals are improving.

The better ponies made nothing of their loads, and my own Snippets had over 700 lbs., sledge included. Of course, the surface is greatly improved; it is that over which we came well last year. We are all much cheered by this performance. It shows a hardening up of ponies which have been well trained; even Oates is pleased!

As we came to camp a blizzard threatened, and we built snow walls. One hour after our arrival the wind was pretty strong, but there was not much snow. This state of affairs has continued, but the ponies seem very comfortable. Their new rugs cover them well and the sheltering walls are as high as the animals, so that the wind is practically unfelt behind them. The protection is a direct result of our experience of last year, and it is good to feel that we reaped some reward for that disastrous journey.

The incidence of this blizzard had certain characters worthy of note:

Before we started from Corner Camp there was a heavy collection of cloud about Cape Crozier and Mount Terror, and a black line of stratus low on the western slopes of Erebus. With us the sun was shining and it was particularly warm and pleasant. Shortly after we started mist formed about us, waxing and waning in density; a slight southerly breeze sprang up, cumulo-stratus cloud formed overhead with a rather windy appearance (radial E. and W.).

At the first halt (5 miles S.) Atkinson called my attention to a curious phenomenon. Across the face of the low sun the strata of mist could be seen rising rapidly, lines of shadow appearing to be travelling upwards against the light. Presumably this was sun-warmed air. The accumulation of this gradually overspread the sky with a layer of stratus, which, however, never seemed to be very dense; the position of the sun could always be seen. Two or three hours later the wind steadily increased in force, with the usual gusty characteristic. A noticeable fact was that the sky was clear and blue above the southern horizon, and the clouds seemed to be closing down on this from time to time. At intervals since, it has lifted, showing quite an expanse of clear sky. The general appearance is that the disturbance is created by conditions about us, and is rather spreading from north to south than coming up with the wind, and this seems rather typical. On the other hand, this is not a bad snow blizzard; although the wind holds, the land, obscured last night, is now quite clear and the Bluff has no mantle.

Before we felt any air moving, during our a.m. march and the greater part of the previous march, there was dark cloud over Ross Sea off the Barrier, which continued over the Eastern Barrier to the S.E. as a heavy stratus, with here and there an appearance of wind. At the same time; due south of us, dark lines of stratus were appearing, miraged on the horizon, and while we were camping after our a.m. march, these were obscured by banks of white fog (or drift?), and the wind increasing the whole time. My general impression was that the storm came up from the south, but swept round over the eastern part of the Barrier before it became general and included the western part where we were.

I am writing late in the day and the wind is still strong. I fear we shall not be able to go on to-night. Christopher gave great trouble again last night – the four men had great difficulty in getting him into his sledge; this is a nuisance which I fear must be endured for some time to come. The temperature, –5° is lower than I like in a blizzard. It feels chilly in the tent, but the ponies don't seem to mind the wind much.

The failure of Scott's motor sledges was a good idea incompetently applied. It was almost an allegory of the collapse of British industrial power. The research was bungled, and trials skimped. Insularity blocked foreign knowledge that at low temperatures metal becomes brittle. This was one cause of failure. Another was the use of air instead of liquid cooling. The design of the engine was poor and the workmanship, shoddy. The breaking of the big ends (the bearings of the piston rods on the crankshaft) revealed execrable metallurgy. It was in other words a botched job, hoping for the best. It needed a few years' patient research and design and extensive field trials in civilization before the machine could become dependable.

Amundsen's 'boiling point observation' referred to a system of measuring altitude. It depended on the fact that the boiling point of a liquid – water in this case – falls as atmospheric pressure drops, and hence altitude rises. At sea level, water boils at 100°C., dropping 0.1°C. for each rise in altitude of about 25 m. The instrument for making these measurements is called a hypsometer. Basically, it was simply a spirit burner, a container with a little water, and a specialized, highly sensitive thermometer to measure the temperature of the steam. No GPS then, and at the time it was the only portable way of accurately determining altitude. Like other explorers, Amundsen did have pocket aneroid barometers, and hence altimeters, but they were unreliable, needing constant calibration. By 'zero point observation' Amundsen meant that he had fixed the height above sea level of the depot at 82° S, to make it the base line for subsequent altitudes.

Scott was now 215 nautical miles behind. Amundsen could not know this, but he was pacing himself. Regular rest was vital to conserve strength, both for men and dogs – something that Scott never understood. Bjaaland was in his element. As a Nordic ski racer, in the age of sequential starting, he was used to the loneliness of racing against the clock. Anyway he knew that he was a better skier than any Englishman, so he had no concern on that score.

Being also a craftsman, it was also natural that Bjaaland should solder the tap on the paraffin tank. Amundsen knew from his own experience, and his reading of polar history, that for mysterious reasons paraffin escaped from tins, threatening disaster. The stopper was one obvious cause. Amundsen had special tanks made up, with silver soldered seams. The tanks were sealed by metal discs silver soldered to the spout. Ordinary solder, based on lead, was unreliable in deep cold. These precautions escaped Scott, although the same history and technical knowledge were at his disposal.

Amundsen worked with huge margins of safety in fuel – 500% at a conservative estimate. Water was one reason. From his life with the Eskimos, he knew that dehydration was the real enemy of a cold climate. It too could have fatal consequences. On that account, he wanted the means to melt any amount of snow so that his men could drink their fill.

The decision to travel 20 nautical miles a day instead of the usual 15 was due to recalculation which indicated a realistic possibility that this would save man-hauling on from 86° S on the way back. That was incentive enough for a bit of racing.

TUESDAY, NOVEMBER 7TH, 1911
Amundsen

Tuesday 7 November
An absolutely wonderful day. Fine weather –19°. Clear with a light airs from SSE. At the first cairn after 82° we had to shoot 'Lussi'. She had just begun to come on heat and caused such disorder in the team that I decided that despatching was the only way to deal with it. She was deposited on the top of the cairn. In the depot at 82° we now have some chocolate, six tins of biscuits, 13 kg dried milk, some pieces of seal steak, 20 l of paraffin, 10 kg of human pemmican, 2 dogs, 1 sledge and some equipment. Now the journey has begun in earnest. At 2 p.m. we passed *Discovery* exp. e'most lat. 82°17' and have stopped now at 82°22'. The Barrier generally gives the impression of being completely flat. Nonetheless there are a few small wave-like formations. The skiing has been brilliant. Partly rock hard, partly just a little soft, but always good snow. No sastrugi. We have taken ¼ hour per nautical mile today. The dogs are now properly trained and in fine condition.

Bjaaland

7 Nov. Unfortunately we had to shoot Jaala because she didn't whelp soon enough. She had three boys inside her. Weather and skiing good, started around 8 o'clock with lightning speed, but Bjørn fell under a runner of Hassel's sledge and overturned his load. The Sheep took the opportunity to serve Lussi, who in consequence got a lead bullet in the forehead and was put on the depot. Distance 20 nautical miles in 8 hours.

Scott

Nov. 7th. **Tuesday** – Camp 4. The blizzard has continued throughout last night and up to this time of writing, late in the afternoon. Starting mildly, with broken clouds, little snow, and gleams of sunshine, it grew in intensity until this forenoon, when there was heavy snowfall and the sky overspread with low nimbus cloud. In the early afternoon the snow and wind took off, and the wind is dropping now, but the sky looks very lowering and unsettled.

Last night the sky was so broken that I made certain the end of the blow had come. Towards morning the sky overhead and far to the north was quite clear. More cloud obscured the sun to the south and low heavy banks hung over Ross Island. All seemed hopeful, except that I noted with misgiving that the mantle on the Bluff was beginning to form. Two hours later the whole sky was overcast and the blizzard had fully developed.

This Tuesday evening it remains overcast, but one cannot see that the clouds are travelling fast. The Bluff mantle is a wide low bank of stratus not particularly windy in appearance; the wind is falling, but the sky still looks lowering to the south and there is a general appearance of unrest. The temperature has been −10° all day.

The ponies, which had been so comparatively comfortable in the earlier stages, were hit as usual when the snow began to fall.

We have done everything possible to shelter and protect them, but there seems no way of keeping them comfortable when the snow is thick and driving fast. We men are snug and comfortable enough, but it is very evil to lie here and know that the weather is steadily sapping the strength of the beasts on which so much depends. It requires much philosophy to be cheerful on such occasions.

In the midst of the drift this forenoon the dog party came up and camped about a quarter of a mile to leeward. Meares has played too much for safety in catching us so soon, but it is satisfactory to find the dogs will pull the loads and can be driven to face such a wind as we have had. It shows that they ought to be able to help us a good deal. The tents and sledges are badly drifted up, and the drifts behind the pony walls have been dug out several times. I shall be glad indeed to be on the march again, and oh! for a little sun. The ponies are all quite warm when covered by their rugs. Some of the fine drift snow finds its way under the rugs, and especially under the broad belly straps; this melts and makes the coat wet if allowed to remain. It is not easy to understand at first why the blizzard should have such a withering effect on the poor beasts. I think it is mainly due to the exceeding fineness of the snow particles, which, like finely divided powder, penetrate the hair of the coat and lodge in the inner warmths. Here it melts, and as water carries off the animal heat. Also, no doubt, it harasses the animals by the bombardment of the fine flying particles on tender places such as nostrils, eyes, and to lesser extent ears. In this way it continually bothers them, preventing rest. Of all things the most important for horses is that conditions should be placid whilst they stand tethered.

By an eerie coincidence, Scott was recording one of his violent mood changes to depression, as Amundsen passed his Furthest South record. That dated from 29 December 1902. It is also strange that Scott is still showing mistrust of dogs, while Bjaaland records the Norwegian dog teams cheerfully doing a third of a degree of latitude in eight hours. Both Amundsen and Bjaaland had their own priorities in what they wrote down. This day, the essentials were that the skiing was good, and they were enjoying it.

Amundsen was now 235 nautical miles ahead of Scott.

WEDNESDAY, NOVEMBER 8TH, 1911
Amundsen

Wednesday 8 November
Same wonderful weather, terrain and skiing. We are running like greyhounds over the endless flat snow plain, only broken now and then by a long, gentle wave formation running E-W. We have built snow cairns every third nautical mile the whole way. Each cairn consists of 60 blocks. All told we will build 200 such cairns. They are more than a man's height and with a fairly broad front. At each whole degree we place a depot for the return journey, and with these intermediary cairns we are safe. In this way we can drive homewards with almost empty sledges. We can see almost no effect on the dogs after the day's run. Today we also covered a nautical mile in 15 minutes – '"The girl" is shielded ashore, let her come on board' etc. Our last lady ended her life yesterday evening because of frivolity. She had also came on heat. All in all we now have 44 dogs. 'Else' was deposited at 82°20' S.Lat.

Bjaaland

8th. 82°40' –23 –15.1. Crystal clear with southerly wind. Today the terrain has been wave formed, East to West for 15 m. smooth as a ballroom floor, had the impression that it ran upwards. Elisa, belonging to Hassel, lost her life yesterday evening for immmoral behaviour. Constantly building cairns as marks. Were those ice peaks or clouds we saw ahead to the right?

Scott

Nov. 8th Wednesday. Camp 5. Wind with overcast threatening sky continued to a late hour last night. The question of starting was open for a long time, and many were unfavourable. I decided we must go, and soon after midnight the advance guard got away. To my surprise, when the rugs were stripped from the 'crocks', they appeared quite fresh and fit. Both Jehu and Chinaman had a skittish little run. When their heads were loose Chinaman indulged in a playful buck. All three started with their loads at a brisk pace. It was a great relief to find that they had not suffered at all from the blizzard.

They went out 6 geographical miles, and our section going at a good round pace found them encamped as usual. After they had gone, we waited for the rear-guard to come up and joined with them. For the next 5 miles the bunch of seven kept together in fine style, and with wind dropping, sun gaining in power, and ponies going well, the march was a real pleasure. One gained confidence every moment in the animals; they brought along their heavy loads without a hint of tiredness. All take the patches of soft snow with an easy stride, not bothering themselves at all. The majority halt now and again to get a mouthful of snow, but little Christopher goes through with a non-stop run. He gives as much trouble as ever at the start, showing all sorts of ingenious tricks to escape his harness. Yesterday when brought to his knees and held, he lay down, but this served no end, for before he jumped to his feet and dashed off the traces had been fixed and he was in for the thirteen miles of steady work. Oates holds like grim death to his bridle until the first freshness is worn off, and this is no little time, for even after 10 miles he seized a slight opportunity to kick up. Some four miles from this camp Evans loosed Snatcher's bridle momentarily. The little beast was off at a canter at once and on slippery snow; it was all Evans could do to hold to the bridle. As it was he dashed across the line, somewhat to its danger.

Six-hundred yards from this camp there was a bale of forage. Bowers stopped and loaded it on his sledge, bringing his weights to nearly 800 lbs. His pony Victor stepped out again as though nothing had been added. Such incidents are very inspiriting of course, the surface is very good; the animals rarely sink to the fetlock joint, and for a good part of the time are borne up on hard snow patches without sinking at all. In passing I mention that there are practically no places where ponies sink to their hocks as described by Shackleton. – *I imagine he confused hock & fetlock or wilfully exaggerrated.* On the only occasion last year when our ponies sank to their hocks in one soft patch, they were unable to get their loads on at all. The feathering of the fetlock joint is borne up on the snow crust and its upward bend is indicative of the depth of the hole made by the hoof; one sees that an extra inch makes a tremendous difference.

We are picking up last year's cairns with great ease, and all show up very distinctly. This is extremely satisfactory for the homeward march. What with pony walls, camp sites and cairns, our track should be easily followed the whole way. Everyone is as fit as can be. It was wonderfully warm as we camped this morning at 11 o'clock; the wind has dropped completely and the sun shines gloriously. Men and ponies revel in such weather. One devoutly hopes for a good spell of it as we recede from the windy northern region. The dogs came up soon after we had camped, travelling easily.

THURSDAY, NOVEMBER 9TH, 1911

Amundsen

Thursday 9 Nov.
Same fine weather. Yesterday we saw some wisps of cloud in the SW quarter, but thought little of it. This morning however, they persisted in the same place, and upon closer examination with the telescope we could clearly make out land. The bearing of the most prominent part – a dome-like peak – was ENE by ½ E (by compass). As far as we could see, the land ran from this peak – which was the N'most of the visible land – in a SE'ly direction. After having covered 20 nautical miles to the south today the bearing is exactly the same, although the mountain range seems closer and more distinct – but that might well be due to the light conditions. According to the map this must be the mountain range that Sh. saw and has surveyed, which ran SE from the Beardmore Glacier. The last of the land that we can see towards the S. we observed NE by E ½ E (by compass) (S. by W. true). Right in our course – south – we can see not a trace of land and that promises well for the climb. The skiing has been excellent but the surface considerably harder. It has assumed a gleaming, hard appearance everywhere. Quite small sastrugi. There is no doubt that it has blown persistently from the S. quarter. Probably no snowfall. It is now absolutely clear as usual with a rather

stiff breeze from the S. but t. is high −13°, and everything has the appearance of summer. The dogs have kept the same speed today as usual − 4 miles [per hour] − and do not seem to be worn out any more. We are now at 83° S.Lat. and stay put tomorrow to build a depot and rest. Took an azimuth observation this afternoon and fixed the compass error at 135° NE.

Bjaaland

9th. 83° S −18 −13. Thursday. Arrived here 3 p.m. Weather fine with southerly wind. Have now covered the degree in 3 days. It was land that we saw alright yesterday, we have closed it a lot, so that we can see it clearly, some of it far to the SW.

Scott

Nov. 9th. Thursday. Camp 6. Sticking to programme, we are going a little over the 10 miles (geo.) nightly. Atkinson started his party at 11 and went on for seven miles to escape a cold little night breeze, which quickly dropped. He was some time at his lunch camp, so that starting to join the rearguard we came in together the last 2 miles. The experience showed that the slow advance guard ponies are forced out of their pace by joining with the others, whilst the fast rearguard is reduced in speed. Obviously it is not an advantage to be together, yet all the ponies are doing well. An amusing incident happened when Wright left his pony to examine his sledgemeter. Chinaman evidently didn't like being left behind and set off at a canter to rejoin the main body. Wright's long legs barely carried him fast enough to stop this fatal stampede, but the ridiculous sight was due to the fact that old Jehu caught the infection and set off at a sprawling canter in Chinaman's wake. As this is the pony we thought scarcely capable of a single march at start, one is agreeably surprised to find him still displaying such commendable spirit. Christopher is troublesome as ever at the start; I fear that signs of tameness will only indicate absence of strength. The dogs followed us so easily over the 10 miles that Meares thought of going on again, but finally decided that the present easy work is best.

Things look hopeful. The weather is beautiful − temp. +12°, with a bright sun. Some stratus cloud about Discovery and over White Island. The sastrugi about here are very various in direction and the surface a good deal ploughed up, showing that the Bluff influences the wind direction even out as far as this camp. The surface is hard; I take it about as good as we shall get.

There is an annoying little southerly wind blowing now, and this serves to show the beauty of our snow walls. The ponies are standing under their lee in the bright sun as comfortable as can possibly be.

Amundsen and Bjaaland are recording their first discovery of new land. It was a continuation of what we know as the Transantarctic Mountains. The Norwegians were now 250 nautical miles in front of Scott, and travelling twice as fast, and drawing ahead at 10 nautical miles a day.

In some ways it was an illusory lead. Scott was going to cross a known mountain range along a route pioneered and mapped by Shackleton. Amundsen had hoped that the Pole lay on a continuation of the Barrier. He now knew that he would have to find a new route across unknown mountains. Theoretically, his timetable allowed him four days. From his point of view, the race now hung in the balance. All he could do was continue following a meridian of longitude for the shortest possible distance, and hope for the best. It was enough to temper the joys of setting eyes on land that no one else had seen before.

FRIDAY, NOVEMBER 10TH, 1911
Amundsen

Friday 10 Nov. In port today. Had a storm from the S. during the night. It blew well. Eased towards the small hours. Got a meridian sight. We were four men – HH W. Hs. and me – and a splendid sun. The results were a little different for the two instr. The average was 83°1'S. Lat. Land was visible most of the day. It must be a very high mountain range. We are probably 100 nautical miles off shore, but on certain occasions seem able to see details of the mountain ridges. Have done my best to make a sketch of the range. A fine piece of work it is not, but when one has done what one can, one cannot do any better. Bj. has a touch of snowblindness in his left eye, but it is better this afternoon. Built our depot during the forenoon. It has a quadrilateral form with sides of 2 m, and 2 m high. Then on top a small dark blue pennant. In the pyramid there are supplies for five human beings and 12 animals for four days – 24 kg dog pemmican 6 kg human pemmican 2 kg chocolate, four bags of milk, 800 biscuits and a box of matches. W. and I made a trip this evening to the last cairn built yesterday – 2 nautical miles from here – to examine the effect of the storm on it. It was still standing, but bent right over by the wind. We shall give the cairns a new form hereafter. Three of Bj's best dogs came after us, went past and continued northwards in the track and quickly out of sight. They were Lussi's lovers. I am afraid they have taken the road back to where we shot her.

Bjaaland

10th –13 – 10. A storm blew up yesterday evening, and lasted until the morning, and dropped around 8 o'clock. Clear weather. Have put out a depot here at 83° for the return journey. Four days' ration for people and 12 dogs, which it is thought will survive the journey. Took a picture of the cairn with HH on top. During the afternoon, the Captain and Wisting went out to examine the last cairn that we built, how it looked after the storm. It had leant over a little, away from the wind. Unfortunately Karenius and the Sheep and Sv [. . .] went off and vanished into the distance towards the north, probably they wanted to look for Lussi who lay 57 m behind.

Scott

Nov. 10th. Friday – Camp 7. A very horrid march. A strong head wind during the first part – 5 miles (geo.) – then a snowstorm. Wright leading found steering so difficult after three miles (geo.)[46] that the party decided to camp. Luckily just before camping he rediscovered Evans' track (motor party) so that, given decent weather, we shall be able to follow this. The ponies did excellently as usual, but the surface is good distinctly. The wind has dropped and the weather is clearing now that we have camped. It is disappointing to miss even 1½ miles.

Christopher was started to-day by a ruse. He was harnessed behind his wall and was in the sledge before he realised. Then he tried to bolt, but Titus hung on.

Amundsen's 'meridian sight' was a time-honoured and elegant way of finding latitude. It involved taking the altitude of the sun at local noon, when it was at its zenith. The calculations were simple, involving no mental strain. This is important. The brain is the single organ taking the greatest share of the metabolism. Therefore, as Amundsen realized, at the limits of survival, the brain must be protected from overwork so as not to waste energy.

The meridian sight does not give longitude very well. At high latitudes, this matters little. At 83° S. the degree of longitude is only 7.3 nautical miles against 60 at the Equator. Before GPS and laptops, finding longitude demanded much observation of the sun, tedious arithmetic and looking up tables. Here in the Antarctic it was not worth racking your brains for a few hundred yards of meaningless accuracy. The specialized form of navigation approaching the Pole had the simpler requirements of latitude and direction. Fixing the Pole itself was going to require a complicated set of observations anyway.

The hidden irony here is that these principles were enunciated by A. R. Hinks, of the Royal Geographical Society in London. Amundsen, or rather Prestrud took note, but Scott did not. He acted as if he were on a ship at sea, at low latitudes.

By 'two instr.[ments]', Amundsen meant his sextants, which he was using for navigational observations The sextant is really a maritime instrument, because it does not need levelling – a little difficult on board ship – but works by lining up a heavenly body with the horizon through a system of mirrors. On land, this is unsatisfactory, because it is virtually impossible to reproduce the unbroken horizon of the sea. An artificial horizon is necessary. This is simply a horizontal reflecting surface at which the sextant is pointed. Amundsen had two types. One was a tray of mercury, which found its own level; the other, a top-silvered glass mirror which needed levelling. It is typical of Amundsen's thoroughness that in case of accidents he took two of the latter, besides three pocket chronometers, and a pair of sextants.

The instrument of choice on land is the theodolite, being theoretically more accurate. Amundsen had two, but both were damaged. Scott used a theodolite exclusively. Amundsen had all four navigators 'shoot the sun', both with mercury and glass artificial horizons to compensate for instrumental error. (Bjaaland could not navigate.)

SATURDAY, NOVEMBER 11TH, 1911

Amundsen

Saturday 11 Nov.

Magnificent going today over huge, smooth surface. The dogs have actually galloped. A few small sastrugi, but flat for the most part. The weather has been brilliant. Calm – partly overcast, partly clear. Around midday we saw in the telescope high, broken land to the S. It was miraged up, and probably 150 nautical miles away. A climb will apparently be unavoidable, but we will scarcely meet it before we have reached 86°. Bj.'s three doggies unfortunately did not come back. He got a dog from Hassel. Bj.'s eye is better today, but he is very careful. It is calm and mild this evening ca. –20°. All the dogs are lying on their sides and enjoying themselves.

Bjaaland

11 November Saturday 83°20'. My dogs which fled yesterday did not return today, and I received Uros from Hanssen and Ulrik from Hassel instead. The going was good and the terrain flat, foul high sastrugi. Distance 20 nautical miles. Hassel had Ulrik back.

Scott

Nov. 11ᵗʰ. Saturday – Camp 8. It cleared somewhat just before the start of our march, but the snow which had fallen in the day remained soft and flocculent on the surface. Added to this we entered on an area of soft crust between a few scattered hard sastrugi. In pits between these in places the snow lay in sandy heaps. A worse set of conditions for the ponies could scarcely be imagined. Nevertheless they came through pretty well, the strong ones excellently, but the crocks had had enough at 9½ miles. Such a surface makes one anxious in spite of the rapidity with which changes take place. I expected these marches to be a little difficult, but not near so bad as to-day. It is snowing again as we camp, with a slight north-easterly breeze. It is difficult to make out what is happening to the weather – it is all part of the general warming up, but I wish the sky would clear. In spite of the surface, the dogs ran up from the camp before last, over 20 miles, in the night. They are working splendidly so far.

SUNDAY, NOVEMBER 12ᵀᴴ, 1911

Amundsen

Sunday 12 Nov.
Fine weather. Gentle breath of air from NW. Partly clear, partly overcast. The sky's appearance changes very quickly. A few moments, and everything has altered. On several occasions, the land seemed very clear today. Now we have travelled 60 nautical miles since we first caught sight of the B range and got a bearing on the northernmost summit of ENE by ½ E. Today we found the bearing of the same mountain to be E by N – i.e. only a ½ point difference. The distance must be very great. The dogs also saw land today. They swung round and headed for it, but HH managed to get them on to the old course.[47] Terrain and going have been the same. We have raced in wild career all day. We polish off our 20 nautical miles in 5 hours. With cairn building, 6½ hours in all. The

night is thus long. It doesn't seem to strain the dogs. They are a little thinner, but in better condition than ever. All feet have healed. Here in the tent we hear some bangs in the ice this evening – the first bangs we have heard. But they are far away, probably near land. – Took a stroll outside this evening at 9.45. A wonderfully beautiful sight met the eye. The land was bathed for us in the loveliest light, standing out clear and sharp. We could then observe considerably more to the West. The most important that we observed was W by ½ N (true) or the land round Sh.'s climb. Therefore the mountain chain we have had in sight for the past few days must be completely new land.

Bjaaland

Sunday 12 83°40 –24 –19 –20.2 Sun and summer, skiing splendid. Can see that we are coming closer and closer land to the west. The Captain believes that he saw land ahead. Did he see correctly? Heard unpleasant rumbling in the ice in the distance, now and then it seemed as if it was beneath us. It began at 4 o'clock, but by 8 nothing was heard. Can it be the tide, or is it the glacier that is advancing? Proposed that we do 25 m. a day, but the answer was that we dare not, for the dogs' sake.

Figure 12 Norwegians 'shooting the sun' on the way to the Pole, October–November 1911. The figure in the centre background can be seen sighting downwards, because he is using an artificial horizon.

– National Library of Norway

Scott

Nov. 12th. Sunday – Camp 9. Our marches are uniformly horrid just at present. The surface remains wretched, not quite so heavy as yesterday, perhaps, but very near it at times. Five miles out the advance party came straight and true on our last year's Bluff depôt marked with a flagstaff. Here following I found a note from Evans, cheerful in tone, dated 7 a.m. 7th inst. He is, therefore, the best part of five days ahead of us, which is good. Atkinson camped a mile beyond this cairn and had a very gloomy account of Chinaman. Said he couldn't last more than a mile or two. The weather was horrid, overcast, gloomy, snowy. One's spirits became very low. However, the crocks set off again, the rearguard came up, passed us in camp, and then on the march about 3 miles on, so that they camped about the same time. The Soldier thinks Chinaman will last for a good many days yet, an extraordinary confession of hope for him. The rest of the animals are as well as can be expected – Jehu rather better. These weather appearances change every minute. When we camped there was a chill northerly breeze, a black sky, and light falling snow. Now the sky is clearing and the sun shining an hour later. The temperature remains about +10° in the daytime.

Amundsen had achieved his planned rhythm. Travel 6 or 7 hours, and rest the remainder of the day and night, however interminable it might seem. He thus conserved energy in men and dogs.

Both Amundsen and Bjaaland are obviously more concerned with the dogs than the men. This is quite logical. In the first place, they were all from the same culture and descent, and knew each others' minds intimately to form a homogenous party, so there was little to remark upon. In the snows, they could do without the men, but not the dogs. Also, the dogs were more entertaining – understandable, not only in Antarctica.

Bjaaland's remark about the tides was the prediscovery of a now accepted phenomenon. The Barrier being afloat, it rises and falls with the tides. At the junction with the mainland, the strains in the ice cause noise and distortion. So Bjaaland's rumble in the ice meant that Antarctic terra firma was in the offing. Which all goes to show that it is not necessary to be an accredited scientist to make acute scientific observations.

MONDAY, NOVEMBER 13TH, 1911

Amundsen

Monday 13 Nov. Same glorious weather. Faint breeze from the NNE quarter. The land appeared to us in the most glorious hues. Glittering white, shining blue, raven black lit by the sun, the land looks like a fairy tale. Pinnacle after pinnacle, peak after peak – crevassed, wild as any land on our globe, it lies, unseen and untrodden. It is a wonderful feeling to travel along it. If B range is the same that Sh. has mapped then, as far as I can make out, it lies in a more ESE'ly direction. Made a great discovery in the forenoon. The S'most and E'most point of C range, which I assumed must lie around 86°, and where our climb must take place, suddenly turned out to be the w'most cape of a huge bight running south, at least C range finishes there, and land only appears again a whole point more E'ly. We cannot see land between these two capes, and therefore I assume that we cannot come up against it before 87°. According to the new compass error we have established today, our course runs straight between the capes. We are naturally very excited.

Reached 84° today, and ought really to have a rest day tomorrow, but we have agreed to profit by the fine weather. The dogs do not give the impression of being exhausted. We put out a depot during the afternoon. It contains 24 kg dog pemmican, 6 kg human pemmican, 2 kg chocolate, four bags of dried milk, 800 biscuits, one can of paraffin (17 l.) 1 box of matches, five seal steaks, one whip, a few carabiners and some items of clothing. It is about 2 m high and marked with a big empty packing case on the top. Last night repeatedly heard bangs and the cannon roars in the ice. They came separately. Noticed today – in a short distance – some really narrow cracks – ca. 1 inch wide – in the ice. This shows that there has been great pressure just in this place – that is to say, quite locally.

Bjaaland

Monday 13 84° –19 –17. Skiing good, and weather fine. Vigtoria [sic] Land now rising lovely and proud to the west. We are running along the land which seems to run in a SE'ly direction. Distance 20.7 m.

Scott

Nov. 13th Monday. Camp 10. Another horrid march in a terrible light, surface very bad. Ponies came through all well, but they are being tried hard by the surface conditions. We followed tracks most of the way, neither party seeing the other except towards camping time. The crocks did well, all things considered; Jehu is doing extremely well for him. As we camped the sun came out and the cold chilly conditions of the march passed away, leaving everything peaceful, calm, and pleasant. We shall be in a better position to know how we stand when we get to One Ton Camp, now only 17 or 18 miles, but I am anxious about these beasts – very anxious, they are not the ponies they ought to have been, and if they pull through well, all the thanks will be due to Oates. I trust the weather and surface conditions will improve; both are rank bad at present.

3 p.m. It has been snowing consistently for some hours, adding to the soft surface accumulation inch upon inch. What can such weather mean? Arguing it out, it is clearly necessary to derive this superfluity of deposition from some outside source such as the open sea. The wind and spread of cloud from the N.E. and the exceptionally warm temperature seem to point to this. If this should come as an exception, our luck will be truly awful. The camp is very silent and cheerless, signs that things are going awry. The temperature in the middle of our tent this morning when the sun was shining on it was +50°! outside −10°.

TUESDAY, NOVEMBER 14TH, 1911

Amundsen

Tuesday 14 Nov.
Heard no noise in the ice during the night. No cracks in sight. Unfortunately the little light N'ly breeze managed to force the fog in. We have thus travelled in fog all day – our 20 nautical miles. It is sad to travel blind along unknown land – but there is nothing to be done about it. We hope that the fog will not last long. The doggies are still behaving in the same way – sprightly and satisfied. Skiing and terrain the same – excellent.

Bjaaland

14th 84°20' –22 –19.3 Oh well, today the land has vanished before our eyes, we are running in fog. It would be fun to be an artist, and paint these lovely mountains in their various smouldering colours. Sometimes they are green, now and then a little blue, then white with black stripes, fairy tale mountains in the highest degree. At 84° I left behind one pair of mittens, one pair of fur kamikks, one pair of socks. At 82° fur kammiks, two pairs, 81° Anorak trousers (fur).

Scott

Nov. 14th. Tuesday – Camp 11. The surface little improved, but a slightly better and much more cheerful march. The sun shone out midway, and although obscured for a time, it is now quite bright again. Now it is thoroughly warm, the air breathlessly still, and the ponies resting in great comfort. If the snow has finished, the surface deposit, which is three to four inches thick, ought to diminish rapidly. Yet it is painful struggling on through this snow, though the ponies carry it gallantly enough. Christopher has now been harnessed three times without difficulty. After One Ton Camp it ought to be possible to stop him for a midnight halt and so get through the easier on long marches. Nearly 12 statute miles without a stop must be a big strain on the rearguard animals. One Ton Camp is only about 7 miles farther. Meanwhile we passed two of Evans' cairns to-day and one old cairn of last year, so that we ought to have little difficulty in finding our depôt.

Although we have been passing the black land of the Bluff I have not seen a sign of this land for four days. I had not thought it possible that misty conditions could continue for so long a time in this region; always before we have seen the land repeatedly. Either the whole sky has been clear, or the overhanging cloud has lifted from time to time to show the lower rocks. Had we been dependent on land marks we should have fared ill. Evidently a good system of cairns is the best possible travelling arrangement on this great snow plain. Meares and Demetri up with the dogs as usual very soon after we camped.

This inpouring of warm moist air, which gives rise to this heavy surface deposit at this season, is certainly an interesting meteorological fact, accounting as it does for the very sudden change in Barrier conditions from spring to summer.

WEDNESDAY, NOVEMBER 15ᵀᴴ, 1911

Amundsen

Wednesday 15 Nov. The same fog persisted this morning, but luckily it retreated in the face of a light SE'ly breeze. Once more we had the most glorious view. We have achieved quite a lot the last two days. The bight that we had discovered towards the S. now showed high ground behind. Our course is now pointing exactly towards a high mountain – we call it the Beehive Mountain[48] – on account of its resemblance to a beehive. It is still so far off that one can say nothing with certainty, but the shapes seem so fine and rounded that I definitely believe that a way up is possible there. Probably we will reach it at about 86° S. lat. Today we estimated that ranges B and C were ca. 20 nautical miles away. We could see small details of the mountains with the telescope. The bay that separates ranges B and C proved to be an extremely big glacier running NE-SW. Range D runs into the E'ly range E in a NE'ly direction. The land mass that we can see in further in small sections, continue in a NE'ly direction. Ranges C, D & E are thus, without doubt the S'most mountains in the world. They are fantastically

Figure 13 Amundsen ready for the Pole.

Author's collection

beautiful this p.m. Calm and clear, the land is bathed in the sun – wonderfully lovely. Today the terrain has been better than ever. Long stretches like a ball-room floor. Skiing brilliant. Meridian altitude gave 84°29' – navigational error 3 nautical miles too little.

Bjaaland

15 Nov. Wednesday. 84°40' –24 –22.3 Fog and mist in the morning, but around midday our Dear Victoria lifted her veil and displayed her charming contours. We are quite near land, 30–40 m., with land ahead that is rather undulating, with glaciers which spill out over the ice. Really believe that it is ancient sea ice we are now travelling on, which has grown for thousands of years and thickened until it has touched bottom in certain places. Passed the first high summit today at 84°30'. Course NE by ½ S. Took a picture of the mountain. Three pictures have now been taken on the film.

Figure 14 Captain Scott ready for the Pole. The pouch slung to his left like a holster is where he carried his diaries.

Getty Images

Scott

Nov. 15th Wednesday. Camp 12. Found our One Ton Camp without any difficulty. About 7 or 8 miles. After 5½ miles to lunch camp, Chinaman was pretty tired, but went on again in good form after the rest. All the other ponies made nothing of the march, which, however, was over a distinctly better surface. After a discussion we had decided to give the animals a day's rest here, and then to push forward at the rate of 13 geographical miles a day. Oates thinks the ponies will get through, but that they have lost condition quicker than he expected. Considering his usually pessimistic attitude this must be thought a hopeful view. Personally I am much more hopeful. I think that a good many of the beasts are actually in better form than when they started, and that there is no need to be alarmed about the remainder, always excepting the weak ones which we have always regarded with doubt. Well, we must wait and see how things go.

A note from Evans dated the 9th, stating his party has gone on to 80° 30', carrying four boxes of biscuit. He has done something over 30 miles (geo.) in 2½ days – exceedingly good going. I only hope he has built lots of good cairns.

It was a very beautiful day yesterday, bright sun, but as we marched, towards midnight, the sky gradually became overcast; very beautiful *halo rings* formed around the sun. Four separate rings were very distinct. Wilson descried a fifth – the orange colour with blue interspace formed very fine contrasts. We now clearly see the corona ring on the snow surface. The spread of stratus cloud overhead was very remarkable. The sky was blue all around the horizon, but overhead a cumulo-stratus grew early; it seemed to be drifting to the south and later to the east. The broken cumulus slowly changed to a uniform stratus, which seems to be thinning as the sun gains power. There is a very thin, light fall of snow crystals, but the surface deposit seems to be abating the evaporation for the moment, outpacing the light snowfall. The crystals barely exist a moment when they light on our equipment, so that everything on and about the sledges is drying rapidly. When the sky was clear above the horizon we got a good view of the distant land all around to the west; white patches of mountains to the W. S. W. must be 120 miles distant. During the night we saw Discovery and the Royal Society Range, the first view for many days, but we have not seen Erebus for a week, and in that direction the clouds seem ever to concentrate. It is very interesting to watch the weather phenomena of the Barrier, but one prefers the sunshine to days such as this, when everything is blankly white and a sense of oppression is inevitable.

The temperature fell to −15° last night, with a clear sky; it rose to 0° directly the sky covered and is now just +16° to +20°. Most of us are using goggles with glass of light green tint. We find this colour very grateful to the eyes, and as a rule it is possible to see everything through them even more clearly than with naked vision.

The hard sastrugi are now all from the W.S.W. and our cairns are drifted up by winds from that direction; mostly, though, there has evidently been a range of snow-bearing winds round to south. This observation holds from Corner Camp to this camp, showing that apparently all along the coast the wind comes from the land. The minimum thermometer left here shows −73°, rather less than expected; it has been excellently exposed and evidently not at all drifted up with snow at any time. I cannot find the oats I scattered here − rather fear the drift has covered them, but other evidences show that the snow deposit has been very small.

THURSDAY, NOVEMBER 16TH, 1911

Amundsen

Thursday 16 Nov. Fine weather all day. Light SE'ly breeze −24° and absolutely clear. It nonetheless feels quite sharp in our faces, and we cannot avoid little spots of frostbite here and there. The terrain has been rather undulating. Huge wave formations. In the trough of one of these we found a maze of huge crevasses and holes, but as these are so firmly drifted over there was no danger. A particularly high ridge in the barrier runs along the land, and it is so high, that from where we are now we can't see much more than steep land and heights. We are now lying on the edge of a very deep depression, which we must cross early tomorrow to surmount a very high ridge. The bight to the S. gives the impression more and more of offering a good climb. We have now built our depot, similarly to the others, and taken the necessary bearings. The depot is marked by a large piece of garbardine towards the S. The dogs have become fairly ravenous now. Thus they ruthlessly attack all lashings and rope ends, so we shovel snow round the sledges. The skiing has been fine, as usual. Quite flat with a few sastrugi.

Bjaaland

16 Nov. 85° −24.6 −22 −19. Arrived at 85° at 2.30 on Thursday. Have had slightly undulating terrain today. About 84°54' crossed a hollow full of vile crevasses and holes, but got through safe and sound. Built a depot cairn and go on further tomorrow. Now we are doing a degree without rest, but still the dogs are lively.

Scott

Nov. 16th. Thursday – Camp 12. Resting. A stiff little southerly breeze all day, dropping towards evening. The temperature –15°. Ponies pretty comfortable in rugs and behind good walls. We have reorganised the loads, taking on about 580 lbs. with the stronger ponies, 400 odd with the others.

Amundsen was now 300 nautical miles ahead. In other words, he had gained 100 miles in just over a fortnight, keeping men and dogs well within their powers. Bjaaland at least was just idling along. It was hardly the 50 km event at Holmenkollen.

FRIDAY, NOVEMBER 17TH, 1911

Amundsen

Friday 17 Nov. An eventful day. We soon reached the wave mentioned yesterday. It was very high – 300 ft. according to the barometer. We had the finest view of land. A four point bearing showed it to be ca. 6 nautical miles distant. After reaching the height of this valley, we drove a bit on the plain. The terrain was completely flat and even, like the finest floor. We found an old crevasse, 3 m broad, but almost completely filled with snow. We avoided it easily and quickly. We crossed yet another wave, and landed on the flat at the foot of C range, 3 nautical miles from the closest visible land. Here for the first time we had a real opportunity of seeing into the bight towards which we have been steering for so long – between C and D ranges. It turned out to be filled with low mountains and steep rock walls. By contrast, the Beehive Mountain promised a good climb. I immediately decided on the latter. As a result we immediately – 11 a.m. – made camp, took a meridian observation – 85°5' and set about preparing our main depot. It consists of full provisions for five men for 30 days, a can of paraffin (17 l) 20 boxes of matches some items of clothing and equipment. We take south with us food for 5 men for 60 days

We have 438 kg of dog pemmican left. That allows us to use all our dogs for another eight days – for the whole climb, one hopes. Thereafter we take 16 dogs to the Pole. From the Pole 12 dogs. Got our longitude during the afternoon, so the position is fixed. When everything was in order, ca. 5 p.m., four of us went in towards land to investigate the climb. We must definitely have been very lucky indeed. All formations are old here and completely filled. The going in the heights was splendid. Just enough loose snow for the dogs' paws, and a gradient

not steeper than they can manage – the first day, at any rate. We were ca. 8 nautical miles inland and ca. 2,000 ft. up. From there had the pleasure of being able
to establish with certainty that the mountain range – beginning with range D
and as far as the eye could see – ran in a NE'ly (true) direction – probably the
same as indicated by Sh. to the SE.

On the way back, Bj. and I climbed the first bare rock. There was no difficulty
whatsoever in reaching it. No trouble on the slope. The hill consisted of loose
scree. We took some samples. This summit does not lie much above the surface of
the snow, but nonetheless towers 1,000 ft. above sea level. I have named it 'Mount
Betty'. I have called the mountain range running SE, King Håkon's mountains.
That running NE – Queen Maud's. The bight that these two form – Crown
Prince Olav's bight. Presumably these mountains are the S'most mountains in
the world. The land gives the impression of being covered for the most part by a
mighty layer of snow. There are no active glaciers. All unevenness has long since
been drifted over. All disturbance completely stopped. Round 'Mount Betty'
there was a little flow of blue ice only a few feet. Presumably caused by melt
water. Have taken a complete fix and some photographs from our camp. The
weather is fine this evening – 11 o'clock the same fine clear, light S'ly breeze, –
12°. Pure summer. We are all equipped with fine reindeer fur clothing for the
plateau. According to a boiling point observation. we are 900 ft. asl.

Bjaaland

Friday 17 Nov. 85°5' –11 deg. –12.5. Did 9 nautical miles today. First met some
long waves, which, opposite a huge glacier, were horribly broken by crevasses
20–30 ft. wide, then had a real tobogganing slope, and then waves again. After
having driven 9 m. the Captain decided to start the climb in a SW'ly direction,
which seems particularly good. We put out a depot for 30 days and lightened
our clothing bags as much as we could. Afterwards we went out 5–6 nautical
miles towards the mountains and surveyed the crossing – 3 nautical miles of
steep slopes but smooth and fine so that perhaps the dogs will manage the loads.
Wisting stumbled and fell, and on the return had cramp in his leg and had to
rest a little. The Captain and I went over to a rocky knoll and set foot on solid
earth after 14 months dodging about on sea and ice. I took a few stones for fun.
The mountain is full of loose stones, it is really made up of them.

Scott

Nov. 17th Friday. Camp 13. Atkinson started about 8.30. We came on about 11, the whole of the remainder. The lunch camp was 7½ miles. Atkinson left as we came in. He was an hour before us at the final camp, 13½ (geo.) miles. On the whole, and considering the weights, the ponies did very well, but the surface was comparatively good. Christopher showed signs of trouble at start, but was coaxed into position for the traces to be hooked. There was some ice on his runner and he had a very heavy drag, therefore a good deal done on arrival; also his load seems heavier and deader than the others. It is early days to wonder whether the little beasts will last; one can only hope they will, but the weakness of breeding and age is showing itself already.

The crocks have done wonderfully, so there is really no saying how long or well the fitter animals may go. We had a horribly cold wind on the march. Temp. –18°, force 3. The sun was shining but seemed to make little difference. It is still shining brightly, temp. 11°. Behind the pony walls it is wonderfully warm and the animals look as snug as possible.

A red letter day for Amundsen – with reservations. On the one hand, this was the end of the Barrier, and the arrival at Antarctic continental land; on the other, it was the end of halcyon days for the men. They had come 400 nautical miles since leaving Framheim, but ski-jored much of the way. Now they would have to exert themselves and climb.

Amundsen named Mount Betty after his much-loved old nursemaid. The name is still on the map. It is one of Amundsen's discoveries which have kept their original names.

Håkon VII was the first King of an independent Norway since the Middle Ages. Maud, his consort, was an English Princess, daughter of Edward VII. Crown Prince Olav was the future King Olav, a respectable ski jumper who ran at Holmenkollen.

SATURDAY, NOVEMBER 18TH, 1911

Amundsen

Saturday 18 Nov.
Started our climb this morning. It began ESE ¼E. The dogs have done work today that has surpassed my greatest expectations. We have covered a distance of 10 nautical miles and climbed ca. 2,000ft. in altitude. We are now lying between

mountain summits and old dead glaciers in the loveliest camp site in the world. We have passed several huge crevasses but all full of old snow. So as not to run into these on the return journey, we have today built eight high, wide snow cairns, two by two on each side of our track, so that we cannot make a mistake. Took six photographs of the mountains at the foot of the climb. They are from No.1 to No.6 on film No.3. All visible mountains seem to be loose scree. On the snow round each summit we can see a strong reddish-yellow colour. Presumably some gravel containing iron that has been drifted over. The weather has been wonderful – pure summer. We are lightly clad and are enjoying the summer warmth. On all dark objects the snow is very hard. Clear and absolutely calm. On the steepest pitches, we had to relay the sledges two by two, with 16 dogs in front of each. It went like a dream. HH & W. have gone out to look at the terrain ahead. Also Bj.

Bjaaland

18. –14. The terrible climb has begun at last. Now I am here 10 m up on the glacier between sheer mountains and old worn out glaciers. The snowfield where we went was fine and smooth, but the climb was so steep that we had to have 16–17 dogs for the load. The crossing promises well on condition that behind these mountains there is no awkward obstacle of parallel mountains! Took two pictures of the caravan with mountains and glacier in the background together with the pass.

Covered 10 m. today, are now on a plain 2,400 ft. asl. Was up by the side of the Beehive summit, and saw the plateau which we will cross to the Pole. Hanssen says he thinks we can reach the plateau in 2 days. If we do so, well . . .

Scott

Nov. 18th Saturday. Camp 14. The ponies are not pulling well. The surface is, if anything, a little worse than yesterday, but I should think about the sort of thing we shall have to expect henceforward. I had a panic that we were carrying too much food and this morning we have discussed the matter and decided we can leave a sack. We have done the usual 13 miles (geo.) with a few hundred yards to make the 15 statute. The temperature was –21° when we camped last night, now it is –3°. The crocks are going on very wonderfully. Oates gives Chinaman at least three days, and Wright says he may go for a week. This is slightly inspiriting, but how much better would it have been to have had ten really reliable beasts! It's touch and go whether we scrape up to the Glacier; meanwhile we get along somehow. At any rate the bright sunshine makes everything *look* more hopeful.

Amundsen was now going to attempt something quite extraordinary. Before him lay an unknown mountain range, untrodden by any human being. It was truly virgin land. He had to find a crossing, which was difficult enough. He had to do so quickly. He was faced by summits at least as high as the Alps, and probably more tangled by unplumbed ice streams of unimagined menace. He was haunted by the phantom of Scott, with his route surveyed to the heights. For all Amundsen knew, Scott might already be half-way up.

Amundsen had to do in days what normally could have taken weeks. It was a challenge at which a lesser man might have balked. Amundsen decided simply to drive straight ahead, keeping as close to due south as he could. The diaries, with their peculiar brand of understatement, veil his courage. The only comparable act was Shackleton's bravery in striking up the then-unknown Beardmore Glacier almost exactly three years before. Unlike Amundsen, however, Shackleton had not been confronted with a race. Amundsen could only stare at the ice-bound peaks looming up ahead, and trust to his skis, his men, his dogs, and his lucky star.

SUNDAY, NOVEMBER 19ᵀᴴ, 1911

Amundsen

Sunday 19 Nov.

Continued the climb. The first short sharp slopes led us to the uppermost pass between the closest coastal mountains. They are about 4,000 ft. high. We built – a little on the other side of the pass – a cairn for the return journey. From there I took bearings on all the surrounding mountain summits. I estimated the three highest peaks to be ca. 15,000 ft., the highest of the coastal mountains to be 7,000 ft. (little beehive). After having passed the first pass, we had a long descent – ca. 800 ft. Thereafter up again over a crevassed glacier with many huge chasms – but almost completely drifted over. Here we had an extraordinarily steep climb – had to hitch all the dogs to two sledges at a time – and still they found it hard. At the top of this glacier we arrived at an altitude – according to the aneroid – of 4,400 feet. Then again a harsh descent. These downhill runs are dangerous. If one does not take proper care to brake, the dogs quickly take command, and charge off, threatening anyone who strays into the vicinity. Finally we came down via an old drifted up glacier. There were many huge and treacherous holes in it, but we happily avoided them. Our course continued towards Håkonshallen, which we thought was the only one we saw during the climb. On coming down to the above-mentioned glacier, a huge mighty glacier appeared – absolutely fjord like – running W-E (true) from Håkonshallen out into Olavs Bight. So if we had continued in to Olavs Bight, towards which we originally had steered, we could have followed this glacier directly up to the camp we have this evening. Ah well, we couldn't have done it that way under two days either. This is the glacier that will be our way back when we come down from the plateau. We are now lying on a little glacier between Håkonshallen and the N. summit, and I hope that we can find a good way up here. We are now lying under the sky-high Håkonshallen, a magnificent sight. A large part of the summit is snow-free, while the flanks are clad in a chaos of huge ice blocks. The N. summit makes a gentler impression. Here, by contrast with Håkonshallen, the entire long flat top is encased in a smooth, solid layer of ice, while the sides gleam in blue-black. Of the lower peaks – 5–7000 ft. – all flanks facing south are bare, while those towards the N. are covered in ice. That shows that the prevailing wind is from the S. Among these high mountains, oddly enough, we have found much loose and deep snow. On that account, our dogs have had an extremely strenuous day. As usual, the weather has been clear, calm and boiling hot – HH & Bj. are out on reconnaissance this evening.

Figure 15 Amundsen and companions at the foot of the Transantarctic Mountains, 19 November 1911. The peak in the centre is probably Mount Pedro Christophersen.

– Author's collection

Bjaaland

19th **Sunday.** After a stiff march upwards, which we managed nonetheless with single dog teams, we ran down nearly to the bottom of the valley, with lightning speed so that we had to put brakes on the sledges. We went up yet another glacier, so steep that we had to have 20 doggies on each sledge. Then again a descent. More violent than the first, so dogs and sledges ran into each other. Broke the bow of my sledge, and the stern of Hassel's. Did 9 miles and now find ourselves down on the bay again after 2 days' climbing over ridges 4,000 ft. high. Camped at the foot of Haakonshallen. On one side, Olavs Høy on the other mighty ridges that stretched their 15,000 f. up to God. I took two pictures of it.

Scott

Sunday Nov. 19th. Camp 15. We have struck a real bad surface, sledges pulling well over it, but ponies sinking very deep. The result is to about finish Jehu. He was terribly done on getting in to-night. He may go another march, but not more, I think. Considering the surface the other ponies did well.

The ponies occasionally sink halfway to the hock, little Michael once or twice almost to the hock itself. Luckily the weather now is glorious for resting the animals, which are very placid and quiet in the brilliant sun.

The Sastrugi are confused, the underlying hard patches appear as before to have been formed by a W.S.W. wind, but there are some surface waves pointing to a recent SE^ly wind. Have been taking some photographs, Bowers also.

As usual, Bjaaland was right, and they had fallen victim to the tricks of mountain perspective. Amundsen had really gone astray. He had crossed a spur of Olavshøi (now Mount Fridtjof Nansen, see map p. xiii), and now had to run down again to the unexpected glacier for the road to the heights. He would have to pay for disobeying the dogs. He could have saved all the trouble if only Helmer Hanssen had listened to his team, and not pulled them away from their chosen course. They wanted to make a beeline for the glacier where it debouched on to the Barrier, and the real start of the climb. They had known the way all along, as dogs do.

Luckily for Amundsen he had struck the Transantarctic Mountains at one of their narrowest points, so the crossing would be short and concentrated. Unluckily for him, it was also a notably turbulent part of the ice cap, like the headwaters of a frozen cataract where it flowed over the mountains down towards the Barrier and the sea.

With a little more time to spare, he could have reconnoitred and found an easier climb nearby, up the Liv Glacier, for example. Under the circumstance, he had no alternative but to hold his course, and storm the ramparts of the glacier on which he had stumbled.

Reconciling Amundsen's discoveries with modern maps has meant a piece of detective work.[49] Concentrating his all on the Pole, he took bearings, and did a few rough sketches, but had no time for a proper running survey. There are present-day equivalents of the main features that Amundsen named in haste as he travelled past. Håkonshallen is Mount Don Pedro Christophersen today. On the spur of the moment Amundsen called it Håkonshallen after a medieval castle in Bergen, whose gabled end resembled the distinctive north face of the mountain. Bjaaland writes Haakonshallen, which was an accepted older spelling. They have the same pronunciation, and mean the same thing: Håkon's Hall. Likewise other features, being named by the spoken word, were written down anyhow according to personal taste, with Bjaaland sometimes using dialect. Thus what Amundsen variously calls Olavshøi and Olavsfjell, Bjaaland writes as Olavs Høy, Olavshøyen, Olavshaug or Olavshaugen. They all mean roughly 'Mount Olav', after the then young Crown Prince of Norway, but today is Mount Fridtjof Nansen. The Great Bee Mountain, or Great Beehive are alternative forms of the Beehive, and all mean Mount Ruth Gade. At that juncture, with who knew what dangers lay ahead, orthography was hardly Amundsen's or Bjaaland's main concern. See map on p. xiii.

MONDAY, NOVEMBER 20ᵀᴴ, 1911

Amundsen

Monday 20 Nov.

HH & Bj. had found an excellent route up the glacier. There were many crevasses and chasms, but we found good bridges everywhere. The glacier – Folgefonni – was fairly steep in a number of places, and relaying with double teams had to be resorted to. We got a good photo of one of these 'claw drives'. (no. 9 Film 3). We don't hear a sound from the glacier. It is certainly quite still. On the other hand, there have been heavy stone falls from Olavshøi the whole afternoon – a veritable cannonade. We have our camp on a shattered ledge on the opposite side. We came here at 2 p.m. and halted in order to find a way out of the terribly chaotic crevasses that surround us. Enormous blocks of ice, mighty abysses and huge crevasses blocked the way everywhere. It seemed really rather difficult to find any route ahead, but after a trip of five hours, HH Bj. and myself were able to find a reasonably acceptable pass at the head of the glacier. This pass went

Figure 16 The Axel Heiberg Glacier; a fearsome, unexplored cataract of ice through which
Amundsen threaded his way up to the polar plateau. The gabled massif in the
background is Mount Don Pedro Christophersen. See the map on p. xiii.

– U.S. Navy for U.S. Geological Survey

between Olavshøi and a lesser mountain at the head. We now have our camp
site at about 6,000 ft. above sea level. The pass just discovered presumably lies at
8,000ft. Through the pass we could just about glimpse the summit of a mountain
– with the same ridge-like appearance of Håkonshallen – sticking up out of the
snow. Conditions seemed quite decent. Not a crevasse or unevenness to be seen.
Presumably it is the plateau, and we will be up there tomorrow evening. 'Fain
would I know, what I once may see over the mountains high' someone burst out
here the other day. 'Oh well', someone else answered, 'Only snow will meet the
eye.' It came out drily, and caused roars of mirth. The temperature has fallen to
−20° this evening. But so far the heat between the mountains the last few days
has been sheer discomfort. Calm, absolutely calm, crystal clear and boiling hot
all day. Our dogs are in splendid working condition but hungry as wolves. They
gnaw and chew everywhere. Olavshøi seems to be the only 8,000 ft. to consist
of granite. From 8–15,000 feet the mountains consist of horizontal strata and
seem quite crumbling. All the bare summits give the same crumbled impression.

Bjaaland

20th. Today was the first day of the climb, and we got up to 5,500. We heard the foul rumbling of avalanches of vile blocks of ice over on Olavs Høy. Afterwards Hanssen and I and the Chief went out and looked for the climb for tomorrow, and found it far to the East. We were eight miles up, and what a stiff march it was.

Scott

Nov. 20th Monday. Camp 16. The surface a little better. Sastrugi becoming more and more definite from S.E. Struck a few hard patches, which made me hopeful of much better things, but these did not last long. The crocks still go still [sic]. Jehu seems even a little better than yesterday, and will certainly go another march. Chinaman reported bad the first half march, but bucked up the second. The dogs found the surface heavy. To-morrow I propose to relieve them of a forage bag. The sky was slightly overcast during the march, with radiating cirro-stratus S.S.W. – N.N.E. Now very clear and bright again. Temp. at night –14°, now +4°. A very slight southerly breeze, from which the walls protect the animals well. I feel sure that the long day's rest in the sun is very good for all of them. Our ponies marched very steadily last night. They seem to take the soft crusts and difficult plodding surface more easily. The loss of condition is not so rapid as noticed to One Ton Camp, except perhaps in Victor, who is getting to look very gaunt. Nobby seems fitter and stronger than when he started; he alone is ready to go all his feed at any time and as much more as he can get. The rest feed fairly well, but they are getting a very big strong ration. I am beginning to feel more hopeful about them. Christopher kicked the bow of his sledge in towards the end of the march. He must have a lot left in him though.

'Folgefonni' – or 'Folgefonden' as Bjaaland writes it – is a west Norwegian glacier, and would have been a natural choice on the spur of the moment. It was eventually called the Axel Heiberg Glacier, after one of Amundsen's patrons. Amundsen had other things on his mind than the appropriate naming of his discoveries. He was making the critical ascent of the ice falls of the glacier. (See map p. xiii.) His matter-of-fact style conceals a relentless frozen cataract, more suited to a mountaineer. Nonetheless, he and Bjaaland record the consummate forcing of the ramparts by dogs and men on skis. In the end, it was not so impressive after all; this was a good season, and there

was enough snow cover to make them feel at home. They had reached the upper terrace of the glacier, and the gateway to the heights.

The quotation beginning 'Fain would I know . . .' is from a somewhat hackneyed poem known to every Norwegian schoolchild. It is by Bjørnstjerne Bjørnson, a nineteenth century Norwegian literary figure, a contemporary of Ibsen, and the national poet. The effect of these lines is a bit like 'To be or not to be . . .' in English.

TUESDAY, NOVEMBER 21ST, 1911

Amundsen

Tuesday 21 November
So we won through. We are on the polar plateau at 10,000 ft. altitude. It has been a hard day's work – for the dogs most of all. But they have also – 24 of our brave companions – had the bitter wage – death. On arrival at 8 o'clock this evening, these were shot and the entrails taken out. We will skin them tomorrow. We have 18 – the best – left. We have divided these into three teams, six in each. It was a sheer marvel of work that the dogs accomplished today. Seventeen nautical miles and 5000 ft. climb. Come and say that dogs cannot be used here. In four days we have reached the plateau from the coast – 44 nautical miles – 10,600 ft. It was a wonderful piece of work. We found a pass – the only approach to the plateau here – between A and B ranges together with Olavsfjell. It was a splendid climb. Quite a smooth snow wall, which almost without interruption ran right down and gently merged with Folgefonni. The plateau seems quite flat, but intersected with rock-hard, knife-edged sastrugi SE-NW. The mountains through which we have travelled, run as a long, ridged scar in the plateau. We are lying on a ridge in D range. This ridge has received the name of the Butcher's shop.[50] We will stay here for two days to feed up the doggies. Many of them have already tucked into the entrails of their comrades. Many of the mountains running NW have come into view up here. The Great Bee Mountain is the SE'most of the chain that we have yet seen. It is quite clear. A light, bitter breeze from SE −26.5°.

Bjaaland

21st Tuesday. −19.1 −26.3 Barom. 10,500 feet high. Hypsom. 10,600 feet. Got out of the thousands of metres deep crevasses where we had our camp. The excitement was great as we approached the side of Olavshaugen, not knowing if it was snow covered and passable, and it was a pleasant surprise, We got up

Figure 17   Amundsen watching Martin Rønne, the sailmaker, at his sewing machine on the deck of Fram *in the Tropics. The awning was for the benefit of the dogs. Amundsen pampered not only the dogs, but also his skis, because the entire expedition depended on both.*

– National Library of Norway

with single teams, it was heavy, but we managed. It was the hardest day we have had. After we had managed the hillock, we went over wave after wave with disgusting sastrugi hard as flint, around 8 o'clock we reached top of a wave behind Haakonshallen and made camp and slaughtered 23 doggies and took out the innards and then you can bet that pemmican and chocolate went down and then into the sleeping bag; heigh ho, polar life is a grind.

Scott

Nov. 21ˢᵗ Tuesday. Camp 17. Lat. 80 35. The surface decidedly better and the ponies very steady on the march. None seems overtired, and now it is impossible not to take a hopeful view of their prospect of pulling through. (Temp. –14°, night.) The only circumstance to be feared is a reversion to bad surfaces, and that ought not to happen on this course. We marched to the usual lunch camp and saw a large cairn ahead. Two miles beyond we came on the Motor Party in

Lat. 80° 32'. We learned that they had been waiting for six days. They all look very fit, but declare themselves to be very hungry. This is interesting as showing conclusively that a ration amply sufficient for the needs of men leading ponies is quite insufficient for men doing hard pulling work; it therefore fully justifies the provision which we have made for the Summit work. Even on that I have little doubt we shall soon get hungry. Day looks very thin, almost gaunt, but fit. The weather is beautiful – long may it so continue! (Temp. +6°, 11 a.m.)

It is decided to take on the Motor Party in advance for three days, then Day and Hooper return. We hope Jehu will last three days; he will then be finished in any case and fed to the dogs. It is amusing to see Meares looking eagerly for the chance of a feed for his animals; he has been expecting it daily. On the other hand, Atkinson and Oates are eager to get the poor animal beyond the point at which Shackleton killed his first beast. Reports on Chinaman are very favourable, and it really looks as though the ponies are going to do what is hoped of them.

Amundsen's praise of the dogs against unnamed sceptics is a hidden dig against Scott. It is also a matter of giving credit where credit is due. Amundsen does not elaborate on his own achievement. In four days, he has pioneered a crossing of an unknown mountain range. The 44 nautical miles of his advance in the heights through the unknown compares with 52 miles covered by Scott on the flat over mapped terrain. In this context, the fact that Amundsen's lead has slipped from 314 nautical miles to 306 seems irrelevant.

WEDNESDAY, NOVEMBER 22ND, 1911

Amundsen

Wednesday 22 Nov.
We had violent gusts of wind during the night. Quite calm until the small hours. Gale from ESE true until midday with thick drift. Just shot the sun. Latitude 85°36'S' A better result than I had expected. The climb that we have done has thus generally gone in a S'ly direction. During the a.m. we skinned 10 doggies, carved them and served them. It seemed that they tasted excellent to the survivors. We human beings did not scorn the beasts either. We have had the most delicate doggy-cutlets for dinner. I myself ate five, but then had to stop because no more remained. My companions undoubtedly found the dish appetising as well. Afterwards, we treated ourselves to an extra dish in the form of pudding made of biscuit crumbs – our favourite dish. We also had time to do some small

jobs before the gale arrived. Fourteen unskinned doggies remain here in the depot. In addition, we leave everything superfluous. We leave here with three sledges and supplies for people for 60 days. We will use 18 dogs in three teams to the Pole. From the Pole, 12 dogs in two teams. Hassel's sledge will be left here. We have all tallied our stores today and everyone knows exactly what he has on his sledge. We still have ca. 54 litres of paraffin left.

Bjaaland

22 November −26 with wind from the south-east and fog and drift. Skinned 12 doggies and carved them up and those dogs that escaped death are now eating their companions. Repaired my sledge with new bow from Hassel's sledge, which itself will be dumped. The good weather is finished. Rime frost in the tent.

Scott

Nov. 22ⁿᵈ Wednesday. Camp 18. Everything much the same. The ponies thinner but not much weaker. The crocks still going along. Jehu is now called 'The Barrier Wonder' and Chinaman 'The Thunderbolt'. Two days more and they will be well past the spot at which Shackleton killed his first animal. Nobby keeps his pre-eminence of condition and has now the heaviest load by some 50 lbs.; most of the others are under 500 lbs. load, and I hope will be eased further yet. The dogs are in good form still, and came up well with their loads this morning (night temp. −1.4°). It looks as though we ought to get through to the Glacier without great difficulty.

The weather is glorious and the ponies can make the most of their rest during the warmest hours, but they certainly lose in one way by marching at night. The surface is much easier for the sledges when the sun is warm, and for about three hours before and after midnight the friction noticeably increases. It is just a question whether this extra weight on the loads is compensated by the resting temperature. We are quite steady on the march now, and though not fast yet get through with few stops. The animals seem to be getting accustomed to the steady, heavy plod and take the deep places less fussily. There is rather an increased condition of false crust-that is, a crust which appears firm till the whole weight of the animal is put upon it, when it suddenly gives some 3 or 4 inches. This is very trying for the poor beasts. There are also more patches in which the men sink, so that walking is getting more troublesome, but, speaking broadly, the crusts are not comparatively bad and the surface is rather better than it was. If the hot sun continues this should still further improve. One cannot see any reason why the crust should change in the next 100 miles. Temp. + 2°

The land is visible along the western horizon in patches. Bowers points out a continuous dark band. Is this the dolerite sill.

THURSDAY, NOVEMBER 23RD, 1911

Amundsen

Thursday 23 Nov.
The gale has lasted all day. Luckily the bad weather chose a rest day – the gale has eased somewhat this evening, and the prospect of getting off tomorrow is good. From here we will build a cairn every other mile. At each degree we will lay a depot with human food for seven days and dog food for six days – a weight of 90 kg. This will quickly lighten the sledges of ours.

Bjaaland

23 Nov. Thursday. 85°36'. −24 −26. A blizzard blew up which lasted all night, so that we had no sleep until early morning now, around 8 o'clock, better weather. By crossing the mountains and losing 2 days, we strained the dogs badly. The Barrier bay towards which we steered has one branch in a SW'ly direction between Haakonshallen to the East and Olavshøyen to the west, and then another branch runs between H-H and the Beehive with, as I believe, a low ridge in between.

Scott

Nov. 23rd Thursday – Camp 19. Getting along. I think the ponies will get through; we are now 150 geographical miles from the Glacier. But it is still rather touch and go. If one or more ponies were to go rapidly down hill we might be in queer street. The surface is much the same I think; before lunch there seemed to be a marked improvement, and after lunch the ponies marched much better, so that one supposed a betterment of the friction. It is banking up to the south T. +9° and I'm afraid we may get a blizzard. I hope to goodness it is not going to stop one marching; forage won't allow that.

FRIDAY, NOVEMBER 24ᵀᴴ, 1911

Amundsen

Friday 24 Nov.
The gale had veered NE'ly and eased by morning. We were out and packed the sledges by 7 a.m. When we had finished with this – having loaded everything on to the three sledges, it blew, with drift, worse than ever. We had to make a virtue of a necessity and turn in again. But first we took a good load of dog meat. The fact is that we all prefer this to our favourite dish – pemmican. We always boil it, as we have nothing to fry it in. The dogs have distinctly recovered. The ravenous hunger they previously showed, has now completely disappeared. They stroll around fat, full and satisfied. We all benefit from the rest we have here – even if it is boring. We have to spend the time in our sleeping bags, and that is not pleasant in the long run. Thick drift all day with occasional glimpses of the sun. Somewhat calmer this evening. –26°

Bjaaland

Friday 24 Nov. –27 –26. It turned into a real black Friday. The wind just about eased, and we got up and packed our sledges, but before we had finished, it drifted up so that you saw only 50 m. It became a rest day which we used to cook joints of Reks [sic] in Pemm. We have now had three splendid dinners out of our good Greenland dogs, and I must say that they tasted good, a little tough perhaps, they were not boiled enough. Have enjoyed H. biscuit pudding made with dried milk. Bugger this lying still. Hope we can get off tomorrow.

Scott

Nov. 24ᵗʰ Friday. Camp 20. There was a cold wind changing from south to S.E. and overcast sky all day yesterday. A gloomy start to our march, but the cloud rapidly lifted, bands of clear sky broke through from east to west, and the remnants of cloud dissipated. Now the sun is very bright and warm. We did the usual march very easily over a fairly good surface, the ponies now quite steady and regular. Since the junction with the Motor Party the procedure has been for the man-hauling people to go forward just ahead of the crocks, the other party following 2 or 3 hours later. To-day we closed less than usual, so that the crocks must have been going very well. However, the fiat had already gone forth, and this morning after the march poor old Jehu was led back on the track and shot. After our doubts as to his reaching Hut Point, it is wonderful to think that he has actually got eight marches beyond our last year limit and could have gone more. However, towards the end he was pulling very little, and on the whole it is merciful to have ended his life. Chinaman seems to improve and will certainly last a good many days yet. The rest show no signs of flagging and are only moderately hungry. The surface is tiring for walking, as one sinks two or three inches nearly all the time. I feel we ought to get through now. Day and Hooper leave us to-night.

SATURDAY, NOVEMBER 25TH, 1911

Amundsen

Saturday 25 Nov.
Had to stay put today as well. Same gale from NE with heavy, thick drift. It has eased a little this evening and also backed ENE'ly. Drift nearly stopped. Prospects good for tomorrow. As usual, we have enjoyed the dog meat together with the dogs. We are all keen on it.

Bjaaland

Saturday 25 Nov. −24 −22. Wind eased, signs of good weather tomorrow. Stratus 10 Bloody horrible lying still, you can hardly breathe at this altitude.

Scott

Nov. 25th Sat'y. Camp 21. The surface during the first march was very heavy owing to a liberal coating of ice crystals; it improved during the second march, becoming quite good towards the end T. −2°. Now that it is pretty warm at night it is obviously desirable to work towards day marching. We shall start two hours later to-night and again to-morrow night.

Last night we bade farewell to Day and Hooper and set out with the new organisation T. −8°. All started together, the man-haulers, Evans, Lashly, and Atkinson, going ahead with their gear on the 10-ft. sledge. Chinaman and James Pigg next, and the rest some 10 minutes behind. We reached the lunch camp together and started therefrom in the same order, the two crocks somewhat behind, but not more than 300 yards at the finish, so we all got into camp very satisfactorily together. The men said the first march was extremely heavy T. + 2°.

The sun has been shining all night, but towards midnight light mist clouds arose, half obscuring the leading parties. Land can be dimly discerned nearly ahead. The ponies are slowly tiring, but we lighten loads again to-morrow by making another depôt. Meares has just come up to report that Jehu made four feeds for the dogs. He cut up very well and had quite a lot of fat on him. Meares says another pony will carry him to the Glacier. This is very good hearing. The men are pulling with ski sticks and say that they are a great assistance. I think of taking them up the Glacier. Jehu has certainly come up trumps after all, and Chinaman bids fair to be even more valuable. Only a few more marches to feel safe in getting to our first goal.

SUNDAY, NOVEMBER 26TH, 1911

Amundsen

Sunday 26 Nov.

Instead of improving, the Nor'Easter assumed the force of a storm in the course of the night. It eased somewhat in the morning, but nonetheless was a heavy gale with thick drift when we turned out at 8 o'clock. Now we were all fed up with this long lie-in at home, and therefore I decided – in spite of the bad weather – to set off. To begin with, it went badly. We had to overcome huge sastrugi, and it was just about impossible to see them. Nor did the dogs have any desire to work. They had overeaten on their comrades. In the meantime the sastrugi became gradually smaller and smaller, and finally we had the finest, smoothest terrain. The going was extremely bad – sticky as glue. Difficult for the dogs. The drift was so thick – mixed with falling snow – that we could hardly see the doggies in front of the sledges. At the start they gave the impression of going on a sheer plain. Sometimes they gave the impression of going slightly downwards. Around 1 o'clock meanwhile they began to go more downhill and in the end they were hurtling wildly down a fairly steep slope. It would have been the work of a madman to continue this charge completely blind – one could have fallen down, with all that might have meant – and however unwillingly we had to stop in the middle of the slope.[51] It is there that we have now pitched our tent. It is blowing from the NE with whirling drift just as much as before. What is there at the bottom of the slope? Is it only a ridge that runs out on to the plateau, or is it a descent between the mountains. Personally I believe it is a ridge, and I believe we will soon be clear of it. But we will see. According to the aneroid we have descended 1,000 ft. today. We should now be at 9,600 ft. Oddly enough we can all notice it in our breathing. At 'the butcher's shop' we all had unpleasant hacking coughs and shortness of breath when we lay in our sleeping bags. For my part, I never noticed anything outside. These hacking coughs have completely disappeared here. Presumably we are on Håkonshallen's ridge. Definitely calmer this evening. –23.5°. By boiling we now prove to be at 10,000 ft. a.s.l. The aneroid showed the same as soon as we arrived here. The other reading of the barometer was taken some hours later. Without exception, all the dogs had much blood in their stools – after enjoying dog meat.

Bjaaland

26 Nov. Sunday. –26.7 –22.5. Started off in a real gale from NE, skiing sticky as dough. Distance 10 m., then we ran down a steep slope and had to stop because we saw nothing. I think this is the ridge which is a continuation of Haakonshallen.

Scott

Nov. 26th Sunday – Camp 22. Lunch camp. Marched here fairly easily, comparatively good surface. Started at 1 a.m. (midnight, local time). We now keep a steady pace of 2 miles an hour, very good going. The sky was slightly overcast at start and between two and three it grew very misty. Before we camped we lost sight of the men-haulers only 300 yards ahead. The sun is piercing the mist. Here in Lat. 81° 35' we are leaving our 'Middle Barrier Depôt', one week for each returning unit as at Mount Hooper.

Camp 22. Snow began falling during the second march; it is blowing from the W.S.W., force 2 to 3, with snow pattering on the tent, a kind of summery blizzard that reminds one of April showers at home. The ponies came well on the second march and we shall start 2 hours later again to-morrow, i.e. at 3 a.m. T. + 13°. From this it will be a very short step to day routine when the time comes for man-hauling. The Sastrugi seem to be gradually coming more to the south and a little more confused; now and again they are crossed with hard westerly sastrugi. The walking is tiring for the men, one's feet sinking two or three inches at each step. Chinaman and Jimmy Pigg kept up splendidly with the other ponies. It is always rather dismal work walking over the great snow plain when sky and surface merge in one pall of dead whiteness, but it is cheering to be in such good company with everything going on steadily and well. The dogs came up as we camped. Meares says the best surface he has had yet.

MONDAY, NOVEMBER 27ᵀᴴ, 1911

Amundsen

Monday 27 Nov.
There was a short clear interval in the small hours at 3 o'clock, and we went out to investigate the conditions. We were on a slope with a fairly steep gradient along our course. On the other hand, by moving to the E one had a fine, even descent. And that is what we did when we set off this morning around 8 o'clock in an E'ly gale with heavy drift so that we could not see our hands before our face. We soon got down to level ground. Without doubt the ridge on which we lay is Håkonshallen's transition to the 'Vidda'.[52] Later we crossed a rather gentle ridge – probably from the Great Beehive and since then we have not noticed anything. Smooth lies the Vidda before us – without sastrugi – flat as a living room floor. We have won a victory. Dragged ourselves through storm and drift and are lying now on the Vidda in sunshine and fine weather. We reached 86° S. Lat. and are extremely pleased with our prospects. The going in the forenoon was like sand. It was real misery to move ahead both for animals and men. It was rather better in the p.m. and it was soon helped when the sun shone a little on us. The dogs' stomachs were completely in order again today after pemmican feeding yesterday. Today I started to take over my position as 'forerunner'. It was necessary in order to make the dogs advance. This evening boiling gave 9,200 ft. In other words a descent of 800ft. today. Well now the road to the Pole is clear – may we soon be there. Have built a number of cairns along the way.

Bjaaland

27 Nov. 86° –24 –20. Blew worse than before, from the east. It went reasonably downhill with brakes under the sledge runners. Today the skiing was so bloody sticky it was like walking on sand. Here the plateau is flat and fine as a bed-sheet and luckily the weather was good, so now there is hope of good skiing. Biscuit crumb pudding here at 86° tasted good.

Scott

Monday, Nov. 27ᵗʰ. Camp 23. T. + 8, 12 p.m.; + 2, 3 a.m.; + 13, 11 a.m.; + 17, 3 p.m. Quite the most trying march we have had. The surface very poor at start. The advance party got away in front but made heavy weather of it, and we caught

them up several times. This threw the ponies out of their regular work and prolonged the march. It grew overcast again, although after a summery blizzard all
yesterday there was promise of better things. Starting at 3 a.m. we did not get
to lunch camp much before 9. The second march was even worse. The advance
party started on ski, the leading marks failed altogether, and they had the greatest
difficulty in keeping a course. At the midcairn building halt the snow suddenly
came down heavily, with a rise of temperature, and the ski became hopelessly
clogged (bad fahrer? [sic] as the Norwegians say). At this time the surface was
unspeakably heavy for pulling, but in a few minutes a south wind sprang up and
a beneficial result was immediately felt. Pulling on foot, the advance had even
greater difficulty in going straight until the last half mile, when the sky broke
slightly. We got off our march, but under the most harassing circumstances
and with the animals very tired. It is snowing hard again now, and heaven only
knows when it will stop.

If it were not for the surface and bad light, things would not be so bad. There
are few sastrugi and little deep snow. For the most part men and ponies sink
to a hard crust some 3 or 4 inches beneath the soft upper snow. Tiring for the
men, but in itself more even, and therefore less tiring for the animals. Meares just
come up and reporting very bad surface. We shall start 1 hour later to-morrow,
i.e. at 4 a.m., making 5 hours' delay on the conditions of three days ago. Our
forage supply necessitates that we should plug on the 13 (geographical) miles
daily under all conditions, so that we can only hope for better things. It is several
days since we had a glimpse of land, which makes conditions especially gloomy.
A tired animal makes a tired man, I find, and none of us are very bright now
after the day's march, though we have had ample sleep of late.

TUESDAY, NOVEMBER 28ᵀᴴ, 1911

Amundsen

Tuesday 28 Nov.
Fairly violent gusts of wind from the N. quarter during the night. As usual we
were on our way around 8 'oclock. But the weather was not of the best kind.
Fog and snow. A little sun now and then. At 86°3' S. Lat. we had – in a little
break in the fog – a glimpse of a mountain summit NW by W by compass (ESE
true). We could not see it for long – nor much of it either. But it revealed not a
little black/yellow colours. Presumably this summit is the S'most of our mountain ranges, Presumably it might be ca. 10 miles away. We passed right under a
ridge. As usual it ran S. (true). The terrain has run up and down in huge waves

as before. The going has been extremely variable. Good and utterly bad. For the most part the surface has been as smooth as a floor – except for a few quite small sastrugi. The place where we are lying this evening consists of huge, old rock-hard sastrugi, presumably formed during the winter – but filled in between by loose snow – fallen in quite calm weather and presumably quite recently. This new snow has filled in the terrain between sastrugi so that everything seems quite flat. These hard sastrugi and loose snow make travelling here heavy and sluggish – At 86°9' there was a little break in the fog and not far away – ca. 4 nautical miles – we caught sight of two long, fairly high snow-clad ridges – presumably 10,000 above sea level. We took the necessary bearings, and soon after they had disappeared. They lay to the west of us, and the range ran N-S (true). I have the impression that these snow mountains are completely independent of our other mountain ranges. We could not trace any connection, and its direction (N-S) also seems to indicate this. These mountains will be splendid landmarks for us on the return journey. We have not yet met any obstacles in our course – but who knows? We have fallen 1,000 ft. quite gently today, and are now lying at 8,200 ft asl. This is rather peculiar, I feel, but we must be prepared for one thing or another among these high mountain ranges. We have done 16 nautical miles today, and are now at 86°17' S.Lat.

Bjaaland

Tuesday 28 Nov. 86°16' –26.5 –18.5 Fine weather, not quite clear. At 86°3' we passed a big ice-covered mountain to the East, and after 9 m. we were level with a mountain or ridge 5–6 miles to the West. Today we broke the Norwegian record in polar exploration in that we reached 86°16'. Nansen reached 86°14' N.Lat. Yesterday were 9,200 f. asl., have descended a little today.

Scott

Tuesday, Nov. 28th. Camp 24. The most dismal start imaginable. Thick as a hedge, snow falling and drifting with keen southerly wind. The men pulled out at 3.15 with Chinaman and James Pigg. We followed at 4.20, just catching the party at the lunch camp at 8.30. Things got better half way; the sky showed signs of clearing and the steering improved. Now, at lunch, it is getting thick again. When will the wretched blizzard be over?

The walking is better for ponies, worse for men; there is nearly everywhere a hard crust some 3 to 6 inches down. Towards the end of the march we crossed a succession of high hard SE^{ly} Sastrugi, widely dispersed. I don't know what to make of these.

Second march almost as horrid as the first. Wind blowing strong from the south, shifting to S.E. as the snowstorms fell on us, when we could see little or nothing, and the driving snow hit us stingingly in the face. The general impression of all this dirty weather is that it spreads in from the S.E. We started at 4 a.m., and I think I shall stick to that custom for the present. These last four marches have been fought for, but completed without hitch, and, though we camped in a snowstorm, there is a more promising look in the sky, and if only for a time the wind has dropped and the sun shines brightly, dispelling some of the gloomy results of the distressing marching.

Chinaman, – The Thunderbolt! – has been shot to-night. Plucky little chap, he has stuck it out well and leaves the stage but a few days before his fellows. We have only four bags of forage (each 130 lbs.) left, but these should give seven marches with all the remaining animals, and we are less than 90 miles from the Glacier.

Bowers tells me that the barometer was phenomenally low both during this blizzard and the last.

This has certainly been the most unexpected and trying summer blizzard yet experienced in this region. I only trust it is over. There is not much to choose between the remaining ponies. Nobby and Bones are the strongest, Victor and Christopher the weakest, but all should get through. The land doesn't show up yet.

WEDNESDAY, NOVEMBER 29TH, 1911

Amundsen

Wednesday 29 Nov.
Fog, fog and fog again, and in addition fine crystals that make the going impossible. Poor beasts, they have struggled hard to get the sledges forward today – But it has been a red-letter day. It was calm this morning. The weather was mild and pleasant. The sun shone and gave warmth. But at the same time this unbearable snowfall and the impenetrable weather. Indeed, the impenetrable weather is almost the worst of all. One can pass right under the biggest mountain without seeing it. Two nautical miles from our camp a huge mountain – in a SE'ly (true) direction – suddenly appeared – ca. 5 nautical miles distant. It proved to be – as we came closer, to be a mighty mountain range running N-S (true). This range has received the name of F range. After having covered a distance of 6 nautical miles, we stopped and set to work building a depot. With land and difficulties

ahead, it was necessary to lighten the sledges. Meanwhile the fog had settled thickly over all land. We built a solid, high depot, and placed a black packing case on top. The depot contains food for 5 men for 6 days and for 18 doggies for 5 days. This lightened each load by 25 kg. When we had built the depot, the weather lifted just enough for us to have a view of land. I drew a sketch of it from the depot and took bearings. At this second lifting of the weather, we had another surprise. To the NE of F range an enormous mountain suddenly appeared – also running N-S true. Unfortunately the fog would not lift from the N'ly of this last range to come into view – G range. Huge glaciers tumbled down them and looked magnificent. Both ranges ran N-S, but NE-SW in relation to each other. Through the telescope I could indistinctly see the ranges continue towards the NE. Without doubt they are a continuation of the E range. Between both ranges there was a monstrous glacier. Towards the F range, the ice seemed more confused than anything I had yet seen. It looked as if a huge mass of enormous blocks of ice had been lifted up and dropped down. But one could definitely see that this happened many, many years ago. Snow and warmth had rounded off and filled in a great deal. The highest summit was rather peculiar. An approximately 10,000 ft. high cupola crowned with huge ice crystals – crystals of giant size. A grander and more beautiful headdress can scarcely be imagined. The biggest and most unpleasant surprise was however an enormous, mighty glacier running E-W (true) from F. range, as far as the eye could see. In other words, right in our course. We soon discovered that the best way of tackling it – by looking through the telescope – was to set our course for the glacier, despite the fog, which had once again settled over everything. A latitude that Hass. fixed at the depot was 86°21' S.Lat, about the same as dead reckoning of 86°23'. We soon arrived at the glacier in the thickest fog, and advanced as best we could. On all sides, there were masses of greater and lesser crevasses, together with enormous chasms, and we had to inch our way through, going about from the one tack to the other. Hass. and I went ahead, roped together, and the three others followed behind. It went far better than expected, despite the complete darkness which we were working in – Only with one 'narrow escape' for W., who nearly fell off a snow bridge that was in the process of collapsing. After climbing a few hundred feet, we encountered such confusion, that we were forced to stop and make camp with crevasses and chasms on all sides. While the others got everything in order, HH and I went out roped together in order try and find a way out of the mousetrap. We were lucky enough to find one. Towards E. – in towards land, the glacier is impassable. But moving a little S'ly, it becomes better. Of course there are enormous cracks and huge chasms – but they are more drifted up and not nearly so dangerous to move over. The terrain is also more even. I don't think that I am much mistaken when I believe that all these mountain ranges running NE-SW meet Sh.'s range running SE-NW at 87° S. Lat. Time will tell. Without doubt the mountain summit of which we took a bearing at 86°3' is a continuation towards the NE of F & G ranges. Deep and sticky snow all day – horrible going. It is splendid in the tent. Everything good and dry. The sun shines through, drying everything. But what good does that do? – the fog remains persistent. It is calm outside this evening, but despite the ca. –23°, outside it feels like summer, here inside the tent. We have climbed 200 ft. We are now at 8,400 ft. above sea level. What will be the next surprise?

Bjaaland

Wednesday 29 Nov. –23 –20.1 The Devil's Glacier. Fine weather, visibility 2 m. To our surprise caught sight of a huge mountain to the SE with horrible crevassed glacier tumbling down and probably pressing on the vidda round the Pole. The glacier is horribly broken and full of cracks and holes on all sides. The Captain dubbed it the Devil's Glacier. The fog lifted, soon came down again and we saw no more of it. It was a lovely sight when the fog lifted again and

Figure 18 On the Devil's Glacier.

– Author's collection

mountains and glacier came through in the most wonderful tints, no artist could achieve anything so magical; the blue green reflection in the fog, how splendid – Think I saw mountains SW, will find out one of these days.

Scott

Wednesday, Nov. 29th. – Camp 25. Lat. 82 21. Things much better. The land showed up late yesterday; Mount Markham, a magnificent triple peak, appearing wonderfully close, Cape Lyttelton and Cape Goldie. We did our march in good time, leaving about 4.20, and getting into this camp at 1.15. About 7½ hours on the march. I suppose our speed throughout averages 2 stat. miles an hour.

The land showed hazily on the march, at times looking remarkably near. Sheety white snowy stratus cloud hung about overhead during the first march, but now the sky is clearing, the sun very warm and bright. Land shows up almost ahead now, our pony goal less than 70 miles away.

The ponies are tired, but I believe all have five days' work left in them, and some a great deal more. Chinaman made four feeds for the dogs, and I suppose we can count every other pony as a similar asset. It follows that the dogs can be employed, rested, and fed well on the homeward track. We could really get through now with their help and without much delay, yet every consideration makes it desirable to save the men from heavy hauling as long as possible. So I devoutly hope the 70 miles will come in the present order of things.

Snippets and Nobby now walk by themselves, following in the tracks well. Both have a continually cunning eye on their driver, ready to stop the moment he pauses. They eat snow every few minutes. It's a relief not having to lead an animal; such trifles annoy one on these marches, the animal's vagaries, his everlasting attempts to eat his head rope, &c. Yet all these animals are very full of character. Some day I must write of them and their individualities.

The men-haulers started 1½ hours before us and got here a good hour ahead, travelling easily throughout. Such is the surface with the sun on it, justifying my decision to work towards day marching. Evans has suggested the word 'glide' for the quality of surface indicated. 'Surface' is more comprehensive, and includes the crusts and liability to sink in them. From this point of view the surface is distinctly bad. The ponies plough deep all the time, and the men most of the time.

The Sastrugi are rather more clearly S.E.; this would be from winds sweeping along the coast. We have a recurrence of 'sinking crusts' – areas which give way with a report. There has been little of this since we left One Ton Camp until yesterday and to-day, when it is again very marked. Certainly the open Barrier conditions are different from those near the coast. Altogether things look much better and everyone is in excellent spirits. Meares has been measuring the holes made by ponies' hooves and finds an average of about 8 inches since we left One Ton Camp. He finds many holes a foot deep. This gives a good indication of the nature of the work. In Bowers' tent they had some of Chinaman's undercut in their hoosh yesterday, and say it was excellent.

I am cook for the present.

Have been discussing pony snow-shoes. I wish to goodness the animals would wear them – it would save them any amount of labour in such surfaces as this.

In naming the glacier after the Devil, Amundsen was having an untranslatable little joke. On the one hand, the ice clearly deserved it. On the other hand, Devil in Norwegian – Fanden – has the force of a four letter word, and never fails to shock. Its full force, as so often, is lost in translation. At the same time, its use is also sometimes touched with humour, as Amundsen would have intended in this case.

Strictly speaking, the Devil's Glacier is a particularly violent patch of disturbance in the ice cap. It too has kept its original name. Amundsen's 'F range' appears on the map today as the group of peaks around the Norway Glacier. 'G Range' is the Nilsen Plateau, named after Fram's captain, Thorvald Nilsen. See map on p. xiii.

THURSDAY, NOVEMBER 30TH, 1911
Amundsen

Thursday 30 Nov.
The fog finally relented in the course of the night. Lovely, fine morning. Sparkling sunshine and clear. The huge new land lay there bathed in the rays of the morning sun – a wonderful fairy tale in blue and white. Now for the first time we could reasonably determine the altitude of G range. We agreed that the highest summit could not be under 8,800 ft. The highest – 12,000 ft. The necessary observations have been taken. The clear weather gave us greater visibility. New ranges have appeared in a NE'ly direction and confirm my assumption. All these ranges are a continuation of E range. H range – bearings not yet taken – estimated between 12–20,000 ft. asl. – We also had a glimpse of the 'Great Beehive'. We could also see the continuation of this range towards the NW, but did not recognize it because it was not entirely clear. – We have not gone fast today – all of 5 nautical miles. 'The Devil's Glacier' has lived up to its name. One has to move two miles to advance one. Chasm after chasm, abyss after abyss has

to be circumvented. Treacherous crevasses and m[asses] o[f]. hummocks make progress extremely difficult. The dogs struggle, and the drivers not less. It is tiring for us two who go ahead. HH and I went out when we made camp this afternoon to survey the route for tomorrow. The terrain wasn't better – some places worse. This might take time. – Saw the continuation of F range towards the S. this afternoon. This seems a bit odd. – 8,700 ft.

Bjaaland

Thursday 30 Nov. –26 –24. Clear weather. Have shuffled along for 5 m, twisting and turning in all directions, really the devil of a glacier, with cracks closely packed. The dogs struggled horribly over crests and hollows and loose snow. There were mighty mountains that appeared to the East, certainly 15 to 20,000 feet high. They ran in a SW'ly direction.

Scott

Thursday, Nov. 30th. Camp 26. A very pleasant day for marching, but a very tiring march for the poor animals, which, with the exception of Nobby, are showing signs of failure all round. We were slower by half an hour or more than yesterday. Except that the loads are light now and there are still eight animals left, things don't look too pleasant, but we should be less than 60 miles from our first point of aim. The surface was much worse to-day, the ponies sinking to their knees very often. There were a few harder patches towards the end of the march. In spite of the sun there was not much 'glide' on the snow.

The dogs are reported as doing very well. They are going to be a great standby, no doubt.

The land has been veiled in thin white mist; it appeared at intervals after we camped and I had taken a couple of photographs.

FRIDAY, DECEMBER 1ST, 1911

Amundsen

Friday 1 Dec.
How often has it not happened to me, that a day that one had expected nothing at all of – brought a great deal. – Gale from SE during the night and in the

morning more drift and almost no visibility. Admittedly I had decided on a rest day for the doggies. But – in a little lull – we all agreed nonetheless to set off and try. It was grim to start with and it went agonizingly slowly. In the course of the night the wind had swept large areas of the glacier absolutely bare. It looked really gruesome. We had left our crampons at 'The Butcher's shop'. Without them, climbing on sheer ice is supposed to be an impossibility. A thousand thoughts ran through my brain. The pole lost, perhaps, because of such an idiotic blunder. But it went inch by inch, foot by foot, sledge length by sledge length, first E, then W, then N., then S., round huge open chasms and treacherous crevasses on the verge of collapsing. Then up a steep twisted ice ridge, then down another, so that one might expect to see the sledges splinter. But – we managed, and after a while we had worked our way up to the place HH and I reached yesterday evening. So far our prospects had not seemed particularly bright. But henceforth – despite the fog – things would brighten for us. We reached a somewhat even stretch, and through fog, gale and drift, and once again, after a long time, had the opportunity – for a long distance – to steer directly South. That brightened things. We were climbing quite gently the whole time. Gradually the huge chasms were filled with snow. The crevasses ebbed out and little by little they became more and more a rarity, until we reached the plateau, where they stopped completely. Here the violent pressure which had caused the heavy disturbance through which we had just passed, now had another effect – rather milder. Big, haycock-like mounds were strewn about in all directions. Some as high as a man, some smaller, others bigger. Up here the terrain is somewhat different. The whole foundation is of bare rather finely cracked ice, broken by big sastrugi running SE-NW. We have not yet been able to see the immediate surroundings, but we know with certainty that we are past the glacier, and therefore we are in a party mood. We may still meet obstacles but we will just have to accept that. Boiling this evening gave 9,100 ft. asl., and at this altitude, I assume with certainty that we are on the 'vidda'. We are longing to see how the land runs. The going up here is much better for the dogs, and they are moving along splendidly.

Bjaaland

Friday 1 December −22.6 −23. A gale blew up which raged against the tent as if it wanted to crush it. Turned out at 9.30, when it eased a little, and it had improved conditions, which were too slippery for paws on the slope, and it was an everlasting grind to get the load up all the hummocks and ridges that we had to cross. Then we got out of the Devil's Glacier, and thank God for that. It has been an awful bother now for three days. Hope it will be better as long as we don't run into any mountains. Here we are lying with crevasse after crevasse and small domes and sastrugi which are formed by the flow of the glacier. Have travelled 24 nautical miles across the Devil's Glacier, which we could have avoided by driving round to the west, but no-one could believe that it looked like that; that we came through without loss of men or animals, is a miracle. The lovely mountains are lying there towards the East, huge and solid like the highest in the world. Ca. 20 to 22,000 feet.

Scott

Friday, Dec. 1st. Camp 27. Lat. 82 47. The ponies are tiring pretty rapidly. It is a question of days with all except Nobby. Yet they are outlasting the forage, and to-night against some opinion I decided Christopher must go. He has been shot; less regret goes with him than the others, in remembrance of all the trouble he gave at the outset, and the unsatisfactory way he has gone of late. Here we leave a depôt so that no extra weight is brought on the other ponies; in fact there is a slight diminution.

Three more marches ought to bring us through. With the seven crocks and the dog teams we *must* get through I think. The men alone ought not to have heavy loads on the surface, which is extremely trying.

Nobby was tried in snow-shoes this morning, and came along splendidly on them for about four miles, then the wretched affairs racked and had to be taken off. There is no doubt that these snow-shoes are *the* thing for ponies, and had ours been able to use them from the beginning they would have been very different in appearance at this moment. I think the sight of the land has helped the animals, but not much. We started in bright warm sunshine and with the mountains wonderfully clear on our right hand, but towards the end of the march clouds worked up from the east and a thin broken cumulo-stratus now overspreads the sky, leaving the land still visible but dull.

A fine glacier descends from Mount Longstaff. It has cut very deep and the walls stand at an angle of at least 50°. Otherwise, although there are many cwms on the lower ranges, the mountains themselves seem little carved. They are rounded massive structures. A cliff of light yellow-brown rock appears opposite us, flanked with black or dark brown rock, which also appears under the lighter colour. One would be glad to know what nature of rock these represent. There is a good deal of exposed rock on the next range also.

Bjaaland is commenting obliquely on Amundsen's behaviour. Consumed by his goal, Amundsen was driving ruthlessly through terra incognita, *taking risks to the point of foolhardiness. Since he was leading by consent, his companions had to share at least some of the blame, as Bjaaland also hints.*

SATURDAY, DECEMBER 2ND, 1911

Amundsen

Saturday 2 Dec.
The 'vidda' over which we are now travelling resembles a frozen sea – a domed cupola of ice. Covered by quite small, covered crevasses. A few minor sastrugi here and there. Excellent conditions for a skater, but unfortunately unsuitable for our dogs and ourselves. I drag myself with my sticks ahead on skis. It is not easy. The dog drivers are off their skis, at the side of their sledges, ready to help the animals, when they can no longer get a grip with their claws. And that has unfortunately mostly been the case all day long. It has been a struggle both for doggies and human beings. Added to that, there is a storm from the SE with thick, intense drift and falling snow, so that one absolutely cannot see anything at all. We have travelled completely blind today. We are almost unrecognizable from frostbitten faces. Some have huge, hard cheeks, others have had to sacrifice noses, and yet others, chins. It has been an unpleasant day – stormy; drift and frostbite – but we have moved ahead – 13 nautical miles closer to our goal. Stiff gale this evening from SE. –24°. Boiling gave 9,300 ft. We are constantly climbing.

Bjaaland

2 December. The Devil's name-day[53]
Turned out in a raging gale from SE with biting snow so that we couldn't see in front of our nose tips and our faces were white and hard as wax candles. The Chief's nose is like that of a country bumpkin, Wisting's jaw looks like the snout of a Jersey cow. Helmer has thick scabs and skin as rough as a file. It was a bloody hard day, the doggies slid on the ice, and stopped when the sledges hit a sastruga, but we forced our way 13 nautical miles in the face of a wind of 10–15 m. which burned like a flame, oh, oh what a life. Are now 9,300 f. asl.

Scott

Saturday, Dec. 2ⁿᵈ. – Camp 28. Lat. 83. Started under very bad weather conditions. The stratus spreading over from the S.E. last night meant mischief, and all day we march in falling snow with a horrible light. The ponies went poorly on the first march, when there was little or no wind and a high temperature. They were sinking deep on a wretched surface. I suggested to Oates that he should have a roving commission to watch the animals, but he much preferred to lead one, so I handed over Snippets very willingly and went on ski myself. It was very easy work for me and I took several photographs of the ponies plunging along-the light very strong at 3 (Watkins actinometer). The ponies did much better on the second march, both surface and glide improved; I went ahead and found myself obliged to take a very steady pace to keep the lead, so we arrived in camp in flourishing condition. Sad to have to order Victor's end-poor Bowers feels it. He is in excellent condition and will provide 5 feeds for the dogs. (Temp. +17°). We must kill now as the forage is so short, but we have reached the 83 parallel and are practically safe to get through. To-night the sky is breaking and conditions generally more promising – it is dreadfully dismal work marching through the blank wall of white, and we should have very great difficulty if we had not a party to go ahead and show the course. The dogs are doing splendidly and will take a heavier load from to-morrow. We kill another pony to-morrow night if we get our march off, and shall then have nearly three days' food for the other 5.

In fact everything looks well if the weather will only give us a chance to see our way to the Glacier. Wild, in his Diary of Shackleton's Journey, remarks on December 15th, that it is the first day for a month that he could not record splendid weather. With us a fine day has been the exception so far. However, we have not lost a march yet. It was so warm when we camped that the snow melted as it fell, and everything got sopping wet. Oates came into my tent yesterday, exchanging with Cherry-Garrard.

The tents now: Self, Wilson, Oates, and Keohane. Bowers, [P.O.] Evans, Cherry, and Crean.

Man-haulers: Evans, Atkinson, Wright, and Lashly.

We have all taken to horse meat and are so well fed that hunger isn't thought of.

SUNDAY, DECEMBER 3RD, 1911

Amundsen

Sunday 3 Dec.

Had really decided on a rest day. But when the wind eased during the a.m., we agreed to give it a try. After taking a latitude observation which gave 86°47', we set off. But we might just as well have remained where we were. It soon began to blow again, and in a short while a full storm was blowing from the SE. We couldn't see our hands in front of our faces. Had the terrain been smooth, we would have continued, but an unfortunate and, considering the weather, a dangerous change had occurred. The pressure on this area had been rather greater than where we had been the past couple of days. The ice was broken by huge crevasses. Admittedly all these crevasses are filled up with snow, but on both sides, along the solid edges, this crust is rather thin and dangerous. We could not use our skis today, it was just sheer ice all over and we had to help the doggies. After several quite dangerous stretches in thick fog, we had to give up and make camp. We had only done 2 nautical miles. But we could have risked people, doggies and sledges in this filthy weather – and that is too costly for a miserable few nautical miles. Our tent is now pitched on bare ice – narrow crevasses everywhere. To reduce our loads, we left all our fur clothing at our previous camp this morning. However, we kept our anorak hoods, which we cut off the anoraks. –21° and storm from SE. Boiling point this evening gave 9,500 ft. asl.

Bjaaland

Sunday 3 Dec. –23 –19 –21. A little easing of the weather got us out of our sleeping bags in a hurry, but we really shouldn't have done so, for first there was slippery ice, and such pressure that we had to be two or three to drag the sledges across. When we had done 2 nautical miles, it was so bad that we made camp to wait for good weather. Today we dumped all our fur clothing to lighten our loads.

Scott

Sunday, Dec. 3rd. Camp 29. Our luck in weather is preposterous. I roused the hands at 2.30 a.m., intending to get away at 5. It was thick and snowy, yet we could have got on; but at breakfast the wind increased, and by 4.30 it was blowing a full gale from the south. The pony wall blew down, huge drifts collected, and the sledges were quickly buried. It was the strongest wind I have known here in summer. At 11 it began to take off. At 12.30 we got up and had lunch and got ready to start. The land appeared, the clouds broke, and by 1.30 we were in bright sunshine. We were off at 2 p.m., the land showing all round, and, but for some cloud to the S.E., everything promising. At 2.15 I saw the south-easterly cloud spreading up; it blotted out the land 30 miles away at 2.30 and was on us before 3. The sun went out, snow fell thickly, and marching conditions became horrible. The wind increased from the S.E., changed to S.W., where it hung for a time, and suddenly shifted to W.N.W. and then N.N.W., from which direction it is now blowing with falling and drifting snow. The changes of conditions are inconceivably rapid, perfectly bewildering. In spite of all these difficulties we have managed to get 11½ miles south and to this camp at 7 p.m. – the conditions of marching simply horrible.

The man-haulers led out 6 miles (geo.) and then camped. I think Evans had had enough of leading. We passed them, Bowers and I ahead on ski. We steered with compass, the drifting snow across our ski, and occasional glimpse of south-easterly sastrugi under them, till the sun showed dimly for the last hour or so.

The whole weather conditions seem thoroughly disturbed, and if they continue so when we are on the Glacier, we shall be very awkwardly placed. It is really time the luck turned in our favour – we have had all too little of it. Every mile seems to have been hardly won under such conditions. The ponies did splendidly and the forage is lasting a little better than expected. Victor was found to have quite a lot of fat on him and the others are pretty certain to have more, so that we should have no difficulty whatever as regards transport if only the weather was kind.

Amundsen's lead had now dropped to 232 nautical miles. He had dumped his fur clothing, because it was now too warm for skiing, and also too cumbersome. Henceforth, he used his Burberry cloth versions of the Netsilik garments, which allowed unconstrained movement. He kept the fur anorak hoods because it is vital to keep the head warm if the brain is to function properly, and hence preserve judgement unimpaired. In extreme conditions, this affects the chances of survival.

The day also reveals another profound contrast between the opponents. Scott is forever complaining about his luck. Amundsen rarely uses the word. As he himself once put it: 'Victory awaits those who have everything in order – people call it luck. Defeat is certain for those who have forgotten to take the necessary precautions in time – people call that bad luck.'[54] *Scott resents the weather as if there is some special kind to which he is entitled. (Nothing much has changed since then amongst his compatriots.)*

Amundsen and Bjaaland, who had seen enough caprice in the elements, simply accepted the dictates of Nature. It was beneficial for their mental balance. Resentment is a dangerous travelling companion.

MONDAY, DECEMBER 4ᵀᴴ, 1911

Amundsen

Monday 4 Dec.

We have been lucky, as usual. The wind backed – after having blown at storm force from the SE – to N. and eased and cleared up. We lost no time in turning out and setting off. We first had to cross the Devil's ballroom. Shiny bare ice with snow-filled crevasses here and there. This ballroom was not particularly difficult to negotiate. Naturally there was no question of using skis. We all had to support the sledges and help the dogs. The next section promised good going, and we congratulated ourselves on having overcome all difficulties. But we spoke too soon! It was not over so quickly. A high ridge suddenly rose before us, and the hollow into which we had to go down quickly showed us that here were difficulties aplenty. The one serac after the other indicated the violent turmoil that had been here. And that was soon revealed. Oops – there was W.'s sledge with one runner down in a huge bottomless crevasse. A rather awkward situation. Bj. took a photo. We were able to get it up again without damage. Then this happened to W. All his dogs fell in and disappeared, and were hauled up again – it happened from one minute to the next. Well – somehow we worked our way across unscathed and got up to the ridge. Again it consisted of bare ice, but so filled up with hidden crevasses that one literally could not put a foot down anywhere without treading through. Luckily almost all these crevasses were filled, but some were dangerous enough. It was a very hard job for the doggies. Bj. fell through, but managed to cling to his sledge. Without that, he would have been irretrievably lost. At last we got over this 'nether region', and little by little we arrived at the real, genuine Vidda – without the disturbance of land. In fact we last saw land W. by N. and W. by S.½ S., compass bearing. This was F range – the southernmost. In other words, this was the southernmost land we have seen. It was at 87° S. lat. that at long last we reached the vidda. We had a good long day's march in the most heavenly weather. Light SE breeze and crystal clear. Advanced 20 nautical miles and are now at 87°9' S. lat. by dead reckoning. The going is good here on the vidda. A few sastrugi – SE-NW – but no hindrance. No more crevasses and fissures.

Bjaaland

4 Decemb. 87°9'– 9,800 feet above sea level. –22.5 –22.3 –22. We headed into a storm, so we didn't expect that we would put 20 nautical miles behind us as we did. There was much slippery ice from the start, and countless crevasses and holes. Wisting drove his sledge into a horrible crevasse badly, so that four men were needed to right it again. There was disturbance of several m. from the East, pressure from glaciers to land. Fell into a crevasse, so if I had not grabbed the end of a rope on the sledge, I would have gone to rest for good. Now we have finally come on to the Vidda, but there are vile sastrugi and it is uneven, so that it is horrible to manage the loads. Wisting capsized 3 times today.

Scott

Monday, Dec. 4th – Camp 29, 9 a.m. I roused the party at 6. During the night the wind had changed from N.N.W. to S.S.E.; it was not strong, but the sun was obscured and the sky looked heavy; patches of land could be faintly seen and we thought that at any rate we could get on, but during breakfast the wind suddenly increased in force and afterwards a glance outside was sufficient to show a regular white floury blizzard.

We have all been out building fresh walls for the ponies – an uninviting task, but one which greatly adds to the comfort of the animals, who look sleepy and bored, but not at all cold. The dogs came up with us as we camped last night and the man-haulers arrived this morning as we finished the pony wall. So we are all together again. The latter had great difficulty in following our tracks, and say they could not have steered a course without them. It is utterly impossible to push ahead in this weather, and one is at a complete loss to account for it. The barometer rose from 29.4 to 29.9 last night, a phenomenal rise. Evidently there is very great disturbance of atmospheric conditions. Well, one must stick it out, that is all, and hope for better things, but it makes me feel a little bitter to contrast such weather with that experienced by our predecessors.

Camp 30. The wind fell in the forenoon, at 12.30 the sky began to clear, by 1 the sun shone, by 2 p.m. we were away, and by 8 p.m camped here with 13 miles to the good. The land was quite clear throughout the march and the features easily recognised. There are several uncharted glaciers of large dimensions, a confluence of three under Mount Reid. The mountains are rounded in outline, very massive, with small excrescent peaks and undeveloped 'cwms' T. + 18°. The cwms are very fine in the lower foot-hills and the glaciers have carved deep channels between walls at very high angles; one or two peaks on the foot-hills stand bare and almost perpendicular, probably granite; we should know later. Ahead of us is the ice-rounded, boulder-strewn Mount Hope and the gateway to the Glacier. We should reach it easily enough on to-morrow's march if we can compass 12 miles.

The ponies marched splendidly to-day, crossing the deep snow in the undulations without difficulty. They must be in very much better condition than Shackleton's animals, and indeed there isn't a doubt they would go many miles yet if food allowed. The dogs are simply splendid, but came in wanting food, so we had to sacrifice poor little Michael, who, like the rest, had lots of fat on him. All the tents are consuming pony flesh and thoroughly enjoying it.

We have only lost 5 or 6 miles on these two wretched days, but the disturbed condition of the weather makes me anxious with regard to the Glacier, where more than anywhere we shall need fine days. One has a horrid feeling that this is a real bad season. However, sufficient for the day is the evil thereof. We are practically through with the first stage of our journey. Looking from the last camp towards the S.S.E., where the farthest land can be seen, it seemed more than probable that a very high latitude could be reached on the Barrier, and if Amundsen journeying that way has a stroke of luck, he may well find his summit journey reduced to 100 miles or so. In any case, it is a fascinating direction for next year's work if only fresh transport arrives.[55] The dips between undulations seem to be about 12 to 15 feet. To-night we get puffs of wind from the gateway, which for the moment looks uninviting.

TUESDAY, DECEMBER 5ᵀᴴ, 1911

Amundsen

Tuesday 5 Dec. Have gone completely blind all day. Breeze from N. with thick drift, and greater, more constant snowfall than I have yet seen in these regions. It has gone very well. The terrain has allowed us to get ahead, albeit with some trouble. Some large sastrugi that has given rise to some capsizing and other troubles. We have worked our way ahead by 20 nautical miles in this impenetrable weather, and at the moment are 10,200 ft. asl. by boiling point. During the am there were still large stretches of ice between the sastrugi, but during the afternoon we finally lost them. I saw the moon here a couple of days ago. I don't know that this has happened to me before – the moon and midnight sun simultaneously. Left a black packing case at the camp site this morning.

Bjaaland

Thursday 5 Dec. –18 –15 We did not have the fine weather for long, today there was drift and NE wind and snow and horrible sastrugi, so horrible that one has to take great care not to capsize. Hanssen and Wisting capsized today also. Put 20 nautical miles behind us today.

Scott

Tuesday, Dec. 5ᵗʰ. Camp 30. Noon. We awoke this morning to a raging, howling blizzard. The blows we have had hitherto have lacked the very fine powdery snow – that especial feature of the blizzard. To-day we have it fully developed. After a minute or two in the open one is covered from head to foot. The temperature is high, so that what falls or drives against one sticks. The ponies-head, tails, legs, and all parts not protected by their rugs-are covered with ice; the animals are standing deep in snow, the sledges are almost covered, and huge drifts above the tents. We have had breakfast, rebuilt the walls, and are now again in our bags. One cannot see the next tent, let alone the land. What on earth does such weather mean at this time of year? It is more than our share of ill-fortune, I, think, but the luck may turn yet. I doubt if any party could travel in such weather even with the wind, certainly no one could travel against it.

Is there some widespread atmospheric disturbance which will be felt everywhere in this region as a bad season, or are we merely the victims of exceptional local conditions? If the latter, there is food for thought in picturing our small party struggling against adversity in one place whilst others go smilingly forward in the sunshine: How great may be the element of luck! No foresight – no procedure – could have prepared us for this state of affairs. Had we been ten times as experienced or certain of our aim we should not have expected such rebuffs.

11 p.m. It has blown hard all day with quite the greatest snowfall I remember. The drifts about the tents are simply huge. The temperature was + 27° this forenoon, and rose to + 31° in the afternoon, at which time the snow melted as it fell on anything but the snow, and, as a consequence, there are pools of water on everything, the tents are wet through, also the wind clothes, night boots, &c.; water drips from the tent poles and door, lies on the floor-cloth, soaks the sleeping-bags, and makes everything pretty wretched. If a cold snap follows before we have had time to dry our things, we shall be mighty uncomfortable. Yet after all it would be humorous enough if it were not for the seriousness of delay – we can't afford that, and it's real hard luck that it should come at such

a time. The wind shows signs of easing down, but the temperature does not fall and the snow is as wet as ever – not promising signs of abatement.

> *Keohane's rhyme*!
> The snow is all melting and everything's afloat,
> If this goes on much longer we shall have to turn the *tent* upside down and use it as a boat.

Scott's 'others go smilingly forward' is his second reference, albeit veiled, to Amundsen in as many days. Nonetheless it is Shackleton, the ghostly rival, who looms largest over Scott. Scott's remark about no one else being able to travel in such weather is obviously wishful thinking. It is also another of the grim ironies that punctuate the story. In equally bad weather, at high altitude, Amundsen was now 260 nautical miles in the lead, and drawing ahead once more.

WEDNESDAY, DECEMBER 6TH, 1911
Amundsen

Wednesday 6 Dec.
Have travelled absolutely blind all day. In such conditions. HH has to drive ahead with his dog team. Hass. and I, who otherwise would take turns in going ahead, cannot do so in this kind of weather, since we would simply come a cropper on the sastrugi. Some of these are quite big – but nothing to make a song and dance about. With a little exhortation the dogs take the sledges over with flying colours. If we had to haul ourselves, it would have been a dangerous job. The oldest of these sastrugi run SE-NW, but many of those more recently formed run N-S and E-W. We have had snowfall (fine) all day – absolutely no visibility. And despite this we have done our 20 nautical miles. Boiling gave 10.750 ft. asl. The dogs are in surprisingly good form. It must be due to the good pemmican and the mild weather.

Bjaaland

6th. –15 –17. Fog. The Devil's own sastrugi terrain, up to 6–7 feet high. H. and W. upset their loads. Put 20 nautical miles behind us, it wears you out going and fussing with the dogs all day, scanty dinner and ditto chocolate. 10800 ft. asl.

Scott

Wednesday, Dec. 6ᵗʰ. Camp 30. Noon. Miserable, utterly miserable. We have camped in the 'Slough of Despond.' The tempest rages with unabated violence. The temperature has gone to +33°; everything in the tent is soaking. People returning from the outside look exactly as though they had been in a heavy shower of rain. They drip pools on the floorcloth. The snow is steadily climbing higher about walls, ponies, tents, and sledges. The ponies look utterly desolate. Oh! but this is too crushing, and we are only 12 miles from the Glacier. A hopeless feeling descends on one and is hard to fight off. What immense patience is needed for such occasions.

11 p.m. At five there came signs of a break at last, and now one can see the land, but the sky is still overcast and there is a lot of snow about. The wind also remains fairly strong and the temperature high. It is not pleasant, but if no worse in the morning we can get on at last. We are very, very wet.

THURSDAY, DECEMBER 7ᵀᴴ, 1911

Amundsen

Thursday 7 Dec. Same weather. Heavy snowfall. Sky and horizon melt into each other. Can see absolutely nothing at all. Despite this we have done our 20 nautical miles and consequently have passed 88° S. Lat. Are now at 88°9' by dead reckoning. Tomorrow we will do another 20 mile march and then exceed Sh.'s record. Then we will stop for a day and recuperate. Of that we are sorely in need, both men and animals. The terrain has much improved today. Completely flat and fine everywhere. No sastrugi but much loose snow. And this evening the hypsometer shows that we have not climbed at all. Are we now on the final high plain? I think so. That does not quite agree with Sh. But possibly he did not have a hypsometer for his final spurt.

Bjaaland

Thursday 7 December. 88°9'. –18 –19 Snowstorm from the *East*, going sticky, my dogs dead tired. Intend breaking Mr. *Chackleton's* [sic] record tomorrow, he reached 88°23'. Degree pudding this evening. This plateau will be called *Grisevidda.*[56]

Scott

Thursday, Dec. 7th. Camp 30. The storm continues and the situation is now serious. One small feed remains for the ponies after to-day, So that we must either march tomorrow or sacrifice the animals. That is not the worst; with the help of the dogs we could get on, without doubt. The serious part is that we have this morning started our Summit rations – that is to say, the food calculated from the Glacier depôt has been begun. The first supporting party can only go on a fortnight from this date and so forth. The storm shows no sign of abatement and its character is as unpleasant as ever. The promise of last night died away about 3 a.m., when the temperature and wind rose again, and things reverted to the old conditions. I can find no sign of an end, and all of us agree that it is utterly impossible to move. Resignation to misfortune is the only attitude, but not an easy one to adopt. It seems undeserved where plans were well laid and so nearly crowned with a first success. I cannot see that any plan would be altered if it were to do again, the margin for bad weather was ample according to all experience, and this stormy December – our finest month – is a thing that the most cautious organiser might not have been prepared to encounter. It is very evil to lie here in a wet sleeping-bag and think of the pity of it, whilst with no break in the overcast sky things go steadily from bad to worse T. + 32. Meares has a bad attack of snow blindness in one eye. I hope this rest will help him, but he says it has been painful for a long time. There cannot be good cheer in the camp in such weather, but it is ready to break out again. In the brief spell of hope last night one heard laughter.

Little or no improvement. The barometer is rising – perhaps there is hope in that. Surely few situations could be more exasperating than this of forced inactivity when every day and indeed one hour counts. To be here watching the mottled wet green walls of our tent, the glistening wet bamboos, the bedraggled sopping socks and loose articles dangling in the middle, the saddened countenances of my companions – to hear the everlasting patter of the falling snow and the ceaseless rattle of the fluttering canvas – to feel the wet clinging dampness of clothes and everything touched, and to know that without there is but a blank wall of white on every side – these are the physical surroundings. Add the stress of sighted failure of our whole plan, and anyone must find the circumstances unenviable. But yet, after all, one can go on striving, endeavouring to find a stimulation in the difficulties that arise.

FRIDAY, DECEMBER 8ᵀᴴ, 1911

Amundsen

Friday 8 Dec.

One of our big days. It did not seem exactly favourable in the morning – thick and with no visibility as usual. But the wind had dropped during the night. What little remained, came from NE. Terrain and going were of the best kind. Flat – quite flat without the slightest hint of sastrugi. The awkward patches of loose drift snow that had been so obstructive the previous day had completely disappeared, and the skiing was absolutely A1*. We had not travelled long, before it began to clear round the whole horizon. But the vault of heaven itself remained veiled. A thick layer of stratus made everything impenetrable and the sun showed not the least sign of itself. At 11.15 a.m., we had one of our usual halts – we had then covered 7 nautical miles, and by dead reckoning were at 88°16' S. Lat. Precisely at that moment the sun appeared, but not more than a pat of butter. We had not had an obs. since 86°16' S. Lat, and it meant a great deal for us to fix our position precisely. It took some time before 'Her Grace' was prepared to reveal herself. But eventually she appeared – not in all her glory, but modest and pretty – excellent for a good view. We shot her – we made no mistake – and the result – Well, it was almost exactly 88°16'. A brilliant victory after 1½° march in thick fog and snow drift. In other words, observation and dead reckoning agreed to a minute. Later in the afternoon we took two separate observations for compass variation, at very different times – 5 o'clock and 8 o'clock – with the same result. So we are ready to take the Pole in any kind of weather on offer. It was only 7 nautical miles from our observation site to the Englishmen's (Sh's) world record (88°23'). I had given HH our Pole flag, which he would hoist on his sledge – the leading sledge – as soon as that latitude had been crossed. I was myself the forerunner at that time. The weather had improved more and more, and the sun was in the process of breaking through in dead earnest. My snow goggles bothered me from time to time. Light airs from the S. made them cloud over, making it difficult to see. Then suddenly I heard a stout, hearty cheer behind me. I turned round. In the light breeze from the S., the brave, well-known colours were flying from the first sledge, we have passed and put behind us the Englishmen's record. It was a splendid sight. The sun had just burst through in all its glory and illuminated in a lovely manner the beautiful little flag – a present from Helland-Hansen and Nordahl Olsen. My goggles clouded over again, but this time it was not the south wind's fault. We halted at 88°23'2 and congratulated each other. We were all happy and content. Took a photo – No.10 film no.3 – of the sledges as the moved on and stopped.

Then we continued our journey again and stopped at 88°25' S. lat. We had the best weather for a long time. Sunshine and almost calm. −18°. It was pure summer inside the tent. Everything of ours that is damp, dries in the course of a few hours. We stay here tomorrow in order to rest ourselves and our dogs. – The snow conditions on the plateau – for the hypsometer shows that we are on the plateau, the result this evening being exactly the same as on the previous two. The snow here is deep and loose, so that it was difficult enough to find a place to pitch the tent. It seems that any wind – at least a strong one – is a rarity here on the plateau. The dogs are quite ravenous – eat anything they can get hold of – especially the lashings on the sledges. Therefore we must strip the sledges bare at night.

Bjaaland

8 Dec. 88°25' −17 −18.5. The greatest day we have had for a long time, calm and flat and fine, a little fog in the morning which lifted. The sun peeped through around midday, so the observers got a good sight, and discovered that we were now at 88°16' S. Lat.

Today broke the world record in high latitude in that we broke Chackletons [sic] previous 88°23' by 2', we reached 88°25'. As my dogs were horribly worn, I was 1 mile behind and when I reached 88°23' the Norwegian flag was flying, and I seemed to walk on springs. I congratulated the Captain, he was in a brilliant humour, you can be sure. Extra chocolate in honour of the occasion. Tomorrow rest day. The sun is shining. The *Vidda* now lay before us, fine and smooth. Perhaps it will be like this right up to the Pole.

Scott

Friday, Dec. 8th. Camp 30. Hoped against hope for better conditions, to wake to the mournfullest snow and wind as usual. We had breakfast at 10, and at noon the wind dropped. We set about digging out the sledges, no light task. We then shifted our tent sites. All tents had been reduced to the smallest volume by the gradual pressure of snow. The old sites are deep pits with hollowed-in wet centres. The re-setting of the tent has at least given us comfort, especially since the wind has dropped. About 4 the sky showed signs of breaking, the sun and a few patches of land could be dimly discerned. The wind shifted in light airs and a little hope revived. Alas! as I write the sun has disappeared and snow is again falling.

Our case is growing desperate. Evans and his man-haulers tried to pull a load this afternoon. They managed to move a sledge with four people on it, pulling in ski. Pulling on foot they sank to the knees. The snow all about us is terribly deep. We tried Nobby and he plunged to his belly in it. Wilson thinks the ponies finished, but Oates thinks they will get another march in spite of the surface *if it comes to-morrow*. If it should not, we must kill the ponies to-morrow and get on as best we can with the men on ski and the dogs. But one wonders what the dogs can do on such a surface. I much fear they also will prove inadequate. Oh! for fine weather, if only to the Glacier. The temperature remains +33°, and everything is disgustingly wet.

11 p.m. The wind has gone to the north, the sky is really breaking at last, the sun showing less sparingly, and the land appearing out of the haze. The temperature has fallen to +26°, and the water nuisance is already abating. With so fair a promise of improvement it would be too cruel to have to face bad weather to-morrow. There is good cheer in the camp to-night in the prospect of action. The poor ponies look wistfully for the food of which so very little remains, yet they are not hungry, as recent savings have resulted from food left in their nosebags. They look wonderfully fit, all things considered. Everything looks more hopeful to-night, but nothing can recall four lost days.

Amundsen and Bjaaland illuminate once more the contest between the inner and the outer man. Of course Amundsen was pleased at having broken the record for the furthest south. His emotions were however more complex. He was moved by his

Figure 19 Amundsen passing Shackleton's Furthest South, 8 December 1911.

– Author's collection

achievement, but he too was touched by the ghostly figure of Shackleton. Amundsen's respect for Shackleton was boundless, so he felt a twinge of melancholy at beating a worthy opponent. The Old Norse sagas have moments such as this. The hunter and the hunted, after all, are bound symbiotically. The hidden irony was that now, through Amundsen, Scott had taken revenge on Shackleton at last. By the same token, Shackleton had avenged himself on Scott, who was now 315 nautical miles adrift, with Amundsen steadily pulling away.

Helland-Hansen, a friend of Amundsen and Nansen, was an oceanographer and one of the founders of modern meteorology. Nordahl Olsen was a Norwegian author and local historian from Bergen.

The figures do not quite express Scott's predicament. Only now has he begun unreservedly to accept the rôle of skis in the snow, but still has to prove to himself that men on skis can pull a load. He could have done it all at base. This is learning on the job with a vengeance. Scott was still a slave to the dictum that 'gentlemen don't practise.' It is hard to see the point of having brought Tryggve Gran on the expedition. Likewise, Scott cannot yet bring himself to believe in dogs. Yet once more, Amundsen points the contrast.

SATURDAY, DECEMBER 9TH, 1911

Amundsen

Saturday 9 Dec. Haved stayed put today, rested, and prepared for the final onslaught. We have put down a depot here to lighten the sledges. HH keeps his sledge unchanged, while the two others have been lightened. Bj.'s dogs have weakened a lot recently, and yesterday evening one of W.'s – The Major – a steady old dog, disappeared. Presumably he had gone away to die. Each of these two sledges has been lightened by ca. 50 kg. Bj. has got rid of 42.5 kg dog and human pemmican. W. has unloaded his case of biscuits containing – 2,200, together with 11.5 kg pemmican. In addition a tin of alcohol[57] and a ball of string have been left in this depot. This depot is marked transversely E-W. 60 planks from packing cases have been laid out on each side 100 paces from each other. Every other plank carries a black pennant. Those planks to the E. all have a notch under the pennant to indicate the direction they lie in relation to the depot. The weather has been really good today. On several occasions the sun has been absolutely clear. –24° this evening. Light SE'ly breeze. We leave here well supplied to get back here – ca. 30 days for humans, ca. 20 days for dogs. Three of us – HH, W, and I look quite awe-inspiring since our faces were frostbitten in the SE storm a few days ago. Bj. & Hass., who went last, got off Scot free. The dogs have begun to be quite dangerous and must be considered as mortal enemies when one leaves the sledges. Oddly enough they have not tried to break in. In addition to the transverse marking we will put up a few snow blocks every other nautical mile on the way south.

Bjaaland

Saturday 9 Dec. 88°25' −20.6 −24. Weather remained fine, afternoon overcast with cirrus clouds. Built a depot, and put in 108 rations of dog food and ca. 2,200 biscuits. From there, we marked out 3 nautical miles on each side, E. and W. with pennants and posts of boards from sledge cases marked with a notch to the east, to the west nothing. The temperature is falling.

Scott

Sat. Dec. 9th. – Camp 31. I turned out two or three times in the night to find the weather slowly improving; at 5.30 we all got up, and at 8 got away with the ponies – a most painful day. The tremendous snowfall of the late storm had made the surface intolerably soft, and after the first hour there was no glide. We pressed on the poor half-rationed animals, but could get none to lead for more than a few minutes; following, the animals would do fairly well. It looked as we could never make headway; the man-haulers were pressed into the service to aid matters. Bowers and Cherry-Garrard went ahead with one 10-foot sledge – thus most painfully we made about a mile. The situation was saved by P.O. Evans, who put the last pair of snowshoes on Snatcher. From this he went on without much pressing, the other ponies followed, and one by one were worn out in the second place. We went on all day without lunch. Three or four miles T. +23° found us engulfed in pressures, but free from difficulty except the awful softness of the snow.

By 8 p.m. we had reached within a mile or so of the slope ascending to the gap which Shackleton called the Gateway. I had hoped to be through the Gateway with the ponies still in hand at a very much earlier date and, but for the devastating storm, we should have been. It has been a most serious blow to us, but things are not yet desperate, if only the storm has not hopelessly spoilt the surface. The man-haulers are not up yet, in spite of their light load. I think they have stopped for tea, or something, but under ordinary conditions they would have passed us with ease.

At 8 p.m. the ponies were quite done, one and all. They came on painfully slowly a few hundred yards at a time. By this time I was hauling ahead, a ridiculously light load, and yet finding the pulling heavy enough. We camped, and the ponies have been shot. Poor beasts they have done wonderfully well considering the terrible circumstances under which they worked, but yet it is hard to have to kill them so early. The dogs are going well in spite of the surface, but here again one cannot get the help one would wish. T. + 19°. I cannot load the animals heavily on such snow. The scenery is most impressive; three huge pillars of granite form the right buttress of the Gateway, and a sharp spur of Mount Hope the left. The land is much more snow-covered than when we saw it before the storm. In spite of some doubt in our outlook, everyone is very cheerful to-night and jokes are flying freely around.

SUNDAY, DECEMBER 10TH, 1911

Amundsen

Sunday 10 Dec. −28° Breeze from the south and crystal clear. It has been a little cool to go up wind, but nothing to make a fuss over. Terrain and going the same old kind – first class. Quite even and flat the Vidda lies before us. Sledges and ski glide easily and pleasantly. But the dogs are tired, and they do not run fast, but they run evenly, and we have covered the stipulated 16 nautical miles. Another 5 days, and it is our intention to arrive. The Vidda does not give the impression of being enriched by strong winds. The snow covering is quite loose. Difficult enough to find a decent camp site. Got a splendid altitude at midday which gave 88°30' S. lat., or 1' more than dead reckoning. That's fine. A splendid azimuth during the p.m.

Bjaaland

Sunday 10 Dec. −28 −28 −29 Fine-fine weather but bloody stinging snow from the south. The dogs were a little better today after the rest day. The Vidda lay before us, flat as a ballroom floor in all directions. Just before evening the snow sank with a roar, as if 1,000 of tons had fallen down. Distance 16.1 nautical miles.

Scott

Sunday, Dec. 10ᵗʰ. Camp 32. I was very anxious about getting our loads forward over such an appalling surface, and that we have done so is mainly due to the ski. I roused everyone at 8, but it was noon before all the readjustments of load had been made and we were ready to start. The dogs carried 600 lbs. of our weight besides the depôt (200 lbs.). It was greatly to my surprise when we – my own party – with a 'one, two, three together' started our sledge, and we found it running fairly easily behind us. We did the first mile at a rate of about two miles an hour, having previously very carefully scraped and dried our runners. The day was gloriously fine and we were soon perspiring. After the first mile we began to rise, and for some way on a steep slope we held to our ski and kept going. Then the slope got steeper and the surface much worse, and we had to take off our ski. The pulling after this was extraordinarily fatiguing. We sank above our finnesko everywhere, and in places nearly to our knees. The runners of the sledges got coated with a thin film of ice from which we could not free them, and the sledges themselves sank to the crossbars in soft spots. All the time they were literally ploughing the snow. We reached the top of the slope at 5, and started on after tea on the down grade. On this we had to pull almost as hard as on the upward slope, but could just manage to get along on ski. We camped at 9.15, when a heavy wind coming down the glacier suddenly fell on us; but I had decided to camp before, as Evans' party could not keep up, and Wilson told me some very alarming news concerning it. It appears that Atkinson says that Wright is getting played out and Lashly is not so fit as he was owing to the heavy pulling since the blizzard. I have not felt satisfied about this party & very dissatisfied with its management. The finish of the march to-day showed clearly that something was wrong. They fell a long way behind, had to take off ski, and took nearly half an hour to come up a few hundred yards. True, the surface was awful and growing worse every moment. It is a very serious business if the men are going to crack up. As for myself, I never felt fitter and my party can easily hold its own. [P.O.] Evans, of course, is a tower of strength, but Oates and Wilson are doing splendidly also.

Here where we are camped the snow is worse than I have ever seen it, but we are in a hollow. Every step here one sinks to the knees and the uneven surface is obviously insufficient to support the sledges. Perhaps this wind is a blessing in disguise, already it seems to be hardening the snow. All this soft snow is an aftermath of our prolonged storm. Hereabouts Shackleton found hard blue ice. It seems an extraordinary difference in fortune, and at every step S.'s luck becomes more evident. I take the dogs on for half a day to-morrow, then send them home. We have 200 lbs. to add to each sledge load and could easily do it on a reasonable surface, but it looks very much as though we shall be forced to relay if present conditions hold. There is a strong wind down the glacier to-night.

For Scott, it is the end of a stage. He has left the Barrier this day and, crossing the Gateway, reached the foot of the Beardmore Glacier – the Glacier to him. Before him is a long hard climb of 120 miles, all man hauling, up that frozen Amazon of an ice stream to the polar plateau.

This is a revealing entry by Scott. In the same breath, he exposes the masochistic cruelty of man-hauling, and the Dionysian side of his personality, proud of his own strength, with a belief that brute force can overcome Nature. Too late, he has finally grasped the use of dogs, but put Meares, and others, at risk by taking him further than the lines of communication can reasonably bear.

Above all, Scott's obsession with Shackleton continues. In a strange dream world it is Shackleton, not Amundsen, who somehow seems the real adversary.

Amundsen was now 325 nautical miles ahead.

MONDAY, DECEMBER 11ᵀᴴ, 1911

Amundsen

Monday 11 Dec.
Fine weather again. Light SSE'ly breeze and −28°. Sometimes quite clear. Sometimes a passing patch of mist. A lovely big ring round the sun. A meridian altitude gave 1 minute less than dead reckoning. Made up for it by doing 17 instead of 16 nautical miles. Now lying at 88°56' S. lat. Terrain and going the same. We notice alright that it is hard to work up here on the heights. We'll get our breath back, if only we win. Oh well, we'll manage. Looking forward to getting down to normal altitudes some time.

Bjaaland

Monday 11 Dec. −28 −28 88°58'. Sunny weather SE wind. *Grisevidda*, was just as fine and flat. Four long days and the Pole's there. Hanssen furious because I am running so slowly.

Scott

Monday, Dec. 11th. Camp 33. A very good day from one point of view, very bad from another. We started straight out over the glacier and passed through a good deal of disturbance. We pulled on ski and the dogs followed. I cautioned the drivers to keep close to their sledges and we must have passed over a good many crevasses undiscovered by us, thanks to ski, and by the dogs owing to the soft snow. In one only Seaman Evans dropped a leg, ski and all. We built our depôt before starting, made it very conspicuous, and left a good deal of gear there. The old man-hauling party made heavy weather at first, but when relieved of a little weight and having cleaned their runners and re-adjusted their load they came on in fine style, and, passing us, took the lead. Starting about 11, by 3 o'clock we were clear of the pressure, and I camped the dogs, discharged our loads, and we put them on our sledges. It was a very anxious business when we started after lunch, about 4.30. Could we pull our full loads or not? My own party got away first, and, to my joy, I found we could make fairly good headway. Every now and again the sledge sank in a soft patch, which brought us up, but we learned to treat such occasions with patience. We got sideways to the sledge and hauled it out, Evans getting out of his ski to get better purchase. The great thing is to keep the sledge moving, and for an hour or more there were dozens of critical moments when it all but stopped, and not a few in it brought up altogether. The latter were very trying and tiring. But suddenly the surface grew more uniform and we more accustomed to the game, for after a long stop to let the other parties come up, I started at 6 and ran on till 7, pulling easily without a halt at the rate of about 2 miles an hour. I was very jubilant; all difficulties seemed to be vanishing; but unfortunately our history was not repeated with the other parties. Bowers came up about half an hour after us. They also had done well at the last, and I'm pretty sure they will get on all right. Keohane is the only weak spot, and he only, I think, because blind (temporarily). But Evans' party didn't get up till 10. They started quite well, but got into difficulties, did just the wrong thing by straining again and again, and so, tiring themselves, went from bad to worse. *It is most awfully trying – I had expected failure from the animals but not from the men – I must blame Lieut. Evans much – he shows a terrible lack of judgement –, instead of having his people trained & drilled he lets things go on any way – half of them have their ski shoes down at the heel and as a rule only three out of the four pull the other man wrestling with his ski of course this is fatal –* So just as I thought we were in for making a great score, this difficulty overtakes us – it is dreadfully trying. The snow around us to-night is terribly soft, one sinks to the knee at every step; it would be impossible to drag sledges on foot and very difficult for dogs. Ski are the thing, and here are my tiresome fellow-countrymen too prejudiced to have prepared themselves for the event.[58]

The dogs should get back quite easily; there is food all along the line. The glacier wind sprang up about 7; the morning was very fine and warm. To-night there is some stratus cloud forming – a hint no more bad weather in sight. A plentiful crop of snow blindness due to incaution-the sufferers Evans, Bowers, Keohane, Lashly, Oates – in various degrees.

This forenoon Wilson went over to a boulder poised on the glacier. It proved to be a very coarse granite with large crystals of quartz in it. Evidently the rock of which the pillars of the Gateway and other neighbouring hills are formed.

Meares and his dogs having turned, henceforth it is exclusively man-hauling all the way for Scott to the Pole and back.

TUESDAY, DECEMBER 12TH, 1911

Amundsen

Tuesday 12 Dec. Lovely weather. Almost calm and partly clear. Ca. –25°. Same fine going and terrain. According to the hypsometer, we are descending, although quite gently. Possibly it is only the weather conditions that explain this. The meridian altitude, which was shot under the most favourable conditions – calm, clear sharply defined sun and horizon likewise gave 89°6'. That is to say dead reckoning was once more in agreement. We have done our usual 17 nautical miles and are now lying at 89°15' – 3 day's march from our goal.

Bjaaland

Tuesday 12 Dec. –24 –26 –26° 89°15' – 15. The Pole is in sight. Fine weather, good observations. Distance 17 nautical miles along our course, but one reservation, hope and pray to my God that the weather continues fine. Oatmeal pudding this evening. Have whipped the dogs on to draw level with HH's dogs. We are moving at 11,000 ft. asl.

Scott

Tuesday, Dec. 12th. Camp 34. We have had a hard day, and during the forenoon it was my team which made the heaviest weather of the work. We got bogged again and again, and, do what we would, the sledge dragged like lead. The others were working hard but nothing to be compared to us. At 2.30 I halted for lunch, pretty well cooked, and there was disclosed the secret of our trouble in a thin film with some hard knots of ice on the runners. Evans' team had been sent off in advance, and we didn't – couldn't – catch them, but they saw us camp and break camp and followed suit. I really dreaded starting after lunch, but after some trouble to break the sledge out, we went ahead without a hitch, and in a mile or two recovered our leading place with obvious ability to keep it. At 6 I saw the other teams were flagging and so camped at 7, meaning to turn out earlier to-morrow and start a better routine. We have done about 8 or perhaps 9 miles (stat.) – the sledgemeters are hopeless on such a surface.

It is evident that what I expected has occurred. The whole of the lower valley is filled with snow from the recent storm, and if we had not had ski we should be hopelessly bogged. On foot one sinks to the knees, and if pulling on a sledge to half-way between knee and thigh. It would, therefore, be absolutely impossible to advance on foot with our loads. Considering all things, we are getting better on ski. A crust is forming over the soft snow. In a week or so I have little doubt it will be strong enough to support sledges and men. At present it carries neither properly. The sledges get bogged every now and again, sinking to the crossbars. Needless to say, the hauling is terrible when this occurs.

We steered for the Commonwealth Range during the forenoon till we reached about the middle of the glacier. This showed that the unnamed glacier to the S.W. raised great pressure. Observing this, I altered course for the 'Cloudmaker' and later still farther to the west. We must be getting a much better view of the southern side of the main glacier than S. got, and consequently have observed a number of peaks which he did not notice. We are about 5 or 5½ days behind him as a result of the storm, but on this surface our sledges could not be more heavily laden than they are, in fact we have not nearly enough runner surface as it is. Moreover, the sledges are packed too high and therefore capsize too easily. I do not think the glacier can be so broad as S. shows it. Certainly the scenery is not nearly so impressive as that of the Ferrar, but there are interesting features showing up – a distinct banded structure on Mount Elizabeth, which we think may well be a recurrence of the Beacon Sandstone – more banding on the Commonwealth Range. During the three days we have been here the wind has blown down the glacier at night, or rather from the S.W., and it has been calm in the morning – a sort of nightly land-breeze. There is also a very remarkable difference in temperature between day and night. It was + 33 when we started, and with our hard work we were literally soaked through with perspiration. It is now + 23°. Evans' party kept up much better to-day; we had their shoes into our tent this morning, and P.O. Evans put them into shape again.

WEDNESDAY, DECEMBER 13ᵀᴴ, 1911

Amundsen

Wednesday 13 Dec.
Our best day up here. It has been calm for most of the day – with burning sunshine. The going and terrain have been the same. Luckily the snow crust is so hard that sledges and doggies sink in very little. The hypsometer still shows us descending, albeit very gently, so that it must be assumed that we have not only established the highest point of the plateau, but also are sinking down towards the other side. We have done 15 nautical miles today, and according to the midday obs. are now at 89°30'30". Obs. and dead reckoning agree brilliantly every day. We can only trust one of our sextants – the *Fram* sextant – the other one has unfortunately suffered a blow and proved not to be reliable. HH W. & I now share the *Fram* sextant.

Bjaaland

Wednesday 13 Dec. –23.5 –23.5. Sunny weather, fine-fine day 15 nautical miles. The terrain is perhaps a little undulating, rising a little. Lying now at 89°30'. Two days' travel from the Pole. The Captain is in a good mood and is unusually pleasant to me. Had a fine dream the other night. A girl, a little angel came to me with food and flowers, among them a big red rose.

Scott

Wednesday, Dec. 13ᵗʰ. Camp 35. A most *damnably* dismal day. We started at 8 – the pulling terribly bad, though the glide decidedly good; a new crust in patches, not sufficient to support the ski, but without possibility of hold. Therefore, as the pullers got on the hard patches they slipped back. The sledges plunged into the soft places and stopped dead. Evans' party got away first; we followed, and for some time helped them forward at their stops, but this proved altogether too much for us, so I forged ahead and camped at 1 p.m., as the others were far astern. During lunch I decided to try the ten foot runners under the crossbars and we spent three hours in securing them.

There was no delay on account of the slow progress of the other parties. Evans passed us, and for some time went forward fairly well up a decided slope. The sun was shining on the surface by this time, and the temperature high. Bowers started after Evans, and it was easy to see the really terrible state of affairs with them. They made desperate efforts to get along, but ever got more and more bogged – evidently the glide had vanished. When we got away we soon discovered how awful the surface had become – added to the forenoon difficulties the snow had become wet and sticky. We got our load along, soon passing Bowers, but the toil was simply awful. We were soaked with perspiration and thoroughly breathless with our efforts. Again and again the sledge got one runner on harder snow than the other, canted on its side, and refused to move. At the top of the rise I found Evans reduced to relay work, and Bowers followed his example soon after. We got our whole load through till 7 p.m., camping time, but only with repeated halts and labour which was altogether too strenuous. The other parties certainly cannot get a full load along on the surface, and I much doubt if we could continue to do so, but we must try again to-morrow.

I suppose we have advanced a bare 4 miles to-day and the aspect of things is very little changed. Our height is now about 1,500 feet; I had pinned my faith on getting better conditions as we rose, but it looks as though matters were getting worse instead of better. As far as the Cloudmaker the valley looks like a huge basin for the lodgement of such snow as this. We can but toil on, but it is woefully disheartening. I am not at all hungry, but pretty thirsty. T. + 15°. I find our summit ration is even too filling for the present. Two skuas came round the camp at lunch, no doubt attracted by our 'Shambles' camp.

In a short sentence Bjaaland says worlds about Amundsen's personality and their attitude to one another.

Meanwhile Scott exposes the shadows hanging over him. Again, there is the violent mood swing between elation and depression. Then he has condemned his men to soul-destroying struggle. They are exhausted after being on the trail for 11 hours – against Amundsen's 6½ hours – man-hauling all the time for a derisory distance. More ominous still, Scott is starting to complain about thirst. He lacks the fuel to melt enough water. He is facing dehydration, the perils of which he does not understand.

Amundsen was now leading by 350 nautical miles.

THURSDAY, DECEMBER 14ᵀᴴ, 1911

Amundsen

Thursday 14 Dec.
Fine weather all morning. Clouded over after we had taken the altitude, and snow showers arrived from the SE. The meridian altitude – both with mercury and glass – gave 89°37'. 89°38'.5 by dead reckoning. This is really very good. –23° all day. Afterwards we did 8 nautical miles, and are now lying 15 nautical miles from the Pole.

Bjaaland

Thursday 14 Dec. –23 –23 –23. Slight snowfall, but sunshine SE wind 2–3 m/s. Covered 16 nautical miles. The dogs are so hungry they're eating their own crap, and if they can get at it, they eat the lashing on the sledges and bite deep into the wood. Somehow they move along, but they have to taste whip and whip handle. We can now lie and look towards the Pole, and I hear the axle creaking, but tomorrow it will be oiled. The excitement is great. Shall we see the English flag – God have mercy on us, I don't believe it.

Scott

Thursday, Dec. 14ᵗʰ. Camp 36. T. +13° Indigestion and the soggy condition of my clothes kept me awake for some time last night, and the exceptional exercise gives bad attacks of cramp. Our lips are getting raw and blistered. The eyes of the party are improving, I am glad to say. We are just starting our march with no very hopeful outlook.

Evening. Height about 2,000 feet. Evans' party started first this morning; for an hour they found the hauling stiff, but after that, to my great surprise, they went on easily. Bowers followed without getting over the ground so easily. After the first 200 yards my own party came on with a swing that told me at once that all would be well. We soon caught the others and offered to take on more weight, but Evans' pride wouldn't allow such help. Later in the morning we exchanged sledges with Bowers, pulled theirs easily, whilst they made quite heavy work with ours. I am afraid Cherry-Garrard and Keohane are the weakness of that team, though both put their utmost into the traces. However, we all lunched together after a satisfactory morning's work. In the afternoon we did still better, and camped at 6.30 with a very marked change in the land bearings. We must have come 11 or 12 miles (stat.). We got fearfully hot on the march, sweated through everything and stripped off jerseys. The result is we are pretty cold and clammy now, but escape from the soft snow and a good march compensate every discomfort. At lunch the blue ice was about 2 feet beneath us, now it is barely a foot, so that I suppose we shall soon find it uncovered. To-night the sky is overcast and wind has been blowing up the glacier. I think there will be another spell of gloomy weather on the Barrier, and the question is whether this part of the glacier escapes. There are crevasses about, one about eighteen inches across outside Bowers' tent, and a narrower one outside our own. I think the soft snow trouble is at an end, and I could wish nothing better than a continuance of the present surface. Towards the end of the march we were pulling our loads with the greatest ease. It is splendid to be getting along and to find some adequate return for the work we are putting into the business.

FRIDAY, DECEMBER 15TH, 1911

Amundsen

Thursday 15 Decbr. (actually 14th)[59]

So we arrived, and were able to raise our flag at the geographical South Pole – King Håkon VII's Vidda. Thanks be to God! The time was 3 p.m. when this happened. The weather was of the best kind when we set off this morning, but at 10 a.m., it clouded over and hid the sun. Fresh breeze from the SE. The skiing has been partly good, partly bad. The plain – King H VII's Vidda – has had the same appearance – quite flat and without what one might call sastrugi. The sun reappeared in the afternoon, and now we must go out and take a midnight observation. Naturally we are not exactly at the point called 90°, but after all our excellent observations and dead reckoning we must be very close. We arrived here with three sledges and 17 dogs. HH put one down just after arrival. 'Helge' was worn out. Tomorrow we will go out in three directions to circle the area round the Pole. We have had our celebratory meal – a little piece of seal meat each. We leave here the day after tomorrow with two sledges. The third sledge will be left here. Likewise we will leave a little three man tent (Rønne)[60] with the Norwegian flag and a pennant marked *Fram*.

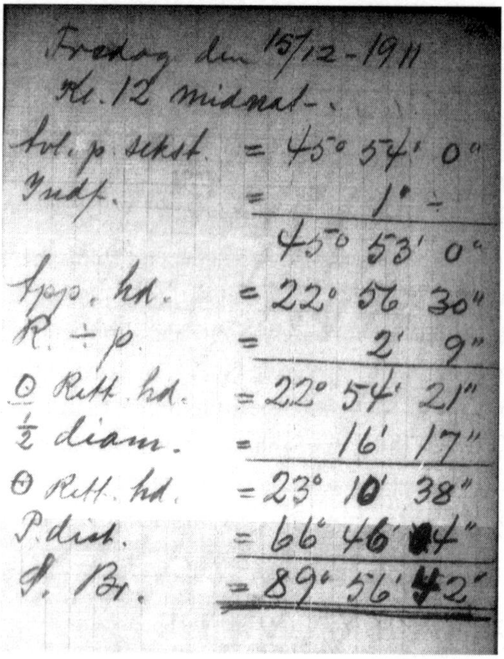

Figure 20 Amundsen's first observation on reaching the South Pole, at midnight on 15th December 1911. Under the Midnight Sun, with the orb circling the horizon, a meridian sight for latitude can be taken at midday or midnight. Amundsen was about 3 miles from the mathematical point.

– National Library of Norway

Bjaaland

Friday 15 Dec. 90° We reached the South Pole at 2.30 today, tired and hungry, thank God we have enough food for the return journey. So now we have attained the goal of our desires, and the great thing is that we are here as the first men, no English flag is flying, but a three-coloured Norwegian. Unfortunately the weather was such that we only had a bad observation. We have now eaten our fill of what we can manage; seal steak, and biscuits and pemmican and chocolate. Yes, if only you knew *Mother*, and Saamund and Torne and Svein and Helga and Hans, that now I'm sitting here at the South Pole and writing, you'd celebrate for me. Here it's as flat as the lake at Morgedal and the skiing is good. The Captain photographed us under the flag. Everyone was together when we planted the flag, which is flying so that the silk cloth is tearing. –21 –23 –21 Have travelled 735 nautical miles from Framheim. ca. 1400 km.

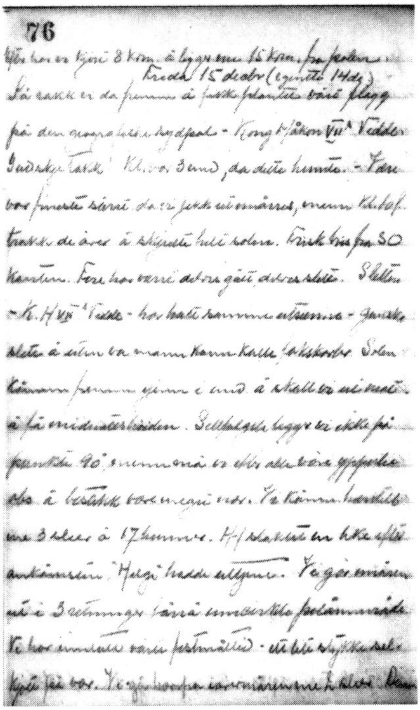

76

Fredag 15 decbr (egentlig 14de)

Figure 21 Amundsen's diary on reaching the South Pole, 15/14 December 1911. The entry begins 'So we arrived, and were able to raise our flag at the geographical South Pole.'

– National Library of Norway

Scott

Friday, Dec. 15th. Camp 37. Height about 2500. Lat. about 84° 8'. Got away at 8; marched till one; the surface improving and snow covering thinner over the blue ice, but the sky overcast and glooming, the clouds ever coming lower, and Evans' is now decidedly the slowest unit, though Bowers' is not much faster. We keep up and overhaul either without difficulty. It was an enormous relief yesterday to get steady going without involuntary stops, but yesterday and this morning, once the sledge was stopped, it was very difficult to start again – the runners got temporarily stuck.

This afternoon for the first time we could start by giving one good heave together, and so for the first time we are able to stop to readjust footgear or do any other desirable task. This is a second relief for which we are most grateful.

At the lunch camp the snow covering was less than a foot, and at this it is a bare nine inches; patches of ice and hard neve are showing through in places.

I meant to camp at 6.30, but before 5.0 the sky came down on us with falling snow. We could see nothing, and the pulling grew very heavy. At 5.45 there seemed nothing to do but camp – another interrupted march. Our luck is really very bad. We should have done a good march to-day, as it is we have covered about 11 miles (stat.).

Since supper there are signs of clearing again, but I don't like the look of things; this weather has been working up from the S.E. with all the symptoms of our pony-wrecking storm. Pray heaven we are not going to have this wretched snow in the worst part of the glacier to come.

The lower part of this glacier is not very interesting, except from an ice point of view. Except Mount Kyffen, little bare rock is visible, and its structure at this distance is impossible to determine. There are no moraines on the surface of the glacier either. The tributary glaciers are very fine and have cut very deep courses, though they do not enter at grade. The walls of this valley are extraordinarily steep; we count them at least 60° in places. The ice-falls descending over the northern sides are almost continuous one with another, but the southern steep faces are nearly bare; evidently the sun gets a good hold on them. There must be a good deal of melting and rock weathering, the talus heaps are considerable under the southern rock faces. Higher up the valley there is much more bare rock and stratification, which promises to be very interesting, but oh, for fine weather; surely we have had enough of this oppressive gloom.

Bjaaland's 'Here it's as flat as the lake at Morgedal and the skiing is good' is the ulti-mate historical sound bite. In a few words, he tells you all you need to know. Coming from Morgedal, with its skiing tradition, and, as a good Telemarking unimpressed by what he saw, he simply demythologized the Antarctic ice cap to his home terrain. Family was part of the process. The names that Bjaaland cites are those of his brother, sister, brother-in-law, sister and brother-in-law respectively.

When Bjaaland says that 'everyone was together when we planted the flag', he meant that all five, Amundsen, Hassel, Helmer Hanssen, Wisting and him-self, gripped the pole together in driving it into the snow. It was a symbolic act by Amundsen to show that as they had shared the risks, they should share the prize, and no one man claim it, be he the leader or not.

Scott was now trailing by 360 nautical miles. In other words, since the Englishman started, Amundsen had increased his lead by 160 miles. He had outstripped his rival. Victory was unarguable. Scott's every action now seems futile. Amundsen's work, how-ever, was only half done. He still had to get his men home safe and sound.

Scott meanwhile was gambling on an accident to Amundsen. It was his only hope. Scott admitted as much in a letter to Joseph Kinsey, his agent in New Zealand. Amundsen, wrote Scott, 'perhaps deserves his luck if he gets through – But he is not there yet!'[61]

SATURDAY, DECEMBER 16ᵀᴴ, 1911
Amundsen

Saturday 16 Decbr.

An extremely agitated day. We turned out at 12 midnight to take an altitude. We managed that alright. Calculations gave lat. 89°56'. That didn't seem too bad. At 2.30 a.m. Bj. W. and Hass. went off on ski to circle the pole. Bj. continued our original course NE by N, (comp.) while Hass. went off NW by W (comp.) and W. SE by E (comp.). They were to cover a distance of ca. 10 nautical miles. They each carried a post (spare sledge runner) with a black flag. A little bag was securely lashed to each post, containing directions to where our 'Polheim' was to be found. The weather was lovely. Calm – a little hazy. HH and I remained behind to take observations. Our intention was to take an observation every sixth hour. At 6 a.m. we took the first obs. after the midnight altitude. To my surprise this gave a much lower altitude than the above mentioned midnight altitude. During our march from 88° S. Lat., we had clearly deviated somewhat from our meridian. The fact was simply that since passing that latitude, we could not get a grip on the azimuth. Now it was a matter of finding which meridian we were on. We began taking hourly sights both with glass and mercury hor. Luckily the weather held, so we were able to get excellent sights. Glass and mercury agreed well. It was only between 5 and 5.30 p.m. – Framheim time – that we found our meridian. That showed that we had strayed over to the 123ʳᵈ meridian E of Gr. – not so odd at these latitudes where one cannot establish one's direction. The meridian sight gave 89°54' 38" S. lat. and a compass bearing gave the Pole's position NW ¼ W. It was an invaluable day, and well worth the trouble. We are now able to find the position of the pole with a fair degree of accuracy. At 10 p.m., the three returned, having accomplished their tasks. The weather has remained wonderful all day. The two sledges with which we will continue, are now quite ready, and the third, together with sledgemeter No.2 will remain here.

Helge, who was killed yesterday, was gulped down with gusto by his comrades. Tomorrow we will set off for the exact point of the Pole 5 ½ nautical miles from here. We now have food for us human beings for 18 days, for the dogs, 10. I think we will be all right back to our depot at 88°25', and from there to the depot at 'the Devil's Glacier'. It is quite interesting to see the sun wander round the heavens at so to speak the same altitude day and night. I think somehow that we are the first to see this curious sight.

Bjaaland

S. Pole **16 Dec.** −22. Cleared up to the most glorious sunny weather, so the observers ran about with their instruments to fix the position. Have gone a little westerly, 5 nautical miles. Today went 10 m. north with a flag, which I planted, Wisting went west, and Hassel east. Thank God I am quit the fuss and bother of my dogs. Wisting gets my sledge and four dogs, Hanssen the other two. Tomorrow we go hunting for the pole point, so it will have to be the day after tomorrow that we start for home. We have too little chocolate, so will have to go short, have enough pemmican. No English flag to be seen anywhere.

Scott

Saturday, Dec. 16th. Camp 38. A gloomy morning, clearing at noon and ending in a gloriously fine evening. Although constantly anxious in the morning, the light held good for travelling throughout the day, and we have covered 11 miles (stat.), altering the aspect of the glacier greatly. But the travelling has been very hard. We started at 7, lunched at 12.15, and marched on till 6.30 – over 10 hours on the march – the limit of time to be squeezed into one day. We began on ski as usual, Evans' team hampering us a bit; the pulling very hard after yesterday's snowfall. In the afternoon we continued on ski till after two hours we struck a peculiarly difficult surface – old hard sastrugi underneath, with pits and high soft sastrugi due to very recent snowfalls. The sledges were so often brought up by this that we decided to take to our feet, and thus made better progress, but for the time with very excessive labour. The crust, brittle, held for a pace or two, then let one down with a bump some 8 or 10 inches. Now and again one's leg went down a crack in the hard ice underneath. We drew up a slope on this surface and discovered a long icefall extending right across our track, I presume the same pressure which caused Shackleton to turn towards the Cloudmaker. We made in for that mountain and soon got on hard, crevassed, undulating ice with quantities of soft snow in the hollows. The disturbance seems to increase, but the snow to diminish as we approach the rocks. We shall look for a moraine and try and follow it up to-morrow. The hills on our left have horizontally stratified rock alternating with snow. The exposed rock is very black; the brownish colour of the Cloudmaker has black horizontal streaks across it. The sides of the glacier north of the Cloudmaker have a curious cutting, the upper part less steep than the lower, suggestive of different conditions of glacier-flow in succeeding ages.

We must push on all we can, for we are now six days behind Shackleton, all due to that wretched storm. So far, since we got amongst the disturbances we have not seen such alarming crevasses as I had expected; certainly dogs could have come up as far as this. At present one gets terribly hot and perspiring on the march, and quickly cold when halted, but the sun makes up for all evils. It is very difficult to know what to do about the ski; their weight is considerable and yet under certain circumstances they are extraordinarily useful.

Everyone is very satisfied with our summit ration. The party which has been man-hauling for so long say they are far less hungry than they used to be. It is good to think that the majority will keep up this good feeding all through.

Amundsen's 'It is quite interesting to see the sun wander round the heavens at so to speak the same altitude day and night. I think somehow that we are the first to see this curious sight' is another classic of its kind. In lapidary fashion, he captures the essence of being at a Pole of the earth. More to the point, he shows – what he never said in public – that he does not believe that either Cook or Peary reached the North Pole. Therein lies a double irony. Amundsen originally wanted the North Pole. Anything more perverse than going south to the opposite Pole of the Earth, as he himself declared, could not be imagined. All the while, in secret, he believed that the other Pole was still waiting to be conquered.

Amundsen knew that his switch from north to south laid him open to accusations of falsifying his results. That was partly why he decided to stay at the Pole for a few days to fix its position as precisely as he could and make sure that he had reached the spot. It also explains why he risked the lives of Bjaaland, Hassel and Wisting by sending them out alone, with only a few biscuits for food, in order to box the Pole.

SUNDAY, DECEMBER 17TH, 1911
Amundsen

Saturday 17 Dec.
Another remarkable day. We struck camp this morning and set off for the Pole point. Bj.'s sledge was left behind, his six dogs divided between HH & W. and he himself appointed forerunner. I myself followed behind to see how he managed

to keep to the course. The weather was of the finest kind. A very light breeze from the W. −25°. Absolutely clear, and a burning sun high in the heavens. It was pure pleasure to see Bj. keep his course. He moved as if he had a marked line to follow. By 11 a.m. we had covered our 5½ nautical miles, stopped, and pitched our tent. At 11.30 a.m. my instruments were ready, and got to work. The time is now 8 p.m., and we have had the most peculiar results. From 11.30 a.m. to 1 p.m. the sun remained at 46°4'. Thereafter it rose to 46°6'50", and remained there right up to 4 p.m. Then it rose to 46°9'30" and has remained there since. At a longitude of 105° E of Greenwich, and after the last observations, we are lying at 89°58'20" S.lat. − HH and Bj have gone out in a continuation of this meridian to cover the remaining 1'40". They had pennants to mark the spot. We are going to take sights all night, as these results are rather odd. All in all, we must consider this place as the pole. We will pitch our little tent here tomorrow and leave the place and head N. Boiling gave an altitude of 11,000 ft. above sea level. So here we are at the South Pole − an enormous flat plain. Hardly an irregularity to be seen. The sun is moving round the horizon at practically the same height and shines and warms from a cloudless sky. It is calm this evening and so peaceful. All the dogs are lying stretched out in the heat of the sun and enjoying life despite the poor rations − apparently in good condition. It has been so clear today that we can see for many nautical miles around. We have all used the telescope industriously to see if there is any sign of life in any direction − but in vain. We are the first here all right.

Bjaaland

17 Dec. −21. From observations discovered that we were 5 m. W. Can thank the Captain and Hanssen and partly Wisting for this pinpointing of the Pole. Hassel shoots the sun incessantly. Today we had a good cigar which Fru Rambek sent me for Christmas. Today went out 2 m East with a pennant, Hanssen and I. Tomorrow we set off for our home on the Barrier. Thank God for that. All small items have been marked South Pole.

Scott

Sunday, Dec. 17th. Camp 39. Soon after starting we found ourselves in rather a mess; bad pressure ahead and long waves between us and the land. Blue ice showed on the crests of the waves; very soft snow lay in the hollows. We had to cross the waves in places 30 feet from crest to hollow, and we did it by sitting on

*Figure 22 Olav Bjaaland and dogs on reaching the South Pole. As he wrote in his diary,
'Here it's as flat as the lake at Morgedal and the skiing is good.' Note the dog in the
background giving his opinion of the proceedings. The photographer surely angled
the shot with intent.*

– National Library of Norway

the sledge and letting her go. Thus we went down with a rush and our impetus
carried us some way up the other side; then followed a fearfully tough drag to
rise the next crest. After two hours of this I saw a larger wave, the crest of which
continued hard ice up the glacier; we reached this and got excellent travelling
for 2 miles on it, then rose on a steep gradient, and so topped the pressure ridge.
The smooth ice is again lost and we have patches of hard and soft snow with
ice peeping out in places, cracks in all directions, and legs very frequently down.
We have done very nearly 5 miles (geo.).

Evening. Temp. –12°. Height about 3500 above Barrier. After lunch decided
to take the risk of sticking to the centre of the glacier, with good result. We travelled on up the more or less rounded ridge which I had selected in the morning,
and camped at 6.30 with 12½ Stat. miles made good. This has put Mount Hope
in the background and shows us more of the upper reaches. *– as we advance
we see that there is great & increasing error in the charting of the various points.
Shackletons watch must have greatly altered its rate which throws everything out
including his variation – If we can keep up this pace, we gain on him,* and I don't

see any reason why we shouldn't, except that more pressure is showing up ahead. For once one can say 'Sufficient for the day is the good thereof.' Our luck may be on the turn – I think we deserve it. In spite of the hard work everyone is very fit and very cheerful, feeling well fed and eager for more toil. Eyes are much better except poor Wilson's; he has caught a very bad attack. Remembering his trouble on our last Southern journey, I fear he is in for a very bad time.

We got fearfully hot this morning and marched in singlets, which became wringing wet; thus uncovered the sun gets at one's skin, and then the wind, which makes it horribly uncomfortable.

Our lips are very sore. We cover them with the soft silk plaster which seems about the best thing for the purpose.

I'm inclined to think that the summit trouble will be mostly due to the chill falling on sunburned skins. Even now one feels the cold strike directly one stops. We get fearfully thirsty and chip up ice on the march, as well as drinking a great deal of water on halting. Our fuel only just does it, but that is all we want, and we have a bit in hand for the summit.

The pulling this afternoon was fairly pleasant; at first over hard snow, and then on to pretty rough ice with surface snowfield cracks, bad for sledges, but ours promised to come through well. We have worn our crampons all day and are delighted with them. P.O. Evans, the inventor of both crampons and ski shoes, is greatly pleased, and certainly we owe him much. The weather is beginning to look dirty again, snow clouds rolling in from the east as usual. I believe it will be overcast to-morrow.

Making Bjaaland the forerunner of this singular procession was deliberately an honour. Amundsen wanted him to be first at the Pole out of respect for a great skier and also because he personified the reason for victory. The fight for the South Pole had turned out to be a ski race in the end. Bjaaland was the hero of this saga.

After Bjaaland came Hassel, followed by Helmer Hanssen's leader dog, the third living creature at the mythic point of 90° S. That too was as it should be. Skis and dogs had together brought triumph. Amundsen deliberately came last, to show how much he owed his companions and their dogs.

Even now, Amundsen could not be certain that he had found the exact point. All four navigators, Hassel, Helmer Hanssen, Wisting and Amundsen himself now began a series of observations round the clock. They countersigned each other's navigation books. Amundsen could hardly do more to satisfy carping critics on his return.

Bjaaland did not smoke himself. He had brought the cigars as a gift for his companions at the Pole.

Scott's 'ski shoes' were a misnomer. In reality they were improvised bindings. It was one more addition to his technical inferiority. Lacking Amundsen's stable ski boots for low temperatures, Scott resorted to finnesko. These were too soft for the fixed ears and tensioned heelstraps of the Huitfeldt-Høyer-Ellefsen binding, which, like Amundsen, he also used. So Scott adopted a kind of overshoe made of stiff canvas, into which the finneskoe was strapped, the whole assembly then being clipped into the Huitfeldt binding. To call P.O. Evans their 'inventor' was taking Scott's obvious favouritism too far. Evans had made the bindings to a design by Tryggve Gran. It was the best Gran could do, with the materials at hand. Still it was an improvisation. The binding wobbled sideways, wasting energy and straining muscles, with a fateful loss of speed and distance in the end.

MONDAY, DECEMBER 18ᵀᴴ, 1911

Amundsen

Monday 18 Dec.

Well now we are finished here, we have done what we can. We have taken a series of observations every hour right round the clock. It is very difficult to arrive at a definitive result. But we can say with certainty that we are south of 89°59'. We have boxed the remaining few seconds of arc. I think our observations will be of great interest for the experts. We started our observations here yesterday at 12 noon Fr. time and finished them today at 12 noon (Fr. time) – We leave here this evening at 7 o'clock and henceforth we will use the night to travel so that we have the sun behind us. We have pitched the little tent[62] and the Norwegian flag with the '*Fram* pennant' beneath it flying from the top of the tent pole. Several things have been deposited in the tent: my sextant with artificial glass horizon, a hypsometer, three reindeer fur foot bags, some kamikks and mittens, and also a few miscellaneous items. I have left a folder with a letter to the King and a few words to Scott, who I must assume will be the first to visit the place after us. We have fixed a plate on which we have all written our names. – And so farewell dear Pole – we won't meet again.

Bjaaland

18 Dec. –22 Thank God we started homewards at 8 o'clock this evening, we will now travel at night. A mass of observations have been made, and the Pole fixed, and the Norwegian Polheim has been pitched with gear and instruments.

700 miles will be quite tough, but I'll manage. We have had the most wonderful weather here at the Pole, so we could see for miles around.

Scott

Monday, Dec. 18th. Camp 40. Lunch nearly 4000 feet above Barrier. Overcast and snowing this morning as I expected, land showing on starboard hand, so, though it was gloomy and depressing, we could march, and did. We have done our 8 stat. miles between 8.20 and 1 p.m.; at first fairly good surface; then the ice got very rugged with sword-cut splits. We got on a slope, which made matters worse. I then pulled up to the left, at first without much improvement, but as we topped a rise the surface got much better and things look quite promising for the moment. On our right we have now a pretty good view of the Adams Marshall and Wild Mountains and their very curious horizontal stratification. Wright has found, amongst bits of wind-blown debris, an undoubted bit of sandstone and a bit of black basalt. We must get to know more of the geology before leaving the glacier finally. This morning all our gear was fringed with ice crystals which looked very pretty.

Afternoon. Night camp No.40, about 4500 above Barrier. T. –11°. Lat. about 84 34. After lunch got on some very rough stuff within a few hundred yards of pressure ridge. There seemed no alternative, and we went through with it. Later, the glacier opened out into a broad basin with irregular undulations, and we got on to a better surface, but later on again this improvement nearly vanished, so that it has been hard going all day, but we have done a good mileage (over 14 stat.). We are less than five days behind S. now. There was a promise of clearance about noon, but later more snow clouds drifted over from the east, and now it is snowing again. We have scarcely caught a glimpse of the eastern side of the glacier all day. The western side has not been clear enough to photograph at the halts. It is very annoying, but I suppose we must be thankful when we can get our marches off. Still sweating horribly on the march and very thirsty at the halts.

By '700 miles will be quite tough', Bjaaland meant that he had been made forerunner for the whole way back. This was a doubtful honour to a Nordic competition skier like himself. He wanted to be at the back of the field, where the best racers were, so that they could judge those who had started before, and knew how to cope with the opposition. Skiing first meant the physical and mental burden of opening the track and dealing with the unknown. Amundsen, however, reckoned that Bjaaland, as the best skier of them all, would raise their speed by constantly being out in front. Speed, and hence time, was of the essence. Amundsen wanted to be back at base before the autumn chill. More: he had to catch Fram *and then beat* Terra Nova *to the cablehead. Without satellite links, internet, webcams, or even simple radio, the cable was the only way of making contact with the outside world. This was the old-fashioned race within a race, Amundsen knew that it was not enough to be first at the Pole; he had to be first with the news as well.*

TUESDAY, DECEMBER 19TH, 1911
Amundsen

Tuesday 19 Dec.
We set off yesterday evening at 7.30 after having said farewell to our dear little Polheim. We saluted our flag and then we were off. It was so clear, and the visibility so good that we were able to see the upended sledge at the other camp site – 5½ nautical miles away. We set a course there, and after two hours we were there. The skiing was brilliant, the weather splendid – −19°, clear and a mild, summer-like wind from our last host – the Pole. We have been uncomfortably warm – everyone is warm today. It is also unusual for us to have the wind behind us. We have always had it in our snouts. In Bj. we have a forerunner beyond compare. He can see like nobody else, and move like nobody else. Thus he has been able to follow our old tracks northwards all day, although they are very indistinct. The small cairns we erected every other nautical mile turned out to be invaluable. They light up like small beacons and I believe – as long as the weather holds, that with their help, we will easily find our way back to our depot. Wonderful weather. The sun is still just as high, it is still warming just as well night and day.

Bjaaland

19th **Tuesday.** We have got away in the most wonderful weather one could possibly wish for. −19 must be said to be fine at the South Pole. The dogs, poor devils, have not been overfed at the Pole, yet they are quick and lively. We covered 15.6 nautical miles in 7 hours. The first evening we arrived, they had their ration, the second day they had their companion Helga from Hanssen's team, which went down, hide and hair. Third day their ration, but then nothing the 18th before the small hours on the 19th after a march of 15 m. Started from the Pole with two sledges and 16 dogs, of which 2–3 are finished. I am now roaming ahead and looking for our old tracks. The cairns are shining brightly in the sun, so we see them 2 miles off.

Scott

Tuesday, Dec. 19th. Lunch, rise 650. Dist. 8½ geo. Camp 41. Things are looking up. Started on good surface, soon came to very annoying criss-cross cracks. I fell into two and have bad bruises on knee and thigh, but we got along all the time until we reached an admirable smooth ice surface excellent for travelling. The last mile, neve predominating and therefore the pulling a trifle harder, we have risen into the upper basin of the glacier. Seemingly close about us are the various land masses which adjoin the summit: it looks as though we might have difficulties in the last narrows, *the charting of which is evidently much out*. We are having a long lunch hour for angles, photographs, and sketches. The slight south-westerly wind came down the glacier as we started, and the sky, which was overcast, has rapidly cleared in consequence.

Night. Height about 5800. Camp 41. We stepped off this afternoon at the rate of two miles or more an hour, with the very satisfactory result of 17 (stat.) miles to the good for the day. It has not been a strain, except perhaps for me with my wounds received early in the day. The wind has kept us cool on the march, which has in consequence been very much pleasanter; we are not wet in our clothes tonight, and have not suffered from the same overpowering thirst as on previous days. T. +11. Min. +5. Evans and Bowers are busy taking angles; as they have been all day, we shall have material for an excellent chart. Days like this put heart in one.

WEDNESDAY, DECEMBER 20TH, 1911

Amundsen

Wednesday 20 Dec.
Same magnificently beautiful weather. Almost calm and partly clear. We have done our regulation 15 nautical miles. Put 'Lasse' down this evening. He was one of our best dogs, but wore himself out. He was divided into 15 parts. The others are now like mad creatures after dog meat. The skiing has been particularly good. We have followed our tracks all day. The ski tracks prove to have lasted best. We can see from cairn to cairn, although they are only ca. 3 ft. high.

Bjaaland

20th −24.3° −21.2°. Calm and fine 15 miles. The Captain's favourite dog Lasse gave his life for the sake of his companions, who devoured him hair and hide.

Scott

Wednesday, Dec. 20th. Camp 42. 6500 ft. about Lat. 84.59.6. Just got off our best half march – 10 miles 1150 yards (geo.), over 12 miles stat. With an afternoon to follow we should do well to-day; the wind has been coming up the valley. Turning this book. seems to have brought luck. We marched on till nearly 7 o'clock after a long lunch halt, and covered 19½ geo. miles, nearly 23 (stat.), rising 800 feet. This morning we came over a considerable extent of hard snow, then got to hard ice with patches of snow: a state of affairs which has continued all day. Pulling the sledges in crampons is no difficulty at all. At lunch Wilson and Bowers walked back 2 miles or so to try and find Bowers' broken sledgemeter, without result. During their absence a fog spread about us, carried up the valleys by easterly wind. We started the afternoon march in this fog very unpleasantly, but later it gradually drifted, and to-night it is very fine and warm. As the fog lifted we saw a huge line of pressure ahead; I steered for a place where the slope looked smoother, and we are camped beneath the spot to-night. We must be ahead of Shackleton's position on the 17th *but his latitudes are out by 7 miles or so.* All day we have been admiring a wonderful banded structure of the rock; to-night it is beautifully clear on Mount Darwin.

I have just told off the people to return to-morrow night: Atkinson, Wright, Cherry-Garrard, and Keohane. All are disappointed – poor Wright rather bitterly, I fear. I dreaded this necessity of choosing – nothing could be more heartrending. I calculated our programme to start from 85° 10' with 12 units of food and eight men. We ought to be in this position to-morrow night, less one day's food. After all our harassing trouble one cannot but be satisfied with such a prospect.

'Turning this book seems to have brought luck' – Scott wrote on one side of each page. On reaching the end of the volume, he turned it around, to continue writing on the blank, reverse sides, back to front, as it were. He made that switch on this day, hence the remark.

THURSDAY, DECEMBER 21ST, 1911

Amundsen

Thursday 21 Dec.
Started in bad weather. Breeze from the SE quarter. Could not follow our tracks. Luckily it soon cleared up. It became dead calm. Easily found the first cairn. Have had the loveliest weather since then. Calm, with burning sun, so that we have to go bare headed and in shirt sleeves. That is something at 89° S. Lat. and 11,000 ft. above sea level. One of W's dogs, 'Per' gave up today[63] and had to be put down. He was a splendid dog, but has worn himself out. Now we start around 8 o'clock in the evening, and have done our 15 nautical miles by 3 in the morning. It is boiling hot in the tent now. The sun shines on. Can't remember the day when rime frost formed inside. Skiing splendid. The plain even and rising gently towards N. We have now made ourselves as light as possible. Abandoned our inner sleeping bags (at the Pole) and everything else superfluous. Our last paraffin can (17 l) has lasted from 26 Nov. until today, 21 Dec. – Cooking for five men.

Bjaaland

21 December –24 –24.2 –24.2. SE wind, hazy over the horizon, cleared around 8.30 to the most wonderful weather. Per, from Wisting's team, couldn't manage any more, and received an axe blow to the head with pleasure as reward. The Chief raised the pemmican ration from 3½ to 4 portions. God bless him for that. Now I'm so full and satisfied, I can't express it in words.

Scott

Thursday, Dec. 21ˢᵗ. Camp 43. Lat. 85 7. Long. 163° 4'. Height about 8000 feet. Upper Glacier Depôt. Temp. –2. We climbed the ice slope this morning and found a very bad surface on top, as far as crevasses were concerned. We all had falls into them, Atkinson and Teddy Evans going down the length of their harness. Evans had rather a shake up. The rotten ice surface continued for a long way, though I crossed to and fro towards the land, trying to get on better ground.

At 12 the wind came from the north, bringing the inevitable fog up the valley and covering us just as we were in the worst of places. We camped for lunch, and

Figure 23 Iconic snapshot of the Norwegians at the South Pole, 15/14 December 1911. (l. to r.) Wisting, Helmer Hanssen, Hassel, Amundsen.

– National Library of Norway

were obliged to wait two-and-a-half hours for a clearance. Then the sun began to struggle through and we were off. We soon got out of the worst crevasses and on to a long snow slope leading on part of Mount Darwin. It was a very long stiff pull up, and I held on till 7.30, when, the other team being some way astern, I camped. We have done a good march, risen to a satisfactory altitude, and reached a good place for our depôt. To-morrow we start with our fullest summit load, and the first march should show us the possibilities of our achievement. The temperature has dropped below zero, but to-night it is so calm and bright that one feels delightfully warm and comfortable in the tent. Such weather helps greatly in all the sorting arrangements, &c., which are going on to-night. For me it is an immense relief to have the indefatigable little Bowers to see to all detail arrangements of this sort.

We have risen to a great height to-day and I hope it will not be necessary to go down again, but it looks as though we must dip a bit even to go to the S.W.

FRIDAY, DECEMBER 22ND, 1911

Amundsen

Friday 22 Dec.
Wonderful, lovely weather right up until midnight. Calm, clear and burning hot – although the T. was –25°. But then bitterly cold, damp air blew up from NE with fine snowfall. The sun, however, was too strong to be fooled. It ripped off the dirty cloth and is shining again in all its usual glory. We did our usual 15 nautical miles by 3 a.m. Have followed our tracks and cairns the whole way. The dogs had extra feed today – besides their pemmican, they have also had 'Per'. Yesterday I also increased our own pemmican ration to 400 g per man.

Bjaaland

22 Dec. Friday. –24 –25.5 Pure summer today. Absolutely calm, sunshine, tracks indistinct but cairns gleaming like electric beacons. The dogs received Per as an extra feed this evening, which they accepted with delight. 15 nautical miles. 55 m. from the Pole.

Scott

Vol. II Starting with Summit Journey Ages: 43 Self, 39 Wilson, 37 Evans, 32 Oates, 28 Bowers. Average 36.

Friday, Dec. 22nd.
Camp 44, about 7100 feet. T. –1°. Bar. 22.3. This, the third stage of our journey, is opening with good promise. We made our depôt this morning, then said an affecting farewell to the returning party, who have taken things very well, dear good fellows as they are.

Then we started with our heavy loads about 9.20, I in some trepidation – quickly dissipated as we went off and up a slope at a smart pace. The second sledge came close behind us, showing that we have weeded the weak spots and made the proper choice for the returning party.

We came along very easily and lunched at 1, when the sledgemeter had to be repaired, and we didn't get off again till 3.20, camping at 6.45. Thus with 7 hours' marching we covered 10½ miles (geo.) (12 stat.).

Obs.: Lat. 85° 13½'; Long. 161°55'; Var. 175°46' E.

To-morrow we march longer hours, about 9 I hope. Every day the loads will lighten, and so we ought to make the requisite progress. I think we have climbed about 250 feet to-day, but thought it more on the march. We look down on huge pressure ridges to the south and S.E., and in fact all round except in the direct on in which we go, S.W. We seem to be travelling more or less parallel to a ridge which extends from Mt Darwin. Ahead of us to-night is a stiffish incline and it looks as though there might be pressure behind it. It is very difficult to judge how matters stand, however, in such a confusion of elevations and depressions. This course doesn't work wonders in change of latitude, but I think it is the right track to clear the pressures – at any rate I shall hold it for the present.

We passed one or two very broad (30 feet) bridged crevasses with the usual gaping sides; they were running pretty well in N. and S. direction. The weather has been beautifully fine all day as it was last night. (Night Temp. –9°.) This morning there was an hour or so of haze due to clouds from the N. Now it is perfectly clear, and we get a fine view of the mountain behind which Wilson has just been sketching

Scott has just reached the headwaters of the Beardmore Glacier, and is emerging on to the polar plateau. It has taken him 12 days to do what Amundsen did in four on the more violent contours of the Axel Heiberg Glacier.

SATURDAY, DECEMBER 23ᴿᴰ, 1911
Amundsen

Saturday 23 Dec.

Bitter this morning. SE'ly breeze and biting cold. Almost overcast. Very difficult to see the terrain. Bj. therefore soon lost our tracks. Luckily it eased and cleared up. We were heading directly for one of our cairns. The sledgemeters agreed precisely with the distances run between each cairn. A little snowfall made the skiing bad. It was sticky in some places so that one could scarcely move the skis forward. In some places, however, they did slide. At midnight it was –27°. After midnight the weather cleared more and more, and now at 3 a.m., it is almost wholly clear and calm. Lovely weather. It is now 26 nautical miles to the depot.

Bjaaland

23 Dec. −24 −27 −26 SE'ly wind light mist above the horizon. Tracks horribly indistinct so one could hardly follow them. 15 m. Travel around 7 hours. The extra that I had for dinner seems to have had an effect. Now have two meals a day, and am satisfied.

Scott

Saturday, Dec. 23rd. Lunch. Bar. 22.01. Rise 370 ? Started at 8, steering S.W. Seemed to be rising, and went on well for about 3 hours, then got amongst bad crevasses and hard waves. We pushed on to S.W., but things went from bad to worse, and we had to haul out to the north, then west. West looks clear for the present, but it is not a very satisfactory direction. We have done 8½ (geo.), a good march. T. −3°. Southerly wind, force 2. The comfort is that we are rising. On one slope we got a good view of the land and the pressure ridges to the S.E. They seem to be disposed 'en echelon' and gave me the idea of shearing cracks. They seemed to lessen as we ascend. It is rather trying having to march so far to the west, but if we keep rising we must come to the end of the obstacles some time.

Sat. night. Camp 45. T. −3°. Bar. 21.61. ? Rise. Height about 7750. Great vicissitudes of fortune in the afternoon march. Started west up a slope – about the fifth we have mounted in the last two days. On top, another pressure appeared on the left, but less lofty and more snow-covered than that which had troubled us in the morning. There was temptation to try it, and I had been gradually turning in its direction. But I stuck to my principle and turned west up yet another slope. On top of this we got on the most extraordinary surface – narrow crevasses ran in all directions. They were quite invisible, being covered with a thin crust of hardened névé without a sign of a crack in it. We all fell in one after another and. sometimes two together. We have had many unexpected falls before, but usually through being unable to mark the run of the surface appearances of cracks, or where such cracks are covered with soft snow. How a hardened crust can form over a crack is a real puzzle – it seems to argue extremely slow movement.

DR, 85° 22'16" S., 159° 31' E.

In the broader crevasses this morning we noticed that it was the lower edge of the bridge which was rotten, whereas in all in the glacier the upper edge was open.

Near the narrow crevasses this afternoon we got about 10 minutes on snow which had a hard crust and loose crystals below. It was like breaking through a glass house at each step, but quite suddenly at 5 p.m. everything changed. The hard surface gave place to regular sastrugi and our horizon levelled in every direction. I hung on to the S.W. till 6 p.m., and then camped with a delightful feeling of security that we had at length reached the summit proper. I am feeling very cheerful about every-thing to-night. We marched 15 miles (geo.) (over 17 stat.) to-day, mounting nearly 800 feet and all in about 8½ hours.

My determination to keep mounting irrespective of course is fully justified and I shall be indeed surprised if we have any further difficulties with crevasses or steep slopes. To me for the first time our goal seems really in sight. We can pull our loads and pull them much faster and farther than I expected in my most hopeful moments. I only pray for a fair share of good weather. There is a cold wind now as expected, but with good clothes and well fed as we are, we can stick a lot worse than we are getting. I trust this may prove the turning-point in our fortunes for which we have waited so patiently.

SUNDAY, DECEMBER 24TH, 1911

Amundsen

Sunday 24 Dec.
Wonderful weather when we set off this evening at 7.30. Absolutely calm and burning sunshine. 5 minutes later, and it was partly overcast. Stratus – the changes that happen so often here on K.H. VII *Vidda*. Around midnight it was almost completely clear again. Light breeze from S. During the night, the skiing has been rather better. Today, for the first time since leaving the Pole, we have found a proper camp site – hard enough. Hitherto, the snow has been too loose. The strongest wind we have recorded on this plateau has been 8 m – and then only once. It has consistently been between 2–4 m. Everlasting good weather surely reigns here. 'Svartflekken' put down this evening. It didn't want to do any more, although it did not seem too bad. Bad character. As a human being, would have begun in a reformatory to end in prison – The snow is now beginning to be firmer, and the dogs are working better. Our usual 15 nautical miles during the night in 7 hours.

Bjaaland

Christmas Eve –23 –26 –25 Today has been fine-fine, the finest we have had for ever so long, my skis were gliding well. It was vilely difficult to find the tracks the first 2–3 nautical miles, but then it brightened to the loveliest sunny weather. 15 m. 7 hours' march. Framheim's real Christmas Eve 88°25'.

Scott

Sunday, Dec. 24ᵗʰ. Lunch. Bar. 21.48. Rise ? 160 feet. Xmas Eve. 7½ miles geo. due south, and a rise, I think, more than shown by barometer. This in five hours, on the surface which ought to be a sample of what we shall have in the future. With our present clothes it is a fairly heavy plod, but we get over the ground, which is a great thing. A high pressure ridge has appeared on the 'port bow.' It seems isolated, but I shall be glad to lose sight of such disturbances. The wind is continuous from the S.S.E., very searching. We are now marching in our wind blouses and with somewhat more protection on the head.

21.41. Camp 46. Rise for day? about 250 ft. or 300 ft. Hypsometer, 8000 ft.

The first two hours of the afternoon march went very well. Then the sledges hung a bit, and we plodded on and covered something over 14 miles (geo.) in the day. We lost sight of the big pressure ridge, but to-night another smaller one shows fine on the 'port bow,' and the surface is alternately very hard and fairly soft; dips and rises all round. It is evident we are skirting more disturbances, and I sincerely hope it will not mean altering course more to the west. 14 miles in 4 hours is not so bad considering the circumstances. The southerly wind is continuous and not at all pleasant in camp, but on the march it keeps us cool. T .–3°. The only inconvenience is the extent to which our faces get iced up. The temperature hovers about zero.

We have not struck a crevasse all day, which is a good sign. The sun continues to shine in a cloudless sky, the wind rises and falls, and about us is a scene of the wildest desolation, but we are a very cheerful party and to-morrow is Christmas Day, with something extra in the hoosh.

MONDAY, DECEMBER 25ᵀᴴ, 1911

Amundsen

Monday 25 Dec.
Light S'ly breeze. Partly clear, partly overcast – changing quickly. We followed tracks and cairns the whole way, and at 12 midnight reached our depot at 88°25' in good form. All honour to Bj. for the way he has managed his post as fore-runner. HH is possibly a mite better – he is more accustomed – but could not have managed to drive the dogs and follow the tracks simultaneously – they are too faint for that. Lovely and clear now towards morning – the finest Christmas Eve weather. Well now you are lighting the candles at home. We are together with you, even if the distance is great. But wait a little – after not too long, you

will have us back again, and then with victory in our hands. We celebrate our Christmas this evening. In reality it is the 24th, although we must write the 25th. There is not much we can do to mark the day. A little extra pudding of Sætre biscuits is all. It will be served at 8 o'clock in the morning, and everyone is longing for it. It is quite odd. After all we are on full rations, but nonetheless we accept everything extra with pleasure. – The boys are out now packing the depot on the sledges, while I lie alone inside writing. The primus is roaring in honour of the day, something we otherwise never allow. On leaving here, we have food for ourselves and the dogs for 12 days. We reckon on 8 days to the depot at 86°21', so we are well supplied. I am now putting aside a sample of each of our articles of food that has been at the Pole. Presumably the suppliers will appreciate it. One bag of milk (dried milk), one slab of chocolate, six biscuits in a little box – another sign of the day's festivity is that three of us are smoking cigars. In fact Bj. had brought a holder with 8 cigars all the way from home. He surprised us with these at the Pole. We each received one. I also had one, so we set off with the three remaining cigars. We are smoking them now today. There was no smoking in the tent until arrival at the Pole. However I was the only one who had a pipe. But the others were not without resource. Our ski sticks are of bamboo, but they are too long. Pipes were made out of the superfluous pieces. W. had English plug tobacco, so now we have a little smoke morning and evening. We have been climbing gradually every day until now, and according to our previous observations should now be at an altitude of 10,750 ft. This altitude will continue for a few days more towards N., and then start to fall. I am looking forward to get down again from these altitudes. Not infrequently I feel tightness in my chest, and have to divide my breathing into several stages.

Bjaaland

25 Dec. –25 –27. Well now it's the South Pole Christmas Eve, and we're celebrating it at 88°25'. W. and Hanssen are busy with the Christmas gruel. We have had wonderful skiing today. We found the depot in order, and now we have food for 12 days for people and dogs. Ah how are you doing Mother, hope you are well and enjoying life, will soon be seeing you. If only I could travel with 7 league boots oh mother of mine, and sit a tiny little moment with you. Now we are 100 m. from the Pole and 600 m. from Framheim. It will be a long hard yomp.[64]

Scott

Monday, Dec. 25th, XMAS. Lunch. Bar.21.14. Rise 240 feet. The wind was strong last night and this morning; a light snowfall in the night; a good deal of drift, subsiding when we started, but still about a foot high. I thought it might have spoilt the surface, but for the first hour and a half we went along in fine style. Then we started up a rise, and to our annoyance found ourselves amongst crevasses once more – very hard, smooth neve between high ridges at the edge of crevasses, and therefore very difficult to get foothold to pull the sledges. Got our ski sticks out, which improved matters, but we had to tack a good deal and several of us went half down. After half an hour of this I looked round and found the second sledge halted some way in rear-evidently someone had gone into a crevasse. We saw the rescue work going on, but had to wait half an hour for the party to come up, and got mighty cold. It appears that Lashly went down very suddenly, nearly dragging the crew with him. The sledge ran on and jammed the span so that the Alpine rope had to be got out and used to pull Lashly to the surface again. Lashly says the crevasse was 50 feet deep and 8 feet across, in form U, showing that the word 'unfathomable' can rarely be applied. Lashly is 44 to-day and as hard as nails. His fall has not even disturbed his equanimity.

After topping the crevasse ridge we got on a better surface and came along fairly well, completing over 7 miles (geo.) just before I o'clock. We have risen nearly 250 feet this morning; the wind was strong and therefore trying, mainly because it held the sledge; it is a little lighter now.

Night. Camp No.47. Bar. 21.18. T. –7°. I am so replete that I can scarcely write. After sundry luxuries, such as chocolate and raisins at lunch, we started off well, but soon got amongst crevasses, huge snowfields roadways running almost in our direction, and across hidden cracks into which we frequently fell. Passing for two miles or so along between two roadways, we came on a huge pit with raised sides. Is this a submerged mountain peak or a swirl in the stream? Getting clear of crevasses and on a slightly down grade, we came along at a swinging pace – splendid. I marched on till nearly 7.30, when we had covered 15 miles (geo.) (17¼ Stat.). I knew that supper was to be a 'tightener' and indeed it has been – so much that I must leave description till the morning.

DR Lat. 85° 5°" S.; Long. 159° 8'2" E. Bar. 21.22.

Towards the end of the march we seemed to get into better condition; about us the surface rises and falls on the long slopes of vast mounds or undulations-no very definite system in their disposition. We camped half-way up a long slope.

In the middle of the afternoon we got another fine view of the land. The

Dominion Range ends abruptly as observed, then come two straits and two other masses of land. Similarly north of the wild mountains is another strait and another mass of land. The various straits are undoubtedly overflows, and the masses of land mark the inner fringe of the exposed coastal mountains, the general direction of which seems about S.S.E., from which it appears that one could be much closer to the Pole on the Barrier by continuing on it to the S.S.E. We ought to know more of this when Evans' observations are plotted.

I must write a word of our supper last night. We had four courses. The first, pemmican, full whack, with slices of horse meat flavoured with onion and curry powder and thickened with biscuit; then an arrowroot, cocoa and biscuit hoosh sweetened; then a plum-pudding; then cocoa with raisins, and finally a dessert of caramels and ginger. After the feast it was difficult to move. Wilson and I couldn't finish our share of plum-pudding. We have all slept splendidly and feel thoroughly warm – such is the effect of full feeding.

In celebrating Christmas, Amundsen and Bjaaland are correcting the fault in their calendar, and dropping the extra day. This is important to them, since they celebrate Christmas Eve, and not Christmas Day as in England. Thus by a quirk, the British and Norwegian expeditions are observing Christmas on the same day for once.

TUESDAY, DECEMBER 26TH, 1911

Amundsen

Tuesday 26 Dec.
Breeze from SE quarter –26°. Brilliant skiing. Quite flat here on the plateau. Have done our 15 nautical miles in one go – without stopping. The doggies seemed to manage well. In our tent again 1.30 a.m. Sunshine, but quite bitter. Cold, raw air in N.–NE. Presumably the mountains are pressing and menacing.

Bjaaland

Christmas Day 26th Dec. –26 –26. SE wind, good skiing. 15 m. at a stretch without stopping. Followed the track for 12 m. then I lost it. Oh my old pals at home, how are you doing? You don't need to envy me yet. Here it looks as if it's going to be cold henceforth. I wish to God we were down on the Barrier, here it is hard to breathe, and the nights are bloody long. Now only eating two meals a day.

Scott

Tuesday, Dec. 26th. Lunch. Bar. 21.11. Four and three-quarter hours, 6¾ miles (geo.). Perhaps a little slow after plum-pudding, but I think we are getting on to the surface which is likely to continue the rest of the way. There are still mild differences of elevation, but generally speaking the plain is flattening out; no doubt we are rising slowly.

Camp 48. Bar. 21.02. The first two hours of the afternoon march went well; then we got on a rough rise and the sledge came badly. Camped at 6.30, sledge coming easier again at the end.

It seems astonishing to be disappointed with a march of 15 (stat.) miles, when I had contemplated doing little more than 10 with full loads.

We are on the 86th parallel. Obs.: 86° 2' S.; 160° 26' E. Var. 179,4 W. The temperature has been pretty consistent of late, –10 to –12 at night, –3° in the day. The wind has seemed milder to-day – it blows anywhere from S.E. to south. I had thought to have done with pressures, but to-night a crevassed slope appears on our right. We shall pass well clear of it, but there may be others. The undulating character of the plain causes a great variety of surface, owing, of course, to the varying angles at which the wind strikes the slopes. We were half an hour late starting this morning, which accounts for some loss of distance, though I should be content to keep up an average of 13' (geo.).

Bjaaland's apparent mistake in calling this Christmas Day, is in reality correcting the calendar, as explained above. The 'true' date would be 25 December.

WEDNESDAY, DECEMBER 27TH, 1911

Amundsen

Wednesday 27 Dec.
Wonderful weather. Light breeze from S. and crystal clear. Splendid skiing –27°. Just before midnight, passed 88° S. Lat. There it changed from absolutely smooth to small, hard sastrugi. The sun has clearly shone here for several days, and there were many smooth, shiny surfaces to see. The dogs particularly liked these conditions, and they charged ahead in full cry. At 88° we also raised land – ca. SW by ½ W. (Compass). It seems as if we will be more fortunate with the weather on the N. journey. Dried my sleeping bag on the sledge load today. The underside was full of rime.

Bjaaland

Wednesday 27 Dec. −25.3 −27 88°5' S. SE wind. Very good skiing, low drift 15 m. 6 hours travel. Sastrugi'd and smooth, old familiar mountains hove into view ahead and to the right today.

Scott

Wednesday, Dec. 27ᵗʰ. Lunch. 21.02, The wind light this morning and the pulling heavy. Everyone sweated, especially the second team, which had great difficulty in keeping up, We have been going up and down, the up grades very tiring, especially when we get amongst sastrugi which jerk the sledge about, but we have done 7¼ miles (geo.). A very bad accident this morning. Bowers broke the only hypsometer thermometer. We have nothing to check our two aneroids. *I am very much annoyed*

Night camp 49, 20.82. T. −6.3, We marched off well after lunch on a soft, snowy surface, then came to slippery hard sastrugi and kept a good pace; but I felt this meant something wrong, and on topping a short rise we were once more in the midst of crevasses and disturbances. For an hour it was dreadfully trying – had to pick a road, tumbled into crevasses, and got jerked about abominably. At the summit of the ridge we came into another 'pit' or 'whirl,' which seemed the centre of the trouble – ? is it a submerged mountain peak. During the last hour and a quarter we pulled out on to soft snow again and moved well. Camped at 6.45, having covered. 13 ⅓ miles (geo,), Steering the party is no light task. One cannot allow one's thoughts to wander as others do, and when, as this afternoon, one gets amongst disturbances, I find it is very worrying and tiring. I do trust we shall have no more of them. We have not lost sight of the sun since we came on the summit; we should get an extraordinary record of sunshine. It is monotonous work this; the sledge meter and theodolite govern the situation.

I start cooking again tomorrow morning.

The breaking of Scott's only hypsometer thermometer is one of those incidents that illuminate whole histories. A thermometer, being made of glass, is prone to breakage, especially at extremes of temperature. Taking only one hints at a touch of insouciance. Amundsen had four such thermometers. It is not known how many were broken, but there were enough to take all the necessary altitudes.

THURSDAY, DECEMBER 28TH, 1911

Amundsen

Thursday 28 Dec.
Same magnificent weather. Brilliant skiing. After 9 nautical miles, we entered a heavily sastrugi'd district. But now we are coping much better than going S'wards. Burning sunshine again, splendid going which puts the doggies in a good mood. They are running well, and the dogs really seem to be getting into form again. We lost our tracks immediately after 88°25'. Have crossed them several times today. We are still moving on the high plateau, but tomorrow we will descend quickly. Steadily approaching land. Sastrugi running N-S and NW-SE

Bjaaland

Grisesletta[65] **28 Dec.** −22 −22. Same weather as yesterday, without drift, skiing easy but stupid to do 15 m. without stopping. Asked the Captain for a little more pemmican,[66] and had ½ a ration extra. Southerly wind. The plain looks like a frozen sea. I start cooking again to-morrow morning.

Scott

Lunch, **Dec. 28th**. 20.77. We've had a troublesome day but have completed our 13 miles (geo.). My unit pulled away easy this morning and stretched out for two hours – the second unit made heavy weather. I changed with Evans and found the second sledge heavy – could keep up, but the team was not swinging with me as my own team swings. Then I changed P.O. Evans for Lashly.

Night T −6 20.66. We seemed to get on better, but at the moment the surface changed and we came up over a rise with hard sastrugi. At the top we camped for lunch. What was the difficulty? One theory was that some members of the second party were stale. Another that all was due to their bad stepping and want of swing; another that the sledge pulled heavy. In the afternoon we exchanged sledges, and at first went off well, but getting into soft snow, we found a terrible drag, the second party coming quite easily with our sledge. So the sledge is the cause of the trouble, and talking it out, I found that all is due to want of *seaman-like* care. The runners ran excellently, but the structure has been distorted by bad strapping, bad loading, etc. The party are not done, and I have told them plainly that they must wrestle with the trouble and get it right for themselves. There is no possible reason why they should not get along as easily as we do.

Obs.: 86°27' 2" S.; 161° 1'15" E.; 179° 33' E. 20.64.

FRIDAY, DECEMBER 29ᵀᴴ, 1911

Amundsen

Friday 29 Dec. Same lovely, lovely weather. Clear, with fresh breeze from SSE –25°. At first, the sastrugi'd terrain continued like yesterday. Fairly big sastrugi. W. had hoisted a sail on his sledge. With the fresh breeze and good going, it went like a dream, even although the sastrugi were quite big. With his sail, W. managed to keep up with HH. The doggies are howling with enthusiasm and pleasure. After some time – 3 hours – we got out of the big sastrugi, and since then have only had to deal with smaller ones. We have also caught sight of new land today. It is a mountain range that runs in a SE'ly direction – probably a continuation of F range. We got a bearing on the S'most peak from 87°35' S. Lat. of W by N. (compass). There is not much more that can be said about its appearance, since a bank of fog has constantly covered it. Did our 15 nautical miles in 5½ hours. Raised pemmican to 450 gm. per man. Left K.H VII Vidda this morning at 87°40' S. Lat – Have descended ca., 300 ft. today.

Bjaaland

Friday 29 –22 –25.3. Clear, sunshine with S. Easterly wind 5–6 m. Wisting set a mainsail today, and he said that he ski-jored all day. Partly bad sastrugi, sometimes dangerously slippery, have had land ahead to the right all day, came much closer. It is land that we didn't see on our way southwards, because then we were out in a gale every day. 15 m. today. 4½ pemmican went down in a trice. Incidentally I had the same amount today as before. We have a really clean cook, he licks the soup ladle after it has been used.

Scott

Friday, Dec. 29ᵗʰ. 20.52. Lunch. Height 9050 about. The worst surface we have struck, very heavy pulling; but we came 6½ miles (geo.). It will be a strain to keep up distances if we get surfaces like this. We seem to be steadily but slowly rising. The satisfactory thing is that the second party now keeps up, as the faults have been discovered; they were due partly to the rigid loading of the sledge and partly to the bad pacing.

Night camp 51. 20.49. T. –6°. Had another struggle this afternoon and only managed to get 12 miles (geo.). The very hard pulling has occurred on two rises. It appears that the loose snow is blown over the rises and rests in heaps on the north-facing slopes. It is these heaps that cause our worst troubles. The weather looks a little doubtful, a good deal of cirrus cloud in motion over us, radiating E. and W. The wind shifts from S.E. to S.S.W., rising and failing at intervals; it is annoying to the march as it retards the sledges, but it must help the surface, I think, and so hope for better things tomorrow. The marches are terribly mono-tonous. One's thoughts wander occasionally to pleasanter scenes and places, but the necessity to keep the course, or some hitch in the surface, quickly brings them back. There have been some hours of very steady plodding to-day; these are the best part of the business, they mean forgetfulness and advance.

SATURDAY, DECEMBER 30ᵀᴴ, 1911

Amundsen

Saturday 30 Dec.

A fresher breeze from a S'ly quarter. Fine and clear –20°. Fog obscured the land, but cleared during the course of the day. It is strange to see what we covered blind here the last time. We are now lying before an extraordinary, huge range (X range) not more than 10 nautical miles away. Many of its peaks reach up to 13 or 14,000 ft. Bearings of them from here at 87°10' S.Lat. are: S. peak W by ¼ N. N. peak SW by W ½ W. (Compass). Much bare land and much snow covered in this range also. I have no doubt now that a continuous mountain range from K.E. VII and Victoria Land runs in a SE'ly direction. Yesterday we could see the summits disappear around 88°S. lat. in the same direction. The terrain in which we are now, is a mixture of sastrugi and blue ice surfaces, and heavily undulating. We have descended 800 ft. today. It has gone like lightning. We skiers now have our work cut out to keep up with the sledges. The sledge drivers lean on the sledges, are pulled along, and have halcyon days. Did our 15 nautical miles today in 5 hours. Finished at 1 a.m. Fabulous weather.

Bjaaland

Saturday 30 Dec. 87°5' –20 –21. Stiff south easterly wind with drift all night. Today it has eased a little, but the skiing is as easy as it could possibly be. Had my work cut out to keep ahead of Helmer's dogs. Just as I thought they were well behind, I found them sticking their noses in front, just next to me. Five hours' march, 15.5 m. Are nearly abreast the newly discovered mountains 20 m. away, our old mountains in sight ahead to the right, partly awkward sastrugi.

Scott

Saturday, Dec. 30th. Lunch. Night camp 52 Bar. 20.36. Rise about 150. A very trying, tiring march, and only 11 miles (geo.) covered. Wind from the south to S.E., not quite so strong as usual; the usual clear sky.

We camped on a rise last night, and it was some time before we reached the top this morning. This took it out of us at the start and the second party dropped. I went on 6½ miles (when the second party was some way astern) and lunched. We came on in the afternoon, the other party still dropping, camped at 6.30 – they at 7.15. We came up another rise with the usual gritty snow towards the end of the march. For us the interval between the two rises, some 8 miles, was steady plodding work which we might keep up for some time. To-morrow I'm going to march half a day, make a depôt and build the 10 ft. sledges. The second party is certainly tiring; it remains to be seen how they will manage with the smaller sledge and lighter load. The surface is certainly much worse than it was 50 miles back. T. –10. We have caught up Shackleton's dates. Everything would be cheerful if I could persuade myself that the second party were quite fit to go forward.

SUNDAY, DECEMBER 31ST, 1911

Amundsen

Sunday 31 Dec. The same splendid weather continues. –19° this morning and crystal clear. It went like a flash – much snow and much over smooth, shining surfaces. The S. sastrugi – the big ones – have stopped today. The terrain is wave-like in the highest degree. And then suddenly we see land quite close. Next moment everything disappears. Since yesterday – early in the day – we have seen a high, broken ice summit a little to the E. of our course. With huge spikes, it completely resembles a Crown of Thorns. Without doubt this must be the high, broken summit in G range estimated to be15,000 ft. We will see tomorrow. The dogs are in splendid form now. Hale and hearty. Passed 87° S.Lat. last night at 11 o'clock. As usual we have done our 15 nautical miles in 5 hours. W. always sets sail on his sledge and it helps him a great deal. Unfortunately he has been suffering much from toothache recently.[67] A root-filled tooth that has flared up.

Bjaaland

Sunday 31 Dec. 86°55' −19 −21. Same weather and skiing, do. Wind and low drift. The easiest day we have had. Our mountains in sight, have descended 700 ft. 15 m. 5½ hours' march.

Scott

Sunday, Dec. 31ˢᵗ. – New Year's Eve. 20.17. Height about 9126. T. −10. Corrected aneroid. The second party depôted its ski and some other weights equivalent to about 100 lbs. I sent them off first; they marched, but not very fast. We followed and did not catch them before they camped by direction at 1.30. By this time we had covered exactly 7 miles (geo.), and we must have risen a good deal. We rose on a steep incline at the beginning of the march, and topped another at the end, showing a distance of about 5 miles between the wretched slopes which give us the hardest pulling, but as a matter of fact, we have been rising all day.

We had a good full brew of tea and then set to work stripping the sledges. That didn't take long, but the process of building up the 10-feet sledges now in operation in the other tent is a long job. Evans (P.O.) and Crean are tackling it, and it is a very remarkable piece of work. Certainly P.O. Evans is the most invaluable asset to our party. To build a sledge under these conditions is a fact for special record. Evans (Lieut.) has just found the latitude – 86° 56' S. So that we are pretty near the 87th parallel aimed at for to-night. We lose half a day, but I hope to make that up by going forward at much better speed.

This is to be called the '3 Degree Depôt,' and it holds a week's provision for both units.

There is extraordinarily little mirage up here and the refraction is very small. Except for the seamen we are all sitting in a double tent – the first time we have put up the inner lining to the tent; it seems to make us much snugger.

10 p.m. The job of rebuilding is taking longer than I expected, but is now almost done. The 10-feet sledges look very handy. We had an extra drink of

tea and are now turned into our bags in the double tent (five of us) as warm as toast, and just enough light to write or work with. Did not get to bed till 2 a.m.

Obs.: 86 55 47 S.; 165 5 48 E.; Var. 175 40 E. Morning 20.08.

Scott's actions here are bizarre. Firstly, ordering Lt Evans and his party to abandon their skis defies all logic. To a skier, it might seem evidence of mild insanity. However, since Scott made his own party keep their skis, there is a glimpse of mitigating circumstances.

The order probably originated in a clash with Evans. It had surfaced in disparaging remarks scattered throughout Scott's diary, but with rising vehemence over the past few weeks (see entries for 11, 14 and 28 December), This particular antagonism had its roots in a quarrel over P.O. Evans. Before the expedition left New Zealand, Lt Evans wanted to exclude him on grounds of physical and mental failings – notably heavy drinking, and running a bit to fat – which disqualified him for polar travel, and could make him a liability to his companions.

Scott however refused to think ill of his all too obvious favourite. He kept P.O. Evans on the expedition, and took Lt Evans' request as a personal affront. They had been at odds ever since. Although Evans was second in command, Scott now mistrusted him, and proceeded to undermine his position.[68] It got so far that during the winter in the hut, Scott had baited Evans, swearing at him in front of the others.[69] In the meanwhile, Scott had all but promised Evans a place on the final party for the Pole. Scott's solution to that dilemma was clearly to wear Evans out by depriving him of skis and forcing him to struggle along through the snow on foot. That would, in turn, allow Scott to send him back on grounds of fitness without any public hint of rancour.

Nor was the rebuilding of the sledges any more rational. Scott wanted their length reduced from 12 ft. to 10 ft. for ease in hauling. To do the work on the trail, at altitude, in deep cold, with consequent delay, was one more risk in an already risky enterprise.

MONDAY, JANUARY 1ST, 1912

Amundsen

Monday 1 January

Still the same weather and progress. Ca. −19°. Fresh following breeze. We are losing height quickly. Our 15 nautical miles in 5 hours. But for the moment the land here remains a mystery. X range has now merged with G range. Tomorrow we will see what they do. It is impossible to know where we are. Tomorrow we reach the glacier, and then we will see how it agrees with our bearings and depot.

As usual, the terrain is undulating. We found a little glacier to our W., and we have now stopped there. Yesterday the land around 'the Butcher's Shop' hove into view. We have been steering towards it all day.

Bjaaland

New Year 1912 –86° 40' –19 –20. The first day of the year. Dear Diary wasn't it fine and easy; the loveliest day of all. Our mountain range lies to the East and glistens, and then Haakonshallen and Olavshaugen ahead. We expect the Devil's Glacier soon, with the depot and food. What will the New Year bring with pleasure and news and reports from home. Wisting is suffering so much from toothache that it is horrible, he has had it for days. 15 m. 5½ hours' march.

Scott

Monday, Jan. 1ˢᵗ, 1912. NEW YEAR [sic] DAY. Lunch. Bar.20.04. Roused hands about 7.30 and got away 9.30, Evans' party going ahead on foot. We followed on ski. Very stupidly we had not seen to our ski shoes beforehand, and it took a good half-hour to get them right; Wilson especially had trouble. When we did get away, to our surprise the sledge pulled very easily, and we made fine progress, rapidly gaining on the foot-haulers.

Night camp Jan. 1ˢᵗ Monday. 19.98. Risen about 150 feet. Height about 9600 above Barrier. They camped for lunch at 5½ miles and went on easily, completing 11.3 (geo.) by 7.30. We were delayed again at lunch camp Evans repairing the tent, and I the cooker. We caught the other party more easily in the afternoon and kept alongside them the last quarter of an hour. It was surprising how easily the sledge pulled; we have scarcely exerted ourselves all day.

We have been rising again all day, but the slopes are less accentuated. I had expected trouble with ski and hard patches, but we found none at all. T. –14°. The temperature is steadily falling, but it seems to fall with the wind. We are *very* comfortable in our double tent. Stick of chocolate to celebrate the New Year. The supporting party not in very high spirits, they have *mismanaged* matters for themselves. Prospects seem to get brighter – only 170 miles to go and plenty of food left.

TUESDAY, JANUARY 2ND, 1912

Amundsen

Tuesday 2 Jan.

Still the same weather. SSE'ly breeze −19°. There was a stiff gale while we were in bed. One has the impression that here the nights are calmer than the days. We careered at breakneck speed today as well. We had the devil's own luck today. Reached 'the Devil's Glacier' as intended, but considerably closer to land than when we climbed it. We found it more amenable here. In a few hours the whole glacier was conquered. Everything was as good as snow-covered, and no obstacles or deviations got in our way. This glacier must be incredibly old. Have never heard it make any noise. F range has now completely merged together with X range. It is much higher, and is further inland (easterly). X range now proves to be a continuation of G range. The summits vary between 13–15,000 f. asl. F range is now only 3 nautical miles away. Its summits are much lower than I originally believed – 9–21,000 ft. Now have a clear view of the various summits in F range. We reach the depot tomorrow if the weather remains clear.

Bjaaland

2nd January 1912 −19 −21. Same fine weather. We crossed the Devil's Glacier quickly and easily in 2½ hours, where we took three days of the most horrible toil and moil on the way south we found a smooth, sloping strip with an easy downwards slope, which brought us down to the plain, between vile crevasses. The Captain thinks we are east of the depot, so do the others. I, on the other hand, believe just as firmly that we are a little to the west. Tomorrow we shall see.

Scott

Tuesday, Jan. 2nd. T. −17. Camp 55. Height about 9980. At lunch my aneroid reading over scale 12,250, shifted hand to read 10,250. Proposed to enter heights in future with correction as calculated at end of book (−340 feet). The foot party went off early, before 8, and marched till 1. Again from 2.35 to 6.30. We started more than half an hour later on each march and caught the others easy. It's been a plod for the foot people and pretty easy going for us, and we have covered 13 miles (geo.).

T.−11.: Obs. 87°20'8" S.; 160°40'53" E.; Var. 180°. The sky is slightly overcast for the first time since we left the glacier; the sun can be seen already through the veil of stratus, and blue sky round the horizon. The sastrugi have all been from the S.E. to-day, and likewise the wind, which has been pretty light. I hope the clouds do not mean wind or bad surface. The latter became poor towards the end of the afternoon. We have not risen much to-day, and the plain seems to be flattening out. Irregularities are best seen by sastrugi. A *skua gull* visited us on the march this afternoon – it was evidently curious, kept alighting on the snow ahead, and fluttering a few yards as we approached. It seemed to have had little food – an extraordinary visitor considering our distance from the sea.

WEDNESDAY, JANUARY 3RD, 1912
Amundsen

Wednesday 3 Jan. The weather did not look promising when we set off, as usual at ca. 7 p.m., but we could just about make out the summits of which I had taken bearings in F range. However, we had not done more than 6 nautical miles when the weather came down so that we could see absolutely nothing. Already at 10 p.m. we were forced to make camp, before completing our usual day's run, and mission unaccomplished. But the weather changes quickly in these parts, and just as we had got our pemmican down, the sun broke through, and shortly afterwards, we had the finest weather. In a quarter of an hour, we had packed up, and were on our way. Because of the way we had found the glacier on the return journey, and so near land did we seem to be, that we all agreed that we must have come too far to the East, and therefore steered directly W in the hope of finding the depot. But although we tried all the bearings I took when we laid the depot, no depot was there to see. With our scant provisions, we all agreed that it would be best to set our course for 'the Butcher's Shop' immediately, and try to reach our dog depot there as quickly as possible. So, in the loveliest weather, we headed directly N. The mighty mountain range ran SE–NW, bathed in sunlight – in blue and white – a wonderful sight. After a short while, we recognized one of the long, low moraine ridges we passed on the 28 Nov. at 86°9'. That also showed that we had come too far W. and not E., as we thought, and our course would therefore have sent us over to the W. instead of the east. Therefore we steered eastwards to rejoin our old route. When we reached this ridge, from the top we had a view of 'the Devil's Glacier' – for the first time – and immediately recognized where we had climbed. It would have been 8 nautical miles back to our depot.[70] Under the circumstances, it would have been wrong to abandon it without even trying to find it, and everyone was perfectly willing to turn back towards the climb to look for it. I chose HH and Bj. for the job. They turned round immediately – 5 a.m. – with one dog team and an empty sledge, while we others made camp. Until 8 a.m. there has been blazing sunshine, so I am sure they managed it. Expect them back around 1 p.m. It has clouded over a little now, but it is still absolutely clear. Got a bearing on the land around 'the Butcher's Shop' at SW by ¾ W. A sight to check the compass variation at 6 a.m. gave the same result as on the way South.

At 3 p.m., 'the boys' returned and, as I expected, with the contents of the depot on the sledge. They had covered 26 nautical miles all told. In other words, HH's team has covered a distance of 42 nautical miles today at an average speed of 3 nautical miles an hour! I dare anyone to say that dogs are useless in this terrain. They had no difficulty in finding the depot. They recognized our climb to the glacier, and steered accordingly. It appeared from the course they had to keep on the return – S by ½ W – that we had strayed 1½ points from the course we had kept S'wards – NE by N. – The weather has been changeable. Now SE and overcast, then calm. Now it is absolutely calm –17° and burning sunshine. High summer. We have a good view of the mountain to the N. – presumably Håkonshallen[71] – bearing SW by W – the course we will naturally follow from this place. The day began badly but ended well. Now we are only 5 days' march from our depôt at 85°9' S. lat. and have enough food for ourselves and the dogs for 10. It really seemed dismal this morning – slaughtering our dogs, man-hauling etc., and now on the right footing again. It is not the first time that I have noticed help at the right moment. What makes the terrain here so difficult to work in is that there are ridges and wave formations everywhere. One can almost never have a proper overview. The two had encountered so many humps

Figure 24 The real heroes of the South Pole. Dogs at the Bay of Whales.

– Author's collection

on the trail today that Bj. remarked drily: At least we haven't got the hump. The concept of day and night is now starting to lose its meaning for several of the participants. 'It is 6 o'clock' someone says. 'Yes, in the morning', says someone else. 'You're stark raving mad', the former replies, 'it must be evening.' Dates don't come into it. Just as well we can remember the year.

Bjaaland

3 January Wednesday −18 −21. Well we would have made it if the weather had held, but just imagine, 3–4 hours after we had turned in, it clouded over and became worse and worse during the morning so that one saw nothing, think that we have come a little too far on to the glacier. According to the angles on the day we put out the depot, we have now driven 3.4 m. in the direction they believe the depot lies, but have seen nothing. Horribly uncertain if we find it even if it clears up, even more it will be a little test for us, as we only have ¾ rat. biscuits and two days chocolate, but luckily enough pemmican. The dogs will have to look after themselves by eating each other up, and finally in harness and haul ourselves. Have a solid dinner, then W. said that the weather was improving, and we broke camp to look for our larder, which soon ended with the conclusion that we had gone over to the west, my opinion exactly, and the Captain thought that it was useless to look for it any more, so we set a course for the Butcher's Shop. We then moved in that direction some 9 m., then he got the idea that we should get hold of the depot, wherever it bloody well lay, and everybody agreed. H.H. and Bjaaland were chosen to do so. H. with empty sledge and his good Greenlanders, and I on my light skis as forerunner. We set a course of NNW and went back at full speed. The Captain said he thought it was 8 miles, but rubbish I said. We went 11 miles, partly in fog and drift, without seeing any-thing. Luckily it cleared ahead and soon we saw it 2½ miles ahead, and believe me our pleasure was vast. Covered 13.6 m. The return journey went like a bomb. The Captain was beaming with pleasure, and rightly so, because otherwise one of the dog teams would have been condemned to death. After 10 hours on the march we were back at the camp, and then we had covered 42 m. that day all in all, a good distance without rest, but now we are rich in provisions. Wisting is now busy with the New Year pudding, yum yum.

Of provisions, W. has 43 rat. dog p.

> Human p. 73 rat.
> Biscuits 600
> H.H. Dog p. 72 rat.

Human p. 8 "
Chocolate 31½ slabs
Bags of milk 6
Biscuits 1200.

Scott

Wednesday, Jan. 3ʳᵈ. Height: Lunch, 10,110; Night, 10,180. Camp 56. T. –17°. Minimum –18.5. Within 150 miles of our goal. Last night I decided to reorganise, and this morning told off Teddy Evans, Lashly, and Crean to return. They are disappointed, but take it well. Bowers is to come into our tent, and we proceed as a five-man unit to-morrow. We have 5½ units of food – practically over a month's allowance for five people – it ought to see us through. We came along well on ski to-day, but the foot-haulers were slow, and so we only got a trifle over 12 miles (geo.). Very anxious to see how we shall manage to-morrow; if we can march well with the full load we shall be practically safe, I take it. The surface was very bad in patches to-day and the wind strong.

Scott does not explain his sudden change of mind to remove Bowers from Evans' party, and take him on to the Pole as an extra man instead. One is thrown back on deduction. To begin with, it was all man-hauling, so he could do with more traction. As it was, they were pulling more than 200 lbs a man.

Navigation was the crux, however. Approaching Shackleton's Furthest South, Scott was on the verge of uncharted territory. Astronomical navigation would be needed for the last lap over the featureless ice cap, besides locating the Pole itself. In other words, a navigator was vital, but Scott had not taken one among the men originally selected for the Pole. Amundsen and his four navigators make the obvious comparison.

In Scott's party, Wilson, Oates and P.O. Evans could not navigate, while Scott himself was out of practice. He needed someone else. Lt Evans was a specialist in navigation, but for obvious personal reasons did not fill the bill. As it turned out, he had a lucky escape. Bowers was a qualified navigator so now, at the last moment, Scott seized on him instead to fill the gap. This disrupted the whole intricate organization, which was based on groups of four. It left Lt Evans with only three men to get safely home. Scott meanwhile had to eke out four men's food and fuel for five. What is more, Bowers had been ordered to dump his skis with the rest of Evans' party. Scott had unthinkingly condemned him to plough through the snow on foot for several hundred miles. All this suggests that Scott did not understand the consequences of his own actions.

That could certainly not be said of either Amundsen or Bjaaland. Behind the even temper of their entries there looms the crisis of the return from the Pole. Once down on the Barrier, they can miss a string of depots without discomfort, but not up here on the ice cap. To miss even one depot would throw all Amundsen's calculations out of joint. Starvation was not the threat – they had enough in reserve – but the spectre of manhauling, and losing the race to the cablehead. Those were the twin horrors they would do anything to avoid. At almost any cost, they absolutely had to retrieve the depot at the foot of the Devil's Glacier.

Bjaaland had brought a pair of racing skis as spares, partly for personal pleasure, but also in case of a crisis such as this where speed might be the solution. In the end, he made it all seem so easy. With all his years of training and competition, it was just another run and a matter of routine. What Bjaaland had done before, Bjaaland could do again. In ten hours he had covered a round trip of 26 nautical miles, or 48 km. It was not exactly Olympic standard, but at 2.6 nautical miles an hour, twice as fast as Scott, and quite respectable in unknown terrain at an altitude of around 10,000 ft. after 76 days and nearly 1,000 nautical miles on the march.

Once more Amundsen proved that he had the moral and material reserves to deal with the unexpected. By implication he admits that he had lost his way, because on the outward journey, he had other things on his mind than map-making or even proper rounds of angles. His only thought was to beat Scott to the Pole, and now to the cablehead as well. Someone else could do the surveying later on.

After Bjaaland's and Helmer Hanssen's performance, Amundsen might well write 'I dare anyone to say that dogs are useless in this terrain.' Even now, with victory in sight, Scott's (and Shackleton's) patronizing comments still rankled.

THURSDAY, JANUARY 4TH, 1912

Amundsen

Thursday 4 Jan.

We have not had better weather than this morning when we turned out. Dead calm and burning sun −19°. It absolutely felt like a summer's day. Everywhere the land was bathed in blazing light. Giant griddles, smooth rounded, ridges, all forms. Especially in our line of march, the land was crystal clear, so that we had a good view of 'the great Beehive', 'Håkonshallen' and 'Olavsfjell'. It is most interesting to see this terrain in high summer, which we negotiated completely blind on our way S. It is rather strange that we did not then make land. We have now passed quite close. There is also land to our W. – snowclad, rounded eskers – no bare ground to be seen. After travelling 10 nautical miles, one of our cairns hove into view. Since then we have followed our line of cairns, until after marching 20 nautical miles, we stopped beneath the ridge, in the middle of which we were forced to stop – in thick weather on the 26 Nov. Now we are lying here in dead calm and burning sun. A great difference since the last time. We have Håkonshallen right before us, and 12 nautical miles up to 'the Butcher's Shop'. We will arrive there tomorrow, as long as the weather holds, put a few dogs on the sledge, and start the descent. The skiing has been excellent today. X and G ranges turn out to be the same – lying considerably closer to F range. – The doggies have been surprisingly good today, with the comparatively heavy loads and climbing.

Bjaaland

4 January 1912 85°49' −19 −19. Summery weather, unbelievably clear, saw Haakonshallen and the Beehive and Olavshaugen, good skiing. 20 m. 7½ hours on the march. Think of passing the Butcher's Shop tomorrow. Today, for the last time, we saw the colossal mountain range that probably runs from Victoria Land and perhaps past the Pole and perhaps far over to the other side of the Polar Land.

Scott

Thursday, Jan. 4th. – T. −17°, Lunch T. −16.5°. We were naturally late getting away this morning, the sledge having to be packed and arrangements completed for separation of parties. It is wonderful to see how neatly everything stows on a little sledge, thanks to P.O. Evans. I was anxious to see how we could pull it, and glad to find we went easy enough. Bowers on foot pulls between, but behind, Wilson and myself; he has to keep his own pace and luckily does not throw us out at all.

The second party had followed us in case of accident, but as soon as I was certain we could get along we stopped and said farewell. Teddy Evans is terribly disappointed but has taken it very well and behaved like a man. Poor old Crean wept and even Lashly was affected. I was glad to find their sledge is a mere nothing to them, and thus, no doubt, they will make a quick journey back. Since leaving them we have marched on till 1.15 and covered 6.2 miles (geo.). With full marching days we ought to have no difficulty in keeping up our average.

Night camp 57. T. −16°. Height 10,280. We started well on the afternoon march, going a good speed for 1½ hours; then we came on a stratum covered with loose sandy snow, and the pulling became very heavy. We managed to get off 12½ miles (geo.) by 7 p.m., but it was very heavy work.

In the afternoon the wind died away, and to-night it is flat calm; the sun so warm that in spite of the temperature we can stand about outside in the greatest comfort. It is amusing to stand thus and remember the constant horrors of our situation as they were painted *by S*; the sun is melting the snow on the ski, &c. The plateau is now very flat, but we are still ascending slowly. The sastrugi are getting more confused, predominant from the S.E. I wonder what is in store for us. At present everything seems to be going with extraordinary smoothness, and one can scarcely believe that obstacles will not present themselves to make our task more difficult. Perhaps the surface will be the element to trouble us.

FRIDAY, JANUARY 5TH, 1912

Amundsen

Friday 5 Jan.
We did not allow ourselves much time to rest yesterday evening. It was 6 p.m. when we lay down to sleep. We turned out already at 11 p.m. The weather was brilliant, and we dared not rest any longer. It was a matter of crossing 'the Butcher's Shop' while the weather was good. We succeeded beyond all expectation. We started off at 1.15 a.m. and ca. 8 a.m. we were at 'the Butcher's Shop'. We followed our cairns the whole way and found our slaughtered dogs. It was HH who, with his sharp eyes, discovered them. Had that not been the case, I don't quite know what would have happened. The place was completely unrecognizable – just as if we had never seen it before. To the NW there was a huge mountain range that was completely unfamiliar, even although the weather was fairly clear when we arrived at 'the Butcher's Shop'. I had no idea that it was the same 'Olavsfjell' – which on that occasion was partly shrouded in fog. No, to travel blind in these surroundings is fairly dangerous. I thought I recognized the land yesterday, but subsequently it proved to be absolutely wrong. The mountains we were able to see furthest off were 'the Big Beehive' and 'Olavsfjell'. 'Håkonshallen' is considerably lower. All in all, I overestimated the height of the mountains in the misty air on the way south. Most of them are between 10–12,000 ft. 'The Big Beehive' is the only one I would say reaches 15,000 ft. At the 'Butcher's Shop' we divided up one of the dog carcasses and gave the dogs a little extra meal. They hurled themselves over it like ravening wolves. We then slung a carcass on each sledge, and away we went. At the 'Butcher's Shop' it was –23°. According to the barometer, we are 5,000 ft. lower here. Only –13°. We have found summer down here among the mountains. It went downhill like a dream. We had ropes

round the sledge runners as brakes. We could not have managed without them. It was too steep. Bj. set off ahead, but even he often found it difficult to cope. By 11.30 a.m. we were down the first section of the climb. Now we have our tent in a warm and cosy place where the sun is in the process of melting us. The doggies are resting contentedly in the sunshine, having devoured a huge portion of dog meat plus pemmican. We are also on the safe side, and can allow ourselves a little extra. A lot of loose snow is still lying here. Difficult to find a camping place. I hope that in three days we will have reached our main depot at 85°9' S. lat. Well we are down from the Plateau again, and we are all extremely glad. We have been comfortable there, but we long for the 'Barrier' as an old friend. Once down there, we count ourselves as good as home. We have got food all over the place.

Bjaaland

Friday 5 January –26 –23 –13. Turned out at 1 a.m. with the intention of passing the Butcher's Shop and running down the last descent. Everyone was confused when we arrived at the Butcher's Shop, nobody recognized it from before, and we had to think and rethink. Only when we found the depot were our eyes opened a little. At the Butcher's Shop we fed the dogs, and slung 2–3 carcasses on the sledges and we shot off, pell mell, down the slopes, the one worse than the other, but we managed with brakes under the sledge runners. Covered 23.5 m. 9½ hours on the march. The Chief has now come to the reasonable conclusion that these mountains, Haakonhallen and Olavshaug can't be more than 12–13,000 feet high against 18–20,000 ft. which I had found so damned hard to believe. By running down to the end of the bay, not over the mountain, we will learn whether we were lucky or not on our climb. Perhaps we might have found the finest pass to the right of the Hall. Cannot believe that we have over 25 m. from the end of the valley to the depot. Anyway tomorrow we will be down in the valley and able to breathe decently, and have a little kinder temperature, not forgetting all the food and drink we want, we have been a little short of chocolate which, by a miscalculation, had been served too liberally.

Scott

Friday, Jan. 5th. Camp 58. Morning, 10,430; night, 10,320 T. 14.8 Obs, 87 57, 159 13. Min. T. –23.5; T. –21. A dreadfully trying day. Light wind from the N.N.W. bringing detached cloud and constant fall of ice crystals. The surface, in consequence, as bad as could be after the first hour. We started at 8.15, marched solidly till 1.15, covering 7.4 miles (geo.), and again in the afternoon we plugged on by 7 p.m. we had done 12½ miles (geo.), the hardest we have yet done on the plateau. The sastrugi seemed to increase as we advanced and they have changed direction from S. W. to S. by W. In the afternoon a good deal of confusing cross sastrugi, and to-night a very rough surface with evidences of hard southerly wind. Luckily the sledge shows no signs of capsizing yet. We sigh for a breeze to sweep the hard snow, but to-night the outlook is not promising better things. However, we are very close to the 88th parallel, little more than 120 miles from the Pole, only a march from Shackleton's final camp, and in a general way 'getting on'.

We go little over a mile and a quarter an hour now – it is a big strain as the shadows creep slowly round from our right through ahead to our left. What lots of things we think of on these monotonous marches! What castles one builds now hopefully that the Pole is ours Bowers took sights to-day and will take them every third day, We feel the cold very little, the great comfort of our situation is the excellent drying effect of the sun, Our socks and finnesko are almost dry each morning, Cooking for five takes a seriously longer time than cooking for four; perhaps half an hour on the whole day, It is an item I had not considered when reorganising.

SATURDAY, JANUARY 6TH, 1912
Amundsen

Saturday 6 Jan.

I have not seen a more beautiful sight than that which I saw when I came out of the tent at 1 a.m. We had the tent between Olavsfjell and the Igloo Peak. The latter obscured the sun, and our camping place was in the shade. But right opposite us on the other side the upper part of Olavsfjell lay bathed in sunlight. The jagged blocks of ice that covered the upper half, glittered and shone. The lower part – probably granite – still lay in darkness, silent and still. We lay closest to the shadow side of the Igloo Peak – N'wards. This has quite a strange, disturbed appearance. It looks as if huge blocks have been sprinkled over its flank. Above its summit lay a little cirrus cloud, gold-edged in the morning sun. And over there lies Håkonshallen, partly illuminated, partly in the shade. If only I could paint! It was a good day for us skiers. Loose snow, so that the ski sank about 2 inches: iced and grainy so that the skis glided as if on a greased surface. But the loose snow was also necessary so that the skis could be steered. The one slope steeper than the other. We tore down like a rushing wind. A wonderful sport. But it was worse for the doggies. They sank through horribly, but they advanced nonetheless. Our day's march is 11.4 nautical miles. They have had an evening feed, ½ kg pemmican and a plentiful ration of meat. We are now on the little glacier where we stayed on 19 November. Instead of taking our old route over the mountains, we will follow the big glacier – of which this little one is the start – out on to the barrier. It will be somewhat longer, but probably much easier. With luck, we will reach the depot the day after tomorrow.

Bjaaland

Saturday 6th. –23 –12.1. Thank God we are back in the lowlands after six weeks' hard existence in the dry cold air. The skiing was wonderful, softer snow, but it was vile for the dogs, they sank in to their knees. I had many good runs and raced with the Captain. 11.6 m. Where we are now, we lay 47 days ago and had so much toil and so many hard days ahead. Perhaps *Fram* is lying at Manhauen and waiting for the lads, well they'll have us in a month. Hassel is delighted at the prospect of more food that we are longing for. Haakonshallen now seems to be just a little peak, not more than 10–11,000 ft. high.

Scott

Sat. Jan. 6th, 10,470, T, –22.3. Obstacles arising – last night we got amongst sastrugi – they increased in height this morning and now we are in the midst of a sea of fish-hook waves well remembered from our Northern experience. We took off our ski after the first 1½ hours and pulled on foot. It is terribly heavy in places, and, to add to our trouble, every sastrugus [sic] is covered with a beard of sharp branching crystals. We have covered 6½ miles, but we cannot keep up our average if this sort of surface continues. There is no wind.

Camp 59 Lat, 88 7¼, 10,430–10,510, Rise of barometer ? T. –22.5, Minimum –25.8, morning. Fearfully hard pull again, and when we had marched about an hour we discovered that a sleeping bag had fallen off the sledge. We had to go back and carry it on. It cost us over an hour and disorganised our party. We have only covered 10½ miles (geo.) and it's been about the hardest pull we've had. We think of leaving our ski here, mainly because of risk of breakage. Over the sastrugi it is all up and down hill, and the covering of ice crystals prevents the sledge from gliding even on the down-grade. The sastrugi, I fear, have come to stay, and we must be prepared for heavy marching, but in two days I hope to lighten loads with a depôt. We are south of Shackleton's last camp, so, I suppose, have made the most southerly camp.

Amundsen's and Bjaaland's gay abandon in recording their downhill runs is a kind
of understatement. It masks something extraordinary in the world of mountain ski-
ing. That season, crevasses choked with snow, the Axel Heiberg Glacier was a dozing
monster, but a monster just the same. The dogs and their drivers bore witness to that.

SUNDAY, JANUARY 7TH, 1912

Amundsen

Sunday 7 Jan.
A little overcast today. −19° yesterday evening. It was so hot in the tent, that we
had difficulty in coping. Our sleeping bags were wet, although we had several
layers of fur and cloth underneath. We have followed the big glacier down all
day – E. true. The going has been splendid, but a little soft for the doggies. We
have done our 15.5 nautical miles, and are now on the W. shore again. Reach
the depot tomorrow. The glacier was completely filled with snow and formed a
continuous even surface. Consequently we have had no difficulty at all. The time
is now 7 a.m. Baking hot in the tent.

Turned out again at 6 p.m. We followed the land, which ran N (true). At the
first ridge, Bj. said that he could already see the depot down on the Barrier. He
proved subsequently to have been right. After travelling 10 nautical miles, we
made our landfall and were certain of the depot's position. We headed straight
on to the Barrier and arrived at 11 p.m., after a march of 11.4 nautical miles.
This depot had been made extra big and high, but the sun had reduced it to a
rather small mass. The surrounding snow lay deep and loose. No sastrugi, so there
could not have been much wind. Everything in the depot was in order. Only the
pemmican, which was wrapped in a fur anorak, had been melted by the power of
the sun. Now HH and W. – after having loaded the depot on the sledges – are
going up to 'Mount Betty' to build a stone cairn there and deposit a report. A tin
of paraffin (17 l.)[72] together with 2 packets of matches (20 boxes) are to be put in
the cairn. Possibly they will be useful in the future. One of the dogs – 'Frithjof'
– was put down this evening. It was ill. It appeared that it had some kind of
lung disease. The meat was divided among his companions. Now they prefer dog
meat to pemmican, although they also like the latter dish a lot. 'Nigger' – one
of Pr.'s dogs – was put down when we had crossed the sastrugi district up on
the plateau. This feeding with dog meat proved to have an extraordinarily good
effect on the dogs. At the same time, they have their pemmican ration. They
seem to be almost in the same condition now as when we left Framheim – We
leave this place when we have had a few hours' sleep. We will then have food for

35 days on the sledges, besides the depots every degree N'wards. We are now really living among the fleshpots of Egypt. It's just a matter now of eating as much as possible to lighten our sledges as quickly as possible.

Bjaaland

7 January Sunday −12 −12. Følgefonden. Today we have gone East along Følgefonden, the skiing was brilliant, snow a little soft for the dogs. The bay ran along the right side of Haakonshallen where it meets huge glaciers. We have nearly reached the Barrier, and perhaps not more than 10 m to the depot. Tomorrow we will see if my prophecy of 25 m to the depot turns out to be true. The Chief still thinks that I'm not right, but he laughed scornfully at my idea eight days ago.

11 o'clock. Evening 7th the same day −11° 85°9'. After 6–7 hours sleep, we got out of the tent, and were on our way. When we passed a crest near the camp, I asked the Captain if I could make for a white hummock which I saw far ahead, and thought that it could be the depot, so I set a course a little to the left. After a march of 8 m saw some rather high mountains to the north-west, which I thought were familiar, and I asked H.H. if that was not our climb, he said no, but I became more and more certain, and when we reached a high ridge, I caught sight of the depot, I looked at it, and said 'there is the crossing' to the Captain. 'No, I'll bet you a million it isn't', but shortly afterwards he said 'you are right', and so it was. The distance from Følgefonden to the depot was 27 m, 2 m longer than I guessed. We have now loaded the sledges with food and drink, if only we now have permission to use them. H.H. and W. went over to a low hill with a tin of paraffin, matches and a note, and built a cairn as a sign that people had been here. Tomorrow we head for Framheim at a rate of 15 m and the day divided into eight hours' sleep and eight hours' work to avoid the long nights, we are now drinking chocolate in the middle of the night to make time pass more quickly. Basically little pleasure, whatever the reason.

Scott

Sunday, Jan. 7th. 10,560. Lunch. Temp. −21.3. The vicissitudes of this work are bewildering. Last night we decided to leave our ski on account of the sastrugi. This morning we marched out a mile in 40 min. and the sastrugi gradually disappeared. I kept debating the ski question and at this point stopped, and after discussion we went back and fetched the ski; it cost us 1½ hours nearly. Marching again, I found to my horror we could scarcely move the sledge on ski; the first hour was awful owing to the wretched coating of loose sandy snow. However, we persisted, and towards the latter end of our tiring march we began to make better progress, but the work is still awfully heavy. I mean to stick to the ski after this.

Afternoon. Camp 60. T. –23. Height 10,570. Obs.: Lat. 88 18 40 S.; Long. 157 21 E.; Var. 179 15 W. Very heavy pulling still, but did 5 miles (geo.) in over four hours.

This is the shortest march we have made on the summit; but there is excuse. Still, there is no doubt if things remained as they are we could not keep up the strain of such marching for long. Things, however, luckily will not remain as they are. To-morrow we depot a week's provision, lightening altogether about 100 lbs. This afternoon the welcome southerly wind returned and is now blowing force 2 to 3. I cannot but think it will improve the surface.

The sastrugi are very much diminished, and those from the south seem to be overpowering those from the S.E. Cloud travelled rapidly over from the south this afternoon, and the surface was covered with sandy crystals; these were not so bad as the 'bearded' sastrugi, and oddly enough the wind and drift only gradually obliterate these striking formations. We have scarcely risen at all to-day, and the plain looks very flat. It doesn't look as though there were more rises ahead, and one could not wish for a better surface if only the crystal deposit would disappear or harden up. I am awfully glad we have hung on to the ski; hard as the marching is, it is far less tiring on ski. Bowers has a heavy time on foot, but nothing seems to tire him. Evans has a nasty cut on his hand (sledge-making). I hope it won't give trouble. Our food continues to amply satisfy. What luck to have hit on such an excellent ration. We really are an excellently found party.

To a skier, Scott's continued vacillation over skis at this late stage might yet again call his judgement into question. Scott's attitude to Bowers, now deprived of his ski, seems callous, not admitting that the fault might ultimately be his own.

These oddities could have physical causes. Despite Scott's protestations, they were slowly starving. For the serfdom of man-hauling, they were each getting perhaps 1,500 calories a day too little. In addition, they were suffering various protein and vitamin deficiencies, together with dehydration. All this, especially dehydration, has mental side-effects.

To point another contrast, at no stage did Amundsen or his men lack the calories they needed. Now 'among the fleshpots of Egypt', they had a surplus of more than 1,000 calories a day. What Amundsen meant was that they had depots strewn all over the Barrier, and starvation was now a physical impossibility. They were putting on weight, and the dogs too. Each in his own way, the rivals were proving that in the last resort, the race for the Pole was a question of food and drink.

MONDAY, JANUARY 8ᵀᴴ, 1912

Amundsen

Monday 8 Jan.

The weather was vile later in the day. Gale from the S'ly quarter, with thick snowfall – the heaviest we have seen in these regions. At 3 p.m. we set off in this disagreeable weather. Luckily I was wearing my sealskin clothes, which I had left in the depot on the way south, and now they were of great use. We steered SW by S (compass). We did not have clear terrain and could not see our hands in front of our faces, so I thought it best to have two forerunners – Bj. and Hass. – roped together. A few hours after starting, we reached some hard, iced ridges, which hinted at the proximity of the huge crevasses we had passed on the way south. At that moment there was a break in the clouds, and not many metres in front of the leading forerunner (Bj.) lay one of the gaping crevasses. Now it was not hard to avoid them and we found our way easily over places that were filled. Oddly enough, it seems as if these crevasses formed a border both for the weather and skiing. The conditions had hitherto been of the worst kind. Deep, loose freshly fallen snow extremely heavy to advance in, both for man and beast. On the N. side of the crevasses, it hardened, and not long after, we had our dear good old Barrier conditions. Behind us, pitch black, impenetrable banks of clouds. No sight of land. Ahead of us blazing sunshine. It is highly probable that these crevasses, which, on our way south, we could see running E. as far as the eye could see, form the junction of Barrier and land. Not long afterwards, we found one of our cairns right in our line of travel – not bad steering in the blizzard. We reached the depot at 85° S. lat. at 9 p.m. in the loveliest sunshine and everything in order. We have made camp here, given the dogs double rations, and loaded the depot on the sledges. Prospects seem good.

Bjaaland

8 January. Monday. –11 –11. Unpleasant snowfall today with wind of 7–8 m/s SE. Easily found the depot at 85°, where we are now. It turned out that Fridtjof, the best dog in my team did not grow old in Wisting's service. He had to give up his life yesterday. His innards were ugly.

Scott

Monday, Jan. 8th. Camp 60. Noon. T. −19.8. Min. for night −25°. Our first summit blizzard. We might just have started after breakfast, but the wind seemed obviously on the increase, and so has proved. The sun has not been obscured, but snow is evidently falling as well as drifting. The sun seems to be getting a little brighter as the wind increases. The whole phenomenon is very like a Barrier blizzard, only there is much less snow, as one would expect, and at present less wind, which is somewhat of a surprise.

Evans' hand was dressed this morning, and the rest ought to be good for it. I am not sure it will not do us all good as we lie so very comfortably, warmly clothed in our comfortable bags, within our double-walled tent. However, we do not want more than a day's delay at most, both on account of lost time and food and the slow accumulation of ice. Night T. −13.5°. It has grown much thicker during the day, from time to time obscuring the sun for the first time. The temperature is low for a blizzard, but we are very comfortable in our double tent and the cold snow is not sticky and not easily carried into the tent, so that the sleeping-bags remain in good condition. T. −3. The glass is rising slightly. I hope we shall be able to start in the morning, but fear that a disturbance of this sort may last longer than our local storm.

It is quite impossible to speak too highly of my companions. Each fulfils his office to the party; Wilson, first as doctor, ever on the lookout to alleviate the small pains and troubles incidental to the work; now as cook, quick, careful and dexterous, ever thinking of some fresh expedient to help the camp life; tough as steel on the traces, never wavering from start to finish.

Evans, a giant worker with a really remarkable head-piece. It is only now I realise how much has been due to him. Our ski shoes and crampons have been absolutely indispensable, and if the original ideas were not his, the details of manufacture and design and the good workmanship are his alone. He is responsible for every sledge, every sledge fitting, tents, sleeping-bags, harness, and when one cannot recall a single expression of dissatisfaction with anyone of these items, it shows what an invaluable assistant he has been. Now, besides superintending the putting up of the tent, he thinks out and arranges the packing of the sledge; it is extraordinary how neatly and handily everything is stowed, and how much study has been given to preserving the suppleness and good running qualities of the machine. On the Barrier, before the ponies were killed, he was ever roaming round, correcting faults of stowage.

Little Bowers remains a marvel – he is thoroughly enjoying himself. I leave all the provision arrangement in his hands, and at all times he knows exactly how we stand, or how each returning party should fare. It has been a complicated business to redistribute stores at various stages of re-organisation, but not one single mistake has been made. In addition to the stores, he keeps the most thorough and conscientious meteorological record, and to this he now adds the duty of observer and photographer. Nothing comes amiss to him, and no work is too hard. It is a difficulty to get him into the tent; he seems quite oblivious of the cold, and he lies coiled in his bag writing and working out sights long after the others are asleep.

Of these three it is a matter for thought and congratulation that each is sufficiently suited for his own work, but would not be capable of doing that of the others as well as it is done. Each is invaluable. Oates had his invaluable period with the ponies; now he is a foot slogger and goes hard the whole time, does his share of camp work, and stands the hardship as well as any of us. I would not like to be without him either. So our five people are perhaps as happily selected as it is possible to imagine.

Despite Scott's self-congratulation, in the fundamentals of snow travel, the party was not happily constituted. Oates and Bowers had never been on skis before coming to the Antarctic. Scott's, Wilson's, and especially P.O. Evans' state was that of a beginner. Tramping laboriously instead of sliding, they were wasting energy, and more seriously time. In a word, their technique was defective. They were monumentally unsuited to the task in which they were engaged.

TUESDAY, JANUARY 9TH, 1912

Amundsen

Tuesday 9 Jan.
Filthy weather again, although not to the same degree as yesterday. To begin with the going was extremely heavy – deep loose snow. But as we got away from land, it became better and better. We are now down on the lower barrier. The wind is NW'ly and it is overcast. Have passed all our cairns today. The first in thick drift – 10 m, away. But it needs a HH to find it. His eyesight is fantastically good. We had fresh seal steak today. –9.6° this afternoon. Only –6.5° this morning.

Bjaaland

9 January. Tuesday. –6.5 –9.7. Absolutely thick so one could see nothing at all, but nonetheless followed the line of cairns. Fine weather in prospect. NW wind 16 m. A lot of loose snow.

Scott

Tuesday, Jan. 9th. Camp 61. RECORD. Lat. 88° 25'. 10,270 ft. Bar. risen I think. T. −4. Still blowing, and drifting when we got to breakfast, but signs of taking off. The wind had gradually shifted from south to E.S.E. After lunch we were able to break camp in a bad light, but on a good surface. We made a very steady afternoon march, covering 6½ miles (geo.) This should place us in Lat. 88°25', beyond the record of Shackleton's *exaggerated* walk. All is new ahead. The barometer has risen since the blizzard, and it looks as though we were on a level plateau, not to rise much further.

Obs.: Long. 159 17 45 E.; Var. 179 55 W.; Min. T. −7.2.

More curiously the temperature continued to rise after the blow and now, at −4°, it seems quite warm. The sun has only shown very indistinctly all the afternoon, although brighter now. Clouds are still drifting over from the east. The marching is growing terribly monotonous, but one 'cannot grumble as long as the distance can be kept up. It can, I think, if we leave a depôt, but a very annoying thing has happened. Bowers' watch has suddenly dropped twenty six minutes; it may have stopped from being frozen outside his pocket, or he may have inadvertently touched the hands. Any way it makes one more chary of leaving stores on this great plain, especially as the blizzard tended to drift up our tracks. We could only just see the back track when we started, but the light was extremely poor.

WEDNESDAY, JANUARY 10TH, 1912

Amundsen

Wednesday 10 Jan.
Same filthy weather. Snow, snow, snow. Snow and snow again. Will it never end[?] Added to that thick weather, so we couldn't see 10 m. −8°. Melting all over the sledges. Everything is wet. Have not seen a single cairn today in this blinding weather. To begin with, the snow was very deep, and the going extraordinarily heavy, but nonetheless the dogs coped with the sledges splendidly. The going became good towards the time we finished (9.30 a.m.). Most of us have now turned our sleeping bags inside out with the hair facing outwards. In this way they keep dry.

Bjaaland

10 January 12 midnight. −11 −8. Distance 16 m. Snowdrift and snowfall and I have had a bloody job going first. No cairns to be seen, presumably towards the west.

Scott

Wednesday, Jan. 10ᵗʰ. – Camp 62. T. −11°. Last depôt 88° 29' S.; 159° 33' E.; Var. 180°. Terrible hard march in the morning; only covered 5.1 miles (geo.). Decided to leave depôt at lunch camp. Built cairn and left one week's food together with sundry articles of clothing. We are down as close as we can go in the latter. We go forward with 18 days' food. Yesterday I should have said certain to see us through, but now the surface is beyond words, and if it continues we shall have the greatest difficulty to keep our march long enough. The surface is quite covered with sandy snow, and when the sun shines it is terrible. During the early part of the afternoon it was overcast, and we started our lightened sledge with a good swing, but during the last two hours the sun cast shadows again, and the work was distressingly hard. We have covered only 10.8 miles (geo.).

Only 85 miles (geog.) from the Pole, but it's going to be a stiff pull *both ways* apparently; still we do make progress, which is something. To-night the sky is overcast, the temperature (−11) much higher than I anticipated; it is very difficult to imagine what is happening to the weather. The sastrugi grow more and more confused, running from S. to E. Very difficult steering in uncertain light and with rapidly moving clouds. The clouds don't seem to come from anywhere, form and disperse without visible reason. The surface seems to be growing softer. The meteorological conditions seem to point to an area of variable light winds, and that plot will thicken as we advance.

THURSDAY, JANUARY 11ᵀᴴ, 1912
Amundsen

Thursday 11 Jan.

At last the weather has improved. After having snowed all day, it stopped towards evening. It was quite fair when we set off at 10.30 p.m. Calm, and quite clear. After a short while HH discovered a cairn. It was slightly off our course. Ca. 1/10 nautical miles to the W. In it we found the report we had

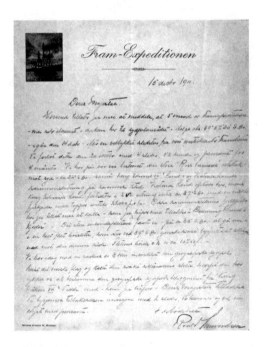

Figure 25 The letter from Amundsen to King Haakon VII of Norway, found by Scott at the South Pole, with a request to have it delivered – in case of accidents. The headed notepaper, carried 1400 kilometres from base, hints at the ultimate precaution of observing the social conventions even at the ends of the Earth. Dated 15 December 1911, the text reads:

Your Majesty

I hereby take the liberty of reporting that 5 men of the Fram Expedition – including myself – reached the South Pole region – according to obs. 89°57'36" S.Lat – yesterday the 14 Dec. – after a successful sledge journey from our winter quarters at 'Framheim'. We left it on 20 October with 4 sledges, 52 dogs and supplies for 4 months. We have determined the Southern most extremity of the great 'Ross Ice Barrier', together with the junction of Victoria Land King Edward VII Land at the same place. Victoria Land finishes here, while King Edward's Land continues in a SW'ly direction to ca. 87° S.Lat. with a mighty mountain range with peaks up to 22,000 ft. asl. I have taken the liberty of calling this continuous mountain range – with permission I hope – 'Queen Maud's Range'. We found that the great inland plateau – at about 88° S.lat. – turned into a completely flat high plain which began to slope gently downwards from 89° S.Lat. The altitude of the plain is ca. 10,750 ft. asl. Today we have encircled the geographic South Pole with a radius of 8 nautical miles, raised the Norwegian flag, and called this gently sloping plain on which we have succeeded in establishing the position of the Geographic South Pole – with I hope Your Majesty's permission – 'King Haakon VII's Vidda'. We start the return journey tomorrow with 2 sledges, 16 dogs and well supplied with provisions.

Your obedient servant,

Roald Amundsen

                                                     – National Library of Norway

deposited – most of which incidentally had melted away – and it showed – 84°26' S. lat. To our great surprise, a few minutes after we had left the cairn, two 'Skua Gulls' came flying overhead and settled on the cairn. Quite remarkable. Our first sight of living creatures, exactly half way between the Pole and open water – ca. 360 nautical miles from the sea. We did not expect this. The weather has improved gradually, and it seems as if we have good weather in prospect. We are lying by the cairn at 84°15', and will reach our depot tomorrow, I hope. We haven't seen much land today. The sun has only illuminated the lower part. Absolutely nothing of the upper part was to be seen. The skiing was heavy to begin with. Brilliant at the end. Completely flattened everywhere. Not *one* sastruga to be seen. We arrived at 4 o'clock this morning.

We have done our second march today. Left our previous camp (84°15' S. lat.) at 3.30 p.m. and arrived here at 9 p.m. In this way we have done 30 nautical miles today. And the dogs are even healthier. Their condition is improving by the day, and are burning with pleasure and the will to work. The way in which we now work is excellent. We have neither day nor night. We do our 15 nautical miles, then turn in and sleep for seven or eight hours, and then turn out again. In this way we save much time. Have followed our cairns all day, and found our depot this evening in order. I have a slight suspicion that the two skua gulls may have made deep inroads into our depots of fresh meat. What a pity for the doggies.

Bjaaland

Thursday 11 January. 84°15'–8. The weather has smartened itself up to sunny, clear, so we soon found a cairn, No. 69, a few clouds helped, so that it was just a matter of holding a course. Had a wonderful message today, with greetings from Framheim. Two crows which surely left there yesterday. We all cheered when they hovered over us. Good day, good day dear skua-crow, how are you doing? When I shot at you with my revolver, and you just gave a bow, I can imagine you've lived well along the way, at 80° on our seal, and [cairns] I and II [after] 80° on our dogs. You go back to Lindstrøm and tell him we'll be back in 20 days and clean up his hot cakes, steaks and fruit, even if it's green plums. It was half-way between Framheim and the Pole that they came to meet us.

10 o'clock, 11 January 84° –8° –12°. Stratus 10 Fine and calm, the best kind of skiing, found the depot after a march of 5½ hours. The Captain impatient; brooks no opposition. Sharp dispute over my goggles. Is he annoyed that I'm not using the Roaldish snow goggles? The wonderful sight of land that we saw yesterday, has disappeared from view today. It looked like a home of the trolls, glittering with silver and fool's gold.

Scott

Thursday, Jan. 11th. – Lunch. 10,540. T. –15.8. It was heavy pulling from the beginning to-day, but for the first two and a half hours we could keep the sledge moving; then the sun came out (it had been overcast and snowing with light SE^{ly} breeze) and the rest of the forenoon was agonising. I never had such pulling; all the time the sledge rasps and creaks. We have covered 6 miles, but at fearful cost to ourselves.

Night camp 63. Height 10,530 Temp. –16.3. Minimum 25.8. Another hard grind in the afternoon and five miles added. About 74 miles from the pole – can we keep this up for seven days? It takes it out of us like anything. None of us ever had such hard work before. Cloud has been coming and going overhead all day, drifting from the S.E., but continually altering shape. Snow crystals falling all the time; a very light S. breeze at start soon dying away. The sun so bright and warm to-night . that it is almost impossible to imagine a minus temperature. The snow seems to get softer as we advance; the sastrugi, though sometimes high and undercut, are not hard – no crusts, except yesterday the surface subsided once, as on the Barrier. It seems pretty certain there is no steady wind here. Our chance still holds good if we can put the work in, but it's a terribly trying time.

Bjaaland gives a neat insight into Amundsen's character. Under strain, Amundsen became quarrelsome. Superficially all seems to be well. Amundsen has brought all his men to the Pole and back with minimum discomfort. Heroism was not required; only speed. Now, safely down from the heights, Amundsen has passed the critical point, and ordered a sprint for home.

Not all is as it seems to be. For one thing, Amundsen is in a hurry to get back to Fram *and sail off to Tasmania and the cablehead. He had been first at the Pole but, for all he knew, Scott might yet be on his tail. Perhaps he only had days to spare. He was hounded by the thought of losing the all-important race to be first with the news. He had no idea that he was now 470 miles ahead. Nor could he know that reading between the lines of Scott's diary, Scott was ailing even before he reached the Pole. His gloom arose from inhuman effort, self-imposed, and not having enough to eat and drink.*

Scott aside, Amundsen was afraid. He had achieved his goal, and would surely have to pay for it. As if fleeing from Nemesis, he wanted to be out of Antarctica as quickly as he could.

Bjaaland had clashed with Amundsen over snow goggles before. Amundsen provided a model with tinted glass. Bjaaland preferred an Eskimo pattern, with slits in opaque eye-pieces.

FRIDAY, JANUARY 12TH, 1912

Amundsen

Friday 12 Jan.
Left at 8 a.m. The skiing has been of the best kind. Ca. 2 inches of loose snow are lying over the old crust and give an excellent surface underfoot. We have crossed several quite narrow crevasses today. The weather has been variable. During the afternoon it cleared and the sun shone. It was then easy to see the cairns. But then it clouded over and the weather thickened again from the N., so that it was impossible to see the cairns out in the terrain. Thus we have not seen the last cairn at 83°46'.

Bjaaland

Friday 12 January 83°15' –10 –7. 2 a.m. Fine weather the first 10 m, now thick, northerly wind. Yes indeed. A few small crevasses appeared. Slept for seven hours, then out to run 15 m until we reach 82° then six hours' sleep until the 80th degree is reached, then 20 m until we arrive at Framheim.

Scott

Friday, Jan. 12th. – Camp 64. T. –17.5. Lat. 88 57 Another heavy march with snow getting softer all the time. Sun very bright, calm at start; first two hours terribly slow. Lunch, 4¾ hours, 5.6 miles geo.; Sight Lat. 88 52 (lunch). Afternoon, 4 hours, 5.1 miles – total 10.7.

In the afternoon we seemed to be going better; clouds spread over from the west with light chill wind and for a few brief minutes we tasted the delight of having the sledge following free. Alas! in a few minutes it was worse than ever, in spite of the sun's eclipse. However, the short experience was salutary. I had got to fear that we were weakening badly in our pulling; those few minutes showed me that we only want a good surface to get along as merrily as of old. With the surface as it is, one gets horribly sick of the monotony and can easily imagine oneself getting played out, were it not that at the lunch and night camps one so quickly forgets all one's troubles and bucks up for a fresh effort. It is an effort to keep up the double figures, but if we can do so for another four marches we ought to get through. It is going to be a close thing.

At camping to-night everyone was chilled and we guessed a cold snap, but to our surprise the actual temperature was higher than last night, when we could dawdle in the sun. It is most unaccountable why we should suddenly feel the cold in this manner; partly the exhaustion of the march, but partly some damp quality in the air, I think. Little Bowers is wonderful; in spite of my protest he *would* take sights after we had camped to-night, after marching in the soft snow all day where we have been comparatively restful on ski.

Night position. Lat. 88 57 25 S.; Long. 160 21 E.; Var. 179 49 W. Min. T. –23.5.

Only 63 miles (geo.) from the Pole to-night. We ought to do the trick, but oh! for a better surface. It is quite evident this is a comparatively windless area. The sastrugi are few and far between, and all soft. I should imagine occasional blizzards sweep up from the S.E., but none with violence. We have deep tracks in the snow, which is soft as deep as you like to dig down.

SATURDAY, JANUARY 13TH, 1912

Amundsen

Saturday 13 Jan.
Set off at 2 a.m. Filthy weather. Couldn't see anything at all. Therefore have done our whole march now – 15 nautical miles – without seeing cairns. It cleared a little from the N. during the morning, and I have the best hopes for the next march. We arrived here at 7.30 a.m. The skiing has been brilliant. Could not be better. Off again at 6.30 p.m., and finished our 15 nautical miles at 11.30 p.m. The weather had cleared in the course of the day, and the first thing we saw when we turned out was a cairn quite close – to the W. of our camp site. Bj. clearly leans to the right, and when we lose sight of our cairns, we can always be certain of having them to our W. We are now lying by the cairn at 83°15' S. lat., and have done 30 nautical miles in our two marches today. Hope to reach the depot at 83° S. lat. – the last critical point – tomorrow.

Bjaaland

Saturday 13th. 83°30' –6 –7.7. Turned out 2 a.m. and covered 15 m. Six hours on the march. Made camp 8 a.m. Thick weather in the morning, but finally after 3 m on the march, a yellow band to follow, which rose higher and higher, skiing splendid. No cairns.

11.30 13 January –4° –11°. 5 hours on the march, 15 m. Splendid weather and skiing. Found the cairn today, saw it 4 m. ahead of us. Tomorrow we will be at the depot at 83°, and load up.

Scott

Saturday, Jan. 13. Lunch 10,390. Barometer low ? lunch Lat. 89° 3' 18". Started on some soft snow, very heavy dragging and went slow. We could have supposed nothing but that such conditions would last from now onward, but to our surprise, after two hours we came on a sea of sastrugi, all lying from S. to E., predominant E.S.E. Have had a cold little wind from S.E. & S.S.E., where the sky is overcast. Have done 5.6 miles and are now over the 89th parallel.

Night camp 65. –10,270 T. –22.5, Min. –23.5. Lat. 89 9 S. very nearly. We started very well in the afternoon. Thought we were going to make a real good march, but after the first two hours surface crystals became as sandy as ever. Still we did 5.6 miles geo., giving over 11 for the day. Well, another day with double figures and a bit over. The chance holds.

It looks as though we were descending slightly; sastrugi remain as in forenoon. It is wearisome work this tugging and straining to advance a light sledge. Still, we get along. I did manage to get my thoughts off the work for a time to-day, which is very restful. We should be in a poor way without our ski, though Bowers manages to struggle through the soft snow without tiring his short legs.

Only 51 miles from the Pole to-night. If we don't get to it we shall be d-d close. There is a little southerly breeze to-night; I devoutly hope it may increase in force. The alternation of soft snow and sastrugi seem to suggest that the coastal mountains are not so very far away.

SUNDAY, JANUARY 14TH, 1912

Amundsen

Sunday 14 Jan.
Have travelled in the thickest fog all day. Found none of our cairns. Stopped at 4 p.m. after having completed our run of 15 nautical miles. As we were pitching our tent, we suddenly saw the depot ca. ½ nautical mile to the W. That was well done in fog. We were quite astonished to see fresh doggie tracks and excrement here at the depot. It or they – perhaps two – had attacked the depot, but it had withstood the attack. It can't be more than a few days at the most since they have been here. The depot – our last – was in order. Have everything on the sledges. The dogs are now fed daily on biscuits and pemmican. Now we have too many biscuits for ourselves and there is no better use for them than to give them to the dogs. They are getting into better condition with each passing day. Now the whip is rarely used. A little flick is enough. It has been so warm in the

tent lately that several of us have had to get out of our sleeping bags. We then lie in thin underclothes on a piece of fur above a big block of ice – for what else is the barrier. We now have masses of food and can give the dogs double feeds.

Bjaaland

Sunday 14 January 83° –1 –10. 4 p.m. Calm but thick, only saw the first cairn. H.H. ran by compass, so I was let off being forerunner. Arrived 1 m to the right of the depot. We found fresh tracks of dogs here, we aren't sure whether one or two, perhaps it is one of those that ran away from me here. Even although the pemmican was not in a box, it was untouched.

Scott

Sunday, Jan. 14th**.** Camp 66. Lunch T. –18°, Night T. –15°. Sun showing mistily through overcast sky all day. Bright southerly wind with very low drift. In consequence the surface was a little better, and we came along very steadily 6.3 miles in the morning and 5.5 in the afternoon, but the steering was awfully difficult and trying; very often I could see nothing, and Bowers on my shoulders directed me. Under such circumstances it is an immense help to be pulling on ski. To-night it is looking very thick. The sun can barely be distinguished, the temperature has risen, and there are serious indications of a blizzard. I trust they will not come to anything; there are practically no signs of heavy wind here, so that even if it blows a little we may be able to march. Meanwhile we are less than 40 miles from the Pole.

Again we noticed the cold; at lunch to-day Obs.: Lat. 89 20 53 S. all our feet were cold, but this was mainly due to the bald state of our finnesko. I put some grease under the bare skin and found it made all the difference. Oates seems to be feeling the cold and fatigue more than the rest of us, but we are all very fit. It is a critical time, but we ought to pull through. The barometer has fallen very considerably and we cannot tell whether due to ascent of plateau or change of weather. Oh! for a few fine days! So close it seems and only the weather to baulk us.

MONDAY, JANUARY 15TH, 1912

Amundsen

Monday 15 Jan,
Unpleasant weather. Fog and falling snow. Passed the second and last cairns. We were about to run into the latter in the thickest fog. Are now lying at 82°45' S. lat. The dog tracks, which were at the depot, also ran past this cairn.

Bjaaland

15 January 82°[45'] −10 −11 SW wind. Thick weather, bloody horrible light. Are on the line of cairns. Saw dog tracks at 46' mile cairn, they were heading north. Skiing good.

Scott

Monday, Jan. 15th. Lunch camp, 9950. Last Depôt. During the night the air cleared entirely and the sun shone in a perfectly clear sky. The light wind had dropped and the temperature fallen to −25°, minimum −27°. I guessed this meant a hard pull, and guessed right. The surface was terrible, but for 4¾ hours yielded 6 miles (geo.). We were all pretty well done at camping, and here we leave our last depôt−only four days' food & a sundry or two. The load is now very light, but I fear that the friction will not be greatly reduced.

Night, Jan. 15. Height 9920. T −25. The sledge came surprisingly lightly after lunch − something from loss of weight, something, I think, from stowage, and, most of all perhaps, as a result of tea. Anyhow we made a capital afternoon march of 6.3 miles, bringing the total for the day to over 12 (12.3). The sastrugi again very confused, but mostly S.E. quadrant; the heaviest now almost east, so that the sledge continually bumps over ridges. The wind is from the W.N.W. chiefly, but the weather remains fine and there are no sastrugi from that direction.

Camp 67. Lunch obs.: Lat. 89 26 57; Lat. dead reckoning, 89 33 15 S.; Long. 160 56 45 E.; Var. 179 E.

It is wonderful to think that two long marches would land us at the Pole. We left our depôt to-day with nine days' provisions, so that it ought to be a certain thing now, and the only appalling possibility the sight of the Norwegian flag forestalling ours. Little Bowers continues his indefatigable efforts to get good sights, and it is wonderful how he works them up in his sleeping-bag in our congested tent, (minimum for night −27.5°). Only *27* miles from the Pole. We *ought* to do it now.

TUESDAY, JANUARY 16ᵀᴴ, 1912

Amundsen

Tuesday 16 Jan. It was baking hot during the last stop. Although I lay on top of the sleeping bag thinly clad, I could not sleep because of the heat. It felt warmer and more uncomfortable than the hottest summer night at home. Had fine weather on our march today. Light NW'ly breeze and clear, so we have been able to follow all the cairns. Arrived at 82°30' S. lat. 1.30 a.m. after a march of 5½ hours. Continue soon after midday when we have had our seven hours' sleep. Splendid skiing. Over-healthy dogs – now they can't manage to eat up their food any more. Have crossed the mysterious dog tracks at several cairns.

[We] were off again around 1 p.m. Splendid weather. Overcast but very clear. We could follow the dog tracks past the first two cairns. Then they swerved a little and disappeared. Have followed the cairns the whole time. Oddly enough, the cairn where 'Else' was laid lay far off our course – as much as ¾ nautical mile to our east. Nonetheless we made the detour, and it was worth it. 'Else' lay there fine and undamaged. Admittedly she had fallen down from the cairn and her fat – she was particularly fat – was somewhat yellow – affected by the sun, but the flesh was tip-top. Oddly enough neither the birds nor the mysterious dogs had touched her. We are now lying at the cairn at 82°15', and have just brought 'Else' out. They were crazy about her.

Bjaaland

82°30' **Tuesday 16 January.** −10.8 −11. Fine and clear, good skiing, found the cairns, saw dog tracks at the 35' m cairn.

16 January. 6 p.m. 30 m per 24 hours. 82°15'. Fine weather, found Else untouched, it was picked up, it smelled a little bad. Saw dog tracks once or twice, it seemed as if there were two.

Scott

Jan. 16ᵗʰ, Tuesday. Camp 68, 9760, T. –23.5, The worst has happened, or nearly the worst. We marched well in the morning and covered 7½. Noon sight showed us in Lat. 89° 42' S., and we started off in high spirits in the afternoon, feeling that to-morrow would see us at our destination. About the second hour of the march Bower's sharp eyes detected what he thought was a cairn; he was uneasy about it, but argued that it must be a sastrugus [sic]. Half an hour later he detected a black speck ahead. Soon we knew that this could not be a natural snow feature. We marched on, found that it was a black flag tied to a sledge bearer; near by the remains of a camp; sledge tracks and ski tracks going and coming and the clear trace of dogs' paws – many dogs. This told us the whole story. The Norwegians have forestalled us and are first at the Pole. It is a terrible disappointment, and I am very sorry for my loyal companions, Many *bitter* thoughts come and much discussion have we had. To-morrow we must march on to the Pole and then hasten home with all the speed we can compass. All the day dreams must go; it will be a wearisome return. We are descending in altitude – certainly also the Norwegians found an easy way up.

Figure 26 Black flag placed by Amundsen to warn Scott that he had lost the race. Sketch by Dr. E.A. Wilson, 16 January 1912.

– From gravure reproduction in *Scott's Last Expedition*, 1913. *Author's collection.*

WEDNESDAY, JANUARY 17TH, 1912

Amundsen

Wednesday 17 Jan. Arrived at the depot at 82° S. lat. at 11 a.m. The fugitive dogs had run riot here. They had managed to attack the pile of packing cases and push them over. They had managed to take off the lid of one of the sledge cases and eat the contents – biscuits and 20 pieces of human pemmican – luckily we did not need them. The two doggy carcasses that lay here had naturally vanished. Luckily they did not manage to remove the lid of the other sledge case. We had masses of seal steak and chocolate in it. Miraculously the bag of dried milk was safe. It lay at half-past eleven on top of a packing case that they had not managed to overturn. Only the jawbone remained of 'Lussi', who was deposited three nautical miles from here. The weather was lovely this morning, and the skiing brilliant. The terrain is quite undulating from 83° S. lat. We have now loaded all edible things on to the sledges. We are leaving equipment behind. The little pennants that attached to packing case planks for transverse marking were just as visible as the day they were put out. Not much snow could have fallen. This evening had special little meal to celebrate our arrival at 'civilization's furthermost outpost in the south.' W. has to be cook on such occasions. He plied us with a mixture of pemmican and seal steak. For dessert: chocolate pudding. The dried milk, which has lain on the top of the depot in a fairly thin bag, exposed to great humidity and blazing sunburn was just as good as the day we got it on board. Sætre biscuits were also just as good as before. Likewise the chocolate.

Bjaaland

82° **17th Wednesday.** –10 –9.6. 11 a.m. Thick weather, which soon turned fine, found the cairns. Lussi, who lay at 82°3', had been taken by the dogs, likewise Jaala and Uranus and 20 rations of pemmican had disappeared, the dried milk and chocolate, however, were untouched. Today we have a special dinner of steak and Pem. Ought to have a lot of pudding here, but I doubt whether we will get it.

Scott

Wednesday, Jan. 17th. Camp 69. T. –22 at start. Night –21. The POLE Yes, but under very different circumstances from those expected. We have had a horrible day –add to our disappointment a head wind 4 to 5, with a temperature –22, and companions labouring on with cold feet & hands.

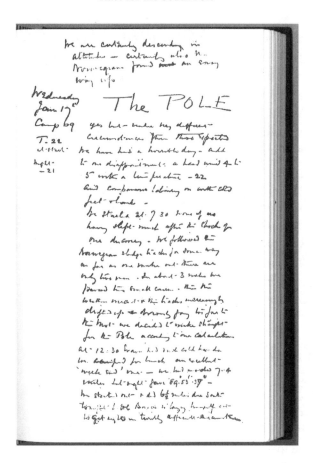

Figure 27 Entry in Scott's diary recording arrival at the South Pole 17 January 1912.

– Cambridge University Library

We started at 7.30, none of us having slept much after the shock of our discovery. We followed the Norwegian sledge tracks for some way; as far as we make
out there are only two men. In about three miles we passed two small cairns.
Then the weather overcast, and the tracks increasingly drifted up and obviously
going too far to the west, we decided to make straight for the Pole according to
our calculations. At 12.30 Evans had such cold hands we camped for lunch –
an excellent 'week-end one.' We had marched 7.4 miles. Lat. sight gave 89° 53'
37". We started out and did 6½ miles due south. To-night little Bowers is laying
himself out to get sights in terribly difficult circumstances; the wind is blowing
hard, T. –21°, and there is that curious damp, cold feeling in the air which chills
one to the bone in no time. We have been descending again, I think, but there
looks to be a rise ahead; otherwise there is very little that is different from the

awful monotony of past days. Great – God this is an awful place and terrible
enough for us to have laboured to it without the reward of priority. Well, it is
something to have got here, and the wind may be our friend to-morrow. We
have had a fat Polar hoosh in spite of our chagrin, and feel comfortable inside
– added a small stick of chocolate and the queer taste of a cigarette brought by
Wilson. Now for the run home and a desperate struggle *to get the news through
first.* I wonder if we can do it.

*In an appropriate coincidence, Scott has finally reached the Pole on the same day that
Amundsen arrived at 'civilization's furthermost outpost in the South', or the last depot
he had put out the previous autumn, and therefore was as good as home. Amundsen is
now 480 miles ahead as the crow flies.*

*Scott also grasps the impact of the headlines, so consoles himself with the thought of
at least beating Amundsen to the cablehead.*

FRIDAY, JANUARY 18TH, 1912

Amundsen

Friday 18 Jan.
Off around 10 o'clock yesterday evening. Have followed the packing case boards
which we used to mark the track in March on our depot journey – each as tall as
ever up to 81°45'. The snow did not seem to have risen around them. Overcast.
Cleared up this morning. –10° Arrived here 4 a.m. Brilliant conditions. A little
loose for the doggies. Off again ca. 2 p.m. The weather was as it has turned out
to be on the barrier in summer – grey. –8°. Skiing brilliant. Grainy snow. Hard
upper crust, which the skis float over. Rather heavy for the dogs, as they break
through. Have followed our packing case marking right up to 81°33' There the
marking finished with two end boards from packing case no.88. These were
placed on a snow pedestal nearly 1 year ago, and looked as if they were put up
yesterday. Pitched our tent at 81°30' S. lat. It was 30 nautical miles today.

Bjaaland

Thursday 18 January –12 –10 Stratus 10. A thin band to the north helped a lot
to hold a course. Found the sledge case planks that were put out last year. Had
the most wonderful chocolate pudding for dessert.

8 p.m. same day. 81°30'. Have done 30 m. today, skiing good but poor marks for route finding. Passed sledge case planks stuck on top of some blocks of snow last year. Southerly wind.

Scott

Thursday morning, Jan. 18th. Decided after summing up all observations that we were 3.5 miles away from the Pole – one mile beyond it and 3 to the right. More or less in this direction Bowers saw a cairn or tent.

We have just arrived at this tent, 2 miles from our camp, therefore about 1½ miles from the Pole. In the tent we find a record of five Norwegians having been here, as follows:

> Roald Amundsen
> Olav Olavson Bjaaland
> Helmer Hansson [sic]
> Sverre H. Hassel
> Oscar Wisting.
> 16 Decr. 1911.

The tent is fine – a small compact affair supported by a single bamboo. A note from Amundsen, which I keep, asks me to forward a letter to King Haakon! *I am puzzled at the object.*

The following articles have been left in the tent: 3 half bags of reindeer containing a miscellaneous assortment of mits and sleeping socks, very various in description, a sextant, a Norwegian artificial horizon and a hypsometer without boiling-point thermometers, a sextant and hypsometer of English make.

Left a note to say I had visited the tent with companions. Bowers photographing and Wilson sketching. Since lunch we have marched 6.2 miles S.S.E. by compass (i.e. northwards). Sights at lunch gave us ½ to ¾ of a mile from the Pole, so we call it the Pole Camp. T. Lunch –21°. We built a cairn, put up our poor slighted Union Jack, and photographed ourselves – mighty cold work all of it – less than ½ a mile south we saw stuck up an old underrunner of a sledge. This we commandeered as a yard for a floorcloth sail. I imagine it was intended to mark the exact spot of the Pole as near as the Norwegians could fix it. Height 9500. A note attached talked of the tent as being 2 miles from the Pole. Wilson keeps the note. There is no doubt that our predecessors have made thoroughly sure of their mark and fully carried out their programme. I think the Pole is about

9500 feet in height; this is remarkable, considering that in Lat. 88° we were about 10,500.

We carried the Union Jack about ¾ of a mile north with us and left it on a piece of stick as near as we could fix it. I fancy the Norwegians arrived at the pole on the 15th Dec. and left on the 17th. *I think it quite evident they aimed to forestall a* date quoted by me in London as ideal, viz. Dec. 22. It looks as though the Norwegian party expected colder weather on the summit than they got; it could scarcely be otherwise from S's *overdrawn* account. Well, we have turned our back now on the goal of our ambition *with sore feelings* and must face our 800 miles of solid dragging-and good-bye to most of the day-dreams!

Obsessed by Shackleton to the bitter end, Scott can afford to look on Amundsen with relative composure. His ghostly rival, rising like a wraith out of the whirling snow, is still the real enemy, and now Scott has beaten him.

Scott might have suspected a veiled insult in Amundsen's request to forward his letter to King Haakon. It was simply a precaution because, as Amundsen himself said: 'The way home was long and so much could happen to prevent us telling about our journey ourselves.'[73]

Figure 28 The British at the South Pole, in front of Amundsen's tent, 18th January 1912. Standing (l. to r.) Wilson, Scott, Bowers. Sitting (l. to r.) P.O. Evans, Oates.

– *National Library of Norway*

The tracks of Amundsen and Scott around the Pole were necessarily tortuous. To disentangle them they appear together in the map on p. xvi. It is based on their own observations. From this comes the ultimate irony. Through mistaking the left-hand flag used by Amundsen to box the Pole for the Pole itself, it seems that Scott never quite reached the mathematical point at all.[74]

FRIDAY, JANUARY 19TH, 1912

Amundsen

Friday 19 Jan.
Unusually fine weather today. Light SSW breeze that cleared the sky during our march. At 81°20' we had our old seracs across our path. We saw many more than ever. They ran in a NE direction as far as the eye could see, with ridges and summits. Shortly afterwards we were greatly surprised to catch sight of high, bare land in the same direction – E. true ca. 25 nautical miles off. And not long after, two high white peaks in a SE'ly direction, presumably around 82°. It was easy to see from the sky that land ran NE-SW (true). This is K.E. Land popping up again. We now have such good material that we can trace the whole chain without hesitation. The terrain towards land is heavily disturbed – crevasses and seracs, waves and dips, confused and criss-cross. We'll close with them tomorrow alright.– Same fine skiing all day. –10.5°. We have been able to see our cairns to the W during the whole march between 82°–81°. Now we are beginning to rejoin them. Now we have seal steak in our pemmican for dinner. That gives it an especially good taste. When we reach 80°, we will be among the fleshpots. We will have everything possible.

Bjaaland

Friday 19 January. –10 –10.5 81°15'. The best day we have had for a long time, with sunshine and south-westerly wind. Glimpsed King Edward VII Land today. Saw several rocky and snowclad mountains, which seemed to run in a NE direction. I think they are 30 m off.

Scott

Friday, Jan. 19ᵗʰ. Lunch 8.1, T. −20.6. Early in the march we picked up a Norwegian cairn and our outward tracks. We followed these to the ominous black flag which has first apprised us of our *unwelcome* predecessors' success. We have picked this flag up, using the staff for our sail, and are now camped about 1½ miles further back on our tracks. So that is the last of the Norwegians for the present. The surface undulates considerably about this latitude; it was more evident to-day than when we were outward bound.

Night camp R. 2. Height 9700. T. −18.5, Min. −25.6. Came along well this afternoon for three hours, then a rather dreary finish for the last 1½. Weather very curious, snow clouds, looking very dense and spoiling the light, pass over-head from the S, dropping very minute crystals; between showers the sun shows and the wind goes to the S.W. The fine crystals absolutely spoil the surface; we had heavy dragging during the last hour in spite of the light load and a full sail. Our old tracks are drifted up, deep in places, and toothed sastrugi have formed over them. It looks as though this sandy snow was drifted about like sand from place to place. How account for the present state of our three day old tracks and the month old ones of the Norwegians?

It is warmer and pleasanter marching with the wind, but I'm not sure we don't feel the cold more when we stop and camp than we did on the outward march. We pick up our cairns easily, and ought to do so right through, I think; but, of course, one will be a bit anxious till the Three Degree Depôt is reached. I'm afraid the return journey is going to be dreadfully tiring and monotonous.

SATURDAY, JANUARY 20ᵀᴴ, 1912

Amundsen

Saturday 20 Jan.
Off at 10 o'clock yesterday evening. Luckily we had clear weather. SW'ly breeze. −19°. It is a really fiendish terrain that we have passed. And when I think that we have already passed here three times, I am surprised that it has gone well. It began at 81°12'. Hollows and haycocks, holes and chasms in such numbers that I have not seen the like. Big pieces of the surface had simply fallen down and left gaping abysses. All went well, except that HH drove his sledge half way into a crevasse. We reached the depot at 4 a.m. We had strayed ca. 1 nautical mile to the east. It was completely in order. No doggies had been here. The doggies have had all they could eat this evening. Now we have double feeds for four days

on the sledges. On a few occasions today the lines of seracs along K.E's Land stood out very clearly. They ran NE-SW as far as the eye could see. [We] were up and on our way at 6 p.m. Wonderful weather. Fine and sunny. −11°. Crossed a few crevasses and are now clear of them until we come down into the 'filthy terrain'. Reached the cairn at 80°45' at 8 p.m. Here lay our first slaughtered dog, 'Bone'. The dogs are now so overfed, that many of them cannot stand the sight of pemmican. 'Bone', on the other hand, went down like hot cakes.

Bjaaland

Saturday 20 81° −19 −15. Raced to the depot at 81° today. 17 m. in six hours' march. Saw land to the east both south and north right down to 80°30', I think. We have run a little too far to the west, and perhaps for that reason not climbed a ridge, and the land would then be hidden. Passed many foul crevasses and disturbance. Arrived a little to the right of the depot.

9 o'clock Saturday 20 January. −11 −15 80°45'. Wonderful weather and skiing, found Bone at a stop, and dug it up. Westerly wind.

Scott

Saturday, Jan. 20th. Lunch camp, 9810. We have come along very well this morning, although the surface was terrible bad −9.3 miles in 5 hrs 20 m. This has brought us to our Southern Depôt, and we pick up 4 days' food. We carry on 7 days from to-night with 55 miles to go. The same sort of weather and a little more wind, sail drawing well.

Night Camp R. 3. 9860. Temp. −18. It was blowing quite hard and drifting when we started our afternoon march. At first with full sail we went along at a great rate; then we got on to an extraordinary surface, the drifting snow lying in heaps; it clung to the ski, which could only be pushed forward with an effort. The pulling was really awful, but we went steadily on and camped a short way beyond our cairn of the 14th. I'm afraid we are in for a bad pull again to-morrow, luckily the wind holds. I shall be very glad when Bowers gets his ski; I'm afraid he must find these long marches very trying with short legs but he is an undefeated little sportsman. I think Oates is feeling the cold and fatigue more than most of us. It is blowing pretty hard to-night, but with a good march we have earned one good hoosh and are very comfortable in the tent. It is everything now to keep up a good marching pace; I trust we shall be able to do so and catch the ship.

SUNDAY, JANUARY 21ST, 1912

Amundsen

Sunday 21 Jan.
Brilliant weather. −17°. Clear light w'ly breeze. Have followed our cairns and are now lying at the cairn at 80°30'. From 81° the skiing has been rather uneven − sometimes sticky, sometimes smooth − but mostly the latter. We like it very much when we can stop at a cairn, because high sastrugi have formed − excellent for a camp, and the sun has changed the cairn itself into pieces of ice, the finest source of water for our cooks.

Bjaaland

Sunday 21. 80°30' −17 −13 15 m. in the tent 11 a.m. W. wind. Wonderful weather.

Scott

Sunday, Jan. 21ˢᵗ. R. 4-. 10,010. T. blizzard, −18 to −11, to −14 now. Awoke to a stiff blizzard; air very thick with snow and sun very dim. We decided not to march owing to likelihood of losing track; expected at least a day of lay up, but whilst at lunch there was a sudden clearance and wind dropped to light breeze. We got ready to march, but gear was so iced up we did not get away till 3.45. Marched till 7.40 − a terribly weary four-hour drag; even with helping wind we only did 5½ miles. The surface bad, horribly bad on new sastrugi, and decidedly rising again in elevation.

We are going to have a pretty hard time this next 100 miles I expect. If it was difficult to drag downhill over this belt, it will probably be a good deal more difficult to drag up. Luckily the tracks are fairly distinct, though we only see our cairns when less than a mile away; 45 miles to the next depôt and 6 days' food in hand-then pick up 7 days' food T. −22 and 90 miles to go to the 'Three Degree' Depôt. Once there we ought to be safe, but we ought to have a day or two in hand on arrival − and may have difficulty with following the tracks. However, if we can get a rating sight for our watches tomorrow we shall be independent of the tracks at a pinch.

MONDAY, JANUARY 22ND, 1912

Amundsen

Monday 22 Jan.

Lovely weather. Calm when we set off yesterday evening in blazing sunshine at 10 o'clock. At 80°23' we passed our last cairn. Weatherbeaten and snowed up, worn away and unassuming, it had done its duty. There stood our last sentinel, grave and silent – a memorial to the hand of man even in these desolate regions. A 'Skua Gull' came to visit us when we made camp at 80°15'. I dare say we will soon see more.

Off again at 12 midnight. The sky was overcast, but it was fine and clear. Light SE'ly breeze ca. –7°. Reached the depot at 80° 11.30 a.m. Everything in order. Report by Pr. that he, Jørg. and Joh. were here the 13 Nov. with two sledges, 16 dogs, and supplies for 30 days. Thus we have a realistic hope of being able to complete the entire west coast of K.E VII according to our observations. Our doggies have now been given unlimited access to the mound of seals that is lying here. They had overeaten so much, that their presence there did not last particularly long. They turned round, going back to their respective sledges. The uppermost boxes of biscuits on the depot must be considered lost, since the sun has split open the boxes which are painted black, humidity has penetrated, and the biscuits have decomposed, so to say. Everything else was in order. Of biscuits in tins, there are seven in all. Here we leave one sledge case of biscuits, ca. 25 kg of chocolate and some bags of dried milk. We have taken 12 pieces of human pemmican, 40 seal steaks from the depot. The depot is marked by a flag on a high pole on the top. The depot itself will naturally become drifted over, but the flag will always show the site. As usual the skiing here on the plain at 80° is extremely loose. Deep, deep snow.

Bjaaland

Monday 22. 3 a.m. 80°15' –17 –13. Fifteen miles march. Had a visit from a skua gull which circled the tent and settled on a snow block. Veering from the N. the wind is now blowing from the south.

6 o'clock 22nd. 80° –7 –5.5 Arrived here 5 p.m. after a journey of 14 m. Saw the depot 3.5 m. off, straight ahead. Found a report from Prestrud and Johannessen and Stubberud, they left here 13/11 1911 heading East towards King Edward the VII'th Land. South East wind, overcast. So now we are four marches from Framheim. It was a damned hard job being forerunner.

Scott

Monday, Jan. 22nd. 10,000. T. −21. I think about the most tiring march we have had; solid pulling the whole way, in spite of the light sledge and some little helping wind at first. Then in the last part of the afternoon the sun came out, and almost immediately we had the whole surface covered with soft snow.

We got away sharp at 8 and marched a solid nine hours, and thus we have covered 14.5 miles (geo.) but, by Jove it has been a grind. We are just about on the 89th parallel. To-night Bowers got a rating sight. I'm afraid we have passed out of the wind area. We are within 2½ miles of the 64th camp cairn, 30 miles from our depôt, and with 5 days' food in hand. Ski boots are beginning to show signs of wear; I trust we shall have no giving out of ski or boots, since there are yet so many miles to go. I thought we were climbing to-day, but the barometer gives no change.

To Bjaaland, the depot at 80° S. was as good as home. The hardship of the forerunner was a skier's own idiosyncratic exit line.

By coincidence, Scott was also deploring less than ideal going, but he was still up on the ice cap, and over 500 miles behind.

TUESDAY, JANUARY 23RD, 1912

Amundsen

Tuesday 23 Jan.
Irritating misty weather when we turned out this morning at 4 o'clock. Temp. was good −11°. Originally I had thought that of doing this last stretch – to Framheim – in stages of 20 nautical miles, but the snow turned out to be so deep, that we had to stop after 15 nautical miles. It was quite enough for man and beast. The seal meat at 80° is now marked by two ski sticks, so now it can safely drift over.

Bjaaland

Tuesday 23 January. 79°45' −11 −10 S.East wind. Ha ha, those fellows who thought they would be pulled 20 m will just have to traipse to Framheim. Have returned to a 15 m. march. Framheim Friday.

Scott

Tuesday, Jan. 23rd. Lowest min. last night −30, Temp. at start −28. Lunch height 10,100. T. with wind 6 to 7, −19. Little wind and heavy marching at start. Then wind increased and we did 8.7 miles by lunch, when it was practically blowing a blizzard. The old tracks show so remarkably well that we can follow them without much difficulty – a great piece of luck.

In the afternoon we had to reorganise. Could carry a whole sail. Bowers hung on to the sledge, Evans and Oates had to lengthen out. We came along at a great rate and should have got within an easy march of our depôt had not Wilson suddenly discovered that Evans' nose was frostbitten – it was white and hard. We thought it best to camp at 6.45. Got the tent up with some difficulty, and now pretty cosy after good hoosh.

There is no doubt Evans is a good deal run down – his fingers are badly blistered and his nose is rather seriously congested with frequent frost bites. He is very much annoyed with himself, which is not a good sign. I think Wilson, Bowers and I are as fit as possible under the circumstances. Oates gets cold feet. One way and another, I shall be glad to get off the summit! We are only about 13 miles from our 'degree & half' depôt and should get there to-morrow. The weather seems to be breaking up. Pray God we have something of a track to follow to the Three Degree Depôt – once we pick that up we ought to be right.

WEDNESDAY, JANUARY 24TH, 1912

Amundsen

Wednesday 24 Jan.
Off at 8 o'clock yesterday evening. It was filthy weather to begin with, but little-by-little it cleared, and 3 nautical miles from the campsite – 18 nautical miles from 80° – we ran into our good old friends, the ridges with spikes on top. We were a little to the east, but very little. Until the ridges, the going had been bad – deep, loose snow, very heavy for the dogs. Difficult for the skiers too, because the snow balled up in big, hard clumps between ski and boots, making it extremely difficult and unstable. N of the ridges, the terrain and snow conditions changed little by little – became good, hard going with ice ridges here and there. It was a great change from the 80° plain, because there was not a *single* irregularity. Only deep, loose even snow. Just before we had done our 15 nautical miles, we arrived at another ridge with spikes running E-W. We ran beneath it along some crevasses – quite narrow. We are a little too far to the east. As soon as we have

passed the 'filth' at 45', we will keep more to the W. to find the old line of flags.

Off again at 11 a.m. The weather was brilliant. Dead calm with baking sunshine −25°. First of all we crossed over a little depression, probably the same where the '45' filth' lies. But we were too far to the E. and saw nothing of it. Then we began the ascent of our old familiar ridge to the E. During this we changed course westwards by ¼ point – S by W. ¼ S – in order to bring us down to the line of flags. Conditions on the climb were beneath contempt. Deep, sticky loose snow. A tedious slog for both man and beast. When we arrived at the top, the conditions immediately changed – good and hard. To my surprise, the barometer showed a climb of 1,000 ft. That proves that we have strayed somewhat too far to the E. – 30 nautical miles today.

Bjaaland

Wednesday 24 2.30 a.m. 79°30' −12 −17. Snowfall and drift that lifted after an hour. Passed our ice mounds at 79°42', are now a few miles to the east, found some ice mounds which we passed to the East. We saw some crevasses.

6 p.m. 24th 79°15' −12 −14. Splendid weather, but bloody heavy and sticky skiing, have come far to the east, have climbed 1,000 feet.

Scott

Wednesday, Jan. 24th. T. lunch T. −8. Things beginning to look a little serious. A strong wind at the start has developed into a full blizzard at lunch, and we have had to get into our sleeping-bags. It was a bad march, but we covered 7 miles. At first Evans, and then Wilson went ahead to scout for tracks. Bowers guided the sledge alone for the first hour, then both Oates and he remained alongside it; they had a fearful time trying to make the pace between the soft patches. At 12.30 the sun coming ahead made it impossible to see the tracks further, and we had to stop. By this time the gale was at its height and we had the dickens of a time getting up the tent, cold fingers all round. We are only 7 miles from our depôt, but I made sure we should be there to-night. This is the second full gale since we left the Pole. I don't like the look of it. Is the weather breaking up? If so, God help us, with the tremendous summit journey and scant food. Wilson and Bowers are my standby. I don't like the easy way in which Oates and Evans get frostbitten.

Amundsen's 30 nautical miles this day must be set against the seven miles of Scott. This encapsulates the whole story. Nonetheless, at a deeper level, it is not the disparity that counts, but what stopped Scott in his tracks. It was a following *wind.*

In detail, it was a stiff gale from the SSE, force 8. It so happens that on 2 December – Bjaaland's 'Devil's name-day' – up on the ice cap, Amundsen had similar conditions, with a south-easterly gale force 8. Since he was still making for the Pole, this meant a head wind. With thick drift, visibility was approximately nil. Nonetheless Amundsen covered his 13 nautical miles for the day.

The difference was technical. Amundsen had prepared for travelling blind, but not Scott. The key lay in the compasses. Amundsen's ship's models, fixed on the sledges, allowed travel in any conditions. Scott only had pocket compasses and portable sundials, both of which assumed good visibility to take the necessary bearings. Nor had he grasped the complexities of man-hauling. In the traces, it was well-nigh impossible to navigate without periodic halts to take compass bearings, and marks in the terrain by which to steer.

To depend on outward tracks in the snow was a risky business. Keeping a course in poor visibility needed someone to follow on behind and call out directions. Scott did not have a man to spare, or the thought did not occur to him. Consequently, as on this particular occasion, he was stopped by a following wind, which otherwise ought to have helped him along. It was one more link in a fateful chain of errors.

Another was Scott's poor judgement in his choice of men. He now recognized the two weak members of his party. P.O. Evans, six feet tall, and barrel-chested, was a big, beefy heavyweight of a figure. This ought to have disqualified him on two counts. In the first place, it meant that he needed more food. Also he was of a type that lacked stamina, being prone to mental breakdown under stress. Oates, for his part, was never really fit enough. In the Boer War, a shot had shattered his left thigh bone, leaving him with a limp that caused him trouble to which he would never admit. Scott, however, was a sentimentalist. He wanted the Army represented at the Pole and, from the Navy, the Lower Deck as well. Oates and Evans filled the bill. As Scott's subordinates had noted, he was indefatigably fond of Evans. Around the turn of the century, they had been shipmates on HMS Majestic. *On that account or otherwise, Scott had never been able to see his faults.*

THURSDAY, JANUARY 25TH, 1912

Amundsen

Thursday 25 Jan.
Off at 4 a.m. Arrived at 10 a.m. Done 21 nautical miles. Brilliant weather to begin with. −22° – fairly cold. Clear. Have descended all day. Going splendid.

The doggies have flown as never before. When we got down, the SW'ster blew up, with drift, fog and other filth, so that we couldn't see anything. Hope it stops in the course of today so that we can reach Framheim early tomorrow morning.

Bjaaland

25th Thursday. 10 a.m. 78°55′ 18 m. from Framheim. Dear God, we have come so close to our dear Framheim. Covered 21 m. today with the best snow we have had for a long time. I also tagged along with a sledge the last 5 m. Are definitely still far East of our route. Our idea is to come home and catch them asleep on Friday morning. The wind freshened to a light gale from SSW. We have almost no food, a few biscuits and chocolate.

Scott

Thursday, Jan. 25th. T. lunch −11°, T. night −16°. Thank God we found our half degree depôt. After lying in our bags yesterday afternoon and all night, we debated breakfast; decided to have it later and go without lunch. At the time the gale seemed as bad as ever, but during breakfast the sun showed and there was light enough to see the old track. It was a long and terribly cold job digging out our sledge and breaking camp, but we got through and on the march without sail, all pulling. This was about 11, and at about 2.30, to our joy, we saw the red depôt flag. We had lunch and left with 9½ days' provisions, still following the track-marched till 8 and covered over 5 miles, over 12 in the day. Only 89 miles (geogr.) to the next depôt, but it's time we cleared off this plateau. We are not without ailments: Oates suffers from a very cold foot; Evans' fingers and nose are in a bad state, and to-night Wilson is suffering tortures from his eyes. Bowers and I are the only members of the party without troubles just at present. The weather still looks unsettled, and I fear a succession of blizzards at this time of year; the wind is strong from the south, and this afternoon has been very helpful with the full sail. Needless to say I shall sleep much better with our provision bag full again. The only real anxiety now is the finding of the 3 degree depôt. The tracks seem as good as ever so far; sometimes for 30 or 40 yards we lose them under drifts, but then they reappear quite clearly raised above the surface. If the light is good there is not the least difficulty in following; Blizzards are our bugbear, not only stopping our marches, but the cold damp air takes it out of us. Bowers got another rating sight to-night – it was wonderful how he managed to observe in such a horribly cold wind. He has been on ski to-day whilst Wilson walked by the sledge or pulled ahead of it.

FRIDAY, JANUARY 26ᵀᴴ, 1912

Amundsen

26 Jan.1912

When we started off yesterday evening at 10 o'clock, the weather was of the most unpleasant kind. Calm with thick snowfall and drift so that one could not see more than the tips of one's skis. Luckily, as we jogged along, it began to lift, and with a light breeze that sprang up from the SE, it brightened properly. We had not seen any of the flags that had been put out, but according to our course, I assumed that we were fairly close to the line of flags. I therefore decided to follow our old course – true N. (W. by S.) After 8 miles march, a large, dark object hove into sight – 2 points off our course – to the west. We struck out for it. It turned out to be one of our sledges, which we had left at the start on the 20ᵗʰ October 1911. Before we knew it, we had reached our point of departure. We saw nothing of *Fram*, but that was hardly to be wondered at because the whole inner part of the bay was covered with ice. Framheim, on the other hand, lay, as we had left it, bathed in the morning sun. It did not take us a long time to cross the bay and at 4 a.m. we were once more in our snug little house – welcomed by our somewhat surprised companions. They had not expected us for a long time yet. News was quickly exchanged and everything declared in order. *Fram* had arrived 9 January, about three months out from Buenos Aires, but because of the ice, forced to keep to the N. side in a small bay (Balloon Bight). After we had had a bite to eat, we set off to visit *Fram*. But we could have saved ourselves the trouble. W'ly winds had driven her out of the bay, but it was not easy to say where. We have set a watch on the nearest height, but this evening at 10.30 she had still not come. She has all our post on board, and naturally we would like to have it as soon as possible. Likewise it is also a matter of getting everything from here on board and setting off as soon as possible. Some Japanese are supposed to by staying in a tent out at the edge of the barrier.[75] What they intend to do, I haven't the slightest idea. They hardly know themselves. Lt. Pr., helped by Joh. & Jørgen have done all the work required of them. They have confirmed the existence of K.E.VII Land and taken rock samples. They have surveyed the land and the western disturbance in the barrier and filmed. There is a whole lot of seal here – Weddell and Crabeater. They have pupped long ago, and those people present have naturally indulged in the extra delicate meat. Only a few penguins have come yet. Today however the ice has disappeared a bit past 'Man's Head' and so we expect both *Fram* and the penguins to come in. We have heard a lot of news. A number of people seem to be indignant over our activities down here – a breach of 'etiquette'? Are these people mad? Is the question of the Pole exclusively reserved to Scott for solution? I don't give a hang for these idiots. Nansen, as usual, with his calm, clear understanding, has cooled emotions. Oh well, people are crazy.

Bjaaland

26th **Friday.** At Framheim again. Well thank God we are here again safe and sound. Came here at 3.30 in the morning, and caught them all in bed; *Fram* was nowhere to be seen, she had gone out because of the gale, so no post yet. Were rousingly greeted by everyone in the best possible way. Lindstrøm served hot cakes and all things good. Afterwards we quaffed a welcoming cup with everyone, a really good swig.

Scott

Friday, January 26th. T. –17. Height 9700, must be high barometer. Started late, 8.50 – for no reason, as I called the hands rather early. We must have fewer delays. There was a good stiff breeze and plenty of drift, but the tracks held. To our old blizzard camp of the 7th we got on well, 7 miles. But beyond the camp we found the tracks completely wiped out. We searched for some time, then marched on a short way and lunched, the weather gradually clearing, though the wind holding. Knowing there were two cairns at four mile intervals, we had little anxiety till we picked up the first far on our right, then steering right by a stroke of fortune, and Bowers' sharp eyes caught a glimpse of the second far on the left. Evidently we made a bad course outward at this part. There is not a sign of our tracks between these cairns, but the last, marking our night camp of the 6th, No.59, is in the belt of hard sastrugi, and I was comforted to see signs of the track reappearing as we camped. I hope to goodness we can follow it to-morrow. We marched 16 miles (geo.) to-day, but made good only 15.4.

It was just as well that Amundsen had been cut off from the outside world since the visit of Terra Nova *to the Bay of Whales a year before. Until now, he had been spared the indignation over his switch from north to south. The 'breach of "etiquette"' came from a leader in the* Daily Mail *on 'the importance of the old rules of Polar etiquette by which, when two or more parties are operating, each keeps to a distinct sphere.'* [76]

Not even this could spoil Amundsen's satisfaction at attaining his ultimate object- ive. He had caught his companions napping as intended. He was almost as pleased, perhaps, as having been first at the Pole. It had required careful timing over the past few days. As the polar party crept inside, Lindstrøm woke with a start, shouting: 'Wake up boys, it's the first cuckoo of spring!' A fitting reception, all things considered.

SATURDAY, JANUARY 27TH, 1912

Amundsen

27 Jan. Saturday

So all the news has been digested. *Fram* came in yesterday just after midday, and lay to in our own bay inside 'Man's Head'. We all went on board to greet our companions. Everything was in the very best order. They were driven out, and had great trouble in beating up to the barrier again. Capt. Nilsen – *Fram's* future commander – had much that was new to report. His description of his stay in B.A. and contact with Christophersen there was of special interest. It is to the intervention of this man that the third *Fram* expedition owes its continued existence. At home, all doors were shut – with the exception of the King and Fridtjof Nansen. May the confidence that they have shown me not be disap- pointed! I admire the King for his manly behaviour. Likewise the other two gentlemen. When everyone turned their backs on me, they came towards me. The King was not afraid to give a contribution to the South Polar expedition, even if parliament – or the majority – wanted *Fram* to be ordered home. But – it didn't go the way those gentlemen wanted. Just wait a bit, we'll soon have a talk. Perhaps you will be pleasanter the next time you hear from *Fram*. The plan is to now to go from here as quickly as possible to Hobart, Tasmania, and thence to B.A – *Fram's* second home, where I have to obtain temporary assistance for the drift. I owe K. N. & Chr. more than I can express. When everyone turned their backs – they stretched out their hand. God bless them! Hope to be ready to leave here Wednesday the 31st inst. – We won't bring more than is absolutely necessary on board. Time is precious, and we've got to reach civilization before anyone else. Start loading on board the day after tomorrow.

Bjaaland

Saturday 27 January. Well, the first night passed in a house, and I must say I slept like a log. Packing and preparation for moving from Framheim starts today. Hassel and I were 3 m. Southwards today to fetch three sledges which had remained there since the spring, then we caught sight of *Fram* far out in the bay, coming in towards the ice, and soon we will have our post at last, and hear the news.

At 1 p.m. *Fram* was at the edge of the ice, and called us down with the siren, where they greeted us with smiles and handshakes, The Captain and W. and H.H. stayed on board until evening. On the homeward journey, the dogs bolted & H. wanted to look for a whip that he had lost, and they just padded off. They were dead scared of ½ a pig they had on the sledge and all the Captain's post that was tied to the sledge. They were discovered safe and sound upside down in a hole near Mount Nilsen. In two to three days set sail for Tasmania and then . . .

Scott

Saturday, Jan. 27th. R. 10. T. –16° (lunch), T. –14.3° (evening). Min. –19. Height 9900. Barometer low ? Called the hands half an hour late, but we got away in good time. The forenoon march was over the belt of storm-tossed sastrugi; it looked like a rough sea. Wilson and I pulled in front on ski, the remainder on foot. It was very tricky work following the track, which pretty constantly disappeared, and in fact only showed itself by faint signs anywhere – a foot or two of raised sledge-track, a dozen yards of the trail of the sledge meter wheel, or a spatter of hard snow-flicks where feet had trodden. Sometimes none of these were distinct, but one got an impression of lines which guided. The trouble was that on the outward track one had to shape course constantly to avoid the heaviest mounds, and consequently there were many zig-zags. We lost a good deal over a mile by these halts, in which we unharnessed and went on the search for signs. However, by hook or crook, we managed to stick on the old track. Came on the cairn quite suddenly, marched past it, and camped for lunch at 7 miles. In the afternoon the sastrugi gradually diminished in size and now we are on fairly level ground to-day, the obstruction practically at an end, and, to our joy, the tracks showing up much plainer again. For the last two hours we had no difficulty at all in following them. There has been a nice helpful southerly breeze all day, a clear sky and comparatively warm temperature. The air is dry again, so that tents and equipment are gradually losing their icy condition imposed by the blizzard conditions of the past week.

Our sleeping-bags are slowly but surely getting wetter and I'm afraid it will take a lot of this weather to put them right. However, we all sleep well enough in them, the hours allowed being now on the short side. We are slowly getting more hungry, and it would be an advantage to have a little more food, especially for lunch. If we get to the next depôt in a few marches (it is now less than 60 miles and we have a full week's food) we ought to be able to open out a little, but we can't look for a real feed till we get to the pony food depôt. A long way to go, and, by Jove, this is tremendous labour.

So soon had victory started to turn sour for Amundsen. For the moment, he almost seems sadly to be echoing Ibsen's words: 'Up here among the fjords I have my native land. But-but-but where do I find my homeland?' It was, after all, an emigré, Don Pedro Christophersen, who had stepped into the breach. In gratitude, Amundsen renamed Haakonshallen, on the crossing of the Transantarctic Mountains, Mount Don Pedro Christopherson. Don Pedro was worth his mountain in the Antarctic.

SUNDAY, JANUARY 28ᵀᴴ, 1912

Amundsen

28 Jan. Sunday
Have kept absolutely quiet today. N. came up to visit us this evening. The weather is fine. Calm. Sunny in the forenoon. A little fog in the p.m. Nice and mild. Have already started carrying little things on board today, bedclothes, the gramophone and chronometers have gone. Tomorrow morning early it begins in earnest.

Bjaaland

Sunday 28 January 1912. There is a party at Framheim today because it is perhaps the last Sunday ashore. And then our good second in command, Lieutenant Nilsen came up and talked at length about all they had done.

Scott

Sunday, Jan. 28th. Lunch, –20°. Height, night, 10,130. R. 11. Supper T. –18°. Little wind and heavy going in forenoon. We just ran out 8 miles in 5 hours and added another 8 in 3 hours 40 mins in the afternoon with a good wind and better surface. It is very difficult to say if we are going up or down hill; the barometer is quite different from outward readings. We are 43 miles from the depôt, with six days food in hand. We are camped opposite our lunch cairn of the 4th, only half a day's march from the point at which the last supporting party left us.

Three articles were dropped on our outward march – Oates' pipe, Bowers' fur mits, and Evans' night boots. We picked up the boots and mits on the track, and to-night we found the pipe lying placidly in sight on the snow. The sledge tracks were very easy to follow to-day; they are becoming more and more raised, giving a good line shadow often visible half a mile ahead. If this goes on and the weather holds we shall get our depôt without trouble. I shall indeed be glad to get it on the sledge. We are getting more hungry, there is no doubt. The lunch meal is beginning to seem inadequate. We are pretty thin, especially Evans, but none of us are feeling worked out. I doubt if we could drag heavy loads, but we can keep going well with our light one. We talk of food a good deal more, and shall be glad to open out on it.

MONDAY, JANUARY 29TH, 1912

Amundsen

29 Jan. – Monday
Have been loading on board with 6 sledges all day. Will probably be ready to depart tomorrow evening. It has been almost calm and very mild – splendid going.

Scott

Monday, Jan. 29th. R. 12. Lunch T. –23. Supper T. –25. Height 10,000. Excellent march of 19½ miles, 10.5 before lunch. Wind helping greatly, considerable drift; tracks for the most part very plain. Some time before lunch we picked up the return track of the supporting party, so that there are now three distinct sledge impressions. We are only 24 miles from our depôt – an easy day and a half.

Given a fine day to-morrow we ought to get it without difficulty. The wind and sastrugi are S.S.E. and S.E. If the weather holds we ought to do the rest of the inland ice journey in little over a week. The surface is very much altered since we passed out. The loose snow has been swept into heaps, hard and wind-tossed. The rest has a glazed appearance, the loose drifting snow no doubt acting on it, polishing it like a sand blast. The sledge with our good wind behind runs splendidly on it; it is all soft and sandy beneath the glaze. We are certainly getting hungrier every day. The day after to-morrow we should be able to increase allowances. It is monotonous work, but, thank God, the miles are coming fast at last. We ought not to be delayed much now with the downgrade in front of us.

TUESDAY, JANUARY 30TH, 1912

Amundsen

30 Jan.– Tuesday

So I'm sitting once more at my desk on board dear old *Fram*, and feel the usual rolling movement. We had finished taking all the necessary victuals and stores on board by 9 o'clock this evening. An hour later we were under way. There was thick fog so a farewell to the barrier there was none. It was a heavy moment to leave Framheim. A more splendid or cosy winter quarters no one has had. When we departed, Lindstrøm had scoured it from top to bottom and it was shining like a new pin. We don't want to be accused of untidiness or dirt if anyone should happen to go there and look.

Bjaaland

Monday and Tuesday 29th and 30th were spent loading on board everything to be used on the N. voyage, and so at 9 p.m. on the 30th we headed out to sea bound for *Hobart*, Tasmania, and leave these regions and Framheim with all their splendour to anyone who wants them, maybe the Japs who are staying here over at the edge of the Barrier. Unfortunately the fog came down so that we saw nothing at all, but farewell then Framheim, your ice and snow and seal and crows and everything. You were fickle and unpleasant and cold now and then but better than I expected.

Scott

Tuesday, Jan. 30th. R. 13. 9860. Lunch T. –25, Supper T. –24.5. Thank the Lord, another fine march – 19 miles. We have passed the last cairn before the depôt, the track is clear ahead, the weather fair, the wind helpful, the gradient down – with any luck we should pick up our depôt in the middle of the morning march. This is the bright side; the reverse of the medal is serious. Wilson has strained a tendon in his leg; it has given pain all day and is swollen to-night. Of course, he is full of pluck over it, but I don't like the idea of such an accident here. To add to the trouble Evans has dislodged two finger-nails to-night; his hands are really bad, and to my surprise he shows signs of losing heart over it – *which makes me much disappointed in him.* He hasn't been cheerful since the accident. The wind shifted from S.E. to S. and back again all day, but luckily it keeps strong. We can get along with bad fingers, but it [will be] a mighty serious thing if Wilson's leg doesn't improve.

WEDNESDAY, JANUARY 31ST, 1912

Scott

Wednesday, Jan. 31st. 9800. Lunch T. –20, Supper T. –20. The day opened fine with a fair breeze; we marched on the depôt, picked it up, and lunched an hour later. In the afternoon the surface became fearfully bad, the wind dropped to light southerly air. Ill luck that this should happen just when we have only four men to pull. Wilson rested his leg as much as possible by walking quietly beside the sledge; the result has been good, and to-night there is much less inflammation. I hope he will be all right again soon, but it is trying to have an injured limb in the party. I see we had a very heavy surface here on our outward march. There is no doubt we are travelling over undulations, but the inequality of level does not make a great difference to our pace; it is the sandy crystals that hold us up. There has been very great alteration of the surface since we were last here – the sledge tracks stand high. This afternoon we picked up Bowers' ski – the last thing we have to find on the summit, thank Heaven! Now we have only to go north and so shall welcome strong winds.

THURSDAY, FEBRUARY 1ST, 1912

Scott

Thursday, Feb. 1st. R. 15. 9778. Lunch T. –20, Supper T. –19.8. Heavy collar work most of the day. Wind light. Did 8 miles, 4¾ hours. Started well in the afternoon and came down a steep slope in quick time; then the surface turned real bad –sandy drifts – very heavy pulling. Working on past 8 p.m. we just fetched a lunch cairn of Dec. 28th, when we were only a week out from the depôt. It ought to be easy to get in with a margin, having 8 days' food in hand (full feeding). We have opened out on the 1/7th increase and it makes a lot of difference. Wilson's leg much better. Evans' fingers now very bad, two nails coming off, blisters burst.

FRIDAY, FEBRUARY 2ND, 1912

Scott

Friday, Feb. 2nd. 9340. R. 16. T.: Lunch –19, Supper –17. We started well on a strong southerly wind. Soon got to a steep grade, when the sledge overran and upset us one after another. We got off our ski, and pulling on foot reeled off 9 miles by lunch at 1.30. Started in the afternoon on foot, going very strong. We noticed a curious circumstance towards the end of the forenoon. The tracks were drifted over, but the drifts formed a sort of causeway along which we pulled. In the afternoon we soon came to a steep slope – the same on which we exchanged sledges on Dec. 28th. All went well till, in trying to keep the track at the same time as my feet, on a very slippery surface, I came an awful 'purler' on my shoulder. It is horribly sore to-night and another sick person added to our tent – three out of five injured, and the most troublesome surfaces to come. We shall be lucky if we get through without serious injury. Wilson's leg is better, but might easily get bad again, Evans' fingers.

At the bottom of the slope this afternoon we came on a confused sea of sastrugi. We lost the track. Later, on soft snow, we picked up [Lt.] Evans' return track, which we are now following. We have managed to get off 17 miles. The extra food is certainly helping us, but we are getting pretty hungry. The weather is already a trifle warmer and the altitude lower, and only 80 miles or so to Mt Darwin. It is time we were off the summit – Pray God another four days will see us pretty well clear of it. Our bags are getting very wet and we ought to have more sleep.

SATURDAY, FEBRUARY 3RD, 1912

Scott

Saturday, Feb. 3rd. – R. 17. Temp.: Lunch –20; Supper –20. Height 9040 f. Started pretty well on foot; came to steep slope with crevasses (few). I went on ski to avoid another fall, and we took the slope gently with our sail, constantly losing the track, but picked up a much weathered cairn on our right. Vexatious delays, searching for tracks, &c., reduced morning march to 8.1 miles. Afternoon, came along a little better, but again lost tracks on hard slope. To-night we are near camp of Dec. 26th, but cannot see cairn. Have decided it is waste of time looking for tracks and cairn, and shall push on due north as fast as we can.

The surface is greatly changed since we passed outward, in most places polished smooth, but with heaps of new toothed sastrugi which are disagreeable obstacles. Evans fingers are going on as well as can be expected, but it will be long before he will be able to help properly with the work. Wilson's leg *much* better, and my shoulder also, though it gives bad twinges. The extra food is doing us all good, but we ought to have more sleep. Very few more days on the plateau I hope.

SUNDAY, FEBRUARY 4TH, 1912

Scott

Sunday, Feb. 4. R.18. 8620 f. Lunch –22; Supper –23. Pulled on foot in the morning over good hard surface and covered 9.7 miles. Just before lunch unexpectedly fell into crevasses, Evans and I together – a second fall for Evans, and I camped. After lunch saw disturbance ahead, and what I took for disturbance (land) to the right. We went on ski over hard shiny descending surface. Did very well, especially towards end of march, covering in all 18.1. We have come down some hundreds of feet. Half way in the march the land showed up splendidly, and I decided to make straight for Mt. Darwin, which we are rounding. Every sign points to getting away off this plateau. The temperature is 20° lower than when we were here before; the party is not improving in condition, especially Evans, who is becoming rather *stupid* & incapable. Thank the Lord we have good food at each meal, but we get hungrier in spite of it. Bowers is splendid, full of energy and bustle all the time. I hope we are not going to have trouble with ice-falls.

MONDAY, FEBRUARY 5TH, 1912

Scott

Monday, Feb. 5th. R. 18 [sic]. Lunch, 8320 ft., Temp. –17; Supper, 8120 ft., –17.2. A good forenoon, few crevasses; we covered 10.2 miles. In the afternoon we soon got into difficulties. We saw the land very clearly, but the difficulty is to get at it. An hour after starting we came on huge pressures and great street crevasses partly open. We had to steer more and more to the west, so that our course was very erratic. Late in the march we turned more to the north and again encountered open crevasses across our track. It is very difficult manoeuvring amongst these and I should not like to do it without ski.

We are camped in a very disturbed region, but the wind has fallen very light here, and our camp is comfortable for the first time for many weeks. We may be anything from 25 to 30 miles from our depôt, but I wish to goodness we could see a way through the disturbances ahead. Our faces are much cut up by all the winds we have had, mine least of all; the others tell me they feel their noses more going with than against wind. Evans' nose is almost as bad as his fingers. He is a good deal crocked up *and very stupid about himself.*

TUESDAY, FEBRUARY 6TH, 1912

Scott

Tuesday, Feb. 6th. Lunch 7900; Supper 7210. T. –15. We've had a horrid day and not covered good mileage. On turning out found sky overcast; a beastly position amidst crevasses. Luckily it cleared just before we started. We went straight for Mt. Darwin, but in half an hour found ourselves amongst huge open chasms, unbridged, but not very deep, I think. We turned to the north between two, but to our chagrin they converged into chaotic disturbance. We had to retrace our steps for a mile or so, then struck to the west and got on to a confused sea of sastrugi, pulling very hard; we put up the sail, Evans' nose suffered, Wilson very cold, everything horrid. Camped for lunch in the sastrugi; the only comfort, things looked clearer to the west and we were obviously going downhill. In the afternoon we struggled on, got out of sastrugi and turned over on glazed surface, crossing many crevasses – very easy work on ski. Towards the end of the march we realised the certainty of maintaining a more or less straight course to the depôt, and estimate distance 10 to 15 miles.

Food is low and weather uncertain, So that many hours of the day were anxious; but this evening, though we are not as far advanced as I expected, the outlook is much more promising. Evans is the chief anxiety now; his cuts and wounds suppurate, his nose looks very bad, and altogether he shows considerable signs of being played out. Things may mend for him on the glacier, and his wounds get some respite under warmer conditions. I am indeed glad to think we shall so soon have done with plateau conditions. It took us 27 days to reach the Pole and 21 days back – in all 48 days – nearly 7 weeks in low temperature with almost incessant wind.

WEDNESDAY, FEBRUARY 7TH, 1912

Scott

END of Summit Journey

Wednesday, Feb. 7th. Mt. Darwin Depôt, R. 21. Height 7100. Lunch T. −9 Supper T. A wretched day with satisfactory ending. First panic, certainty that biscuit-box was short. Great doubt as to how this has come about, as we certainly haven't over-issued allowances. Bowers is dreadfully disturbed about it. The shortage is a full day's allowance. We started our march at 8.30, and travelled down slopes and over terraces covered with hard sastrugi – very tiresome work – and the land didn't seem to come any nearer. At lunch the wind increased, and what with hot tea and good food, we started the afternoon in a better frame of mind, and it soon became obvious we were nearing our mark. Soon after 6.30 we saw our depôt easily and camped next it at 7.30.

Found note from Evans to say 2nd return party passed through safely at 2.30 on Jan. 14th – half a day longer between depots than we have been. *They have taken on their allowance of food.* The temperature is higher, but there is a cold wind to-night.

Well, we have come through our 7 weeks' ice cap journey and most of us are fit, but I think another week might have had a very bad effect on Evans, who is going steadily down hill.

It is satisfactory to recall that these facts give absolute, proof of both expeditions having reached the Pole and places the question of priority beyond discussion.

The last paragraph is on a page of its own, and out of context. It is clearly part of a draft public statement if Scott had been able to beat Amundsen to the cablehead and, as he hoped, get the news through first. See Scott's entry for 17 January p. 246.

THURSDAY, FEBRUARY 8TH, 1912

Scott

RETURN from Summit Depôt

Thursday, Feb. 8th. R. 22. Height 6260. Start T. –11; Lunch T. –5; Supper, zero. 9.2 miles. Started from the depôt rather late owing to weighing biscuit, etc., and rearranging matters. Had a beastly morning. Wind very strong and cold. Steered in for Mt. Darwin to visit rock. Sent Bowers on, on ski, as Wilson can't wear his at present. He obtained several specimens, all of much the same type, a close-grained granite rock which weathers red. Hence the pink limestone. After he rejoined we skidded downhill pretty fast, leaders on ski, Oates and Wilson on foot alongside sledge – Evans detached. We lunched at 2 well down towards Mᵗ Buckley, the wind half a gale and everybody very cold and cheerless. However, better things were to follow. We decided to steer for the moraine under Mᵗ. Buckley and, pulling with crampons, we crossed some very irregular steep slopes with big crevasses and slid down towards the rocks. The moraine was obviously so interesting that when we had advanced some miles and got out of the wind, I decided to camp and spend the rest of the day geologising. It has been extremely interesting. We found ourselves under perpendicular cliffs of Beacon sandstone, weathering rapidly and carrying veritable coal seams. From the last Wilson, with his sharp eyes, has picked several plant impressions, the last a piece of coal with beautifully traced leaves in layers, also some excellently preserved impressions of thick stems, showing cellular structure. In one place we saw the cast of small waves on the sand. To-night Bill has got a specimen of limestone with archeo-cyathus – the trouble is one cannot imagine where the stone comes from; it is evidently rare, as few specimens occur in the moraine. There is a good deal of pure white quartz. Altogether we have had a most interesting afternoon, and the relief of being out of the wind and in a warmer temperature is inexpressible. I hope and trust we shall all buck up again now that the conditions are more favourable. We have been in shadow all the afternoon, but the sun has just reached us, a little obscured by night haze. A lot could be written on the delight of setting foot on rock after 14 weeks of snow and ice and nearly 7 out of sight of aught else. It is like going ashore after a sea voyage. We deserve a little good bright weather after all our trials, and hope to get a chance to dry our sleeping bags and generally make our gear more comfortable.

They were now starting the critical descent of the Beardmore Glacier. To geologize at that point illuminates Scott's bizarre lack of judgement once more. Instinct ought to

have driven him on while the going was good – like Amundsen on 5 January, also on
the verge of leaving the ice cap. He *cut short his sleep, seized the moment, and crossed*
the Butcher's Shop to run down the head of the Axel Heiberg glacier under the mid-
night sun. The comparison is obvious.

FRIDAY, FEBRUARY 9ᵀᴴ, 1912
Scott

Friday, Feb. 9ᵗʰ. R. 23. Height 5,210 ft. Lunch T. + 10; T. + 12.5. About 13 miles. Kept along the edge of moraine to the end of Mᵗ. Buckley. Stopped and geolo-gised. Wilson got great find of vegetable impression in piece of limestone. Too tired to write geological notes. We all felt very slack this morning, partly rise of temperature, partly reaction, no doubt. Ought to have kept close in to glacier north of Mᵗ. Buckley, but in bad light the descent looked steep and we kept out. Eventually got amongst bad ice pressure and had to come down over an ice-fall. The crevasses were much firmer than expected and we got down with some difficulty, found our night camp of Dec. 20ᵗʰ, and lunched an hour after. Did pretty well in the afternoon, marching 3¾ hours; the sledgemeter is unshipped so cannot tell distance traversed. Very warm on march and we are all pretty tired. To-night it is wonderfully calm and warm, though it has been overcast all the afternoon. It is remarkable to be able to stand outside the tent and sun oneself. Our food satisfies now, but we must march to keep in the full ration, and we want rest, yet we shall pull through all right, D.V. We are by no means worn out.

SATURDAY, FEBRUARY 10ᵀᴴ, 1912
Scott

Sat'y. Feb. 10ᵗʰ. R. 24. lunch T. + 12; T. + 10. Got off a good morning march in spite of keeping too far east and getting in rough, cracked ice. Had a splendid night sleep, showing great change in all faces, so didn't get away till 10 a.m. Lunched just before 3. After lunch the land began to be obscured. We held a course for 2½ hours with difficulty, then the sun disappeared, and snow drove in our faces with northerly wind – very warm and impossible to steer, so camped. After supper, still very thick all round, but sun showing and less snow falling. The fallen snow crystals are quite feathery like thistledown. We have two full days' food left, and though our position is uncertain, we are certainly within two outward marches from the middle glacier depôt. However, if the weather doesn't clear by to-morrow, we must either march blindly on or reduce food. It is very trying. Another night to make up arrears of sleep. The ice crystals that first fell this afternoon were very large. Now the sky is clearer overhead, the temperature has fallen slightly, and the crystals are minute.

SUNDAY, FEBRUARY 11TH, 1912

Scott

Sunday, Feb. 11th. R. 25. Lunch Temp. −6.5; Supper −3.5. The worst day we have had during the trip and partly owing to our own fault. We started on a wretched surface with light S.W. wind, sail set, and pulling on ski – horrible light, which made everything look fantastic. As we went on light got worse, and suddenly we found ourselves in pressure. Then came the fatal decision to steer East, hoping to do a good distance, which in fact I suppose we did, but for the last hour or two we pressed on into a regular trap. Getting on to a good surface we did not reduce our lunch meal, and thought all going well, but half an hour after lunch we got into the worst ice mess I have ever been in. For three hours we plunged on ski, first thinking we were too much to the right, then too much to the left; meanwhile the disturbance got worse and my spirits received a very rude shock. There were times when it seemed almost impossible to find a way out of the awful turmoil in which we found ourselves. At length, arguing that there must be a way on our left, we plunged in that direction. It got worse, harder, more icy and crevassed. We could not manage our ski and pulled on foot, falling into crevasses every minute – most luckily no bad accident. At length we saw a smoother slope towards the land, pushed for it, but knew it was a woefully long way from us. The turmoil changed in character, irregular crevassed surface giving way to huge chasms, closely packed and most difficult to cross. It was very heavy work, but we had grown desperate. We won through at 10 p.m. and I write after 12 hours on the march. I *think* we are on or about the right track now, but we are still a good number of miles from the depôt, so we reduced rations to-night. We had 3 pemmican meals left and decided to make them into 4. To-morrow's lunch must serve for two if we do not make big progress. It was a test of our endurance on the march and our fitness with small supper . We have come through well. A good wind has come down the glacier which is clearing the sky and surface. Pray God the wind holds to-morrow. *We ought to have kept the bearings of our outward camps that is where we have failed.* Short sleep to-night and off first thing, I hope.

MONDAY, FEBRUARY 12TH, 1912

Scott

Monday, Feb. 12th. R. 26. In a very critical situation. All went well in the fore-noon, and we did a good long march over a fair surface. Two hours before lunch we were cheered by the sight of our night camp of the 18th Dec. the day after we made our depôt – this showed we were on the right track. In the afternoon, refreshed by tea, we went forward, confident of covering the remaining dis-tance, but by a fatal chance we kept too far to the left, and then we struck uphill and, tired and despondent, arrived in a horrid maze of crevasses and fissures. Divided councils caused our course to be erratic after this, and finally, at 9 p.m. we landed in the worst place of all. After discussion we decided to camp, and here we are, after a very short supper and one meal only remaining in the food bag – the depôt doubtful in locality. We *must* get there to-morrow. Meanwhile we are cheerful with an effort – It's a tight place, but luckily we've been well fed up to the present – Pray God we have fine weather to-morrow.

		Compass		True	
		N	E	S	W
Right Ex. C.M.		211 ·		205	
Left Ex. C.M.		145 ·	45	139 ·	45
Pt. beyond c.m.		72 ·	45	66 ·	45

N 25 E

N 40·15 W

S 66·45 W

Depot Bearings	Compass
P. bey. Right Ex c.m.	N 64 ½ E
Left Ex. C.M.	N 90 ¼ E
Right Ex. C.M.	N.195 ¾ E

These are the bearings of the Mid Glacier Depot, around 84° S. See Map 1 p. xi. C.M. or c.m. means the Cloudmaker Mountain, a prominent landmark to the west of the Beardmore Glacier.

TUESDAY, FEBRUARY 13TH, 1912

Scott

Tuesday, Feb. 13th – Camp R. 27, beside Cloudmaker. T. +10°. Last night we all slept well in spite of our grave anxieties. For my part these were increased by my visits outside the tent, when I saw the sky gradually closing over and snow beginning to fall. By our ordinary time for getting up it was dense all around us. We could see nothing, and we could only remain in our sleeping-bags. At 8.30 I dimly made out the land of the Cloudmaker. At nine we got up, deciding to have tea, and with one biscuit, no pemmican, so as to leave our scanty remaining meal for eventualities. We started marching, and at first had to wind our way through an awful turmoil of broken ice, but in about an hour we hit an old moraine track, brown with dirt. Here the surface was much smoother and improved rapidly. The fog still hung over all and went on for an hour, checking our bearings. Then the whole place got smoother and we turned outward a little. Evans raised our hopes with a shout of depôt ahead, but it proved to be a shadow on the ice. Then suddenly Wilson saw the actual depôt flag. It was an immense relief, and we were soon in possession of our 3½ days' food. The relief to all is inexpressible; needless to say, we camped and had a meal.

Marching in the afternoon, I kept more to the left, and closed the mountain till we fell on the stone moraines. Here Wilson detached himself and made a collection, whilst we pulled the sledge on. We camped late, abreast the lower end of the mountain, and had nearly our usual satisfying supper. Yesterday was the worst experience of the trip and gave a horrid feeling of insecurity. Now we are right up, we must march. In future food must be worked so that we do not run so short if the weather fails us. We mustn't get into a hole like this again. Greatly relieved to find that both the other parties got through safely. Evans seems to have got mixed up with pressures like ourselves. It promises to be a very fine day to-morrow. The valley is gradually clearing. Bowers has had a very bad attack of snow blindness, and Wilson another almost as bad. Evans *having* no power to assist with camping work *is a great nuisance and very clumsy.*

WEDNESDAY, FEBRUARY 14TH, 1912

Scott

Wednesday, Feb. 14th. Lunch T. 0 Supper T. +1. A fine day with wind on and off down the glacier, and we have done a fairly good march. We started a little late and pulled on down the moraine. At first I thought of going right, but soon, luckily, changed my mind and decided to follow the curving lines of the moraines. This course has brought us well out on the glacier. Started on crampons; one hour after, hoisted sail; the combined efforts produced only slow speed, partly due to the sandy snowdrifts similar to those on summit, partly to our torn sledge runners. At lunch these were scraped and sand-papered. After lunch we got on snow, with ice only occasionally showing through. A poor start, but the gradient and wind improving, we did 6½ miles before night camp.

There is no getting away from the fact that we are not pulling strong. Probably none of us: Wilson's leg still troubles him and he doesn't like to trust himself on ski; but the worst case is Evans, who is giving us serious anxiety. This morning he suddenly disclosed a huge blister on his foot. It delayed us on the march, when he had to have his crampon readjusted. Sometimes I fear he is going from bad to worse, but I trust he will pick up again when we come to steady work on ski like this afternoon. He is hungry and so is Wilson. We can't risk opening out our food again, and as cook at present I am serving something under full allowance. We are inclined to get slack and slow with our camping arrangements, and small delays increase. I have talked of the matter to-night and hope for improvement. We cannot do distance without the horses. The next depôt some 30 miles away and nearly 3 days' food in hand.

THURSDAY, FEBRUARY 15TH, 1912
Scott

Thursday, Feb. 15th. – R. 29. Lunch T. –10; Supper T. –4. 13.5 miles. Again we are running short of provision. We don't know our distance from the 1 depôt, but imagine about 20 miles. Heavy march – did 13¾ (geo.). We are pulling for food and not very strong evidently. In the afternoon it was overcast; land blotted out for a considerable interval. We have reduced food, also sleep; feeling rather done. Trust 1½ days or 2 at most will see us at depôt.

FRIDAY, FEBRUARY 16TH, 1912
Scott

Friday, Feb. [1]6th. –12.5 m. Lunch T. –6.1; Supper T. +7. A rather trying position. Evans has nearly broken down in brain, we think. He is absolutely changed from his normal self-reliant self, *and has become impossible* This morning and this afternoon he stopped the march on some trivial excuse. We are on short rations with not very short food; spin out till to-morrow night. We cannot be more than 10 or 12 miles from the depôt, but the weather is all against us. After lunch we were enveloped in a snow sheet, land just looming. Memory should hold the events of a very troublesome march with more troubles ahead. Perhaps all will be well if we can get to our depot to-morrow fairly early, but it is anxious work with the sick man. But it's no use meeting troubles half way, and our sleep is all too short to write more.

SATURDAY, FEBRUARY 17TH, 1912
Scott

Sat'y Feb. [1]7th. A very terrible day. Evans looked a little better after a good sleep, and declared, as he always did, that he was quite well. He started in his place on the traces, but half an hour later worked his ski shoes adrift, and had to leave the sledge. The surface was awful, the soft recently fallen snow clogging the ski and runners at every step, the sledge groaning, the sky overcast, and the land hazy. We stopped after about one hour, and Evans came up again, but very slowly. Half an hour later he dropped out again on the same plea. He asked Bowers to lend him a piece of string. I cautioned him to come on as quickly as he could, and he answered cheerfully as I thought. We had to push on, and the remainder of us were forced to pull very hard, sweating heavily. Abreast the Monument Rock we stopped, and seeing Evans a long way astern, I camped for lunch. There was no alarm at first, and we prepared tea and our own meal, consuming the latter. After lunch, and Evans still not appearing, we looked out, to see him still afar aft. By this time we were alarmed, and all four started back on ski. I was first to reach the poor man and shocked at his appearance; he was on his knees with clothing disarranged, hands uncovered and frostbitten, and a wild look in his eyes. Asked what was the matter, he replied with a slow speech that he didn't know, but thought he must have fainted. We got him on his feet, but after two or three steps he sank down again. He showed every sign of complete collapse. Wilson, Bowers, and I went back for the sledge, whilst Oates remained with him. When we returned he was practically unconscious, and when we got him into the tent quite comatose. He died quietly at 12.30 a.m. On discussing the symptoms we think he began to get weaker just before we reached the Pole, and that his downward path was accelerated first by the shock of his frostbitten fingers, and later by falls during rough travelling on the glacier, further by his loss of all confidence in himself. Wilson thinks it certain he must have injured his brain by a fall. It is a terrible thing to lose a companion in this way, but calm reflection shows that there could not have been a better ending to the terrible anxieties of the past week. Discussion of the situation at lunch yesterday shows us what a desperate pass we were in with a sick man on our hands at such a distance from home.

At 1 a.m. we packed up and came down over the pressure ridges, finding our depôt easily.

Even Scott's lack of sympathy, and expecting too much of the man, does not explain the whole course of events. Wilson probably came close to the truth by his suggestion of brain injury due to a fall. Scott records two falls by Evans into crevasses on 4 February. Evans, under the strain of man-hauling was by then in an advanced state of malnutrition, especially with a lack of vitamin C, from which they were all suffering. Being a big man, with the same rations as his other, lighter companions, any deficiency would have been exacerbated. One effect of vitamin C deficiency is to make blood vessels fragile, so that even a minor fall could cause a slowly developing brain haemorrhage with an eventually fatal outcome. It fits the facts as noted by Scott, in particular mental deterioration with lucid intervals.[77]

This is, however, complicated by dehydration and vitamin B deficiency, especially thiamine. Both have mental effects.

SUNDAY, FEBRUARY 18TH, 1912
Scott

Return Barrier Journey
Sunday, Feb. 18th. R. 32. T. –5.5. At Shambles Camp. We gave ourselves 5 hours' sleep at the lower glacier depot after the horrible night, and came on at about 3 to-day to this camp, coming fairly easily over the divide. Here with plenty of horsemeat we have had a fine supper, to be followed by others such, and so continue a more plentiful era if we can keep good marches up. New life seems to come with greater food almost immediately, but I am anxious about the Barrier surfaces.

MONDAY, FEBRUARY 19TH, 1912
Scott

Monday, Feb. 19th. Lunch T. –16°. It was late (past noon) before we got away to-day, as I gave nearly 8 hours sleep, and much camp work was done shifting sledges and fitting up new one with mast, &c., packing horsemeat and personal effects. The surface was every bit as bad as I expected, the sun shining brightly on it and its covering of soft loose sandy snow. We have come out about 2' on the old tracks. Perhaps lucky to have a fine day for this and our camp work, but we shall want wind or change of sliding conditions to do anything on such a surface as we have got. I fear there will not be much change for the next 3 or 4 days.

R.33. T. –17. We have struggled out 4.6 miles in a short day over a really terrible surface – it has been like pulling over desert sand, not the least glide in the world. If this goes on we shall have a bad time, but I sincerely trust it is only the result of this windless area close to the coast and that, as we are making steadily outwards, we shall shortly escape it. It is perhaps premature to be anxious about covering distance. In all other respects things are improving. We have our sleeping bags spread on the sledge and they are drying, but, above all, we have our full measure of food again. To-night we had a sort of stew fry of pemmican and horseflesh, and voted it the best hoosh we had ever had on a sledge journey. The absence of poor Evans is a help to the commissariat, but if he had been here in a fit state we might have got along faster. I wonder what is in store for us, with some little alarm at the lateness of the season.

TUESDAY, FEBRUARY 20TH, 1912
Scott

Monday, Feb. 20th. R. 34. Lunch T. –13; Supper T. –15. Same terrible surface; four hours' hard plodding in morning brought us to our Desolation Camp, where we had the four-day blizzard. We looked for more pony meat, but found none. After lunch we took to ski with some improvement of comfort. Total mileage for day 7 – the ski tracks pretty plain and easily followed this afternoon. We have left another cairn behind. Terribly slow progress, but we hope for better things as we clear the land. There is a tendency to cloud over in the S.E. to-night, which may turn to our advantage. At present our sledge and ski leave deeply ploughed tracks which can be seen winding for miles behind. It is distressing, but as usual trials are forgotten when we camp, and good food is our lot. Pray God we get better travelling as we are not so fit as we were, and the season is advancing apace.

This should be Tuesday. Two Mondays in a row hint at the turmoil in Scott's mind. Henceforth, the dates are correct, but the days of the week are one behind.

WEDNESDAY, FEBRUARY 21ST, 1912

Scott

Tuesday, Feb. 21st. R.35. Lunch Temp. +9; Supper T. –11. Gloomy and overcast when we started; a good deal warmer. The marching almost as bad as yesterday. Heavy toiling all day, inspiring gloomiest thoughts at times. Rays of comfort when we picked up tracks and cairns. At lunch we seemed to have missed the way, but an hour or two after we passed the last pony walls, and since, we struck a tent ring, ending the march actually on our old pony-tracks. There is a critical spot here with a long stretch between cairns. If we can tide that over we get on the regular cairn route, and with luck should stick to it; but everything depends on the weather. We never won a march of 8½ miles with greater difficulty, but we can't go on like this. We are drawing away from the land and perhaps may get better things in a day or two. I devoutly hope so.

THURSDAY, FEBRUARY 22ND, 1912

Scott

Wednesday, Feb. 22nd. R. 36. Supper T. –2°. There is little doubt we are in for a rotten critical time going home, and the lateness of the season may make it really serious. Shortly after starting today the wind grew very fresh from the S.E. with strong surface drift. We lost the faint track immediately, though covering ground fairly rapidly. Lunch came without sight of the cairn we had hoped to pass. In the afternoon, Bowers being sure we were too far to the west, steered out. Result, we have passed another pony camp without seeing it. Looking at the map to-night there is no doubt we are too far to the east. With clear weather we ought to be able to correct the mistake, but will the weather get clear? It's a gloomy position, more especially as one sees the same difficulty returning even when we have corrected the error. The wind is dying down to-night and the sky clearing in the south, which is hopeful. Meanwhile it is satisfactory to note that such untoward events fail to damp the spirit of the party. Tonight we had a pony hoosh so excellent and filling that one feels really strong and vigorous again.

FRIDAY, FEBRUARY 23RD, 1912
Scott

Thursday, Feb. 23rd. R. 37. Lunch T. –9.8; Supper T. –12. Started in sunshine, wind almost dropped. Luckily Bowers took a round of angles and with help of the chart we fogged out that we must be inside rather than outside tracks. The data were so meagre that it seemed a great responsibility to march out and we were none of us happy about it. But just as we decided to lunch, Bowers' wonderful sharp eyes detected an old double lunch cairn, the theodolite telescope confirmed it, and our spirits rose accordingly. This afternoon we marched on and picked up another cairn; then on and camped only 2½ miles from the depôt. We cannot see it, but, given fine weather, we cannot miss it. We are, therefore, extraordinarily relieved. Covered 8.2 miles in 7 hours, showing we can do 10 to 12 on this surface. Things are again looking up, as we are on the regular line of cairns, with no gaps right home, I hope.

SATURDAY, FEBRUARY 24TH, 1912
Scott

Friday, Feb. 24th-. Lunch. Beautiful day – too beautiful – an hour after starting loose ice crystals spoiling surface. Saw depôt and reached it middle forenoon. Found store in order except shortage oil – shall have to be *very* saving with fuel – otherwise have ten full days' provision from to-night and shall have less than 70 miles to go. Note from Meares who passed through Dec.15th, saying surface bad; from Atkinson, after fine marching (2¼ days from pony depôt), reporting Keohane better after sickness. Short note from Evans, not very cheerful, saying surface bad, temperature high. Think he must have been a little anxious. It is an immense relief to have picked up this depôt and, for the time, anxieties are thrust aside. There is no doubt we have been rising steadily since leaving the Shambles Camp. The coastal Barrier descends except where glaciers press out. Undulation still but flattening out. Surface soft on top, curiously hard below. Great difference now between night and day temperatures. Quite warm as I write in tent. We are on tracks with half-march cairn ahead; have covered 4½ miles. Poor Wilson has a fearful attack snow-blindness consequent on yesterday's efforts. Wish we had more fuel.

Night camp R. 38. T. –17. A little despondent again. We had a really terrible surface this afternoon and only covered 4 miles. We are on the track just beyond a lunch cairn. It really will be a bad business if we are to have this pulling all through.

I don't know what to think, but the rapid closing of the season is ominous. It is great luck having the horsemeat to add to our ration. To-night we have had a real fine 'hoosh.' It is a race between the season and hard conditions and our fitness and good food.

SUNDAY, FEBRUARY 25TH, 1912

Scott

Sat'y, Feb. 25th. Lunch T. –12. Managed just 6 miles this morning. Started somewhat despondent; not relieved when pulling seemed to show no improvement. Bit by bit surface grew better, less sastrugi, more glide, slight following wind for a time. Then we began to travel a little faster. But the pulling is still *very* hard; undulations disappearing but inequalities remain *passed*.

26 Camp walls about 2 miles ahead, all tracks in sight – Evans' track very conspicuous. This is something in favour, but the pulling is tiring us, though we are getting into better ski drawing again. Bowers hasn't quite the trick and is a little hurt at my criticisms, but I never doubted his heart. Very much easier – write diary at lunch – excellent meal – now one pannikin very strong tea – four biscuits and butter.

Hope for better things; this afternoon, but no improvement apparent. Oh! for a little wind – Evans evidently had plenty.

R. 38 T. –20°. Better march in afternoon. Day yields 11. 4 miles – the first double figure of steady dragging for a long time, but it meant and will mean hard work if we can't get a wind to help us. Evans evidently had a strong wind here, S.E. I should think. The temperature goes very low at night now when the sky is clear as at present. As a matter of fact this is wonderfully fair weather – the only drawback the spoiling of the surface and absence of wind. We see all tracks very plain, but the pony-walls have evidently been badly drifted up. Some kind people had substituted a cairn at last camp 27. The old cairns do not seem to have suffered much.

Scott's criticism of Bowers' skiing was hardly justified. He had done nothing to ensure that Bowers was systematically trained. This is implicit admission that the party had not properly learned to ski. That meant lost distance; enough by itself in the end to seal their fate.

MONDAY, FEBRUARY 26ᵀᴴ, 1912

Scott

Sunday, Feb. 26ᵗʰ. Lunch T. −17°. Sky overcast at start, but able see tracks and cairn distinct at long distance. Did a little better, 6½ miles to date. Bowers and Wilson now in front. Find great relief pulling behind with no necessity to keep attention on track. Very cold nights now and cold feet starting march, as day footgear doesn't dry at all. We are doing well on our food, but we ought to have yet more. I hope the next depôt, now only 50 miles, will find us with enough surplus to open out. The fuel shortage still an anxiety.

R. 39. −21. 9 hours' solid marching has given us 11½ miles. Only 4.3 miles from the next depôt. Wonderfully fine weather but cold, very cold. Nothing dries and we get our feet cold too often. We want more food yet and especially more fat. Fuel is woefully short. We can scarcely hope to get a better surface at this season, but I wish we could have some help from the wind, though it might shake us badly if the temp. didn't rise.

They were ineluctably starving, not because the elements were against them, but because the depots were too far apart. Scott had spaced them for animal transport, when he must have known that he would be man hauling on the way back. Between 80° S. and 84° S. he had four depots, at irregular intervals. Over the same distance, Amundsen had five depots, precisely a degree of latitude or 60 nautical miles between each. Scott was taking about eight days for a degree of latitude; Amundsen and his dogs had done it in three. Besides which, Scott had cut things fine. He had not put enough in his depots to get him safely home. He depended on returning parties, and particularly the dogs, to bring out more supplies. His orders were unclear, so that had not been done. Even at the best of times, he allowed for no margin of error. All this explains his lurching from one crisis to another, repeatedly running out of food. He had condemned his men to march or die.

TUESDAY, FEBRUARY 27ᵀᴴ, 1912

Scott

Monday, Feb. 27ᵗʰ. Desperately cold last night: −33° when we got up, with −37° minimum. Some suffering from cold feet, but all got good rest. We *must* open out on food soon. But we have done 7 miles this morning and hope for some 5 this afternoon. Overcast sky and good surface till now, when sun shows again. It is good to be marching the cairns up, but there is still much to be anxious about. We talk of little but food, except after meals. Land disappearing in satisfactory manner. Pray God we have no further set-backs. We are naturally always discussing possibility of meeting dogs, where and when, etc. It is a critical position. We may find ourselves in safety at next depôt, but there is a horrid element of doubt.

Camp R.41. T. −32°. Still fine clear weather but very cold − absolutely calm to-night. We have got off an excellent march for these days (12.2) and are much earlier than usual in our bags. 31 miles to depôt, 3 days' fuel at a pinch, and 6 days' food. Things begin to look a little better; we can open out a little on food from to-morrow night, I think.

Very curious surface-soft recent sastrugi which sink underfoot, and between, a sort of flaky crust with large crystals beneath.

WEDNESDAY, FEBRUARY 28TH, 1912
Scott

Tuesday, Feb. 28th. Lunch. Thermometer went below −40° last night; it was desperately cold for us, but we had a fair night. I decided to slightly increase food; the effect is undoubtedly good. Started marching in −32 with a slight northwesterly breeze − blighting. Many cold feet this morning; long time over foot gear, but we are earlier. Shall camp earlier and get the chance of a good night, if not the reality. Things must be critical till we reach the depôt, and the more I think of matters, the more I anticipate their remaining so after that event. Only 24½ miles from the depôt. The sun shines brightly, but there is little warmth in it. There is no doubt the middle of the Barrier is a pretty awful locality.

Camp 42. Splendid pony hoosh sent us to bed and sleep happily after a horrid day, wind continuing; did 11½ miles. Temp. not quite so low, but expect we are in for cold night. T. −27.

THURSDAY, FEBRUARY 29TH, 1912
Scott

Wednesday, Feb. 29th. Lunch. Cold night. T. −37.5; −30 with NW wind, force 4, when we got up, Frightfully cold starting; luckily Bowers and Oates in their last new finnesko; keeping my old ones for present. Expected awful march and for first hour got it. Then things improved and we camped after 5½ hours marching close to lunch camp 22½. Next camp is our depôt and it is exactly 13 miles.

It ought not to take more than 1½ days; we pray for another fine one. The oil will just about spin out in that event, and we arrive 3 clear days' food in hand. The increase of ration has had an enormously beneficial result. Mountains now looking small. Wind still very light from west – cannot understand this wind.

FRIDAY, MARCH 1ST, 1912
Scott

Thursday, Mar. 1st. Lunch. Very cold last night – minimum –41.5°. Cold start to march, too, as usual now. Got away at 8 and have marched within sight of depôt; flag something under 3 miles away. We did 11½ yesterday and nearly 6 this morning. Heavy dragging yesterday and *very* heavy this morning. Apart from sledging considerations the weather is wonderful. Cloudless days and nights and the wind trifling. Worse luck, the light airs come from the north and keep us horribly cold. For this lunch hour the exception has come. There is a bright and comparatively warm sun. All our gear is out drying.

SATURDAY, MARCH 2ND, 1912
Scott

Friday, Mar. 2nd. Lunch. Misfortunes rarely come singly. We marched to the (Middle Barrier) depôt fairly easily yesterday afternoon, and since that have suffered three distinct blows which have placed us in a bad position. First we found *a bare ½ gallon of oil instead of the full;* with most rigid economy it can scarce carry us to the next depôt on this surface. Second, Titus Oates disclosed his feet, the toes showing very bad indeed, evidently bitten by the late temperatures. The third blow came in the night, when the wind, which we had hailed with some joy, brought dark overcast weather. It fell below –40 in the night, and this morning it took 1½ hours to get our foot gear on, but we got away before eight. We lost cairn and tracks together and made as steady as we could N. by W., but have seen nothing. Worse was to come – the surface is simply awful. In spite of strong wind and full sail we have only done 5½. We are in a *very* queer street since there is no doubt we cannot do the extra marches and feel the cold horribly.

SUNDAY, MARCH 3RD, 1912
Scott

Saturday, Mar. 3rd. Lunch. We picked up the track again yesterday, finding ourselves to the eastward. Did close on 10 miles and things looked a trifle better; but
this morning the outlook is blacker than ever. Started well and with good breeze;
for an hour made good headway; then the surface grew awful beyond words. The
wind drew forward; every circumstance was against us. After 4¼ hours things
so bad that we camped, having covered 4½ miles. One cannot consider this a
fault of our own – certainly we were pulling hard this morning – it was more
than three parts surface which held us back – the wind at strongest, powerless
to move the sledge. When the light is good it is easy to see the reason. The surface, lately a very good hard one, is coated with a thin layer of woolly crystals,
formed by radiation no doubt. These are too firmly fixed to be removed by the
wind and cause impossible friction on the runners. God help us, we can't keep
up this pulling, that is certain. Amongst ourselves we are unendingly cheerful,
but what each man feels in his heart I can only guess. Pulling on foot gear in
the morning is getting slower and slower, therefore every day more dangerous.

*There was a cure for the bad going described by Scott, but unknown to him. The sledge
runners had to be coated with a thin, elastic film of ice. This was done by warming
mouthfuls of water, and carefully squirting in thin layers. It could overcome deep cold
and any kind of snow. It originated with the Netsilik Eskimos of Arctic Canada.
Amundsen had learned the technique from them on the North West Passage and so, in
the Antarctic, was also prepared for the worst.*

MONDAY, MARCH 4TH, 1912
Scott

Sunday, Mar. 4th. Lunch. Things looking *very* black indeed. As usual we forgot
our trouble last night, got into our bags, slept splendidly on good hoosh, woke
and had another, and started marching. Sun shining brightly, tracks clear, but
surface covered with sandy frost-rime. All the morning we had to pull with all
our strength, and in 4½ hours we covered 3½ miles. Last night it was overcast
and thick, surface bad; this morning sun shining and surface as bad as ever. One
has little to hope for except perhaps strong dry wind – an unlikely contingency at
this time of year. Under the immediate surface crystals is a hard sastrugi surface,

which must have been excellent for pulling a week or two ago. We are about 42 miles from the next depôt and have a week's food, but only about 3 to 4 days' fuel – we are as economical of the latter as one can possibly be, and we cannot afford to save food and pull as we are pulling. We are in a very tight place indeed, but none of us despondent *yet*, or at least we preserve every semblance of good cheer, but one's heart sinks as the sledge stops dead at some sastrugi behind which the surface sand lies thickly heaped. For the moment the temperature is on the −20° – an improvement which makes us much more comfortable, but a colder snap is bound to come again soon. I fear that Oates at least will weather such an event very poorly. Providence to our aid. We can expect little from man now, except the possibility of extra food at the next depôt – *a poor one.* It will be real bad if we get there and find the same shortage of oil. Shall we get there ? Such a short distance it would have appeared to us on the summit! I don't know what I should do if Wilson and Bowers weren't so determinedly cheerful over things.

TUESDAY, MARCH 5TH, 1912

Scott

Monday, Mar. 5th. Lunch. Regret to say going from bad to worse. We got a slant of wind yesterday afternoon, and going on 5 hours we converted our wretched morning run of 3½ miles into something over 9. We went to bed on a cup of cocoa and pemmican solid with the chill off.

The result is telling on all, but mainly on Oates, whose feet are in a wretched condition. One swelled up tremendously last night and he is very lame this morning. We started march on tea and pemmican as last night – we pretend to prefer the pemmican this way. Marched for 5 hours this morning over a slightly better surface covered with high moundy sastrugi. Sledge capsized twice; we pulled on foot, covering about 5½ miles. We are two pony marches and 4 miles about from our depôt. Our fuel dreadfully low and the poor Soldier nearly done. It is pathetic enough because we can do nothing for him; more hot food might do a little, but only a little, I fear. We none of us expected these terribly low temperatures, and of the rest of us Wilson is feeling them most; mainly, I fear, from his self-sacrificing devotion in doctoring Oates' feet. We cannot help each other, each has enough to do to take care of himself. We get cold on the march when the trudging is heavy, and the wind pierces our warm garments. The others, all of them, are unendingly cheerful when in the tent. We mean to see the game through with a proper spirit, but it's tough work to be pulling harder than we ever pulled in our lives for long hours, and to feel that the progress is so slow. One can only say God help us & plod on our weary way, cold and very miserable, though outwardly cheerful. We talk of all sorts of subjects in the tent, not much of food now, since we decided to take the risk of running a full ration. We simply couldn't go hungry at this time.

Scott had ample warning of low temperatures the previous southern autumn. He was proving once again that there is no bad weather, only bad clothing. He was not properly dressed for the conditions, with tight garments and too few layers. The critical failing was the outer protective jacket, made of insufficiently windproof fabric, and no fur, not even round the hood to shield the face. Had he worn fur clothing, like Amundsen on his abortive start for the Pole, he would at least have spared himself hypothermia, and arguably saved Oates from something worse.

WEDNESDAY, MARCH 6ᵀᴴ, 1912

Scott

Tuesday, Mar. 6th. Lunch. We did a little better with help of wind yesterday afternoon, finishing 9½ miles for the day, and 27 miles from depôt. But this morning things have been awful. It was warm in the night and for the first time during the journey I overslept myself by more than an hour; then we were slow with foot gear; then, pulling with all our might (for our lives) we could scarcely advance at rate of a mile an hour; then it grew thick and three times we had to get out of harness to search for tracks. The result is something less than 3½ miles for the forenoon. The sun is shining now and the wind gone. Poor Oates is unable to pull, sits on the sledge when we are track-searching – he is wonderfully plucky, as his feet *must* be giving him great pain. He makes no complaint, but his spirits only come up in spurts now, and he grows more silent in the tent. We are making a spirit lamp[78] to try and replace the primus when our oil is exhausted. It will be a very poor substitute and we've not got much spirit. If we could have kept up our 9-mile days we might have got within reasonable distance of the depôt before running out, but nothing but a strong wind and good surface can help us now, and though we had quite a good breeze this morning, the sledge came as heavy as lead. If we were all fit I should have hopes of getting through, but the poor Soldier has become a terrible hindrance, though he does his utmost and suffers much I fear.

THURSDAY, MARCH 7TH, 1912
Scott

Wednesday, Mar. 7th. A little worse I fear. One of Oates' feet *very* bad this morning; he is wonderfully brave. We still talk of what we will do together at home.

We only made 6½ miles yesterday. This morning in 4¼ hours we did just over 4 miles. We are 16 from our depôt. If we only find the correct proportion of food there and this surface continues, we may get to the next depôt but not to One Ton Camp. We hope against hope that the dogs have been to Mt. Hooper; then we might pull through. If there is a shortage of oil again we can have little hope. One feels that for poor Oates the crisis is near, but none of us are improving, though we are wonderfully fit considering the really excessive work we are doing. We are only kept going by good food. No wind this morning till a chill northerly air came ahead. Sun bright and cairns showing up well. I should like to keep the track to the end.

FRIDAY, MARCH 8TH, 1912
Scott

Thursday, Mar. 8th. Lunch. Worse and worse in morning; poor Oates' left foot can never last out, and time over foot gear something awful. Have to wait in night foot gear for nearly an hour before I start changing, and then am generally first to be ready. Wilson's feet giving trouble now, but this mainly because he gives so much help to others. We did 4½ miles this morning and are now 8½ miles from the depôt – a ridiculously small distance to feel in difficulties, yet on this surface we know we cannot equal half our old marches, and that for that effort we expend nearly double the energy. The great question is, What shall we find at the depôt? If the dogs have visited it we may get along a good distance, but if there is another short allowance of fuel, God help us indeed. We are in a very bad way, I fear in any case.

SUNDAY, MARCH 10TH, 1912
Scott

Sat., March 10th. Things steadily downhill. Oates' foot worse. He has rare pluck and must know that he can never get through. He asked Wilson if he had a chance this morning, and of course Bill had to say he didn't know. In point of fact

Figure 29 Front page splash of Amundsen at the South Pole, Aftenposten, *Christiania (Oslo), Norwegian organ of popular journalism, 8 March 1912. The headline reads 'Norway's flag raised at the South Pole! All Well!'*

– *National Library of Norway*

he has none. Apart from him, if he went under now, I doubt whether we could get through. With great care we might have a dog's chance, but no more. The weather conditions are awful, and our gear gets steadily more icy and difficult to manage. At the same time of course poor Titus is the greatest handicap. He keeps us waiting in the morning until we have partly lost the warming effect of our good breakfast, when the only wise policy is to be up and away at once; again at lunch. Poor chap – *poor chap* it is too pathetic to watch him; one cannot but try to cheer him up.

Yesterday we marched up the depôt, Mt. Hooper. Cold comfort. Shortage on our allowance all round. I don't know that anyone is to blame, – *but generosity & thoughtfulness have not been abundant –* The dogs which would have been our salvation have evidently failed. Meares had a bad trip home I suppose. – *It's a miserable jumble.*

This morning it was calm when we breakfasted, but the wind came from the W.N.W. as we broke camp, It rapidly grew in strength. After travelling for half an hour I saw that none of us could go on facing such conditions. We were forced to camp and are spending the rest of the day in a comfortless blizzard camp, wind quite foul.

The shortage of food and fuel was Scott's own fault. By taking a fifth man on to the Pole, and disrupting his lines of retreat, he had forced the returning parties to rearrange the depot. Since he had not organized his supplies in modules, they had to weigh out, measure and repack. Without proper equipment, mistakes were inevitable.

Likewise, Scott had only himself to blame for the absence of the dogs that would have been his salvation. Meares did have a 'bad trip home' because Scott had taken him further than intended. This was the last straw, and Meares went home in Terra Nova, *which had come and gone, disgusted with the whole affair. That left a gap in the chain of command, with Demetri the only dog driver, unable to work on his own.*

Again, Scott was suffering from unclear orders of his own. He had left confused and contradictory instructions for the dogs, repeatedly changed along the way. A critical last-minute order to bring them to between 82° and 83° S to help him home had been lost in transmission. He had mentioned it to Lt Evans before parting at the head of the Beardmore Glacier. Evans had fallen victim to scurvy on the way back, and in the ensuing race for life, understandably forgot what Scott had said. Besides, a depot of dog food Scott mentioned in one of his messages did not in fact exist. So the dogs waited at McMurdo Sound, their masters uncertain what to do, unwittingly leaving Scott and his companions to their fate. Eventually Cherry Garrard and Demetri made a half-hearted attempt with the dogs to meet the polar party, but got no further than One Ton Depot, where they waited in vain before turning back.

MONDAY, MARCH 11TH, 1912

Scott

Sunday, Mar. 11th. Titus Oates is very near the end, one feels. What we or he will do, God only knows. We discussed the matter after breakfast; he is a brave fine fellow and understands the situation, but he practically asked for advice. Nothing could be said but to urge him to march as long as he could. One satisfactory result to the discussion; I practically ordered Wilson to hand over the means of ending our troubles to us, so that anyone of us may know how to do so. Wilson had no choice between doing so and our ransacking the medicine case. We have 30 opium tabloids apiece and he is left with a tube of morphine. So far the tragical side of our story.

The sky completely overcast when we started this morning. We could see nothing, lost the tracks, and doubtless have been swaying a good deal since 3.1 miles for the forenoon – terribly heavy dragging – expected it. Know that 6 miles is about the limit of our endurance now, if we get no help from wind or surfaces. We have 7 days' food and should be about 55 miles from One Ton Camp to-night, 6 × 7 = 42, leaving us 13 miles short of our distance, even if things get no worse. Meanwhile the season rapidly advances.

TUESDAY, MARCH 12ᵀᴴ, 1912
Scott

Monday, Mar. 12ᵗʰ. We did 6.9 miles yesterday, under our necessary average. Things are left much the same, Oates not pulling much, and now with hands as well as feet pretty well useless. We did 4 miles this morning in 4 hours 20 min. – we may hope for 3 this afternoon, 7 × 6 = 42. We shall be 47 miles from the depôt. I doubt if we can possibly do it. The surface remains awful, the cold intense, and our physical condition running down. God help us! Not a breath of favourable wind for more than a week, and apparently liable to head winds at any moment.

THURSDAY, MARCH 14ᵀᴴ, 1912
Scott

Wednesday, Mar. 14ᵗʰ. No doubt about the going downhill, but everything going wrong for us. Yesterday we woke to a strong northerly wind with temp. –37°. Couldn't face it, so remained in camp till 2, then did 5¼ miles. Wanted to march later, but party feeling the cold badly as the breeze (N.) never took off entirely, and as the sun sank the temp. fell. Long time getting supper in dark.

This morning started with southerly breeze, set sail and passed another cairn at good speed; half-way, however, the wind shifted to W. by S. or W.S.W., blew through our wind clothes and into our mits. Poor Wilson horribly cold, could not get off ski for some time. Bowers and I practically made camp, and when we got into the tent at last we were all deadly cold. Then temp. now midday down –43° and the wind strong. We *must* go on, but now the making of every camp must be more difficult and dangerous. It must be near the end, but a pretty merciful end. Poor Oates got it again in the foot. I shudder to think what it will be like to-morrow. It is only with greatest pains rest of us keep off frostbites. No idea there could be temperatures like this at this time of year with such winds. Truly awful outside the tent. Must fight it out to the last biscuit, but can't reduce rations.

SATURDAY, MARCH 16TH OR SUNDAY 17TH, 1912

Scott

Friday, March 16th or Sat. 17th. Lost track of dates, but think the last correct. Tragedy all along the line. At lunch, the day before yesterday, poor Titus Oates said he couldn't go on; he proposed we should leave him in his sleeping-bag. That we could not do, and induced him to come on, on the afternoon march. In spite of its awful nature for him he struggled on and we made a few miles. At night he was worse and we knew the end had come.

Should this be found I want these facts recorded. Oates' last thoughts were of his Mother, but immediately before he took pride in thinking that his regiment would be pleased with the bold way in which he met his death. We can testify to his bravery. He has borne intense suffering for weeks without complaint, and to the very last was able and willing to discuss outside subjects. He did not – would not – give up hope to the very end. He was a brave soul. This was the end. He slept through the night before last, hoping not to wake; but he woke in the morning – yesterday. It was blowing a blizzard. He said, I am just going outside and may be some time. He went out into the blizzard and we have not seen him since.

I take this opportunity of saying that we have stuck to our sick companions to the last. In case of Edgar Evans, when absolutely out of food and he lay insensible, the safety of the remainder seemed to demand his abandonment, but Providence mercifully removed him at this critical moment. He died a natural death, and we did not leave him till 2 hours after his death. We knew that poor Oates was walking to his death, but though we tried to dissuade him, we knew it was the act of a brave man and an English gentleman. We all hope to meet the end with a similar spirit, and assuredly the end is not far.

I can only write at lunch and then only occasionally. The cold is intense, −40° at midday. My companions are unendingly cheerful, but we are all on the verge of serious frostbites, and though we constantly talk of fetching through I don't think anyone of us believes it in his heart.

We are cold on the march now, and at all times except meals. Yesterday we had to lay up for a blizzard and to-day we move dreadfully slowly. We are at

No.14 pony camp, only two pony marches from One Ton Depôt. We leave here our theodolite, a camera, and Oates' sleeping bags. Diaries, etc & geological specimens carried at Wilson's special request, will be found with us or on our sledge.

They had now been on the march for 137 days since leaving base. Given the absence of Vitamin C from their diet, and the fact that it can only be stored for about 100 days, they must therefore have all been suffering from a state of advanced defi-ciency. In all likelihood, scurvy had begun. On the evidence, it was complicated by general malnutrition, notably a lack of protein, undesirable in heavy work at low temperatures.

One effect of Vitamin C deficiency is to make old wounds reopen. Oates, with the horrific Boer War injury to his left femur and surrounding tissue, would have been particularly prone. What he was going through does not bear thinking about. Walking out of the tent would have been about the only way left to put an end to his suffering. Scott's announcement of heroic motives need not be taken literally.

MONDAY, MARCH 18TH, 1912
Scott

Sunday, March 18th. – To-day, lunch, we are 21 miles from the depôt. Ill fortune presses, but better may come. We have had more wind and drift from ahead yesterday; had to stop marching; wind N.W., force 4, temp. –35° No human being could face it, and we are worn out *nearly*.

My right foot has gone, nearly all the toes – two days ago I was proud pos-sessor of best feet. These are the steps of my downfall. Like an ass I mixed a small spoonful of curry powder with my melted pemmican – it gave me violent indigestion. I lay awake and in pain all night; woke and felt done on the march; foot went and I didn't know it. A very small measure of neglect and have a foot which is not pleasant to contemplate. Bowers takes first place in condition, but there is not much to choose after all. The others are still confident of getting through – or pretend to be – I don't know! We have the last *half* fill of oil in our primus and a very small quantity of spirit – this alone between us & thirst. The wind is fair for the moment, and that is perhaps a fact to help. The mileage would have seemed ridiculously small on our outward journey –

TUESDAY, MARCH 19TH, 1912

Scott

Monday March 19th. – Lunch. We camped with difficulty last night and were dreadfully cold till after our supper of cold pemmican and biscuit and a half a pannikin of cocoa cooked over the spirit. Then, contrary to expectation, we got warm and all slept well. To-day we started in the usual dragging manner. Sledge dreadfully heavy. We are 15½ miles from the depôt and ought to get there in three days. What progress! We have two days' food but barely a day's fuel. All our feet are getting bad – Wilson's best, my right foot worst, left all right. There is no chance to nurse one's feet till we can get hot food into us. Amputation is the least I can hope for now, but will the trouble spread? That is the serious question. The weather doesn't give us a chance – the wind from N. to N.W. and – 40 temp. to-day.

THURSDAY, MARCH 21ST, 1912

Scott

Wednesday, March 21st. Got within 11 miles of depôt Monday night; had to lay up all yesterday in severe blizzard. To-day forlorn hope, Wilson and Bowers going to depôt for fuel.

FRIDAY, MARCH 22ND OR SATURDAY 23RD, 1912

Scott

22nd or 23rd. Blizzard bad as ever – Wilson and Bowers unable to start – to-morrow last chance – no fuel and only one or two of food left – must be near the end. Have decided it shall be natural – we shall march for the depôt with or without our effects and die in our tracks.

[MARCH 24TH OR 25TH, 1912][79]

Message to public
The causes of the disaster are not due to faulty organisation, but to misfortune in all risks which had to be undertaken.

1. The loss of pony transport in March 1911 obliged me to start later than I had intended, and obliged the limits of stuff transported to be narrowed.

2. The weather throughout the outward journey, and especially the long gale in 83° S., stopped us.
3. The soft snow in lower reaches of glacier again reduced pace.

We fought these untoward events with a will and conquered, but it cut into our provision reserve.

Every detail of our food supplies, clothing and depots made on the interior ice-sheet and over that long stretch of 700 miles to the Pole and back, worked out to perfection. The advance party would have returned to the glacier in fine form and with surplus of food, but for the astonishing failure of the man whom we had least expected to fail. Edgar Evans was thought the strongest man of the party.

The Beardmore Glacier is not difficult in fine weather, but on our return we did not get a single completely fine day; this with a sick companion enormously increased our anxieties.

As I have said elsewhere we got into frightfully rough ice and Edgar Evans received a concussion of the brain – he died a natural death, but left us a shaken party with the season unduly advanced.

But all the facts above enumerated were as nothing to the surprise which awaited us on the Barrier. I maintain that our arrangements for returning were quite adequate, and that no one in the world would have expected the temperatures and surfaces which we encountered at this time of the year. On the summit in lat. 85° 86° we had −20°, −30°. On the Barrier in lat. 82°, 10,000 feet lower, we had −30° in the day, −47° at night pretty regularly, with continuous head wind during our day marches. It is clear that these circumstances come on very suddenly, and our wreck is certainly due to this sudden advent of severe weather, which does not seem to have any satisfactory cause. I do not think human beings ever came through such a month as we have come through, and we should have got through in spite of the weather but for the sickening of a second companion, Captain Oates, and a shortage of fuel in our depôts for which I cannot account, and finally, but for the storm which has fallen on us within 11 miles of the depôt at which we hoped to secure our final supplies. Surely misfortune could scarcely have exceeded this last blow. We arrived within 11 miles of our old One Ton Camp with fuel for one last meal and food for two days. For *four* days we have been unable to leave the tent – the gale howling about us. We are weak, writing is difficult, but for my own sake I do not regret this journey, which has shown that Englishmen can endure hardships, help one another, and meet death with as great a fortitude as ever in the past. We took risks, we knew we took them; things have come out against us, and therefore we have no cause for complaint, but bow to the will of Providence, determined still to do our best to the last.

But if we have been willing to give our lives to this enterprise, which is for the honour of our country, I appeal to our countrymen to see that those who depend on us are properly cared for.

Had we lived, I should have had a tale to tell of the hardihood, endurance, and courage of my companions which would have stirred the heart of every Englishman. These rough notes and our dead bodies must tell the tale, but surely, surely, a great rich country like ours will see that those who are dependent on us are properly provided for.

R. Scott

FRIDAY, MARCH 29TH, 1912

Scott

March 29th. Since the 21st we have had a continuous gale from W.S.W. and S.W. We had fuel to make two cups of tea apiece and bare food for two days on the 20th. Every day we have been ready to start for our depôt *11 miles* away, but outside the door of the tent it remains a scene of whirling drift. I do not think we can hope for any better things now. We shall stick it out to the end, but we are getting weaker, of course, and the end cannot be far.

It seems a pity, but I do not think I can write more.

R. Scott.

Last Entry
For God's sake look after our people.

A few days later, on 1 April, Terra Nova *reached Akaroa, in New Zealand. As she lay in the roadstead, two men in a boat called out: 'Why didn't you get back sooner? Amundsen got the Pole in a sardine tin on the 14th December.'*[80] Fram *had beaten* Terra Nova *to the cablehead after all, so Amundsen had won that race too. His diary takes up the tale.*

THURSDAY, MARCH 7TH, 1912

Amundsen

7 March – Thursday. Arrived at Hobart 11 a.m. Went ashore with the doctor and the harbourmaster. Booked in at the Orient Hotel.[81] Was treated as a tramp – my peaked cap and blue sweater – given a miserable little room. Immediately visited the Norwegian consul, McFarlane, and very warmly received by the old gentleman. Received my post and read it. No telegrams had come. Thereafter telegraphed to the King. Then to Nansen and L. – Day spent at rest – with the exception of reporters who were intrusive – but they ran up against a brick wall.

The Pole meant nothing until it had been made into news. One unguarded word, and Amundsen could still lose all. His silence was the last lap of the journey which began when he decided to switch from the North Pole to the South. He had to keep the story exclusive if he was to profit by his work. 'L.' is his brother Leon, and his Press agent too.

FRIDAY, MARCH 8TH, 1912

Amundsen

8 March – Friday. This morning received telegram from L. who instructed me to send the main telegram to the *Daily Chronicle*, London. That was done immediately. Since then have kept absolutely silent. When I had gone to bed – 10 o'clock at night – the telegrams began to pour in. The conquest of the Pole had been published. The King's was the first. Then they came from the Storting, Government, Academy of Science, University, Kristiansands Garrison Commander, the City of Christiania, the Geographical Society, King George V, Norwegian Navy, and a mass of organizations. Journalists tried to break open the door of my bedroom, but did not get in.

By using a major newspaper in the English-speaking world, Amundsen could rake in the money, as hoped. Through his silence he had given the Daily Chronicle *its scoop. Now the attainment of the Pole would have a price and Amundsen earn his fee – £2,000, or about £150,000 today. He still needed to lie low, however. After the first sensation and the headlines, he had to guard the feature rights, so that battle would be crowned by victory as well.*

It was a close-run thing. Fram's passage had been hard, perhaps the hardest side

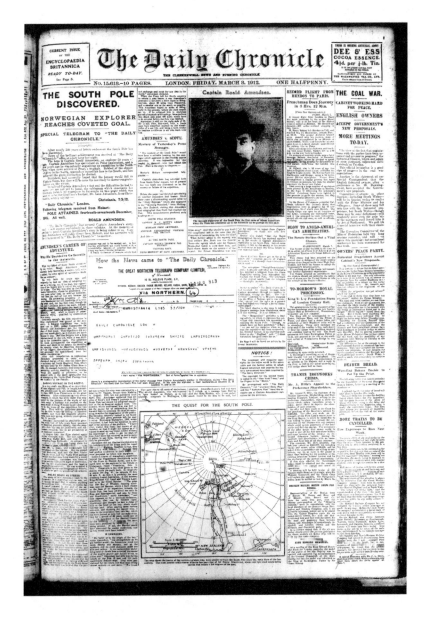

Figure 30 The conquest of the South Pole, Daily Chronicle, *London, 8 March 1912. Their scoop. They paid Amundsen the equivalent of £150,000 today for world rights. The telegram reads, 'POLE ATTAINED fourteenth-seventeenth December 1911. ROALD AMUNDSEN'.*

– Cambridge University Library

of the whole expedition, with uncertainty to the very end. 'Struggling ahead with miserable slow speed, against wind and fog and rain and high seas, so the motor has had to stay still',[82] *as Bjaaland put it. His diary at landfall and the last entry of the voyage from Antarctica fittingly brings the story to a close:*

TUESDAY, MARCH 5ᵀᴴ, 1912
Bjaaland

Tuesday 5 March
It was a stinking job to get into Hobart. Storm and calm followed each other, and when we finally were at the approaches to our goal, so God help me we were blown past, the result being that we had to lay to in a storm with torn sail and splintered gaff.

My birthday, which was celebrated today in the usual way, somewhat different from last year in 40 deg. of frost at 81° South lat.

EPILOGUE

By beating *Terra Nova* into port, Amundsen had the headlines to himself. He won unstinted acclaim, except in England, which offered grudging recognition tempered by hopes that Scott perhaps might yet return victorious after all. Wishful thinking ended when *Terra Nova* arrived in New Zealand without Scott, but with Lt Evans, recovering from scurvy. Evans having parted from Scott on 4 January, still 150 miles from the Pole, confirmed that Scott had indeed lost the race.

That released a torrent of chagrin in the British Press but few suspicions of anything awry. By contrast, when Amundsen heard that *Terra Nova* had left McMurdo Sound on 4 March, and Scott had not yet reappeared, he had intimations of disaster.[83] This could involve undesirable consequences for himself. Having first gone to Argentina to meet his patron Don Pedro Christophersen and finish the book of the expedition on one of Don Pedro's estancias, Amundsen finally arrived back in Christiania on 31 July. He did so incognito, fatigued by a surfeit of publicity. Nonetheless, with his pressing financial obligations, he hastened to exploit his triumph while Scott's fate was still hidden in the Antarctic, and the going was good. With his box of lantern slides, he embarked on the international lecture circuit. Before the advent of television and instant fame, this was the only way of capitalizing on celebrity.

When Amundsen reached England, national huffiness had waned. Although snubbed by the pooh-bahs and panjandrums, by the public he was well received. He won considerable respect for his modesty, and admiration for his deed. He even acquired a certain exotic popularity, to which the diary of a 14-year-old Bristol schoolgirl bears witness:

> 4 December 1912 *Amundsen lecture*. Hardly contain myself the whole day
> ...Amundsen had a simply killing Norwegian accent...having told us that
> many people asked what was the use of getting to the S. Pole etc. etc., he
> then said with the *utmost* scorn, 'Little minds have only room for thoughts
> of bread & butter.'[84]

The critics were indulgent when Amundsen's book about the expedition, translated into English as *The South Pole*, appeared in the autumn. Outside the fray, as it were, the *New York Times* enthused: 'An ancient Norseman's saga sung in the language of the twentieth century; 'Burnt Njal' divested of its blood-feuds, but with all its humour and quaint gossip.'[85] At home, even the *Times Literary Supplement* was downright approving, with oblique digs at Scott, as he revealed himself in his press reports. The Norwegians 'advanced in blizzards which less hardy men would scarcely have ventured to face', the TLS reviewer (The Rev. E.H.R Tatham, Brasenose College, Oxford) observed, 'But . . . the lightheartedness of the party . . . conveys the impression that the whole affair was a sort of pleasure trip.'[86]

Amundsen could scarcely have put it better himself. It was just in time. That review appeared on 28 November. On 10 February 1913, *Terra Nova* returned to New Zealand from her third voyage to the Antarctic. The previous November, a search party had found the tent with the bodies of Scott, Wilson and Bowers immured in the snow. This was the news that the ship brought back, together with diaries and other relics.

Until then, Amundsen was regarded as the natural victor, while Scott was in the process of being dismissed as the loser. Scott's ruin now reversed the rôles, which poses the question of whether it had been premeditated. Amundsen was eclipsed in England by sensational death in the snow. The country wallowed in an orgy of self-indulgent lamentation reminiscent of the British public's response, more recently, to the death of Princess Diana. Prodigies of sophistry erupted to sweep away the taint of defeat by presenting the losers as men who 'snatched victory from the jaws of death',[87] to quote a tragi-banal leader in *The Times*. It had become an approved national calamity, and on 14 February there was a memorial service at St Paul's Cathedral.

Ten months earlier, St Paul's had seen another service in memory of those who had gone down with the *Titanic*. She sank on 14 April 1912, just as the last lingering hopes for the polar party disappeared at McMurdo Sound. It was more than mere coincidence. Both belonged to a historic roll-call of all-British disasters. Among the more apposite in this case was the disappearance of Sir John Franklin in the Arctic, during the 1840s, with all his 130-odd followers. Indeed,

The Times inimitably reinforced the parallel by applying to Scott, Tennyson's lines about Franklin: '. . . thou,/Heroic sailor-soul/Art passing on thine happier voyage now/Toward no earthly pole!'[88]

What these debacles had in common was an immediate aversion to asking the reasons why, publicly at least. Avoidable tragedy was masked instead by stirring tales of 'glorious doom', and 'a fatal display of courage',[89] as *The Times* said at the time of that quintessential British disaster, the Charge of the Light Brigade, with much reference to chivalry like the knights of old. Among Scott's followers there was an unspoken agreement to defend the burgeoning myth and suppress awkward facts.

Atkinson, for instance, published no medical report. The senior naval surgeon of the expedition, he was in the party that found the bodies of Scott and his companions in the tent. He always denied – in private – that scurvy had a hand in the disaster. Nonetheless by 29 March, the date of Scott's last diary entry, the polar party had been on the trail for 150 days by which point, on clinical grounds, scurvy must have appeared. Moreover Tryggve Gran, who was also among those who found the tent, recorded in his diary that the bodies had a yellowish colour.[90] This is a symptom of advanced scurvy. In after years, Atkinson admitted a cover-up, out of loyalty to Scott, since it would have been 'a reflection on his ability as an organizer to say that scurvy had developed'.[91]

Concealment of this or any other kind was underpinned by Scott's 'Message to the Public'. *The Times* ran it in its entirety on 11 February, the day that the news broke. Scott understood his audience. He pandered to the unique English worship of the glorious failure and romantic suffering as an end in itself. His exercise in shifting responsibility and blaming misfortune was manna for a country now seeking excuses for defeat.

There were occasional voices of reason. Lord Curzon, past Viceroy of India, now President of the Royal Geographical Society, declared in public that

> while with good luck the British organization . . . might have stood any strain, the Norwegians' equipment of 120 dogs . . . and of men, not required to pull, and life-trained to the use of ski, was a superior mechanism for swift progress on the plateau, and even on the Barrier itself and might . . . have been a more efficient safeguard against unforeseen misfortunes either of accident or climate.[92]

Oates' mother, Mrs Caroline Oates, made one of the few attempts to elicit the truth. She wanted to know what really happened to her son. There were too many unanswered questions, and his storybook ending as portrayed by Scott did not ring true to her. Taking careful notes, she interviewed members of the expedition. Among them was Lashly whom, in her own words, she asked

> what he thought was the reason of Evans (seaman) first beginning to fail & his opinion was that the man was lonely & fretted once having no one of his own class to talk to that he got depressed which of course never answers![93]

Mrs Oates was concerned with P.O. Evans because, amongst other things, she evidently disapproved of Scott's blaming him and her son for the disaster. From Meares, Atkinson, and the other Evans, now promoted Commander, Mrs Oates learned more about Scott's unstable temper and poor leadership, something of which she already knew from the outspoken letters of her son. It became clear that because of his injury in the Boer War, with his shattered thigh, Oates was unfit for the polar journey. Mrs Oates never forgave Scott for leading her son to his death. She pointedly refused to go to Buckingham Palace for the presentation of medals to the survivors and the families of the dead. It was her one public gesture. Otherwise, she too acquiesced in the conspiracy of silence that descended on the inner history of the expedition.

There were more private reservations. When Scott's sledge was dug out, Tryggve Gran noted in his diary: 'a geological collection of about 20 kg . . . I think they might have saved themselves the weight.'[94] Commander Evans wrote that Scott's sledge

> contained 150 lbs of trash . . . It seems to me extraordinary that . . . they stuck to their specimens. We dumped ours at the first big check . . . I considered the safety of my party before the value of the records . . . apparently Scott did not.[95]

Perhaps Scott was trying to save something from the wreckage at any cost.

One way of hiding awkward truths was by making an heroic virtue of disaster. The moving spirit here was Scott's widow, now Lady Scott. A grateful government (Liberal), which knew a wave of popular opinion when it saw it, had given her the title as if her husband had lived to be knighted. Lady Scott arranged for the swift publication of her husband's diaries as *Scott's Last Expedition*. It purported to be a faithful transcription, but, with its excisions, it too was part of the cover up.

Scott's Last Expedition appeared in the autumn of 1913, to reviews ranging from near hysteria at one extreme to an oddly lukewarm reception in *The Times Literary Supplement* at the other. Perhaps *The Times* critic was reacting to Scott's

tone of self-pity. Perhaps too, it might all have been the outcome of a gentle-
manly code that prescribed both language and behaviour so that, in the words
of one author

> descriptions of heroic events . . . are often so stylised that the event loses
> all reality; it is sometimes hard, when reading Scott's journal or even more
> the accounts of the end of the *Titanic*, to realise that these were actual and
> terrible tragedies, not episodes in a bad novel. [96]

Either way, it was all overtaken by events. Eight or nine months after publication, the Great War broke out, and for the next four-and-a-half years there was
enough disaster to be getting on with.

The Scott myth was a product of the years between the wars. No single tow-
ering Briton had issued from the mass slaughter of the trenches, or the unsatisfactory war at sea, which whetted the public appetite for individual heroes.
Lawrence of Arabia was one; Scott of the Antarctic, another. Both were literary
creations. Out of *The Seven Pillars of Wisdom* came Lawrence. In the other case,
Scott's Last Expedition played a similar rôle. It was, however, only the raw material. It covered the whole expedition, including the long months at base. Various
other books projected the myth of the elegiac hero. The most influential were
Herbert Ponting's *The Great White South* in 1921, and Cherry-Garrard's *The
Worst Journey in the World* in 1922. Ponting had produced an illustrated book of
artless propaganda. Cherry-Garrard wrote an immature but persuasive, highly
charged apologia.

Between them, they created the myth of Scott of the Antarctic, the apothe-
osis of unnecessary self-sacrifice and gallantry without intelligence. Lady Scott
– now after remarriage, Lady Hilton Young – was an imperious accomplice.
She arrogated to herself the role of keeper of the flame and censor of what was
published about Scott, with some success, be it said. They all found opportune
help in Dr George Simpson. The meteorologist with Scott as he was, Simpson
nonetheless joined the tacit agreement to promote the leader's reputation.
When, during the winter of 1911 at Cape Evans, Simpson heard Scott's plans
for the Pole, he prophetically observed in his diary that 'there is little margin,
and a few accidents or a spell of bad weather would not only bring failure but
very likely disaster.'[97] Now, in 1926 he published a book to prove that *unexpectedly* bad weather *alone* was Scott's undoing. Simpson evidently did not know
the dictum that there is no bad weather, only bad clothing, and that furs could
have saved the polar party from extinction, as Amundsen had repeatedly shown.

Ponting and Cherry-Garrard may have formed the legend, but it was

Simpson who founded the cottage industry in exculpating Scott, which has lasted to this day. What the apologists had in common was rallying round the myth and advancing a cult of mindless gallantry. They naturally featured the nobility of Scott's inhuman man-hauling against Amundsen's use of dogs. They promoted Scott's ill-conceived expedition as a modern epic. After the Second World War it was made into a film, with John Mills in the title role. The sound track was by Vaughan Williams, no less, and subsequently turned into a concert version as the *Sinfonia Antarctica*. More hagiographies followed. Intellectual dishonesty was the rule which, to be fair, only mirrored public life. Specialists were long aware of the fraud behind the myth, but they kept up the pretence, while uncovering morsels of the truth. Amundsen was perversely dismissed as the professional, and Scott embraced as the noble amateur, having led better men than himself to their death. Like its government, a country gets the heroes it deserves.

In England at least, Amundsen was written out of the script. It was flying in the face of reality. Nobody, for example, considered his margins of safety. When he left his depot at 85°9' on 8 January 1912, on his return from the Pole, he had enough supplies, *on his proven performance*, to reach his base at Framheim in comfort, even if he missed every remaining depot. This suggests a reserve of at least 500–600 per cent. Of course this fell as his distance from home increased. His lowest ebb was on the return between the depots at 88°25' and 86°9, a journey of nine days. He arrived with three days' food in hand for men and dogs, which, leaving aside his abundance of fuel, gave 30 per cent as the margin of safety. Nowhere on his entire polar journey did Scott approach this figure. Apart from man-hauling, that was Scott's glaring fault, the result of almost wilful incompetence in organizing lines of supply. It was as if avoiding risk was considered unmanly.

Another cause of the disaster was the sheer ineptitude of the men at base. Polar tyros, execrable skiers, and psychologically shackled by Scott's autocratic leadership, they were drained of independent judgement to go out and rescue him. Critics have reproached Amundsen for his caution, on the grounds that only by suffering can heroism be attained. This shows the cultural abyss between the rivals. Scott wanted heroic endeavour, Amundsen conspicuous achievement. Without generous supplies, Amundsen would never have persuaded anyone to follow him, because discomfort was not attractive to his fellow countrymen. By contrast, Scott's companions were touched by masochism.

Eventually Scott's failings were exposed and his prestige declined. In the cold light of day, he had lost more men in the course of a few months than the great Scandinavian polar explorers over 30 years. The agent of change was ironically not so much Amundsen as Scott's old enemy, Shackleton. For a generation, Shackleton was half forgotten; now he supplanted Scott in public esteem. In fact, Shackleton shared most of Scott's technical faults, but he had virtues entirely his own. He was no bureaucrat like Scott, but a model of private enterprise, and anti-Establishment to the core. Shackleton had the fire of leadership; which Scott conspicuously lacked. Shackleton really cared about the lives entrusted to his care. Above all, he was a survivor. It is no accident that his revival belonged to the late 1980s and the 1990s. These were the Thatcher years, the aftermath of the Falklands War, and the collapse of the Soviet empire. Martyrdom was out of fashion and hope was on the wing. Shackleton became a hero of our times. This was due not so much to his Furthest South in 1909, as the saga of the *Endurance*, his ship on an attempt to cross Antarctica in 1914–16. *Endurance* was crushed in the ice, but Shackleton brought his men safely home, every one. It is one of the sagas of the sea.

Clinging to their creed, Scott's apologists eventually counter-attacked. This too was in the spirit of the times, being a form of flagellation begotten by a sour feeling of national self-hatred. The apologists gave an impressive display of twisted logic and intellectual contortion, together with ignorance of primary sources for Amundsen, of historical cold-weather clothing, the mechanics of skiing, and the physics of snow.

One scientific defence of Scott was that sliding on snow was impossible below –40°C, when Amundsen himself recorded skiing in his diary at –55.5°C. although, as he said, the going was 'continually bad'.[98] In fact the sliding mechanism ceases at around –80°C.[99]

Much effort has gone into bolstering Simpson's original contention that an unexpected cold snap in March 1912 finished Scott off. This hides a double hypocrisy. On the one hand, the historical apologists *need* their sacrificial hero; on the other, they wish to absolve him of all blame. They want it both ways. They would have been mortified if Scott had returned defeated and alive.

Weather is no excuse. If Scott really was caught unawares, it suggests estrangement from Nature added to criminal optimism. To make the natural comparison again, Amundsen considered the ferocious vagaries of weather as normal under any circumstances. The Polar Regions are actually cold. He worked on the assumption that one day in four would bring low temperatures and bad weather to pin him down.

The apologists also tried to dismiss the magnitude of Amundsen's victory. He started 11 days ahead of Scott, and beat him to the Pole by 34 days. He had increased his lead by 23 days after travelling for 57 days, including rests. Scott had taken 78 days to reach the Pole which, even allowing for his opponent's starting 60 nautical miles in front, still left him trailing far behind. Amundsen's average daily run to the Pole was 12.6 nautical miles against Scott's 9.9, so that Amundsen was drawing ahead by 2.7 nautical miles a day. Amundsen's average speed was around 3 nautical miles an hour to Scott's 1.8. Scott had quite simply been outclassed. If this had been a mile race, he would have been lapped soon after the bell. The return from the Pole was equally crushing. Amundsen took 39 days at an average daily run of 19 nautical miles. Scott was on the trail for 62 days, averaging 9.6 nautical miles per day.

It is part of the Scott myth that his weather was worse. In plain figures, Amundsen faced an average temperature of −21.8°C. on the way to the Pole whereas Scott faced −18.2. Amundsen had 15 days of gale force winds out of a total journey of 99 days Scott, six out of 139. Scott had 108 fine days to Amundsen's 51. The statistics go on and on. Amundsen's reputation ought to have been secure. He had no image makers, however, and at home he was taken for granted. His reception on returning to Norway in 1912 was more like that of one more ski champion than the conqueror of the South Pole.

From a certain point of view, this was understandable. The attacks by Scott's supporters rankled. His one recorded comment on his eclipse at the hands the Scott cult was that 'the British are bad losers'.[100] What he ought to have said was that against the British penchant for turning defeat into glorious failure, there is little or no defence. Nor did he endear himself to the Scott or kamikaze school of polar exploration by his philosophy, encapsulated on arrival at Hobart by telling the *Daily Chronicle* that 'there was little that was adventurous about the trip'.[101] Amundsen's brand of understatement was beyond the comprehension of a populace steeped in a semi-comic, voyeuristic love of exhibitionist self-punishment.

In the last resort, Amundsen did not care too much about his standing in England. The South Pole was only one episode in his career. The deed was its own reward but Nemesis was waiting in the wings. After the South Pole, anything else would only mean anticlimax. Amundsen wanted to abandon polar exploration and settle in Arctic Canada to study the Eskimos before their culture was finally extinguished. He was a born anthropologist, as his diaries and collections from the North West Passage had proved. Nansen, however, forced him to start on his Arctic drift. This was to redeem his promise that his switch from North to South was only a deviation from his original goal. That, so Nansen insisted, was a point of honour since the death of Scott. In 1918, Amundsen, half unwillingly set out to repeat Nansen's Arctic drift in *Fram* by sailing along the coast of Siberia in a new ship called *Maud*. He reached no further than Wainwright, in Alaska.

It was Amundsen's first failure. On that account or otherwise, single-minded to the point of obsession, he resumed his calling in high latitudes, to the exclusion of all else. The *Maud* expedition did, however, mark the start of something new. In the race for the South Pole, Amundsen had brought the era of dogs and sledges to an end. He understood that the future lay in the air. Already in 1913, he ordered two German aeroplanes for his forthcoming Arctic drift. This was the first known attempt to use heavier than air aircraft – as distinct from balloons and airships – on a polar expedition.

The outbreak of the Great War in 1914 scotched those plans, and Amundsen had to embark on *Maud* using the old methods. Thereafter, he did indeed pioneer the use of aircraft in polar exploration. In 1925 he made the first attempt to fly to the North Pole with two aeroplanes, reaching 87° 15'N. In the process he revived his dwindling reputation by saving all his men from a forced landing in the Arctic pack ice to become a national hero once more. Finally, in 1926, he made the first flight across the Arctic in an airship called *Norge* ('Norway'), passing the North Pole on the way, thus becoming the first man to reach both poles of the earth. He disappeared in 1928 when flying to the rescue of an Italian airship that had crashed in the Arctic. A virtuoso of exploration, he had followed his fate to the end.

Time did not cure the British hostility to Amundsen. He was dismissed as a mere pole seeker, while Scott was blandly presented as the real victor because he was supposed to have led a great scientific enterprise. As Scott himself had declared that he wanted to be first at ninety degrees South, this was hypocrisy on an heroic scale. From another point of view, it mimicked the self-righteous glow of moral superiority assumed by politicians to cover up defeat. Ironically, it was Amundsen's avowedly non-scientific expedition that made an original contribution to science. There was a Russian oceanographer called Aleksandr Stepanovitch Kuchin on *Fram*, and in 1911, while waiting to fetch Amundsen, *Fram* crossed the Atlantic to let him make the first ever line of soundings between South America and Africa.

Scott's defeat at the hands of Amundsen left a scar in the British national psyche that even now, a century after the event, has not quite healed. At its height, any attempt to question the Scott legend, and praise Amundsen was met by a storm of sentimental rage, as this author has every reason to know.

One line of attack on Amundsen, and hence rallying round Scott, has been playing at 'what if', meaning 'if only'. One instance is Amundsen's choice of base on the Ross Ice shelf itself. It could so easily have floated out to sea, so this line of wishful thinking goes, and then Scott would have won the race by default – although whether he would have still returned alive is another matter altogether.

What the critics ignored, but Amundsen fully grasped, was the doctrine of calculated risk. Another issue was Amundsen's boots: he has been derided for taking years over their development, only finishing at the last moment, whereas praise has been lavished on P.O. Evans for his improvised bindings. Then Amundsen's rapid passage of the pack ice on the way to the Bay of Whales was dismissed as 'luck', when Thorvald Nilsen, *Fram's* captain, was exactly one day out in his calculated time of arrival, after a non-stop oceanic voyage of four months and 14,000 nautical miles. The outcome, of course, speaks for itself.

The real story of the British attempt on the South Pole is those who did *not* go. There were men in England who could have given Amundsen a run for his money. Take for example Professor John Walter Gregory who, in 1896, made the first crossing of Spitsbergen with Sir Martin Conway. Gregory – a geologist who discovered and named the Great Rift Valley in Kenya – was an accomplished mountain skier. He had been kept out of the *Discovery* expedition; so too Tom Longstaff. Becoming a notable Himalayan climber, Longstaff was, like Amundsen, an exponent of the small expedition. By whatever arcane mechanism of choice, Amundsen and his men were the best of their kind and suited to their task. They had what the Greeks called *Aretê*, their most prized attribute; functional virtue, or goodness of quality. The British, in the grip of institutionalized mediocrity, preferred someone like Scott who, surrounding himself with a band of followers monumentally unsuited to their purpose, lost the Pole and killed himself and his men into the bargain – a gruesome metaphor of national decay.

In each sphere, the race for the South Pole has had its characteristic aftermath. British adventurers, often alien to snow, and skiing tyros, playing to television, have tried to undo the verdict of history by proving that Amundsen only won because he was lucky. Usually this took the form of attempting some new exploit in Antarctica, for example being the first to achieve a certain factitious goal unsupported, whatever unnecessary horrors or emergency evacuation that entailed. In most cases they were forestalled by Norwegians, like Scott before them, and for many of the same reasons.

A Nordic skier naturally identifies with Amundsen, so his compatriots pioneered a fashion for repeating his exploits with imaginative use of new technology and seeming ease so that, perhaps some of his distinctive genius might rub off on them. As Amundsen was fortified by having one of the world's best skiers in the person of Olav Bjaaland, so were his successors uplifted by the knowledge that by the time of the Vancouver Winter Olympics in 2010, their fellow Norwegians had won more medals – 151 – than any other country in all Olympic Winter Games since their inception in 1924. Because the latter day Antarctic exploits, like the original one, remain ski races on a large scale; thus the first man to ski to the South Pole solo and unsupported was Erling Kagge in 1992; the first woman was Liv Arnesen in 1994, and the first man ever to cross Antarctica from sea to sea unsupported was Børge Ousland in 1997.

More dramatically, there have been TV reconstructions of the race for the South Pole. It all culminated in the Southern summer of 2009, with the first re-run of the race in Antarctica. In each case Amundsen's compatriots, still the better skiers, intervened to take the prize without undue hardship. Like latter-day Amundsens, the British media virtually wrote them out of the script, concentrating on the epic misery of the British contestants, from blisters upwards. They had proved once again, as someone said, that history does indeed repeat itself, the first time as tragedy, the second time as farce.

There seems to have been a curse on the conquest of the South Pole. It killed Scott. It was the last straw that drove Hjalmar Johansen to suicide on his return to Norway in 1913, after a lifetime of depression and disappointment. It left Amundsen successful, famous, but lonely, unhappy, and embittered by what he considered the ingratitude of his fellow-countrymen. Hopeless with money, everlastingly in debt, Amundsen somehow always found patrons to finance his expeditions. Lincoln Ellsworth, an American millionaire, paid for both his polar flights. Amundsen never married, although he is said to have fathered a son by an Eskimo woman on the North West Passage. He had two documented affairs; one around 1909 in Norway and the other in England after the South Pole. Both were with married women. Both ended, discreetly, in disaster.

In the end, Amundsen was dogged by an ironic Fate. So, for example, Scott was glorified in pictures by Ponting, but Amundsen's cameras were damaged, so he had no photographic record of his historic journey. Bjaaland, as so often, saved the day. Luckily he had taken within his personal allowance, besides his racing skis, a folding Kodak pocket camera. The photographs that he took with this remain the only pictures of the conquest of the Pole; but they have the eerie evocativeness of the snapshot that escapes the more polished product.

Bjaaland came out best of them all. After the South Pole, he returned to Morgedal. There he set up a small ski factory – with a loan from Amundsen in the midst of his own financial tribulations, as a point of honour – and led a contented life for nearly 50 years, respected by all as an old ski champion and the first man at the South Pole (in that order). He never wrote a book about his Antarctic experience – unfortunately; it would have been full of humour and worth reading. He married, but had no children. He died in 1961, having kept his polar diary privately at home. It had been written in an almost illegible handwriting, which a nephew spent many years deciphering.

Neither Bjaaland nor Amundsen thought to justify themselves by publishing their diaries. Amundsen's polar journals eventually made their way into the Norwegian national library, where they lay gathering dust, awaiting publication, some day. Bjaaland's modest little volume remained a family heirloom in Morgedal.

Fridtjof Nansen, the founder of modern polar exploration, appropriately has the last word. 'Like everything great, it all seems plain and simple', he wrote in the immediate aftermath of Amundsen's conquest of the South Pole. And in praise of skis and dogs:

> victory did not depend on the great inventions of modern times, and the many new devices in every field; the means are ancient, the same that the nomad knew thousands of years ago, when he advanced over the snow-clad plains of Siberia and Northern Europe.

But also:

> *everything,* both great and small, was carefully thought out – and the plan was brilliantly executed. It is the *man* on which everything depends; here as everywhere else.[102]

GLOSSARY

Anemometer. Instrument for measuring the speed of the wind. It consisted of an impeller with cup-shaped blades, linked to a specialized mechanical speedometer.

Azimuth. The true bearing of the sun, or any other heavenly body. Varying with latitude, date and time of day, before the age of GPS, it was found by tedious arithmetic from navigational tables.

Burberry cloth. The first efficient modern lightweight windproof fabric. It was made of closely woven cotton with a double weave. It takes its name from the original makers. The name survives today as a brand in the fashion industry.

Cwm. A bowl-shaped hollow at the head of a valley or on a mountain slope, originally formed by a glacier.

Dead Reckoning (DR). Estimating position by course steered and elapsed distance without astronomical observations.

Drift snow. Snow in which wind or ablation have converted the original hexagonal crystals into minute, needle-like particles. It resembles, and acts like, the sands of the desert. Skis and sledges do not like it. Skiing on good crystalline snow at −40°C. is far better than drift snow at −10°, proving that snow structure is as important as temperature.

Finnesko. From Norwegian *finnsko* or (earlier) *finsko*, literally 'Lappish shoes'. The light moccasins of the Lapps, made of fur from the legs of the reindeer, with the hair facing outwards. It has turned-up toes to hook into simple toestrap ski bindings. Traditionally, Lapps and early explorers lined the finnesko with *senne-græs*, an arctic sedge that efficiently insulates against cold, and absorbs moisture to keep the feet dry. Its disadvantage was that it had to be regularly dried out, often by body heat.

Kamikk. Soft Eskimo boot, usually made of sealskin. On making camp the Norwegians sometimes used them as *après-ski* boots, so to speak.

Pemmican. Before freeze drying and so on, pemmican was the staple source of concentrated high energy food for polar explorers. Originating among North American Indians, it is basically dried meat ground up and mixed with fat, generally cast into blocks for transport.

Pressure. Disturbance and deformation in ice caused by forces acting on it.

Sastruga, pl. sastrugi. Ridges or waves in the snow formed by wind gouging and deposition. They run parallel to the prevailing wind, and may be from a few centimetres to more than a metre in height.

Serac. Detached tower formed by intersection of crevasses caused by disturbance in the ice. It is important to remember that ice acts like an intensely viscous liquid with a remorseless onward creep. Snow, by contrast, is a crystalline solid. And both are made of water!

Ski-joring. To be pulled along on ski, originally by horses, but later meant any tractive power.

Stratus. Type of cloud, even in colour and thickness, usually low lying. When followed by a figure, it means cloud cover on a scale of 1 to 10. Thus 'Stratus 10' means completely overcast with stratus.

Variation, or magnetic variation. The angle between the bearing by magnetic compass and a true bearing. Before the days of GPS, essential when the compass was the only means of steering a course. It was checked by azimuth observations q.v.

NOTES

1 See Huntford (2008), pp. 161–5.

2 Sir Clements was a man of parts. As a young man, he smuggled the cinchona plant out of South America to India. The cinchona is the source of quinine, which was then the only known treatment for malaria. Sir Clements also helped to abolish flogging in the Royal Navy, besides being probably the first to rehabilitate King Richard III after Shakespeare's political hatchet job.

3 *Diario de Noticias*, 7 September 1910.

4 Roald Amundsen, letter to Fridtjof Nansen, 22 August 1910, NBO Ms.fol. 1924: 5, 3.

5 John Scott Keltie, letter to Fridtjof Nansen, 8 October 1909, RGS correspondence files.

6 Fridtjof Nansen, letter to Sir Clements Markham, 4 April 1913, NBO Brevs. 48.

7 9 September 1909 was the date that Amundsen wrote to the Danish authorities in Copenhagen, ordering his dogs from Greenland – 100 of them – to be delivered in Norway This proved that he was now going South. In his original plan for his Arctic drift, he would have fetched dogs from Alaska, just before passing the Bering Strait. thus avoiding unnecessarily long transport, and a double passage through the Tropics in rounding South America. See Huntford (1993), p. 219 and (2003), p. 209.

8 Amundsen (1912) vol. 1, p. 136.

9 Quoted in Seaver (1933), p. 182.

10 Quoted in Cherry-Garrard (1965), p. 16.

11 Amundsen (1912), vol. 1, p. 147.

12 Ibid, p. 139.

13 Isachsen (1933), p. 51.

14 Sigurd Scott Hansen, *Fram* diary 18 February 1894, NBO Ms.8°3423:1.

15 Sverdrup (1903), vol. 1, p. 19.

16 Amundsen (1912), vol. 1, p. 146.

17 The reversible two-stroke diesel, still in use today.

18 Amundsen (1912), vol. 1, p. 50.

19 M'Cormick (1884), vol. 1, p. 169.

20 Olav Bjaaland, diary, 11 January 1911.

21 Wilson (1972), p. 45.

22 *Erebus* and *Terror* achieved a subsequent morbid fame as the ships of the doomed Sir John Franklin. He disappeared in the Arctic together with both vessels and all his 134 followers in the search for the North West Passage during the mid 1840s.

23 *Morgenbladet*, Christiania, 2 October 1910.

24 *The Times*, 13 September 1909.

25 H. Dickason, diary 4 February 1911, Christies.

26 Amundsen, diary, 10 February 1911, NBO Ms.8°1196.

27 Amundsen (1912), vol 2, pp. 88–9.

28 Amundsen, diary, 15 February 1911.

29 Scott, diary, 19 February 1911

30 Roald Amundsen to Fridtof Nansen, 22 August 1910.

31 Scott, diary, 22 February 1911.

32 Cherry Garrard, diary 24 February 1911, SPRI.

33 Henrik Ibsen, *Kongs-Emnerne* (*The Pretenders*), Act V. Ibsen 1962 p. 312. Author's translation.

34 Cherry-Garrard, diary 24 February 1911, SPRI Ms.559/1.

35 L. E. G. Oates, letter to his mother, 23 November 1910, SPRI.

36 Boynton and Fischer (2005).

37 Amundsen (1907, p. 12).

38 See Huntford (2008), pp. 150–2, 284.

39 The authority for Meares' scorn of Scott is, firstly correspondence between the author and Dr L. R. Phillips, who had met Meares. The other source is a record by Mrs Caroline Oates, Captain Oates' mother, of a conversation with Meares on his return to England. See note 80 and Huntford (1993, 2003, 2009).

40 Amundsen, third *Fram* diary, 5 July 1911, NBO Ms.4°1549.

41 Gran (1961), p. 118.

42 Amundsen (1912), volume 1, p. 389.

43 Interview with author, April 1977.

44 Adolf Hoel, notes on Hjalmar Johansen, NBO Ms.4°2776:13b.

45 F. Hj. Johansen, *Fram* diary, 17 July 1896, NBO 8°2775.

46 Wright could not steer because he only had a pocket compass. Unlike Helmer Hanssen's ship's compass, this needed periodical halts to take a bearing. That was impossible in a snowstorm or a whiteout, which meant interrupted travel. It was one more detail with unforeseeable consequences.

47 As it eventually turned out, he should have let them have their head.

48 Mount Ruth Gade today. Named after the wife of one of Amundsen's patrons, the Norwegian-American Herman Gade. See map p. xiii.

49 See Drewry and Huntford 1979.

50 The Butcher's Shop is one feature that has kept its name. See map on p. xii.

51 As both Amundsen and Bjaaland surmised, they were on a spur of Mount Don Pedro Christophersen. They had camped on the southern slope, overlooking the Bowman Glacier, another outlet of the ice cap. See map on p. xiii.

52 *Vidda* is usually translated as 'plateau', but this is misleading. There is no direct equivalent in English. It represents an aspect of the Norwegian landscape. The word means a wild upland, as distinct from a mountain range. It has connotations of untrammelled space. It is also a metaphor of escape. Ibsen wrote a poem in its praise, of which the defining couplet is:

> Up here on the heights, God and freedom reign,
> Down below the others flounder on.

The word *vidda* is deeply anchored in the Norwegian psyche. To Amundsen, the Antarctic ice cap would simply be a *vidda* writ large. Using the word in that context would be instinctive. It would have a homely ring, so the ice cap would appear as an extension of his native terrain, and hence lose its power to instil a sense of mythic fear.

In using the word *vidda* at this point, Amundsen meant the summit of the ice cap. He spoke too soon.

53 Norway was Lutheran, so Bjaaland would have known the church calendar with its list of saints' or name days. To put the Devil there was Bjaaland's characteristic way of dealing with the weather by a little private joke. Bjaaland followed Amundsen's naming of the glacier with another Norwegian name for the Devil – *Djævlen* – that also has the force of a four letter word. The blasphemy is therefore double, as it were, and hence also Bjaaland's satisfaction.

54 Amundsen (1927), p. 238.

55 Scott meant not dogs, but mules, ordered from India by *Terra Nova* when she left for the southern winter. This is an ambiguous passage. Either Scott had resigned himself to defeat, and was going try and save something from the wreckage, or he thought he would win the race, and add more exploration for

the kudos. Either way, he clearly expected to miss the ship, which in turn meant being out dangerously late in the season.

56 Another typical Bjaaland touch. *Grisevidda* roughly means 'the pig's *vidda*' or 'filthy heights'. This conveyed the wind and generally unpleasant conditions. However, it had a homely ring. There is humour and something of childhood in the choice of epithet. The *effect* is a bit like saying 'Piglet's Plateau'. Bjaaland was unimpressed by the great Antarctic Ice Cap, or anything else for that matter. After all, it was just another *vidda*, such as he had known since he was a boy.

57 For starting the Primus stove. See p. 44.

58 This was shifting responsibility. The prejudice against ski was real enough, but Scott did not set a good example. Around the base, and on the subsidiary journeys, he generally shuffled along on foot. Nor did he make sure that his subordinates learned to ski. He had the authority to do so.

59 When *Fram* was sailing to the Bay of Whales, she crossed the 180th degree of longitude, and hence the International Date Line, but the calendar was not put back a day, as required when moving from west to east. By the time the mistake emerged things had gone too far. Logs and diaries would have needed wholesale revision. Amundsen decided to keep the 'wrong' calendar through-out, while entering the correction, in retrospect, for the arrival at the Pole. The 14 December 1911 is the date that has gone down in history. It is all academic anyway. In the interests of historical authenticity, the original 'wrong' dates in the Norwegian diaries are preserved. Scott did not cross the Date Line, so this issue does not concern him.

60 This was a small lightweight emergency tent for two or three people made of silk. It was of surprisingly advanced design, aerodynamically constructed with a sloping ridge to reduce wind resistance. Amundsen clearly felt that he needed it no longer. Also it was an extra precaution to make clear to Scott that he had beaten him to the Pole. 'Rønne' was Martin Rønne, *Fram*'s sailmaker, who made the tent. He did so on the voyage out, with *Fram* heaving, pitching and tossing, so that he had to cut the cloth on a gyrating chart table.

61 R. F. Scott, letter to Joseph Kinsey, 28 October 1911, SPRI Ms.761/8/33.

62 See note 60.

63 Dehydration was probably the cause, as it finished off other dogs. As was the custom at the time, Amundsen let his dogs slake their thirst by eating snow. He could get away with this at lower altitudes, but not up on the polar plateau. We now understand that eating snow causes dehydration, and that in deep cold at high altitude, dogs need plenty of water, just like their masters.

64 An early use of the word. 'Yomp' is a back formation from the English 'jump', which is the way Bjaaland spells it. 'Yomp' is an approximation to the Norwegian

pronunciation. The origin is obscure but is either Norwegian seaman's slang, or perhaps entered the language from Norwegian emigrants in America. It made its way into English via the Royal Marines, who would have picked it up when doing their Arctic training in Norway.

65 A variation of Bjaaland's *Grisevidda*, see note 49. *Grisesletta* would mean, roughly, 'the pig's (or piglet's) plain.

66 On the grounds that, as forerunner, he needed more food than the others. Nobody objected.

67 In the end, Amundsen had to extract it. Their first aid equipment included a pair of dental forceps. Wisting was the one who had taken a crash course in simple dentistry, so he had to prompt Amundsen in the act, as it were.

68 See Huntford (1993), p. 418.

69 See note 36. On 26 April 1913 Mrs Oates recorded a conversation with Meares, who 'said . . . Captain Scott would swear all day at Commander [then Lieut.] Evans . . . and the worst was it was not possible to get away from the rows.' This was partly quoted in the catalogue of Christie's sale of 26 September 2001, p. 233.

70 See map p. xiii.

71 Mount Don Pedro Christophersen today. See pp. 133, 135 and map p. xiii.

72 Found by Dr Charles Swithinbank nearly 50 years afterwards. It was still full. See Swithinbank (1964), p. 46. Hermetic sealing was the explanation. See author's comment on pp. 108–9. The cairn remains the only surviving trace of Amundsen in Antarctica today.

73 Amundsen (1912), vol. 2, p. 135.

74 See map p. xvi, Hinks (1944) and Huntford (1993), p. 518.

75 This was the *Kainan Maru* (*Opener up of the South*) expedition, named after the expedition ship, under Lieutenant Shirase. It was the first Japanese polar expedition, and part of a process of overhauling the West. A party from the *Kainan Maru* made the first landing on King Edward VII Land from the sea, although Prestrud had been the first actually to reach it on his journey from the Bay of Whales.

76 *Daily Mail*, 21 April 1911.

77 See Rogers (1974).

78 The spirit, or alcohol, was carried to start the Primus stove. See p. 44.

79 Undated in the original, but on internal evidence, it was almost certainly 24 or 25 March.

80 Taylor (1916), p. 434.

81 Hadleys Orient Hotel. It still exists today, as Hadleys Hotel, part of an international group.

82 Olav Bjaaland, diary, 18 February 1912.

83 *Dagbladet* (Christiania) 2 July 1912, *The Times,* 15 February 1913.

84 Mrs D. Irving-Bell, personal communication with the author.

85 *New York Times* 5 January 1913.

86 *Times Literary Supplement* 28 November 1912, p. 545.

87 *The Times*, 12 February 1913.

88 *Ibid.*

89 *The Times*, 14 November 1854.

90 Gran (1915), p. 187.

91 A. H. Macklin, interview with James Fisher (SPRI) *see* Huntford (2009), p. 666.

92 *The Times*, 25 February 1913.

93 Mrs Caroline Oates, conversation with William Lashly, 24 June 1913. Mr Christopher Dennistoun kindly made Mrs Oates' records of her interviews available to the author. They were subsequently sold at Christies, and are now in private ownership. See Huntford (2009), pp. 360–2.

94 Gran (1915), p. 190.

95 E. R. G. R. Evans, letter to Ralph Gifford, 6 February 1913. Sold at Christies on 21 September 2000, partly quoted in the sale catalogue.

96 Girouard (1981), p. 14.

97 George Simpson, Diaries Vol. III, 11 June 1911, SPRI Ms. 704/3.

98 Amundsen, sledging diary, 11 September 1911, Ms.8°1249 NBO, see p. 40.

99 Sliding on snow actually involves two mechanisms. One works by the melting of snow by pressure to form a thin layer of water under the moving surface. This fails at around $-40°C$. The other depends on the behaviour of water molecules near the surface of snow crystals. Depending on the atmospheric pressure and humidity, these molecules escape in varying numbers to produce a water-like substance that acts as lubrication. This ceases at around $-80°C$., when all sliding becomes impossible.

100 Amundsen (1927), p. 69.

101 *Daily Chronicle*, 11 March 1912.

102 Amundsen (1912), vol. 1, p. 3.

BIBLIOGRAPHY

Amundsen, R., Antarctic diaries, NBO Ms.4°1549, Ms.8°1196, Ms.8°1249.

Amundsen, R. (1907), *Nordvestpassagen*. Kristiania: H. Aschehoug & Co.

Amundsen, R. (1912), *Sydpolen*. Kristiania: Jacob Dybwads Forlag.

Amundsen, R. (1921), *Nordostpassagen*. Kristiania: Gyldendalske Boghandel.

Amundsen, R. (1927), *Mitt liv som Polarforsker*. Oslo: Gyldendal norsk Forlag.

Austbø, J. (1945), *Olav Bjåland*. Oslo: Fonna Forlag.

Bjaaland, O., Antarctic diaries, in the possession of the Bjaaland family in Morgedal.

Boynton, A. and W. Fischer (2005), *Virtuoso Teams*. Harlow: Prentice Hall.

Bregman, G. A. (1962), 'Kapitan A. S. Kuchin', in *Letopis' Severa* [*Annals of the North*], 3, 130–47.

Cherry-Garrard, A. (1965), *The Worst Journey in the World*. London: Chatto & Windus.

Drewry, D. J. and R. Huntford (1979), 'Amundsen's route to the South Pole'. *Polar Record*, 19, (121), 329–36.

Girouard, M. (1981), *The Return to Camelot*. New Haven: Yale University Press.

Gran, T. (1915), *Hvor Sydlyset Flammer*. Kristiania: Gyldendalske Boghandel, Nordisk Forlag.

Gran, T. (1961), *Kampen om Sydpolen*. Oslo: Ernst G. Mortensens Forlag.

Gran, T. (1974), *Fra tjuagutt til sydpolfarer*. Oslo: Ernst G. Mortensens Forlag.

Hansen, S. S., *Fram* diaries 1893–96, NBO Ms.8° 3423.

Harrison, A. H. (1912), 'The control of British polar research'. *The Nineteenth Century*, April, 756–66.

Hinks, A. R. (1910), 'Notes on determination of position near the poles'. *Geographical Journal*, 1, (35), 3, 299–312.

Hinks, A. R. (1944), 'The observations of Amundsen and Scott at the South Pole'. *Geographical Journal*, 103, (4), April, 160–80.

Huntford, R. (1993), *Scott and Amundsen*. London: Weidenfeld.

Huntford, R. (2001), *Nansen*. London: Abacus.

Huntford, R. (2003), *Scott and Amundsen*. London: Abacus.

Huntford, R. (2008), *Two Planks and a Passion*. London: Continuum.

Huntford, R. (2009), *Shackleton*. London: Abacus.

Huxley, L. (ed.) (1913), *Scott's Last Expedition*. London: Smith, Elder & Co.

Ibsen, H. (1962), *Ibsens samlede verker*, vol. 2. Oslo: Gyldendal Norsk Forlag.

Isachsen, G. (1933), 'Polarhunden'. *Polar-Årboken*. 1933, 48–51.

Johansen, F. H., *Fram* diaries 1893–96. NBO Ms.8°2775.

Jones, M. (ed.) 2005, *Robert Falcon Scott Journals*. Oxford: Oxford University Press.

M'Cormick, R. (1884), *Voyages of Discovery in the Arctic and Antarctic Seas and Round the World*. London: Sampson Low, Marston, Searle & Rivington.

Nansen, F. (1890), *Paa ski over Grønland*. Kristiania: H. Aschehoug & Co's Forlag.

Nansen, F. (1897), *Fram over Polhavet*. Kristiania: H. Aschehoug & Co's Forlag.

Olav Bjaalands Museum Morgedal (1970), *Ski og Sudpol*. Skien: Erik Tanche Nilssen.

Ponting, H. G. (1921), *The Great White South*. London: Duckworth.

Rogers, A. F. (1974), 'The death of Chief Petty Officer Evans'. *The Practitioner*, April, 1–12.

Ross, Captain Sir J. C., R. N. (1847), *A Voyage of Discovery and Research in the Southern and Antarctic Regions*. London: John Murray.

Scott, R. F., Diaries and other records of the Second Antarctic Expedition, BL Add. Ms. 51024-51042.

Scott, R. F. (1968), *The Diaries of Captain Robert Scott: A Record of the Second Antarctic Expedition 1910–1912*, Facsimile Edition, Tylers Green, Buckinghamshire, University Microfilms Ltd.

Seaver, G. (1933), *Edward Wilson of the Antarctic*. London: John Murray.

Shackleton, E. H. (1909), *The Heart of the Antarctic*. London: William Heinemann.

Simpson, G. C. (1926), *Scott's Polar Journey and the Weather*. Oxford: The Clarendon Press.

Sverdrup, O. (1903), *Nyt Land*. Kristiania: H. Aschehoug & Co. (W. Nygaard).

Swithinbank, C. (1964), 'To the valley glaciers that feed the Ross Ice Shelf'. *The Geographical Journal*, 130, (1), 32–48.

Taylor, G. (1916), *With Scott: The Silver Lining*. London: Smith, Elder & Co.

Wheeler, S. (2001), *Cherry, A Life of Apsley Cherry-Garrard*. London: Jonathan Cape.

Wilson, E. (1972), *Diary of the 'Terra Nova' Expedition to the Antarctic 1910–1912*. London: Blandford Press.

INDEX